TECHNOLOGY AND AGRICULTURAL DEVELOPMENT
IN PRE-WAR JAPAN

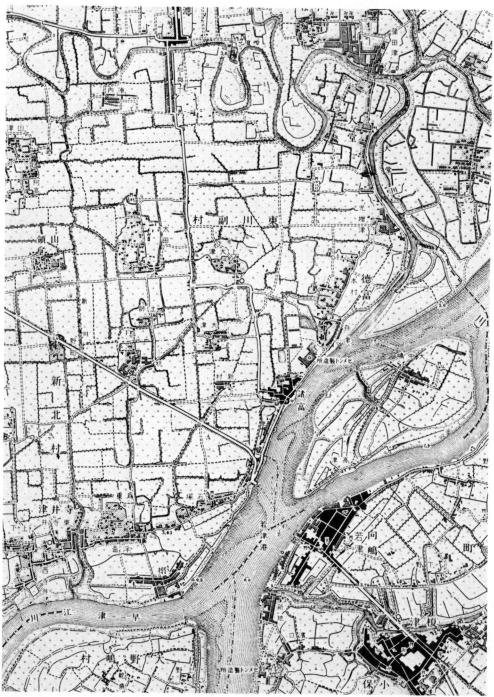

Illustration 1. The Creek Network. Detail from a map published in 1902, showing creeks and fields on the bank of the river Chikugo around hamlets of Kawazoe village.

Technology and Agricultural Development in Pre-War Japan

PENELOPE FRANCKS

Yale University Press

New Haven and London

1984

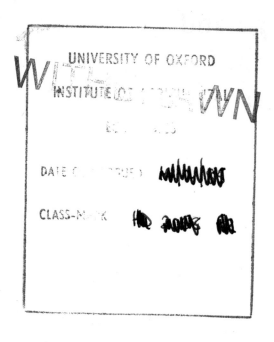
Designed by Caroline Williamson
and set in Compugraphic Baskerville by Red Lion Setters, London WC1.
Printed in Great Britain by Pitman Press Ltd, Bath.

Library of Congress Cataloging in Publication Data

Francks, Penelope, 1949–
  Agriculture in pre-war Japan.
  Bibliography: p.
  Includes index.
  1. Agriculture—Japan—History. 2. Agriculture—Economic aspects—Japan.
3. Agricultural innovations—Japan—History. 4. Rice—Japan—Irrigation—History.
I. Title.
S471.J3F66   1984   338.1'0952'2   82–20306
ISBN 0–300–02927–6

CONTENTS

TABLES, CHARTS AND MAPS

Tables

PREFACE

The aim of this book is to approach certain aspects of Japan's agricultural development from the point of view of the development economist. In it I try to ask the questions which the development economist would ask and apply the theories and techniques which he/she would apply. But the data which must of necessity be used in this are not the modern surveys and statistics which the contemporary development economist can produce, but the information to be derived from the sources of economic history. My method of research has therefore largely been one of assembling and assimilating this information from the work of Japanese local historians, agricultural economists and economic historians, and the existence of this book is in some measure a tribute to the interest and thoroughness with which these scholars and enthusiasts have carried out their work. In making use of the data they have collected, I hope to throw light on some of the issues with which development economists are currently concerned (principally those related to the causes and consequences of technical change) by considering them in relation to the only case of successful agricultural development in Asia for which it is possible to take a long-term view, and at the same time to tell the story of how a group of ordinary Japanese rural communities overcame the problems which stood in the way of their material progress.

This book has its origins in the work I carried out for my doctoral thesis and it would not now exist without the many years of both financial and moral support which I have received from the School of Oriental and African Studies of London University, where I was a postgraduate student and later a research fellow. Of the many members of the School's staff who have helped me in the study of both economics and Japanese, I must especially thank Professors Christopher Howe and W.G. Beasley, who have both given me encouragement and support well beyond the call of duty.

During the course of research I have spent more than two years living in Japan and this book owes perhaps its greatest debt to the two eminent Japanese scholars who cared for me during that time: Professor Shigeru Ishikawa of Hitotsubashi University, who first introduced me to Saga and whose ideas lie behind much of the framework and approach of the study; and Professor Shūjirō Sawada of Fukuoka University, who gave me the benefits not only of his profound knowledge of Japanese agriculture but also of his own and his wife's great kindness and hospitality. I am extremely grateful also to all the staff of the Institute of Economic Research at Hitotsubashi University, where I was based during my first stay in Japan, and to Professor Tsuchiya and the Department of Agricultural Economics at Kyūshū University, especially Mr. Satoshi Kai, for providing me with facilities and help of all kinds and for welcoming me so kindly. In addition, at Saga University Professors Itō and Nagano and Mr. Utsumi gave me hours of help and hospitality in my efforts to find out about Saga Plain agriculture. On the financial side, I must express my thanks to London University for the travelling scholarship which financed my first visit to Japan, and to the British Academy and the Japan Foundation Endowment Fund for support for the second.

As will become clear, this book relies heavily on the work of a number of Japanese scholars who have specialised in the study of Saga agriculture, most notably Professor Tatsuo Yamada, Dr. Shōjirō Miyajima and Dr. Toshihiko Isobe. All three have taken the time and trouble to talk to me and to try to understand and answer my queries and problems, for which I am exceedingly grateful. Needless to say, however, none of them is responsible for the use which I, approaching their work in a foreign language, have made of their books, articles and conversation.

Many other people have of course helped me in all sorts of ways, from the chance suggestion of an article to read, to hours of discussion or days of practical help, and here I can only attempt to list a few of them and offer my thanks: Kenji Chō; Shigemochi Hirashima; Jun Katata; Yukihiko and Ikuko Kiyokawa; Jyūrō Kudō; Ryoshin Minami; Liz Rouse; Professors Charles Dunn, P.G. O'Neill and Kenneth Walker of the School of Oriental and African Studies; and the staff of the Institute of Agricultural Economics at Oxford, especially Margaret Haswell, Richard Castle and Steve Parsons, and many of my students there, from whom I learnt a great deal.

Last but not least, nothing of this would ever have been written without my husband's efforts at organising, typing, photographing, cycling the Saga Plain, conversing politely while eating and drinking with whomever required, and supporting and caring for me throughout the making of a book which is in some ways as much his as mine.

CONVENTIONS USED

Western forms of expression have been employed as far as possible, using the methods of conversion described here. Frequently-used Japanese words for which no convenient English equivalent could be found are listed in the glossary.

Dates: Western dates are given throughout, but occasionally Japanese names are used, following the practice of Japanese writers, to denote periods of time. The Tokugawa period lasted from 1603 until 1867, and the Meiji period from 1868 (the Meiji Restoration) until 1912.

Measurements: Japanese measures have been converted to their metric equivalents. One *Chō* is almost exactly equal to one hectare (ha.), and a *tan* (0·1 *chō*) is therefore taken as equivalent to 10 ares. One *koku* of rice weighs 150 kg and one *koku* of wheat 136·9 kg. Yields originally calculated in *koku/tan* are thus expressed in kg/10 ares.

Currency: The yen is frequently abbreviated to ¥. ¥1 = 100 sen.

Names: Japanese personal names are written in Western fashion, with given names preceding family names in the text and family names followed by initials in the references.

Romanisation: Long vowel sounds are indicated by macrons, except in the cases of very familiar place names.

Footnotes and references: Items in the bibliography are indicated in the footnotes and endnotes by author, short title and (in brackets after the title) number in the bibliography list. Footnotes indicated by letters are placed at the foot of the page and contain material of more general interest. Footnotes containing reference to sources alone are indicated by numbers and placed at the end of the book.

GLOSSARY

bunke	a branch family farming an independent holding but, tied socially and economically to the related main family of which it was once part.
buraku	the natural village or hamlet.
daimyō	a ruling feudal lord.
dōzoku	the hierarchical group of related households stemming from one main household.
gun	the geographical unit here translated as 'county'.
han	a feudal ruling group and its domain.
hatake	a field which cannot be irrigated.
honke	the main household from which other households have been separated to form branches.
ie	the household, including the family and its owned and inherited property and traditions.
kanden	a field which can be drained of water when required.
ken	prefecture.
kogashira	the recruiter, organiser and foreman of a group of workers.
koku	a unit of measurement of capacity, equal to 150 kg of rice or 136·9 kg of wheat.
kumiai	a union, association or co-operative. *Suiri kumiai* are the organisations of users of particular irrigation facilities. *Kōchi seiri kumiai* are organisations of farmers formed to carry out land improvement or the re-organisation of holdings.
Meiji Nōhō	the set of agricultural techniques, centring on the use of high-yielding seed varieties and heavy fertiliser application, which spread during the Meiji period.

mura	the administrative village unit, composed of several natural villages.
nenko	a hired agricultural worker contracted for a period of a year.
nōkai	an agricultural association, one of the official organisations formed at the national, prefectural, county and village levels to disseminate extension advice to farmers.
san-ka meichū	the three-brooded rice-borer, Schoenobius.
shi	the administrative area of a city.
Shinriki	the name of the most successful high-yielding rice variety of the Meiji period.
shitsuden	a field which cannot be drained of water.
tezukuri jinushi	a landowner who both cultivates and lets out parts of his holding.
tokojime	a method of ploughing designed to reduce water loss through the base of a paddy field.

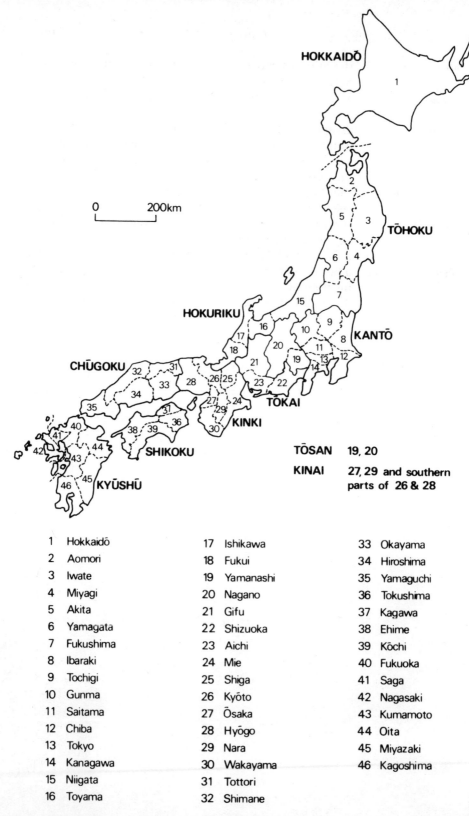

1	Hokkaidō	17	Ishikawa	33	Okayama
2	Aomori	18	Fukui	34	Hiroshima
3	Iwate	19	Yamanashi	35	Yamaguchi
4	Miyagi	20	Nagano	36	Tokushima
5	Akita	21	Gifu	37	Kagawa
6	Yamagata	22	Shizuoka	38	Ehime
7	Fukushima	23	Aichi	39	Kōchi
8	Ibaraki	24	Mie	40	Fukuoka
9	Tochigi	25	Shiga	41	Saga
10	Gunma	26	Kyōto	42	Nagasaki
11	Saitama	27	Ōsaka	43	Kumamoto
12	Chiba	28	Hyōgo	44	Oita
13	Tokyo	29	Nara	45	Miyazaki
14	Kanagawa	30	Wakayama	46	Kagoshima
15	Niigata	31	Tottori		
16	Toyama	32	Shimane		

Map 1. Prefectures and Regions of Japan

CHAPTER ONE
Technical Change and Agricultural Development

This study represents an attempt to use the methods of economics in the analysis of historical data. These data concern the development, introduction and diffusion of new forms of technology in agriculture. In this chapter I want to outline the way in which economists have begun to try to understand technology and its relationship with economic organisation, especially in agriculture, and to discuss some of the gaps in knowledge and understanding which the subsequent case-study might help to fill.[a]

1. The Economist's Approach to Technology

Technology, according to the dictionary, is 'the science of the industrial arts'. In general, it might be thought of as knowledge of the ways of producing useful things. Technology is created by engineers and other applied scientists, and by all practical people who use knowledge of the way things work to develop techniques for producing goods of whatever kind, and technologies are made up of all the individual techniques known for producing something, from the sickle to the combine harvester, from the water-wheel to the nuclear power station. The nature of the technology in use in a particular society has a profound influence on very many aspects of the lives of those who live in that society. In particular, it has a profound influence on the economic structure of that society, on the ways in which the production and distribution of goods and services are organised. Equally though, the society itself, and the

[a] Trained economists will find much of this chapter takes them back to their first years at university, but, if they will bear with it, it will also reveal the approach which I take to the various controversial issues involved.

economic organisation of that society, affect the nature of the technology
developed and used. The understanding of the relationship between
economic organisation, the province of the economist, and technology,
the province of the applied scientist, is therefore an important and
complex task, made more significant by the growing awareness of the
fact that apparent rapid advances in the science of the industrial arts is
not enough to ensure adequate access to the products of those arts for a
substantial proportion of the world's population.

How, then, have economists begun to try to understand the relationships between a society's economic organisation and the technology it
employs? The production techniques in use affect people's lives in very
many ways—through the work they demand of them, the forms of
organisation they impose on them, the noise they make, the architec-
ture they require, and so on. Economists have to abstract out the aspects
of technologies which they consider are most significantly related to the
subject matter of economics. Students of economics, having been told
that their subject is the study of the relationship between scarce resources and unlimited wants, are first presented with the economist's view of
technology in the form of the so-called production function, the standard means of expressing the way in which engineering knowledge affects
the possibilities of converting scarce resources into desirable output.

A production function is a graphical or mathematical expression of
all the possible ways of producing a given quantity of output of something, each way being expressed in terms of the combinations of scarce
inputs which it requires. If, for instance, we work with the case of a good
which can be produced from only two inputs, say, land and labour,
then all the possible ways of producing a certain output of this good
could be expressed as points on a graph whose axes measure quantities
of the two inputs.[b] A, B and C are possible combinations of land and

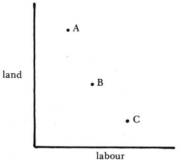

[b] E.g. a given quantity of grain could be produced by very rough cultivation of a large
area by a small labour force, or very careful, intensive cultivation of a small area by a
large labour force, or by combinations in between.

labour, all yielding the same output. If we rule out all those methods which produce the given output using more of both inputs than any other possible method (methods which no rational entrepreneur would ever use), and if we make the further assumption that this still leaves a very large number of possible input combinations producing the given output, then the production function can be expressed as a curve, or as a differentiable equation of the general form $O = f(L, N)$, where O is the quantity of output, L that of land and N that of labour.[c]

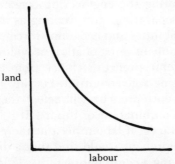

The precise meaning of this function depends on the time-scale under consideration. In the very short term, it can be taken to be expressing the scope for varying input combinations without reducing output with the given production techniques actually in use at that time. Over the longer term it could express the various input combinations implied by the range of different techniques known to engineers at that time, each point on the curve representing a different method of production involving different machinery and so on. Over the very long term, it could be taken to mean the range of techniques which could be developed in the present state of scientific knowledge, but which do not necessarily at present exist in the form of engineers' blueprints. All these cases represent different stages in the relationship between scientific knowledge and the actual production of goods.

The picture which emerges of the relationship between the engineer,

[c] The actual form of the function can be derived *ex post* by determining the equation which best fits available empirical data about input combinations and output levels, but it is more commonly assumed to take a form expressing the characteristics predicted of the relationship between output and inputs, *ex ante*, by economists' theories about the nature of production. For example, it should be able to show diminishing returns to increasing application of one input if the other input is held constant. See Brown, M., *On the Theory and Measurement of Technical Change* (138), pp.29–42. Production functions more commonly express combinations of *capital* and labour, although there is a substantial body of opinion which would argue that there is no logically acceptable way of measuring aggregate quantities of capital goods.

who represents technical knowledge, and the businessman or entrepreneur, who decides on the way in which that knowledge will be used to produce things, is thus of the engineer presenting the entrepreneur with, as it were, blueprints of the known ways of producing a given output, each way involving some different combination of inputs, on the basis of which the entrepreneur decides through some economic maximisation principle (e.g. profit maximisation) which method to use.

This way of representing the engineering constraints on economic production by clearly separating, and treating as independent of one another, technical possibilities and economic forces, is very convenient for dealing with two problems. First of all, it provides a straightforward way of explaining the entrepreneur's choice from among the various possible ways of producing a given output. For any given set of relative prices for inputs, the entrepreneur will select the technique which involves the least-cost combination of inputs. If relative input prices should change — for instance, if labour became more expensive relative to land — then the entrepreneur would find that a different method of production — one involving a combination of less labour and more land to produce the same output — would result in lower costs, and he would seek to change to that method.[d]

Secondly, this representation provides a way of expressing the effect of the appearance of possible new techniques on the choice facing the entrepreneur, and thereby it provides a way of expressing the economic nature of technical change. This is by means of comparing the production function involving the new technical possibilities with the old one. For instance, there might be advances in technical knowledge which make all possible techniques more efficient without affecting the relative combinations of inputs that they use. In this case the new production function would have exactly the same shape as the old, but be nearer to the origin of the graph (for the same output level), and would have no effect on the relative input combinations entrepreneurs used (neutral technical change). Alternatively, an advance in technical knowledge might make certain combinations of inputs more efficient but not others (biassed technical change). For instance, it might be some advance in machinery design which improved techniques using a relatively large amount of capital equipment more than it did those which relied more heavily on labour input. This would then change the shape

---

[d] This is strictly factor substitution (a movement along an existing production function), not technical change (a change in production methods induced by the discovery of new techniques, i.e. by a change in the production function), although in practice it is often hard to make the distinction.

of the curve and lead entrepreneurs to adopt techniques with different relative input combinations at the same set of relative input prices.

The production function can thus be used as a tool for explaining the economic nature of the technology in use, and of changes in that technology, but it is important at this stage to note the assumptions, and hence limitations, which its use involves, since it is out of those limitations that other approaches have emerged. The standard approach assumes:

1. that the range of available techniques is determined by engineering knowledge, independent of economic forces;

2. that there is a relatively wide range of possible efficient techiques from which the entrepreneur can choose;

3. that characteristics of techniques other than the relative input combinations they imply for the production of a given output can be ignored in explaining the entrepreneur's choice from amongst available techniques, i.e. that the 'factor intensity' of techniques, or the 'factor bias' of technical change, is the most important characteristic determining whether or not particular techniques are adopted.

There has been a considerable amount of work on elaborating this standard approach in order to bring it closer to reality, both for theoretical purposes and in order to carry out empirical anlaysis of technical change. On the other hand, there have been efforts to specify production functions in ways which enable them to express the relationship between inputs and output in a more precise way, to describe a wider variety of economically significant characteristics of technologies. For instance, many technologies include techniques with characteristics such that the relationship between inputs and output is not the same at all scales of production (economies/diseconomies of scale). The existence of this characteristic will clearly affect the choice of technique decisions of entrepreneurs and hence the impact of technologies on the economy, and it would be desirable to try to express the way in which this characteristic affects the entrepreneur's choice through the specification of the production function. Alternatively, there have been efforts to increase the scope of this kind of production function approach by disaggregating the inputs to be considered and specifying the available techniques in more detail in terms of a wider variety of sorts of input. For instance, techniques can be described in terms of combinations of skilled and unskilled labour, of educational expenses or managerial resources, of scientific research, and so on.

But despite these elaborations, there are areas which this kind of approach to the relationship between technology and the economy must, by its very assumptions, ignore. The limitations which these assumptions posed presented particular problems to those concerned with technical progress in developing countries. It was often difficult to explain why the introduction of new techniques took the form that it did simply in terms of the relationship between relative factor prices and a production function. While developing countries could clearly be characterised as possessing abundant supplies of labour and limited supplies of capital, so that the price of labour ought to be relatively low and that of capital relatively high, the production techniques which they embodied in their new investment tended to be capital-intensive, labour-saving ones, not unlike those used in developed countries with very different relative factor supplies. Among the many problems arising from this was the failure to provide employment for expanding labour forces, leading to growing urban unemployment, few opportunities for the bulk of the population to become involved in the growth of the modern sector of the economy, and increasing inequality between those who were able to find modern sector employment and those who were not. The explanation which the standard approach required was that markets in developing countries tended to be very imperfect for many reasons,[e] so that the input prices which entrepreneurs actually faced might not reflect the position of relative factor supplies in the economy, leading them to select techniques which were least-cost from their point of view but not from society's. However, there were also areas which the standard approach ignored which might contain other reasons for the failure of technical choice to deal with the employment problem. Firstly, the approach does not attempt to explain what determines the nature of the technology available, why the production function is as it is. It could be that the choice of capital-intensive techniques in developing countries was the result of the characteristics of the available techniques from which entrepreneurs had to choose, for instance if capital-intensive techniques were more efficient, in the sense of using less of all inputs for a given level of output, than any available labour-intensive technique. This could mean also that there was only a limited number of efficient techniques (perhaps only one) from which to choose. Secondly, the emphasis on the factor-intensity characteristics of techniques as determining entrepreneurs' choices might mean ignoring other characteristics of techniques which were important influences for entrepreneurs faced with the particular problems of production and of input supply in developing countries. These possibilities have led economists to look more closely, firstly, at the determinants of available technology, dropping the assumption that advances in technical knowledge occur independently of economic forces, and, secondly, at the way in which choice-of-technique decisions are actually taken.

[e] E.g. governments might subsidise the import of capital goods; minimum wage legislation or the existence of trade unions might force up the wages of labour.

2.   Influences on the Nature of Available Technology

As was pointed out earlier, the standard production function approach is based on the assumption that the scientific knowledge which determines the technology available to entrepreneurs is the result of research unrelated to and uninfluenced by economic forces. 'The production function ideally embodies no economic magnitudes such as prices or interest rates; market variables which provide inducements for the diversion of resources, or which are expressions of equilibrium situations in the economic world should be excluded from the concept of a production function.'[1] As Murray Brown goes on to say, this assumption is made in order that the production function might be seen as expressing the constraints imposed on the entrepreneur from outside by independently gathered technical knowledge. However, it is clear that in much of modern industry these constraints are not accepted, and substantial resources are invested in attempts to remove them. The direction taken by research into the way things work is therefore not just a matter of what scientists and solitary inventors happen to be interested in or discover, and it is valid for the economist to ask whether there might not be economic forces influencing the direction of scientific research and hence changes in the characteristics of the technology available.

What economic forces might these be? Given the way in which economic theory has conceptualised technology, the obvious answer is changes in relative input supplies and prices. This idea was originally suggested by Hicks,[2] who hypothesised that research would be directed towards developing techniques which economised on those inputs which were becoming relatively more expensive. The idea became known as the induced innovation hypothesis, and was the subject of much debate and controversy.[3] For those concerned with developing countries, it opened the way for an explanation of why entrepreneurs might be forced to select capital-intensive techniques: if, as has always been the case, most research into the development of new technology is conducted in developed countries where capital is relatively cheap and labour relatively expensive, it would follow that progress in improving and developing capital-intensive, labour-saving techniques would be likely to be much more rapid than that into labour-using techniques which would not match available relative factor supplies in the economies where research was carried out.[f] As a

[f] Cf. Atkinson and Stiglitz's variant of this idea, which suggests that research and development are concentrated on improving those techniques already in use in developed countries (i.e. capital-intensive ones), and which thus provides a link with 'learning by doing' theories of technical change. See Atkinson, A. and Stiglitz, J., 'A New View of Technological Change' (136).

result, capital-intensive techniques would tend to be absolutely more efficient (use less of all inputs per unit of output) and the only available labour-intensive techniques would be those which had been in use in developed countries in the past, since ignored by those who were improving and developing technology.[4]

For our purposes, the most useful working-out of the induced innovation hypothesis is in the model developed by Hayami and Ruttan,[5] who apply it to agriculture in particular and thereby work out many of its implications for the understanding of the direction of development of new techniques, hence the nature of available technology, in the individual sector with which we are concerned. Starting from the assumption that the direction taken by changes in the nature of available technology is significantly influenced by economic forces, Hayami and Ruttan set out to develop a model to explain the processes whereby a particular choice is made in a country from amongst alternative paths of technical development in agriculture. Working within the production function framework, they characterise these alternative paths according to their relative factor use, as either mechanical (labour-saving) or biological (land-saving), and ask why a country should come to develop its agricultural technology in one direction rather than the other, e.g. towards a mechanised, labour-saving agricultural technology in the United States as opposed to a fertiliser-intensive, land-saving one in Japan.

They hypothesise, firstly, like all those using the induced innovation hypothesis, that private firms conducting research will allocate their funds towards developing new techniques which economise on inputs which are becoming relatively more expensive. But beyond this they argue that, since much of the research relevant to the agricultural sector is carried out by publicly financed organisations, it is necessary to extend the hypothesis to show how public research institutions might be led to respond to changes in relative factor scarcities. They suggest that interaction between researchers and farmers will lead scientists, in response to farmers' demands, to develop techniques which economise on inputs which are becoming relatively scarce, and substitute for them inputs which are becoming relatively abundant. If institutional arrangements stand in the way of achieving the full potential of new techniques so developed, then individuals will be induced, with greater or lesser time lags, to change these arrangements ('institutional innovation'). In addition, innovations induced in one aspect of a technical system will generate bottlenecks and imbalances which will lead to the development of new methods in other parts of the system, and thus the inducement mechanism will generate a cumulative sequence of technical change ('dynamic sequences').

Hayami and Ruttan argue that the efficiency of these inducement mechanisms, which determine the choice of the direction of change in available technology, is a key factor in explaining differences in success in agricultural development. Growth in agriculture in the United States and Japan, they suggest, was the result of the efficiency with which these mechanisms operated, selecting paths of technical development appropriate to the relative availabilities and prices of factors of production in those countries.[g] This efficiency depended on the existence of institutional arrangements whereby research, much of it carried out in the public sector, was directed towards the development of new techniques with suitable factor bias characteristics.[h]

Hayami and Ruttan base their argument on a fairly general discussion of agricultural development at the national level, using Japan and the United States as examples. There are, as yet, comparatively few studies of the generation of particular innovations against which the theory of induced innovation could be tested at the micro-economic level. Rosenberg,[6] in a survey of what was known about the origins of a number of industrial innovations, found firms simply responding to particular immediate problems, some the result of specific historical situations (wars, strikes, government legislation, accidents, etc.), some generated by the use of existing technology itself. 'Complex technologies create internal compulsions and pressures which, in turn, initiate exploratory activity in particular directions.'[7] The two studies of the generation of new techniques most relevant to the present case, those of Clay and Sansom into innovations in irrigation pumping technology, fit into this picture of innovators simply trying to solve particular practical problems.[8] It might well be possible in a number of cases to trace back the causes of these problems to changes in relative factor supplies or prices, or to argue that relative factor availability significantly conditioned the nature of the solutions found. What this micro-economic evidence suggests, however, is that the step from changes in relative factor prices to the innovator's activities, or to the research organisation's allocation of funds, is not a simple one, and making it involves specifying how factor supply problems formulate themselves to the firm or farm (and through them to the research organisation) in a particular technical and institutional environment.

[g] 'Development of a continuous stream of new technology which altered the production surface to conform to long-term trends in factor prices was the key to success in agricultural growth in the United States and Japan.' Hayami, Y. and Ruttan, V., *Agricultural Development* (152), p.135.

[h] 'The success in agricultural growth in both the United States and Japan seems to lie in the capacity of their farmers, research institutions and farm supply industries to exploit new opportunities in response to the information transmitted through relative price changes.' Hayami, Y. and Ruttan, V., *Agricultural Development* (152), p.135.

But beyond this, the variety in the nature of the problems which seem to have stimulated innovatory activity suggests that, while relative input supplies may be an important factor conditioning or constraining the innovations developed, they may not be the only, or the most significant, influence on the nature of the new techniques produced and made available. It suggests that there are other characteristics of techniques which can cause the problems which induce innovation, or condition the nature of the new techniques developed, in significant respects. Successful innovations, for which research organisations and individual innovators are searching, must solve problems or raise output in such a way as to fit in, not only with the factor supply conditions of the economy for which they are intended, but also with, for instance, the prevailing industrial organisation, the existing technology in the processes related to that in which the innovation takes place, the income levels of the consumers for whom the innovation's products are destined, and so on.[9] To take this into account it is necessary to drop the third of the assumptions lying behind the standard production function approach, that relative factor use is the single most significant characteristic by which to define a technology and explain technical choice, and to see the innovations developed, and hence the nature of the technology available, as the products of particular sets of historical and geographical circumstances. As Stewart puts it: 'The development of techniques is essentially a historical process in which one technique with one set of characteristics replaces another in the light of the historical and economic circumstances of the time. The historical nature of technological development means that the time and circumstances in which any particular technique is developed heavily influence its characteristics.[10] It follows from this, for instance, that the available technology developed by research in economically advanced countries may be inappropriate for use in developing countries in a wide range of ways beyond simply its factor bias. But from our point of view it implies most significantly that the inducement mechanisms through which successful paths of technical development arise must be able to transmit the influence not only of relative factor supplies, but also of many other features of the environment of the time and place for which the new techniques are required.

The conclusions of this section are therefore these: the nature of the technology available to entrepreneurs in a particular industry is not independent of economic forces. It is the result of the sets of economic and technical circumstances prevailing when the techniques of which it is made up were each developed. The nature of available technology must therefore be the result of the working of inducement mechanisms through which those carrying out research are made aware of a wide

range of the economic, and other, characteristics of the industry concerned. Empirical studies must thus, as Stewart suggests, try to illuminate the ways in which 'the set of techniques available depends on the
historical development of technology, and specifically the economic/
social conditions of the economy for which the techniques were originally developed,'[11] and this the subsequent case-study will try to do. But
now we must go on to the other determinants of the actual techniques in
use, the mechanisms of the entrepreneur's choice of technique.

3.   The Choice of Technique and its Effects

Assuming now that the set of efficient techniques making up the available technology is given, as a result of the sorts of innovatory process
described in the last section, how does the individual firm or farm select
the technique to use? In section 1 we saw that the standard approach at
its simplest level hypothesises that the entrepreneur would select that
technique which required the lowest-cost combination of inputs, setting
the relative prices of factors of production against the factor intensities
of the possible techniques. It would follow that any other entrepreneur
operating in the same markets, therefore facing the same prices, would
make the same choice, and this would determine the diffusion of new
techniques and the structure of the technology in use in the industry.
This abstracts from differences in the initial situations of firms in the
industry and assumes that they all have the same access to inputs, in
terms of both price and quantity. However, empirical studies suggest
that these assumptions hide forces which, especially in developing countries, and in agriculture, may significantly affect the incentives and
abilities of individual firms (farms) to adopt new techniques.
  The work of Salter and others has shown that, even in developed
countries' industrial sectors, it is necessary to take into account, when
explaining the rate and pattern of the diffusion of new techniques, the
structure and age distribution of the existing capital stock in the industry concerned.[12] The profitability of a given innovation will vary
between firms depending on the age and other characteristics of their
present capital equipment. In agriculture, generations of investment in
land infrastructure can have the same sort of effect. David's work on the
diffusion of the mechanical reaper in Britain and the United States
shows that, despite similar changes in factor prices, the adoption of the
innovation was much slower on British farms, because the reaper was
incompatible with the past investment in roads, hedges, ditches, and so
on.[13] In areas where paddy rice is grown, the past investment in water
supply facilities plays the same sort of role, and differences in access to

water, not only between countries and regions, but also between individual farms, can profoundly affect the ability to adopt innovations such as high-yielding varieties. In general, therefore, it is likely to be impossible to ignore variations in existing investments in infrastructure, equipment, and all the means whereby farmers have sought to control their natural environment, in explaining the patterns of adoption of particular techniques.

Secondly, especially in economies where markets are less well developed than in the countries of economic textbooks, firms may differ from one another in their access to supplies of other kinds of marketed and non-marketed inputs. Resources such as credit, knowledge, education, as well as modern inputs such as fertilisers, are particularly scarce in developing countries and their allocation often is not (e.g. credit) or cannot be (e.g. extension advice) carried out according to market principles. In agriculture, land is perhaps the crucial resource for which this is the case, land markets being generally very imperfect and the ability to command other resources often highly dependent on ownership of land. Griffin has brought together much evidence for the argument that differential access to inputs among farmers in developing countries can mean that farmers with large holdings and those with small will choose to adopt radically different techniques within the same economy.[14] Institutional factors conditioning access to inputs are therefore something else which will probably have to be taken into account in analysing choice-of-technique decisions.

Thirdly, the standard theory will fail to explain the pattern of adoption of new techniques if characteristics other than factor bias are important determinants of entrepreneurs' choices of technique (as well as of the direction of research), i.e. if selection procedures or criteria are different from those assumed by the standard approach. Evidence is beginning to emerge of cases in which the selection of techniques was heavily influenced by characteristics which are hard to accommodate within the standard approach. The tying of aid to the purchase of equipment from the donor country, for instance, can cause this, and there is evidence that aid agencies, staffed by engineers and others from developed countries, are sometimes influenced in their choice of technique by characteristics of production methods which make them desirable in the aid agency's terms rather than those of the receiving country.[15] There is also evidence that indigenous entrepreneurs may be influenced by characteristics such as avoidance of labour management problems, the apparent modernity of the technique, the desire to produce products of developed-country quality, lack of maintenance facilities, and so on. Only the accumulation of evidence concerned with the relative importance of the various characteristics of techniques for those who choose them will show whether or not it would be simpler to abandon the standard approach in favour of, for instance, one based on the institutional requirements of the organisations which choose,[16] or some other selection mechanism.

These limitations of the standard approach lead on to a further problem. If different firms or farms have differential access to, or perceive different relative profitability in, a given available technology, it follows that a change in that technology will result in some firms adopting new techniques and others not, at any given time. This will result in structural changes in the production going on in that industry and in the social and economic organisation underlying it. Just as the nature of available technology is influenced by the social and economic environment in which it is developed, so changes in it will affect that environment and in turn affect further stages in the development of technology. For this reason, if we want to understand the relationship between technology and the economy, we cannot ignore the dynamic and cumulative effects of technical choice on the social and economic structure.

A large amount of work has been carried out on the income distributional and employment effects of the choice of technique in developing countries, and especially on the impact of the Green Revolution on the social and economic structures of rural areas. There has as yet been less opportunity to study the longer-term dynamic effects of the pattern of adoption of new techniques on subsequent technical, economic and social change. A framework for such a study in the case of developing countries' agriculture, based on what is known about the effects of the Green Revolution and on existing efforts to develop longer-term, dynamic models,[17] might be as follows.

A new technique, or set of techniques, with a specific set of characteristics, becomes available in a particular area. The initial economic structure of agriculture in that area, especially the distribution of access to inputs such as land, credit, technical advice and so on, determines which farmers are first willing and able to adopt the new technique (the 'initial innovator group' in Ishikawa's terminology). The emergence of this group results in changes in the economic structure of agriculture in the area, and in the distribution of income and power, these changes depending partly on the extent to which other farmers are able to follow the initial innovators in adopting the new techniques, and partly on the effects of the spread of the new technology on the demand for inputs (especially labour), hence on the distribution of income among the owners of different factors of production. Further changes will occur if, through the kinds of inducement mechanism described in the last section, the changes in economic structure (e.g. the increase in the relative income of the initial innovator group) influence the further development of new techniques. These new techniques represent new available technology, and thus we come round full circle, linking together the choice of technique and the determinants of available technology.

This is essentially the framework used in the analysis of the case-study, an attempt being made there, firstly (chapter 4), to analyse the initial technical and economic structure of an agricultural society as it conditioned the access to inputs, and then to look (chapter 5) at the response to newly available techniques. This leads on (chapter 7) to the factors conditioning the subsequent emergence of further local innovations, and then to their effects (chapter 8). The use of historical data for Japan makes it possible to work over a long enough time-scale to be able to examine the dynamics of several stages of technical change. However, in the case-study, matters are complicated (in chapter 6) by the impact on the area concerned of the concurrent development of the industrial sector, and it is to the issues raised by the interaction between the agricultural and industrial sectors, and their influence over the course of technical change in agriculture, that we now turn.

4. Technical Change in Agriculture in Relation to the Development of the Economy as a Whole

Many of the arguments I have been making up to this point could be reduced to the proposition that it is impossible to isolate the process of technical change from the wider economic environment in which it is taking place. Up to now, we have been considering that environment at the level of the individual firm or industry. But it is also the case that the technology available to and in use in a particular industry or sector will be affected by that sector's position in the economy as a whole and its particular stage of development. This is especially so in the case of agriculture: since almost all countries are predominantly agricultural when they begin their process of economic development, it is the agricultural sector which must, as it were, shoulder the main burden of the changes which industrialisation brings. Technical innovation itself, and the changes consequent upon the shift from community, or household-based, self-subsistent economic relationships to those based on markets or on national planning, must therefore be seen as part of agriculture's process of response to the growth of the non-agricultural sector. Finally, then, let us examine very briefly what economists and development theorists have had to say about the non-agricultural sector's influence on agricultural change.

Until relatively recently there was an accepted view as to the role which agriculture played in the development process.[18] Agriculture, being by far the largest sector in terms of output and employment in an underdeveloped economy, must be the source of the supplies of capital, labour and output required by the expanding non-agricultural sector, and technical change in agriculture, like institutional and organisational change there, must, in cases of successful economic development, be such as to facilitate the release of those resources. In the archetypal development process of Britain, technical and institutional changes in agriculture preceding the industrial revolution were seen as the means whereby this release of resources was made possible. Japan was frequently cited as a case in which these changes occurred concurrently with the outflow of capital and labour resources to industry, while at the same time making possible a substantial contribution of food output and foreign-exchange-earning exports.[19]

It was never denied in this approach that agriculture as an industry had to provide productive employment for those who worked in it, or that the incomes earned from this employment were important as a source of demand for the output of industry. Nor was it denied that it might be necessary to make some investment in agriculture itself. But the basic thrust of the approach was that agriculture could maintain or expand its output, while giving up inputs, through a more efficient allocation of its resources, especially through the release to industry of the marginally unproductive labour which was assumed to be held there in large amounts.[20] Agriculture's role in development was therefore essentially a passive one and technical and institutional change in agriculture were simply vehicles which might be required to enable it to play this role.

This view of agriculture's role was very prevalent in the 1950s and earlier 1960s, both in the academic world and in the policies of governments of both planned and market economies in the Third World. The growth of modern industry was heavily encouraged and investment in agriculture minimised. However, as time went on certain difficulties which this policy created became more and more acute. The first of these was the problem of food shortage, resulting from inadequate growth in agricultural output, which led to rising prices and wages and urban unrest. The second was the problem of the lack of employment opportunities for rapidly growing labour forces, as it became clear that industrial growth, almost however fast, could not provide enough jobs, and even exacerbated the problem by encouraging migration in search of urban employment, so that it began to be more and more important for agriculture to hold its labour force rather than give it up. In addition, the advent of new technological possibilities in agriculture, through for instance higher-yielding seed varieties, raised the possibility that investment in agriculture might be not only necessary but also profitable.[21]

In the light of these developments substantial re-thinking of the role of agriculture in development and of the relationship between agriculture and industry in the development process has begun. Schultz was among the first to challenge the idea that traditional agricultural sectors could achieve output growth simply by allocating resources more efficiently, and he argued that substantial investment from outside would be required to provide farmers with the incentives and the possibilities necessary to raise output.[22] From quite a different direction, Ishikawa's work on Asian agriculture showed that agriculture's ability to respond to output-raising opportunities, especially in paddy rice areas, depended crucially on prior investment in irrigation facilities.[23] In recent years much greater emphasis has come to be placed on agricultural development *per se*, treating agriculture as an industry with growth potential in its own right, in which resources have to be invested, rather than as the source of industry's input requirements.

For our purposes, however, the basic point which arises from this discussion is that both the kinds of approach to agricultural development outlined here are based on the assumption that growth in agriculture has to be stimulated by developments outside the agricultural sector, whether passively through the demands made by the growing industrial sector, or actively as a result of the channelling of outside resources into agriculture. In practical terms, it is extremely hard to think of a case of agricultural growth being sustained without some stimulus from outside.[i] Furthermore, while in principle any outside stimulus could lead to agricultural development, historically it has as a rule been the growth of indigenous commerce, towns and industry which has led to sustained growth in agriculture.[j] The extent to which

[i] See e.g. Boserup, who concludes, on the basis of a survey of historical experience of the relationship between agricultural and industrial growth, that 'In the normal course of events, new things do not originate in the agricultural milieu: a pull or push from outside seems to be needed, be it the pull of foreign demand, the opening of new transport systems, the appearance of new consumer goods to tempt the subsistence peasant, or the drain of manpower away from agriculture.' Boserup, M., 'Agrarian Structure and Take-Off' (137), p.205.

[j] Cf. Geertz, who argues that an outside stimulus leads only to 'involution' where there is no local industry or commerce to sustain agricultural development, and who explains the lack of development in Javanese agriculture, as compared with Japanese, as follows: 'Where Japanese peasant agriculture came to be complementarily related to an expanding manufacturing system in indigenous hands, Javanese peasant agriculture came to be complementarily related to an agro-industrial structure under foreign management . . . The dynamic interaction between the two sectors which kept Japan moving and ultimately pushed her over the hump to sustained growth was absent in Java.' (Geertz, C., *Agricultural Involution* (146), p.135.

governments can substitute for, or assist in, the role of non-agricultural growth in stimulating change in agriculture is something which the Japanese case — transitional, as it were, between the unplanned indus- trialisations of the West and the more consciously initiated ones of later developing countries — can help to illuminate, but at any rate, in what follows I shall start from the assumption that the forces which stimulate and sustain growth and technical change in agriculture originate outside the agricultural sector.

It follows from this that if the stimulus for agricultural growth and technical change comes from outside the agricultural sector, then we have to take into account the nature of that stimulus if we want to explain the pattern of agricultural development. That is to say, in the historical cases where development of the non-agricultural sector was the spur to agricultural change, the form which that development took, as well as its scale and timing, must have been an important determinant of the type of agricultural change which occurred. In terms of the problem of technology, this can be read as saying that the type of technology which is demanded and developed and diffused in agriculture depends on the influence agriculture receives from the outside economy, in both quan- tity and quality. In other words, we have to explain the nature of tech- nical change in agriculture as part of the agricultural sector's response to the way in which the rest of the economy is developing. This means that it is very important to consider the channels of communication between agriculture and non-agriculture, such as markets for output and labour or the institutions of credit and extension, and the way in which they filter the influences of the outside economy into agriculture, or, more generally, the effects on agriculture of being drawn into the circles of influence of the commercial and industrial sectors, if we are to understand why particular techniques are developed and adopted when and where they are. For the case of Japan, this implies the argument that the successful choice of a path of technical devel- opment in agriculture, and the successful diffusion of the newly- developed techniques, cannot be explained without taking into account the nature of Japanese industrialisation and the ways in which it affected agriculture. In chapter 3 I try to develop a framework for looking at the pattern of Japanese agricultural development over time and through regions which is based on changes in the nature of the impact of industrialisation on agriculture. The case-study itself examines in detail, at the micro-economic level, the ways in which the impact of the growing industrial sector influenced the characteristics and diffusion of technical change and the economic structure of agri- culture.

5.   Summary

The basic point which this chapter has tried to make is that economic forces influence technical change. The main questions which have arisen in analysing this point, and with which the case-study tries to deal for one particular agricultural instance, could be summarised as follows:

1. What determines the characteristics of new techniques made available? The case-study provides an opportunity to look at the operation of the mechanisms of induced innovation through public institutions, and to consider what characteristics of techniques might be important in determining the success of the innovations developed.

2. What are the initial and longer-term effects of the appearance and adoption of new techniques? These include the effects on subsequent technical development ('dynamic sequences') and on the economic and social organisation of the agricultural community.

3. How does the nature of a stimulus from outside the agricultural sector influence the development and diffusion of new agricultural techniques? To answer this involves analysing how a particular agricultural economy worked before the stimulus was felt and how the particular stimulus operated on it. The main stimulus considered in the case-study is that of industrial development of a specific kind, but the role of the government in stimulating agricultural growth by making new techniques available is also considered.

Before launching into the case-study itself, however, chapter 2 will give some background to the development of the Japanese agricultural sector as a whole, as a means to seeing it in relation to agricultural development in other places, and chapter 3 will describe the pattern of technical, economic and institutional change over the period between 1868 and 1939, relating it to the pattern of Japanese industrialisation, in order to provide a framework within which to view the case-study itself.

CHAPTER TWO

The Features of Japanese Agriculture

Japan remains the only country to have industrialised to a high level on the basis of an agricultural sector composed of farms growing principally paddy rice. For this reason, it has often been argued that Japan's experience is particularly useful for understanding and promoting growth in the developing countries of Asia. At one point it was felt that this experience could be generalised into a 'model', elements of which could be followed by other developing countries. The model rested on the role which agriculture was felt to have played in Japan's economic development — on relatively rapid growth of agricultural output concurrent with industrial growth; on agriculture's contribution of labour, capital, foreign exchange and food supplies to the growing industrial sector; on the role of the land tax as the main source of the revenue used by the government to promote industrialisation; and on the land-saving nature of technical change in agriculture, which permitted all this without requiring a great deal of investment of resources in the agricultural sector. It was felt to be significant also that agriculture was able to play this role without large-scale institutional change, on the basis of small-scale family farms and a landlord/tenant system.[1]

With the progress of research into Japanese agrarian history, however, more and more evidence came to suggest that the development of agriculture could only be understood in relation to the specific historical conditions of Japan's economic development — conditions which could not easily be reproduced at the present time by today's developing countries. In this chapter therefore, I want to bring together, on the one hand, the general macro-economic outline of the development of Japanese agriculture and of its relationship with industrialisation, the controversial basis for the idea of the desirability and transferability of the Japanese experience; and, on the other hand, the main characteristics of Japanese agriculture conditioning its micro-economic structure and the specific nature of the economic change which took place. This should serve both as an introduction to the more detailed analysis of the history of technical change and economic development in Japanese agriculture as a whole (chapter 3) and to the case-study itself, and as a basis for relating Japan's agricultural development to that of other countries.

1.   The Outline of the Economic Development of Japanese Agriculture

(1)   AGRICULTURE IN THE DEVELOPMENT OF THE ECONOMY

To begin at the broadest level, we can start by considering the position of agriculture in the developing Japanese economy as a whole. In 1868 there occurred the almost bloodless revolution known as the Meiji Restoration, which brought to power a government determined to overthrow the social, economic and political system by which the former Tokugawa rulers had controlled the country, in isolation from the rest of the world, for the previous two hundred years. The new government's aim was to establish a modern state and economy which could resist the military and economic threat of the colonising powers. However, although there are no precise data to prove it, there is little doubt that the base from which they had to launch their new policies was that of a predominantly agrarian society. As I shall suggest in chapter 3, this is not to say that there had not been substantial growth of commerce and rural manufacturing during the Tokugawa period. But the available evidence suggests that 70−80% of the gainfully occupied population were still engaged in agriculture, forestry and fishing at the beginning of the Meiji period.[2] It is likely that a significant proportion of those registered as employed in agriculture were also engaged in some kind of manufacturing by-employment,[3] and industrial and agricultural employment were not clearly separated. Nevertheless, agriculture was by far the most important single industry, providing some employment for something like four out of five of the working population, and inevitably of great significance from the point of view of the new government's policy of promoting industrialisation and economic growth.

The period between 1868 and the end of the century saw the first stages in the enactment of this policy. The opening up of the country to foreign trade led to the expansion of exports of silk and tea and then to the development of a domestic textile industry encouraged by the government, which used its tax revenues and its foreign exchange to

import modern machinery and foreign technical advice, to build railways, model factories and so on. Modern economic growth began,
according to Ohkawa and Rosovsky, somewhere in the mid-1880s, as
the modern textile industry became established following the stabilis-
ation of the financial system under the deflationary policy of Finance
Minister Matsukata (1881–5).[4]

The part that agriculture played in this process has been the subject
of fierce controversy. The controversy hinges on the estimation of the
rate of growth of agricultural output in the Meiji period. If the agricultural growth rate was relatively high, then we may have a remarkable
and interesting case of an agricultural sector simultaneously growing
and contributing resources to the development of the non-agricultural
sector—what Ohkawa has called the concurrent growth of industry and
agriculture. This would be in contrast to the experience of other now-
developed countries, where the achievement of relatively high levels of
agricultural output is thought to have occurred before industrialisation
began and to have been a pre-condition for it.

It might have been thought that in Japan at least this question could
be quite straightforwardly answered, since official government organisations had begun to collect data on agricultural output and inputs from
early on, as a consequence of the levying of taxation on land. These official Ministry of Agriculture figures give an average rice yield for
1878–82 of 180 kg/10 ares,[5] which is relatively high but by no means
outstanding when compared with yields achieved in other Asian countries in the 1950s and early 1960s;[6] when considered alongside the relatively high man/land ratio in Japan, they suggest that output per man
was comparatively rather low. But they imply a growth rate of gross
agricultural output of 2·8% p.a. for the period 1878–1902,[7] which is
relatively high, especially taken in conjunction with the low rate of
population growth. These figures therefore provided the basis for the
'Japanese model' by implying that Japanese agriculture began from a
base in 1868 not unlike that in other Asian developing countries today,
but grew relatively fast at the same time as the first stages of industrialisation were taking place.

Then, in 1966, James Nakamura published a book[8] in which he
argued that the official figures significantly under-estimated the level of
output and yields immediately after the Meiji Restoration, and since
this under-estimation decreased over time, they also over-estimated the
rate of growth in subsequent periods. The cause of this lay in widespread and accepted practices for concealing land and output from
government officials as a means of evading the land tax. The evidence
that these practices existed was incontrovertible. The question was how
significant they were, and how far the growth rate should be reduced to

take account of them. Nakamura himself produced a new series for agricultural production which gave a growth rate of 0·9% p.a. for 1878−1902, and an initial yield level for 1878−82 of 246 kg/10 ares, well above the levels of Asian countries in the 1950s.[9] Ohkawa and his colleagues then reworked the official series as part of their large-scale project on Japanese historical statistics[10] and produced a growth rate of 1·8% p.a. for 1878−1902, almost halfway between Nakamura and the official data.

Because of the doubt remaining about these estimates, it is difficult to say, then, how productive Japanese agriculture was in 1868, and precisely what was happening to output in the second half of the nineteenth century. To say more on this question of growth rates and pre-conditions we need to go below the surface of the macro-level data to look in more detail at the forces determining productivity levels, and some attempt to do this is made in the next chapter. Meanwhile, we can at least say that, between 1868 and the turn of the century, there was steady, though probably not spectacular, growth in agricultural output, that industrial output was growing fast,[11] leading to increasing demand for food, and that the rural nature of much industrial production provided farm households with further opportunities for increasing their incomes. The deflationary period of the 1880s was something of an exception, but in general this trend of linked expansion in industry and agriculture continued into the twentieth century.[12]

After 1900, industry began to move into the second stage of its development with the establishment and growth of modern heavy industries based on urban factory production. On everybody's estimates agricultural growth continued at a faster rate than earlier in the period up to the end of World War I, though at nowhere near the 6·15% p.a. achieved by the industrial sector at this time (1897−1917).[13] There is also general agreement that in the inter-war period agricultural growth slowed up and the gap between it and industrial growth increased.[a] By the 1930s the relative positions of agriculture and industry had been reversed as compared with 1868, so that agriculture by then employed less than half the employed population and produced less than 20% of national output.[14] Real income per gainfully employed person in agriculture continued to rise but, with industrial incomes rising much faster, the gap between the sectors expanded greatly.[b] By the time of

---

[a] Between 1917 and 1939 agricultural output grew at 1·00% p.a. while industrial output grew at 6·29% p.a. Ohkawa, K., Johnston, B. and Kaneda, H., *Agriculture and Economic Growth* (2), p.35.

[b] Primary sector income was 46·4% of secondary in 1908−12 and 24·8% in 1933−7. Ogura, T., *Agricultural Development in Modern Japan* (3), p.37.

World War II, agriculture had thus become a depressed and problematic sector of the now predominantly industrial economy.

How much did agriculture contribute to the development of the industrial sector? The 'Japanese model' approach argues that, up till about 1900, agriculture had to be and was the main source of the resources used to develop the basis for industrialisation. Agriculture provided the labour for the expanding industrial sector; it provided marketed food supplies to meet the demand from the new industrial workers and primary product exports to generate foreign exchange; and through the land tax it was the main source of government revenue to be used for building railways, subsidising new industries, etc. This was possible because of the scope for what Ranis calls 'taking up the slack' in the agricultural sector, making fuller use of the resources of land and labour in agriculture and creaming off the resulting increase in output to redirect towards developing industry.[c] The main mechanisms for achieving this were, on the one hand, the land tax and other institutional means for redirecting agricultural savings towards industrial investment, and, on the other, the simple transfer of labour through small-scale, rural industrialisation. Underlying it was a process of technical change in agriculture which, it is argued, produced substantial increases in output with little increase in investment.[d]

There have been a number of doubts cast on this view of agriculture's role in Japanese development. Early on, Oshima[15] argued that the contribution of the land tax to the growth of industry was not all that great, since much of the revenue was spent on military uses, which it was difficult to argue had much impact on domestic industry. By the time modern industrialisation really began in Japan, the land tax had ceased to be the main source of government revenue. The heavy taxation of agricultural income hindered the development of domestic demand, with all kinds of distorting consequences for the economic, social and political structure. Along similar lines, Sinha has argued that although agriculture may have met the requirements for food and foreign exchange in the 1870s and 1880s, when Japanese industrialisation really got going after 1890 the agricultural sector ceased to fulfil these

[c] Ranis, G., 'The Financing of Japanese Economic Development' (127). In Nakamura's terms, it was less output growth and more redirection of already existing output which made this possible. This does not alter the basic argument, however. In neither case does agriculture require a substantial inflow of resources.

[d] From this description it can be seen why the Japanese example played a large part in the construction of the early two-sector models of agriculture's role in development, mentioned in chapter 1. See e.g. Ranis, G. and Fei, J., *Development of the Labour Surplus Economy* (164), for instance pp.62–3.

functions.[16] Imports of rice began to be necessary and exports of industrially processed products, using imported raw materials, became much more important. There is no question that agriculture did provide the labour force of the expanding industrial sector, but whether it did this as easily and cheaply (from industry's point of view) as the 'model' approach implies is also open to doubt. There has been much debate as to whether there was in Japan anything corresponding to the 'unlimited supplies of labour' from the agricultural sector postulated by dual economy approaches to economic development. That is to say, did agriculture yield up its 'surplus' labour to industry at a constant wage rate little above the subsistence level income, or was it necessary for industrial employers to raise the wages they offered in order to attract more and more labour from agriculture? There is considerable evidence to suggest that industrial employers did not find it easy to recruit a stable factory labour force, and that the agriculture/industry wage differential decreased when industrial employment was expanding. The concept of 'surplus labour' is also difficult to interpret in an agricultural sector undergoing technical change which required, as we shall see, increased labour input.[e]

These doubts hinge largely on the significance of the 1870s and 1880s as a prelude to the later full-scale industrialisation and the creation of a modern factory labour force—i.e. on an understanding of the nature of growth in the industrial sector. More significant from our point of view are the doubts raised by Ishikawa as to the resource requirements of the growth of the agricultural sector and their effect on the net inter-sectoral flow of resources.[17] This is a question which hinges on an understanding of the requirements of technical change of the kind observed in Japanese agriculture in the Meiji period (or earlier, following Nakamura), and on the specific relationship between industrial and agricultural development in Japan. There are two stages to Ishikawa's case:

1. Technical change of the Japanese kind, involving use of improved seed varieties, heavy application of fertiliser, and intensive cultivation practices, generates output growth only where there already exist facilities for adequate and controlled supplies of irrigation water. This

---

[e] For more on this see, for example, Taira, K., *Economic Development and the Labour Market in Japan* (132), and Patrick, H. ed., *Japanese Industrialisation and its Social Consequences* (126) especially the articles by Saxonhouse and by Cole and Tominaga. Taira makes out a convincing case for the argument that the paternalistic practices of Japanese employers (for instance, the life-time employment system), often attributed (e.g. by Abegglen in *The Japanese Factory* (104)) to the peculiarities of Japanese culture, were a response to the high labour turnover experienced by factory owners in the earlier stages of Japanese industrialisation.

finding, presented in chapter 2 of *Economic Development in Asian Perspective*, has been substantially borne out by subsequent experience of the Green Revolution.

2. Much investment in the creation of an adequate irrigation system in Japan had already taken place before 1868, so that the flow of resources into agricultural investment did not need to be as large as in countries which do not have such favourable initial conditions for agricultural growth. But nevertheless the data are not adequate to prove that there were not flows into agriculture offsetting the flow from the land tax the other way, and government investment in riparian work represents part of this offsetting flow not generally allowed for. Flows of wages and of private loans from industry to agriculture are also very difficult to measure and probably substantial.

The conclusion is that it is difficult to show empirically that there was a net flow of resources from agriculture to industry, and even if there was, this was only because the necessary investment in agriculture had been made in earlier periods.[f] Much of what follows in later chapters is concerned with examining and trying to elucidate this relationship between the particular characteristics of technical change and investment in land infrastructure. For the moment, suffice it to say that the existence of the relationship, combined with the extreme difficulty of estimating statistically the volume of investment in irrigation work in Japan, casts doubt on the extent of the net flow of resources from agriculture to industry in Japan and on the comparability of the Japanese case with those of other developing countries.

(2) The Nature of Agricultural Growth

Ishikawa's argument has carried us from the question of agriculture's role in the overall development of the Japanese economy to the question of

---

[f] For the latest discussion of the inter-sectoral resource flow in Japan, see Ohkawa, K. and Mundle, S., 'Agricultural Surplus Flow in Japan' (14), who conclude basically that the significance of resource transfer depends on the time-period under consideration and the viewpoint taken. From the point of view of agriculture, the outflow of resources to the non-agricultural sector represented at times a significant burden, but from industry's point of view, inflows from agriculture were never all that significant as a source of capital. In their estimates, Ohkawa and Mundle make the dividing line between the agricultural and non-agricultural sectors that between agricultural production activities and non-agricultural production activities. This means that the surplus they measure is not that derived from farm *households* (who might also be engaged in non-agricultural activities) and transferred to the non-farm household sector, but that derived from agricultural production and transferred to the non-agricultural production sector.

the nature and sources of agriculture's ability to raise output. This latter question is obviously confused by the problem of the reliability of output and land input data, but we can probably safely say that we need to explain a period of steady output growth, which may or may not date back before the early Meiji period, a speeding up of this growth around 1900−20, and a period of much slower growth between the wars. Here I shall simply summarise the overall changes in inputs and in the macro-level characteristics of technical change which are held to explain this growth.[18] In the next chapter I shall examine the process in much more detail at the micro level.

It is commonly acknowledged that the cultivable area of Japan is proportionately very low, and by the Meiji period the scope for expanding the cultivated area was limited. In the period 1880−1920, cultivated area was still expanding at a rate of about 0·5% p.a.,[19] but most of this increase was in the very north of Honshū and in Hokkaidō, and consisted of marginal upland fields in cold areas. The area of paddy field grew much more slowly and after 1920 the total cultivated area also more or less ceased to grow. The area actually planted to crops (i.e. allowing for double-cropping) grew on average over the entire period before World War II at about the same rate as the cultivated area, but underlying this were various offsetting tendencies affecting the double-cropping rate. Up to 1900, double-cropping practices were spreading in some parts of the country, but the spread slowed up after that for the reasons to be examined in chapter 3, and was also offset to some extent by the expansion of the cultivated area in the north where double-cropping was impossible. In general, therefore, increase in the cultivated area cannot account for any great part of the increase in output.

The agricultural labour force changed little before 1900. It dropped quite sharply during the 1900−20 boom period, and thereafter declined very slowly.[20] Actual input of labour time per worker is another matter, however. Where a worker is engaged in both agriculture and an industrial side-occupation it is very difficult to monitor changes in the amount of his time he spends on each. Tussing, in his study of data from Yamanashi Prefecture in the Meiji period,[21] found that the categorisation of workers according to their primary occupation in the official statistics tended to over-estimate agricultural labour input in the early years, when agriculture was primary and manufacturing secondary for many people, and to under-estimate it in later years, when manufacturing had become primary for many and agriculture secondary. Allowing for this, he estimated that labour input into agriculture was increasing until the late Meiji period, and this is what would be expected from the nature of the technical changes being diffused. Shintani has made estimates of the total labour days in agriculture which also show an increase in the period up to 1920, implying quite a large increase in work-days per worker.[22] As is well known, taking the country as a whole, labour outflow from agriculture to industry in the pre-World-War-II period never made any real impression on the absolute number of farm workers or households, simply absorbing the increase in that population, and it seems more than likely that labour input per man and per hectare was increasing until about World War I.

Turning to capital, Chōki Keizai Tōkei[23] gives estimates of the fixed capital stock in agriculture in terms of machinery and tools, livestock and plants, and farm buildings. This stock changed little over the entire period up to World War II, growing at no more than 1% p.a. This does not include, though, investment in land improvement, the progress of which will be described as far as possible in the next chapter. Current capital inputs, most notably fertiliser, increased rapidly, growing at a little over 3% p.a. over the entire pre-World-War-II period, but faster in the inter-war period than earlier.

As a result of these trends in inputs, factor productivities moved in the direction of higher yields, higher output per man (though not necessarily per hour worked), and probably some decline in output per unit of capital inputs, especially in the inter-war period. The exact size of these changes depends on the estimation of agricultural output growth, but, on the basis of Chōki Keizai Tōkei data, Hayami concludes that land and labour productivities were rising at about the same rate as output, with the same kind of phasing over time.[24]

In general, then, technical change in Japanese agriculture could be characterised as land-saving, probably labour-using in its earlier stages, and certainly variable capital-intensive. It was also closely bound up with investment in irrigation facilities in ways which cannot easily be analysed statistically at the macro level.[25] If this is set against what we know of available factor proportions and prices, which indicates a falling price for current inputs relative to land and labour, then we have the basis for suspecting the existence of some kind of induced innovation mechanism, and Hayami and Ruttan use this evidence, combined with their analysis of the institutional mechanisms, as proof of their induced innovation model (see chapter 1). This leads them to argue that the lessons from Japanese agricultural development lie in the mechanisms of the choice of an appropriate path of technical change to suit the particular factor endowments available, rather than in the specification of a particular growth process.

This has brought us a long way from the original 'Japanese model' and has stripped it down, as it were, to its essence, which Hayami and Ruttan argue lies in the choice-of-technique mechanisms. The case-study which follows is in effect an analysis of these mechanisms, but, as argued in chapter 1, widening the idea of appropriateness beyond simple factor intensities. To make this further step, we need to look beyond available inputs to the micro-economic, institutional and infrastructural factors conditioning the nature of an appropriate technique and the mechanisms whereby it might be chosen. I shall turn now, therefore, to a brief introduction, for the country as a whole, to the institutional and environmental context within which the growth described above took place.

2.   The Characteristics of Japanese Agriculture and its Economic Organisation

In this section I shall outline the main factors conditioning changes in technology and economic organisation in Japanese agriculture in the period before World War II. The features which I describe here were in operation throughout the 1868–1939 period, and I shall concentrate on the aspects of continuity within them.[g] Such changes as occurred in them will as far as possible be ignored until chapter 3. I shall begin by looking at the factors conditioning the agricultural technology in use and then go on to the social and institutional forces influencing the economic organisation of agricultural production.

(1)   RICE CULTIVATION AND ITS ROLE IN JAPANESE AGRICULTURE

Rice has always been and remains to this day the chief crop grown by Japanese farmers. It is thought to have been introduced into Japan in about the first century BC and by the end of the eighth century AD was being grown as far north as the Tōhoku district.[26] From earliest times most of the rice grown in Japan was of the Japonica, as opposed to the Indica, type, Japonica varieties being able to germinate at lower temperatures and to respond to fertiliser application and dense planting by producing more grain rather than more leaves and stem.[h]

Rice is the main item in the Japanese diet and is commonly eaten at all meals. Up till the end of the Tokugawa period, however, it was something of a luxury food, eaten unmixed with other grains only by the upper classes. The mass of cultivators had to make do with wheat or barley, or rice mixed with these inferior grains. The rice they grew

---

[g] I shall use past tenses, although much of what is described here would still be true of present-day villages and farms.

[h] Though Indica varieties, known as 'red rice' in Japan, were still quite commonly grown in areas where conditions were bad in Tokugawa and early Meiji times.

constituted in large part the tax revenue of the feudal nobility. The samurai received their incomes in rice, and rice was the most important medium of exchange and measure of value. Rents for paddy land were paid in rice throughout the pre-World-War-II period. Rice supplies Japanese alcohol, its straw was made into all kinds of household items, babies were fed on the water it was boiled in. It acquired a religious significance to reflect its practical one. As incomes rose in the nineteenth and twentieth centuries, the mass of the population came to be able to substitute rice for other grain and also to begin to demand a wider range of food than the grain, pickled vegetables, soy-bean protein and occasional fish or dairy produce which they had consumed during the Tokugawa period. So consumption of meat, eggs and dairy produce, and of a wider range of fruit and vegetables, has increased, but rice has retained its predominant position in the Japanese diet.

Rice has also always been the most important crop from the point of view of the cultivator. Almost all Japanese farmers grew at least some rice and it has in general been exceptional to use fields with adequate irrigation facilities (about 50% of the cultivated area) for any other crop.[i] Where rice can be grown under irrigated conditions, it can produce a high yield of food grain year after year on the same land, even without the use of fertiliser.[j] It can thus support a dense population which in turn supplies the heavy labour input needed for its cultivation and for the creation and maintenance of the irrigation facilities it demands. In this way it brings into existence an infrastructure of investment in land improvement and of economic and social institutions, tastes, customs, etc., which are incompatible with the cultivation of any other crop.[k]

In most areas, therefore, the cultivation of crops other than rice was subsidiary and had to be fitted into the system of rice-growing. Most farm holdings consisted of a mixture of paddy fields fitted into the village irrigation system and 'upland fields' (*hatake*) which could not be irrigated to the requirements of paddy rice. Rice was sometimes grown in upland fields, but in general they were used to grow non-rice crops — originally the other vegetables, pulses and grain crops necessary for subsistence,

[i] Cotton was grown on paddy fields in advanced areas in the late Tokugawa and early Meiji periods, but not once much cheaper imported supplies became available. The same is true of sugar-cane.

[j] This is due to the nutrients carried in the water, the action of bacteria in the water, the inhibition of weed growth, etc.

[k] Cf. Geertz: 'A Javanese peasant's terrace . . . is both a product of an extended historical process of cultural development and perhaps the most immediately significant constituent of his "natural" environment.' *Agricultural Involution* (146), p.9.

later other commercial crops, such as tea, mulberry, etc., as well. It was also climatically possible outside the northernmost regions (Tōhoku and Hokkaidō) to grow winter crops of non-rice grains on paddy fields, and this practice spread where fields could be suitably drained and where adequate fertiliser was available (see chapter 3). Wheat and barley were the most common of these second crops, and green manure crops were also sometimes grown in the winter on paddies. Livestock have not traditionally been required to play the role of fertiliser producers within a mixed rotation which they have played in Western agriculture, and more land-saving crops such as soya-bean have in general been used instead of animals as the main sources of protein in the Japanese diet. However, in the later nineteenth and twentieth centuries livestock did become important as draught animals, and fodder crops were grown for them. Both horses and oxen were used, and some dairy cattle were also kept, stall-fed in the same way.

In general terms cultivation methods, especially for rice, were extremely labour-using. The laborious but yield-increasing practice of growing seedlings in a nursery and transplanting them on to the paddy was probably used as early as the twelfth century and was universal in the Tokugawa period and after. The preparation of the paddy field before transplanting and the weeding and care of the plants afterwards were all carried out with meticulous care.[1] Before World War II, with the exception of ploughing, for which draught animals were used where conditions permitted, all field operations were carried out by hand or with simple tools. Threshing and husking were also carried out using man-powered tools until the first machine-powered threshers and huskers appeared in the twenty years before World War II.

Traditionally, the labour demands of the standard technical system were very uneven through the year, with peaks at transplanting and harvesting times, and long slack periods during the winter available for general repairs and maintenance to irrigation facilities, buildings, equipment, etc. Double-cropping of the paddy fields made more work in the winter but tended to intensify the harvesting and transplanting bottlenecks by imposing time limits on these operations.

Throughout, the fundamental influence on the nature of Japanese rice-producing technology was the need to obtain high yields per unit of land. In places, as early as the Tokugawa period, some labour-saving practices were developed, but never at the expense of yields. The use of fertilisers to raise yields increased steadily over time. In advanced areas,

---

[1] Note the inbred nature of this attitude to farming revealed in the distaste for mechanised transplanting felt by the older generation of farmers in Dore's *Shinohata* (43), pp.106–7.

commercial fertilisers such as waste fish and vegetable products and human excrement from the towns were being used in the Tokugawa period, but until about 1900 the main sources of fertiliser remained grass, leaves and other vegetable matter, collected in woods and forests and on waste ground with the expenditure of huge amounts of labour time. These sources were replaced in this century by various forms of commercial organic and later chemical fertilisers. The effort to increase and stabilise rice yields is known to have produced, from early on, many different rice varieties, suited to different local environments, producing different qualities of rice with different fertiliser responsiveness, photosensitivity, resistance to cold, etc.

Many significant changes took place in the technology of rice cultivation and in the structure of agricultural production between 1868 and 1939, but it remained true that the farmer of 1868 would probably not have found it hard to adapt to the agricultural technology of 1939. He would have found more or less the same crops grown, the rhythm of seasons and rotations substantially unchanged, and his knowledge of tools and cultivation practices not particularly out of date. By contrast, he would probably, as we shall see, have found the *economic*, as opposed to the technical, nature of production harder to deal with — he would have had to learn to produce for and buy from a market, and to take economic decisions which were not required of him in Tokugawa times. And by even greater contrast, a counterpart working in manufacturing industry, who would have been a craftsman using human or water power, probably in his own home, in 1868, would have been a wage-earner, operating electrically-powered machinery in an urban factory by 1939. In many ways, this relative stability of agricultural technology can be traced back to the requirements of rice cultivation embodied and embedded in the landscape and in the attitudes and institutions of village society.

(2)   THE LAND INFRASTRUCTURE OF RICE CULTIVATION

Paddy rice was probably first grown in Japan on naturally marshy land. However, there is little in the geography of Japan to compare with the great flood plains of other parts of Asia, nor does Japan have a full-scale monsoon.[m] So the spread of paddy cultivation really required the

---

[m] There is a distinct rainy season (*tsuyu*), but rainfall is much more evenly distributed throughout the year than in typical Asian rice-growing regions. See Ogura, T., *Agricultural Development in Modern Japan* (3), p.596, for a comparative rainfall chart. The rainy season also tends to come rather late for transplanting, given the relatively long growing season required under Japanese conditions of temperature and sunlight.

creation of facilities to store rainfall throughout the year and to control and direct the flow of rivers. Because of this requirement, relatively sophisticated irrigation facilities were developed from early on wherever paddy rice could be grown, and the main outlines of the system were constructed in most places well before the Meiji Restoration. Sawada has estimated that 70·9% of the pond or reservoir facilities and 73·7% of the river irrigation systems in existence in the 1960s were first constructed before 1868.[27] This enormous and often technically sophisticated investment embedded in the landscape was a crucial factor determining the social and economic structure of Japanese agriculture and therefore the possibilities for and the nature of technical change. It is therefore highly important, both in general and for the case-study, to understand how the irrigation system, in some ways uniquely Japanese, operated.

The first irrigation facilities developed in Japan generally took the form of ponds or small reservoirs, located above the system of paddy fields, in which water collected. A controlled flow would then be directed on to the paddy fields at the right time by means of gates or barriers, using the force of gravity to drive the water. This sort of irrigation system is most common in the Kinki and Inland Sea area, the original centre of population where agriculture developed earliest. In this area too, the rivers tend to be relatively short and small, and the development of small-scale river irrigation systems, involving the damming of streams, was also comparatively easy to organise.

After the end of the sixteenth century, as the power of the feudal lords (*daimyō*) under the rule of the Tokugawa government became more firmly established, it became institutionally possible to mobilise resources on a larger scale for the construction of more complex and wide-scale irrigation systems. For the *daimyō*, the creation of new paddy fields within their domains was a prime means of increasing revenue and, as engineering technology advanced, they organised schemes which made available large areas of the alluvial plains of larger rivers, extending cultivation further and further downstream as the ability to control rivers improved. In the earlier part of the Tokugawa period, such schemes involved the flooding of the plain in a manner not unlike that in the flood plains of other Asian countries. But from the middle of the Tokugawa period, as cultivation expanded with the growth of population, the development of engineering techniques permitted the construction of much more highly controlled irrigation flows, whereby water was carried direct to the individual paddies and the growing towns and villages were protected by banks and dykes from the flood. The Kantō Plain was the most significant area opened up for cultivation in this way, it having both a large-scale river system and the strong organisational control of the Tokugawa rulers in Tokyo.[28]

As more and more river irrigation systems were built, there remained only the swamps and mudflats of coastal areas and river mouths as potential but undeveloped rice-growing areas, and with the development of flood control upstream, the reclamation of such areas became more and more feasible. By 1868 certain areas of this sort and parts of the very north, including Hokkaidō, constituted more or less the only potential paddy-growing land left to be opened up. After 1868 reclamation of coastal areas, such as the Ariake Bay in Kyūshū, and the development of Hokkaidō continued, but it was to the improvement of the facilities built during the Tokugawa period and earlier that the bulk of investment in land infrastructure was directed.

The form taken by individual irrigation systems depended on the nature of the source of water. Systems based on rivers were most common, covering about 70% of the irrigated area, while pond sources covered about 20%, and other miscellaneous types, such as the creek system in Saga, covered the remaining 10%.[29] River systems vary enormously in their size and scope, but we can conceptualise all systems, including pond ones, as consisting of an original source of water and the various stages at which water from that source is divided up and distributed, working right down to the final user. Thus a system might consist of a river whose flow is partly tapped off at many points by branch channels, and those branch channels may themselves have many branches, and so on. Or a system may simply consist of a pond supplying a channel which directly feeds individual paddy fields. At every branch of every system, however large or small, there must be a mechanism for controlling the allocation of water between the channels, and the rules for the control of this distribution mechanism are crucially important for determining the productivity of individual fields and the area which can be farmed, hence the distribution of income between individual farmers and villages and areas up- or down-stream.

How, then, was this distribution organised?[30] The first point to be emphasised is that, in Japan, the final water-consuming unit has always been the individual plot or field, not the farm or the household.[n] The reasons for this go far beyond anything that can be covered here — into Japanese topography, the reasons behind the development of highly labour-using methods, the absence of large farm units, etc. — but this principle is embodied in the structure of irrigation systems built generations ago. The individual household might farm one plot or many plots, but only in exceptional circumstances would it farm all the plots covered

[n] Compare a flooded plain where there is little or no control over which individual plots are flooded, or use of underground water through private farm-level ownership of a tube-well or pump.

by one water source or even one branch of a source, and water usually flowed from one plot or group of plots to the next around each part of the system. If there was to be a peaceful distribution of water, each household had therefore to come to a co-operative agreement with other users of water from the source, and it was always rare for any individual land-owner to be in such a dominating position as to be able to ignore entirely the interests of other users of water from the source or sources he used.

What therefore emerged was a pyramidal structure of communal groups dependent on each branch of the system. At the base were the communal groups of final users, farmers of the paddy area covered by the final branches. Very often these groups were village communities, where a village's paddy area was separate from that of other villages and dependent on one final branch or source. Where a village had its own independent water source, e.g. a pond, there were no other layers of groups involved. But where it was part of a larger system, individual groups of final users needed to be represented in the communal group which controlled the distribution at the next branch up, and so on at every level up to the original source, and at each level someone would be chosen to represent the group members at the next level up.

These communal groups came to be generally known as *suiri kumiai* (water use associations or unions), and they ranged down from the *kumiai* of representatives of the entire area covered by an irrigation system to the *kumiai* of final users, most often based on the village, to which all farmers belonged. At each layer, the *kumiai* responsible managed the allocation of water at its branch and attempted to regulate the conflicts of interest between the *kumiai* beneath it. They were not always successful in this and, especially when water was in short supply, violent conflicts between *kumiai* up- and down-stream were not uncommon.[o] There were many complex customary rules governing allocation, through the length of time sluices could be open, the size of diversionary barriers that could be built, etc., which served as the standards by which disputes could be judged. To varying degrees there was scope for the more powerful to manage things to their advantage, but this was always tempered by the need to maintain the system on which everyone depended.[p] Each *kumiai*

[o] For examples see Shimpo, M., *Three Decades in Shiwa* (40), p.2. In the area he deals with, 'between 1626 and 1942 water disputes occured once every seven years when, according to available documents, several thousand farmers would confront each other at the river junction and often become involved in bloody fighting'.

[p] In Shimpo's village, Shiwa, village water users were clearly divided into 'haves' (the upstream groups) and 'have-nots' (the downstream groups), but the haves never seem to have gone much further in the use of their privileged position than requiring the have-nots to ask very deferentially for extra water when they were short. *Three Decades in Shiwa* (40), p.7.

was generally responsible for the maintenance of the facilities it controlled and could organise communal labour and levy fees on members,
and *kumiai* responsible for large-scale facilities later came to employ
permanent technical and managerial staff. During the Tokugawa
period, the local *daimyō* could act as a final arbiter of disputes to ensure
peaceful cultivation and tax-paying. After 1868, local government to
some extent took over this role, but customary rules, rather than national
legislation, remained the basis for water management.

At each level, the *kumiai* would police itself by appointing guards, for
instance to make sure that sluices were not open at the wrong times. The
kumiai head had the authority to punish those who were caught breaking the rules, but, in the interests of community solidarity, apologies
were generally thought adequate. The position of *kumiai* head was an
important one, and was usually held by a larger landowner who had the
economic resources to fight for the *kumiai*'s interests at higher levels.

Thus the technical nature of the irrigation system, itself conditioned
by the structure of cultivation within the villages, in turn imposed social
and economic relationships on agricultural communities. This meant
that technical and economic change was conditioned not only by the
embodied investment which the irrigation facilities represented, but
also by the institutional forms which they made necessary. Japanese irrigation *kumiai* have long traditions of, and experience in, communal
action. In this respect their existence potentially provided a valuable
tool through which communal groups of farmers could take part in
technical development. But in other ways, through their continual need
to reconcile conflicting interests, they could stand in the way of changes
such as the re-organisation of plots into larger fields or improvements to
the irrigation system.[q] In either case, the irrigation system and the institutional forms which it determined were fundamental factors conditioning the path of technical change and economic development.

(3)   THE HOUSEHOLD AND ITS ACCESS TO INPUTS

While the irrigation system was, as we have seen, based on the unit of
the individual plot, the economic and social organisation of Japanese
agriculture was based on the unit of the household. The absolute number of farm households in Japan changed very little throughout the
1868–1939 period, remaining at around 15½ million despite the out-
migration of agricultural labour and considerable economic change.

[q] For instance, it took twenty years to obtain the agreement necessary from all the interested groups for the dam-construction project described by Shimpo. *Three Decades in
Shiwa* (40), pp.18–21.

The Japanese word *ie*, here translated as household, in fact has a more complex meaning, involving not just the house building and property and those who live in it, but also the family in its past, present and future generations, a continuing entity which exists apart from as well as within the lives and deaths of individual family members.[31] The household was the basic unit of property ownership and economic decision-taking in Japanese agriculture, but it was also an entity with great social, moral and religious importance, and the social forms which governed the behaviour of the household determined many important aspects of the economic life of Japanese villages. While the spread of the commercial economy and of market relationships introduced new elements into economic dealings, the influence of traditional forms on the allocation of resources, especially land and labour, remained strong throughout the pre-World-War-II period. We shall see this as we come now to consider the determinants of the household's access to inputs.

Originally land in Japan was probably farmed in large holdings, using serf-like labour, by those who had been able to acquire it by military or political means. But under the first Tokugawa rulers, the military classes were removed from direct control of cultivation, going to live in castle towns and becoming purely tax-gatherers and administrators. Although in theory all land remained the property of the Emperor and could not change hands or be privately sold, it was managed by individual village households and in practice, as fortunes changed, land was mortgaged and lost, or transferred from household to household, and tenancy appeared. It has been estimated that at the time of the Meiji Restoration about 20% of households were pure tenants and 35% part-tenants.[32]

The new Meiji government established the principle of private land ownership and began the process of issuing legal title to land. Land could then be legally bought and sold and mortgaged and rented out, and the shifting structure of landownership and cultivation, the changes in which will be described in detail in chapter 3, could respond without legal hindrance to the economic forces affecting agriculture. Once legal ownership of the land had been established, the land tax could be levied, and this was paid in cash by the landowner as a fixed percentage of the assessed value of his holding. As we shall see in chapter 3, tenancy spread after this until almost half of the cultivated area was farmed by tenants. This continued to be the case until the promulgation of the land reform, enforced by the American occupation forces after World War II, which established ceilings on land holdings, expropriated the bulk of absentee and non-cultivating landlords, and fixed the structure of small-scale owner farms which still prevails today.

How, then, within this overall institutional framework, did individual households obtain access to inputs and adjust their land and labour resources to each other?[33] The household's labour force depended in principle on the size of the family, but the first and chief means of balancing labour force to area cultivated was through adjustments to the size of the family which the household supported. During much of the Tokugawa period this was principally achieved by larger land-holding households taking in as household members those whom smaller land-holding households could not adequately employ. Younger sons and daughters of small land-holding households were taken in as resident household servants and agricultural labourers, fed, clothed, perhaps given pocket money, perhaps allowed to marry and establish a family within the overall household, and required to do whatever work was demanded of them. At a higher level, adoption, or the importing into the household of a daughter's husband, were means of ensuring the continuity of an *ie* in which the househead had no son to whom to pass on the headship. Younger sons and poor relations could be kept within the household as required and a household might thus consist of a hierarchy of families, from the househead and his wife at the top, through their successors and their other children and relatives, down to the families of servants.

Small-scale cultivating households with more labour than they could employ thus sought to have their spare workers adopted into richer households, but if this failed, then they had to be sent out to find other work — by-employment within the household or casual labour in other farming areas or in the towns — and the selling of daughters into prostitution was an accepted practice. However, as time went by, especially in the more advanced, commercialising areas of the country, the alternatives to becoming a farm servant became more numerous and attractive, and large-scale households began to find it increasingly difficult to find the labour they needed. Their response was to resort more and more to the traditional practice whereby households had trimmed their size in order to remain effective as cultivating units: this was the creation of branch households.

A main household could establish a branch by setting up one of its member families as an independent household on some of the *ie*'s land. Since the survival of the main household was the primary aim, the new branch was usually given only a relatively small piece of land, along with the tools and equipment and general assistance it needed to get going, and the main household generally retained draught animals and major items of capital equipment, as well as irrigation rights and access to woodland. Thus the main household shed a greater proportion of its dependent members than it did of its economic resources. Among richer households, the forming of branches was often practised as a way of setting up younger sons on their own holdings, but it could also be used as a way of rewarding, and shedding responsibility for, long-serving household servants. The branch household (*bunke*) and the main household (*honke*) remained connected by their common ancestry, real or fictitious, and by mutual economic need. The branch might for many years remain dependent on the main household for the loan of livestock, equipment and sometimes money, and the *honke* would retain the right to call on the labour of the *bunke* if it needed it. With time, branch households themselves might form branches, and a hierarchy of households stemming from a single main household might develop, tied together by social, economic and religious inter-relationships, and known as a *dōzoku* group.[34]

As we shall see in detail in chapter 3, with the development of commercial agriculture and of intensive techniques to go with it, and with the increase in non-agricultural employment opportunities in the late Tokugawa and Meiji periods, it became increasingly difficult to operate large holdings on the basis of the extended household labour force. The possibility of setting up branch households gave larger landowners the means of reducing the area they cultivated under their own management by setting up their dependent families as branches and accepting rent from them. Furthermore, these tenant households also represented a pool of labour which could be drawn on without accepting full responsibility for them — a labour force tied by obligations to the main household and not liable to demand wage rates comparable to those to be earned outside agriculture.

The relationships between landlord and tenant households, even when not strictly those between *honke* and *bunke*, were often coloured by the existence of the *honke/bunke* pattern, with landlords offering protection and assistance to tenants and tenants providing labour when required. The usual system of rental payments, whereby rents which were laid down in terms of a fixed quantity of rice were frequently reduced on a sliding scale according to the state of the harvest, reflected the assumption of the landlord's responsibility to a certain extent for the protection and survival of his tenants.[r]

In areas where the permeation of commercial relations was well advanced and where alternative employment opportunities gave the small farmers and their families greater bargaining power, the social ties of obligation were not enough to ensure a labour force for larger cultivators, and proper wage labour came into being as the available workers demanded cash or kind wages. This trend developed through a

---

[r] Rents for paddy land were always paid in kind in this way. Rents for upland fields were quite commonly converted into cash as the range of crops grown became more diversified.

gradual shortening of the period of time for which workers were bound to their employers — where once it had been for life, it eventually became a period of years, then a single season, then a month or day. The timing of this trend varied over the country with the speed of commercialisation, and in the north traditional extended households and household servants were still to be found at the time of the land reform. The trend was also overtaken, as it were, by the progress of the outflow of agricultural labour to industry, which drew off precisely the younger sons and daughters of small-scale cultivating households who had previously constituted the hired labour force, leaving all farm households to rely more and more on their own family labour or on co-operative labour exchange arrangements. But in the meantime, particularly in the period between 1868 and World War I, villages typically contained small-scale cultivators, often tenants, members of whose households worked as agricultural labourers for some of their time, and larger-scale landowners who farmed some of their land with hired labour and let out the rest. The relationship between employer and employee could range from the full-scale traditional paternal responsibility for the resident worker, to a strictly market relationship between the employer and a son of an almost landless household, working by the day for the highest-paying employer.

It will be argued in the next chapter that there were significant shifts within the distribution of landownership and cultivated holdings in the period between 1868 and 1939. Nevertheless, in summarising the pattern of land-holding which emerged from the mixture of traditional institutional and modern market forces described here, various elements of continuity stand out and are important for an understanding of the Japanese context in comparison with that of other countries.

Firstly, despite the increasing commercialisation of the village economy, land-holding remained the chief *raison d'être* of the rural household. The proportion of households without access to land was always small and in principle even those resident in the village who could not possibly have lived without income from other sources were deemed to be members of cultivating households in some way. In this can be seen the influence of the concept of the *ie* as the unit of village society — it was almost impossible for an individual to live outside a continuing household unit. Furthermore, since the *ie* was something above its individual present members, it could not disappear, and it was incumbent on those members to try to maintain it and its assets intact. The underlying principle remained that the members of the *ie* cultivated the *ie*'s land for their own subsistence and for anything above that which would contribute to the economic and social success of the *ie*, and all members gave their labour, in whatever form required, to the maintenance of the household of which they were part.

Secondly, the size of holding, both owned and cultivated, throughout the period, was exceedingly small in terms of area. The average size of holding cultivated varied little from around one hectare throughout, and a large proportion of holdings were below this. Villages varied enormously, even within small localities, in the structure of their landholdings, but the prototype structure against which variation and change can be viewed would have consisted of one or two larger holdings of 3 hectares or more (the holdings of the main, *honke* families), partly cultivated by their owners and partly let out, a group of middle-sized holdings of about a hectare and a mass of small holdings of a half hectare or less, farmed often by those who supplemented what they owned by renting in or by working at by-employments or for other farmers. In the north, there tended to be more large-scale landowners, sometimes dominating whole villages or areas and sometimes continuing to farm a part of their holding with extended family labour. In the more commercialised south-west, the independent small-scale family holding became gradually dominant, although tenancy remained widespread.

Thirdly, within this pattern of small-scale holdings, the structure of landownership was highly complex and difficult to fit into recognised formulations of rural land-holding structures. There existed every gradation of land-holding status from the smallest pure tenant household to the largest absentee landlord, and tenancy relations were, as we have seen, heavily bound up with social and kinship relations. A large proportion of households both owned and rented in land. Some even rented in and out — e.g. in order to cultivate a more convenient holding. Given the small size of land-holdings, tenants would often cultivate land owned by a number of different landlords. Many of those who became technically absentee or non-cultivating landlords were relatively small-scale landowners who had other occupations, within the village — schoolteachers, priests, etc. — or outside it. Dore estimates that in the 1930s a landlord would have needed the rent from 6½ hectares to give an income equivalent to that of an urban civil servant or teacher,[35] and there were relatively few who owned that much.

Finally, I should briefly mention the household's access to capital assets. The main household, as suggested earlier, tended to retain ownership of major items of capital equipment when branches were formed. This was a useful way of giving smaller-scale cultivators access to larger-scale capital items, such as horses, and later even mechanical equipment such as threshers, which they could not have utilised fully themselves. On the one hand, it left the branch household still dependent and under an obligation to the main household, which limited its freedom of action. The *dōzoku* structure also provided small-scale cultivators with a source of credit — a household's *honke*/landlord would be the first place to turn when a loan was needed, and the combination of the roles of landlord and moneylender, common in developing countries, was thus in Japan part of the complex of hierarchical relationships between households.

What has been described in this section are the institutional means whereby the individual household controlled and allocated its resources. Market mechanisms were to some extent superseding the traditional institutional ones, and the effects of this on the structure of household economies will be traced in detail later, but the allocation of economic resources by farm households remained conditioned by earlier forms of economic relationship in many ways, and the force of institutions such as the *ie* exerted a profound influence on the nature and direction of technical change, as we shall see.

(4)   THE VILLAGE[s] AND THE OUTSIDE WORLD

In the previous section we looked at the factors determining the economic position of the individual household. However, as we began to see there and in the analysis of the organisation of irrigation, the actions of individual households cannot be isolated from their position within the village society. The large majority of Japanese villages are compact settlements composed of around fifty households, and scattered villages, or villages with more than a hundred households or so, are rare.[36] The village was thus a distinct community of its own and, as well as groupings of households within the village, such as the *dōzoku*, the village itself provided a central unit, above the household, to which farmers belonged and with which they identified themselves. In important ways, also, it was through the village as a community that individual households related with outside institutions such as the state. In this section, therefore, I want to consider how the village was organised as a community and how it related with the outside world, since this strongly influenced the technical choices open to it and made by individual farm households.

Full-scale discussion of the causes of the group solidarity observed

[s] Changes in local government terminology have complicated the use of the word 'village' in relation to Japan. The original word for the village (*mura*), as the smallest, geographically concentrated, residential household grouping, came to be used, after the various local government reorganisations of the second half of the nineteenth century, to refer to a wider area, containing several traditional village settlements. These individual village settlements were referred to by various terms (e.g. *buraku*, *ōaza*), but I shall continue to call them 'villages', since this seems to accord best with English usage of the word (they are sometimes referred to as 'hamlets'), and I will use the term 'administrative village' to translate *mura* in its present local government usage.

historically in Japanese villages would take us well beyond the scope of this book. The dependence on an irrigation system which no single household could construct and upon which all households relied has already been suggested as a reason for mutual co-operation.[37] From the point of view of the small-scale cultivator, on the margin of subsistence, submergence of individual wishes in the interests of the group may be the only way of ensuring survival and protection in bad times.[38] Subservience to richer households imposed on the more powerful obligations to protect and help the poorer dependent households.[39] Scott has shown that similar approaches to the functions of hierarchies and to, for instance, the landlord/tenant relationship have operated in other Asian rural societies, and that the dependent household accepts its status only so long as the patron or landlord household fulfils its obligations.[40] It is very difficult to know just how much internal conflict was covered up by the need to present an appearance of solidarity to the outside world and to what extent the typical larger landowning household used the group to further its own individual ends. Nevertheless, I would simply want to point out here that there were economic reasons why all households, both rich and poor, might accept the rights and obligations imposed by approaching as a group a number of the problems posed by agricultural production under Japanese conditions.[t]

What sort of village groups existed and how were they organised? These groups can be divided into groups internal to the village and groups to which the whole village belonged. The *dōzoku* — the hierarchy of households related by real or fictive kinship ties — was one of the main types of internal village grouping. There would generally be several *dōzoku* groupings within an individual village, and it is easy to see that they were designed to operate the kind of mutual security and insurance system just described. Those at the lower levels of the hierarchy would reliably provide the outside labour needed by those higher up — not just agricultural labour but, for instance, help with cooking and serving special meals, repairing the *honke* house, etc. In return, those higher up the hierarchy provided financial and material assistance — such as loans, equipment, clothes and utensils for special occasions, or access to wood or thatch for house repairs. They also provided help with social matters and with

---

[t] For a model illustrating the economic rationale behind the operation of community relationships in agricultural villages, see Ishikawa, S., 'Peasant Families and the Agrarian Community' (157). This paper includes an interesting discussion of the extent of community relationships in villages in Japan and in some developing countries, but above all is able to explain how, under certain conditions, landlords and agricultural workers operating according to economic maximisation principles could rationally decide to act as a community.

dealings with those outside the *dōzoku*, for example by arranging marriages or adoptions. Full-scale *dōzoku* systems tended to be found in the more backward parts of the country, in areas where subsistence was more precarious and where the maintenance of the *honke* as a powerful household with access to many resources was valuable as an insurance for everyone. However, patron/client relationships between households of a less formalised and permanent character were common everywhere where the distribution of land and assets was unequal and where poorer households had few opportunities for securing income outside the village.

Not all groupings, though, were of this hierarchical kind. In villages where there was a less marked differentiation between rich and poor, where incomes from by-employment and/or from commercial agriculture gave individual households the means to be more independent and secure in their survival, groups based on equality were more common. These groups served the same kind of function of mutual assistance and insurance, but were composed of households connected by something other than hierarchical, patron/client relationships — commonly, for instance, by their being neighbours. Groups of all sorts of size and function were possible, but they were usually used for the organisation of funerals — providing utensils and crockery, and help with cooking and entertaining — for house repairs, and so on. They could be based on mutual exchange of labour for farming also, especially for transplanting, and on mutual supply of credit. In areas where *dōzoku* had never existed or had died out, they therefore fulfilled the same kind of function of providing as a group services and insurance which the individual household could not provide for itself, but on the basis of equality rather than hierarchy.

The nature of the internal village groupings was reflected in the organisation of the village group as a whole. The village's group actions and organisation could be heavily dominated by the heads of the *dōzoku* or they could be much more democratically run, or they could be anywhere between the two extremes. But whatever form it took, the co-operative organisation of the village as a whole was a vital part of its life and fulfilled many important functions. There were all kinds of whole-village organisations which were open to all households. Apart from irrigation organisations, there would for example be organisations for the maintenance of village shrines and religious ceremonies, for provision of fire brigade services, young men's groups and young women's groups. Many such groups were highly traditional, but others could be of relatively recent formation. Patriotic groups were widely formed in the 1930s,[u] and there

---

[u] Cf. Dore: 'Perhaps only China since the revolution has ever perfected to the same extent as Japan in the 1930s the art of the "voluntary" organisation that everyone automatically belongs to.' *Shinohata* (43), p.49.

are modern housewives' groups and so on. And most interesting for our purposes, the post-1868 period saw the formation of many village agricultural groups, such as discussion groups and groups for promoting technical improvements, credit and marketing co-operatives, and tenants' groups.

Above this, for all general matters the village as a group was organised under the institution of the village head. The village head was the means for deciding how the village as a whole should react to outside happenings and how it should solve its own internal problems and disputes.[v] There were traditionally many different ways of selecting the village head, ranging from hereditary selection, through rotation among leading households, to election, but it cost money to be village head, as it did to be head of other village organisations, to pay for village entertainment, to wield influence with outside authorities, and so on, so that only relatively well-to-do households could afford the time and money necessary. As a result, there were rarely many eligible candidates and the question of who was to be head was either obvious or could be solved with a little discussion. Village headmen and heads of other village organisations were powerful and influential, but also had many duties and responsibilities.

What is clear from this is that the Japanese village had great experience in group organisation and had developed over the generations the institutions and skills necessary for group action. I want finally to look at some of the ways in which this experience and skill was used in dealing with the outside world. In the Tokugawa period and before, the village group had been used as the basic unit of administration, represented by the village head. Taxes were levied on the village rather than the individual household, and the village as a group was responsible for their payment, and, indeed, for the behaviour of individual members. The Meiji Restoration changed this, but it remains true that in many ways throughout the pre-World-War-II period and beyond, village groups have acted as intermediaries between individual farms and the outside world of markets, government bodies, and so on.

This mediation took place at two levels. First of all, it is clear that it was often through village groups that knowledge about agricultural techniques was brought into the village from outside. The generally accepted view[41] that in the Meiji period it was the larger village landowners, those who rented out land but who also continued to cultivate some themselves, who promoted the spread of new technology can be seen in

---

[v] It was also the means of organising communal work such as roadmending. There were other village officers, such as treasurers, irrigation officers and so on. See Fukutake, T., *Japanese Rural Society* (45), pp.117–23.

this light, for these were the kinds of household who would have been leaders of *dōzoku* groupings or patron/landlord to a number of clients/ tenants, or village heads. In their role as village leaders, they would have come into contact with the outside world, through their rice-marketing, through their social contacts with outside villages, and through the fact that government officials would have worked through them. They would also have been the only type of household having the resources to act as heads of agricultural groups, co-operatives, etc.

At the other level, within the village, the close inter-connections between households, embodied in village groups, promoted the spread of new technology from group leaders to the mass of small farmers. Some landlords clearly encouraged others to adopt new methods out of paternalism or a sense of duty to the group, but such attitudes were not essential to the spread of new methods because the structure of village groups itself promoted it. Thus the improvement of the irrigation system, for instance, necessarily involved and benefited everyone and required the leadership of the more influential farmers; if main households used improved equipment, then branch households borrowing from them also would; if branch households and tenants helped out main households with labour, then they would learn new cultivation methods used by the innovating main households. Landlords also had more obvious economic motives for encouraging improved techniques —e.g. raising the quality or reliability of rent rice payments—and the economic rationale for and consequences of this process will be examined in the next chapter. Here I simply want to point out the institutional mechanisms whereby it occurred.

Where larger-scale cultivating landlords had never been significant, or where they lost interest in village agriculture as industrial and commercial development attracted them away, whole-village groups were there to fulfil the same sort of role as intermediary with the outside world, and to take over functions such as marketing and provision of credit that landlords had previously performed. Thus, marketing co-operatives, fertiliser-buying co-operatives, credit co-operatives and so on, which were open to all village households just as all village households belonged to the shrine association or the fire brigade, mediated between the farmer and the market and between the farmer and the state extension services. Villages as a whole or village groups bought larger pieces of machinery, such as mechanised threshers or hullers, when they became available, and village irrigation associations financed and arranged irrigation improvements.

By no means all village groups, either landlord-dominated or more equal, acted in this progressive way towards technical change. Much depended on the circumstances of individual villages, on the skill and enthusiasm of village leadership, on the attitude of outside authorities. Nevertheless, the institutional organisation of village life had the potential to act as a means of introducing new technology to the mass of small farmers, of overcoming the barriers preventing them from borrowing, investing, marketing, or taking risks, which tend to beset small farmers in developing countries. I have tried to show that this need not be regarded as the result of peculiar qualities of leadership or altruism on the part of the rural elite, nor of magical discoveries by the Japanese in the field of social organisation, but can be seen as stemming from the way in which agricultural production and village society have together evolved over the generations within the Japanese environment.

CHAPTER THREE

Industrialisation, Technical Change and the Economic Development of Japanese Agriculture

In the last chapter, I set out some of the main forces conditioning the technical and economic responses of decision-making units in pre-war Japanese agriculture. In this chapter I shall attempt to summarise the developments to which these decision-makers had to respond and to describe the nature of their response. This involves, in effect, a historical description of the technical and micro-economic changes which took place in Japanese agriculture, in response to the growth of the industrial sector, in the period before World War II. In this I shall attempt to illustrate the hypothesis, suggested in chapter 1, that the characteristics of technical change in agriculture are strongly conditioned by agriculture's relationship with the growing non-agricultural sector. At the same time, the chapter provides the historical background and framework within which to place the particular region of the case-study.

For these purposes, I shall treat the period up to 1939 as two phases. These phases refer to patterns of economic and technical change, occurring at different times in different places, rather than to strict temporal divisions, but the turning-point between the two could be said, on average, to have occurred during the period 1900–20. The justification for this phasing will be clearer from the description itself, but it is perhaps worth making two points about it now. It has been customary, in the analysis of Japanese history, to treat the Meiji Restoration of 1868 as a highly significant turning-point. My main concern in this book is with periods later than this, especially with those after 1900, but in as far as I do deal with the time before this, I shall tend to regard the trends of the 1868–1900 period as going back into the late Tokugawa period. As a result, my analysis has no clear-cut starting date. The Meiji Restoration led to a number of highly significant changes for the economy and for the institutional organisation of agriculture, but for my purposes in analysing agriculture's response to industrial development, it makes more sense to treat Meiji economic growth as Tussing does, as 'a vast increase in the scale of an already functioning economic order in response to population increase, the widening of the market, and a permissive political arrangement',[1] rather than as a revolution involving large-scale change in the nature and structure of industry.

This leads on to the second point in that it is the shift towards a new kind of industrial structure around 1900−20 which justifies my location of a turning-point there. Precise dating of the turning-point is not important. What matters is that from around the turn of the century the characteristics of industrialisation began to change, changing in turn the demands made by the industrial sector on agriculture and the requirements of agriculture's response. Since it is the nature and characteristics of industrial development that represent, as it were, the independent variables in my schema, it is changes in them which constitute the turning-points in my analysis.[a]

In what follows, therefore, I shall first describe briefly the nature of change in the non-agricultural sector in each phase, and then proceed to analyse changes in agricultural technology and in the economic

[a] Ohkawa and Rosovsky are the doyens of phasing Japanese economic growth. Ohkawa, in his article on agricultural growth phases (13) in *Agriculture and Economic Growth* (2), places the period 1905−19 in his first phase (1885−1919). This, like the more complex system of phasing for the economy as a whole in *Japanese Economic Growth* (124), is based largely on analysis of trends in macro-economic variables—growth rates of output, inputs, investment, etc. However, Ohkawa notes that 1904 represents 'the beginning point of an investment spurt, indicating the independent growth of the modern sectors in Japan' (*Agriculture and Economic Growth*, p.20), and in their earlier article (15) in Lockwood's *The State and Economic Enterprise in Japan* (116), Ohkawa and Rosovsky base their phasing more on institutional changes and place the turning-point between their first and second phases of modern economic growth in 1905. After this, they argue, there existed 'a modern sector gradually becoming more independent and capable of growing on its own' (p.76). From this time, (1) the land tax was replaced as the main source of government revenue; (2) the rate of growth of the non-agricultural labour force of agricultural origin slowed down (i.e. natural increase within the modern sector began to be an important source of labour supply to industry); (3) the weight of traditional exports in the total began to decline in favour of modern products; (4) investment in modern technology became a higher proportion of total investment than traditional technology; (5) modern industry began to turn to exports for its markets (pp.75−6). Thus, while from the point of view of agriculture alone 1920 seems to be the best demarcation point, marking the shift from the relatively buoyant conditions of phase 1 to the depression and stagnation of phase 2, from the point of view of the relationship between industry and agriculture, the 1900s and 1910s belong to the second phase, in which industry grows independently of agriculture. Analytically it might be clearest to speak of two phases and a transition period between them, but for the sake of the flow of the narrative I shall deal in terms of two phases only.

organisation of agriculture as responses to that non-agricultural development, using the kind of theoretical framework relating the characteristics of technical change to economic and institutional forces described in chapter 1.

1. Phase 1

(1) COMMERCIAL AND INDUSTRIAL DEVELOPMENT

In this section I shall describe very briefly the development of commerce and manufacturing in late Tokugawa and early Meiji Japan, concentrating on the characteristics of that development which were significant for the agricultural sector. I want to stress two points: firstly, the continuity in the characteristics of the growth of the non-agricultural sector in the period before about 1900, and, secondly, the extent to which, as a result of these characteristics, the development of industry and commerce fitted in with and complemented agricultural growth.

To understand the characteristics of Japan's early industrial growth and its relationship with agriculture, we need to start from the nature of economic development in the Tokugawa period which conditioned it. As research into the Tokugawa economy proceeds, it is becoming clear that the seventeenth and eighteenth centuries were not the stagnant period they were once thought to be.[2] More and more evidence is indicating that trade and commerce were thriving and developing, both in the towns and the country, in many areas of Tokugawa Japan, and a recent study[3] suggests that, with population growing only slowly, the incomes and living standards of a wide stratum of society were growing significantly. It remains difficult to say how large the commercial sector was from the national or macro-economic point of view,[b] and the penetration of the market economy varied widely from region to region, but certainly in some parts of the country a sophisticated and well-developed commercial economy existed before 1868.

Towns and cities were the focal points of this economic development, and, for her day, Japan was a remarkably urbanised country.[c] Tokyo

[b] Crawcour estimates that a half to two-thirds of agricultural output was being marketed, either directly or after having been paid as tax, in the 1860s. Crawcour, E., 'The Tokugawa Heritage' (5), p.41.

[c] Wilkinson estimates that 13–14% of the Japanese population lived in urban areas in the late Tokugawa period, probably a higher proportion than in European pre-industrial countries (*The Urbanisation of Japanese Labour* (135), pp.24–5), and Rozman argues that the proportion of urban dwellers rose from 6–7% to over 16% during the Tokugawa period (*Urban Networks in Ch'ing China and Tokugawa Japan* (128), p.300).

(Edo), which was a fishing village in 1590, was probably the largest city in the world in the first half of the eighteenth century, with over half a million inhabitants.[4] The urban concentration around Ōsaka and Kyōto had grown to almost a million by 1800.[5] Throughout the country there were the castle towns which housed the feudal lords and their retainers, with all those necessary to provide the goods and services they demanded, and probably few farm households lived far from a town of some sort.

What is important about this urbanisation, however, is the extent to which the cities were linked to, and promoted the commercialisation of, the countryside around them. Good communications were an essential part of this, and it is often said that Japan has to thank for this the *sankin kōtai* system whereby feudal lords were required to spend six months of every year in the capital and the other six months in their fiefs. The passage of the lords and their many retainers from distant parts of the country led to improvements in the road system and to development of commercial facilities for them along the way, while keeping the more remote parts of the country in communication with the capital and other urban centres. Coastal and river shipping were also growing with the development of sea-routes between Ōsaka, Tokyo and the Japan Sea coastal provinces.

As the cities grew and internal travel increased, so commercial trade and the use of money spread as the goods required to meet the needs of the urban population were drawn in. The development of markets and commercial trading in simple consumption goods, along with the use of money, was widely remarked.[6] Hanley and Yamamura argue that such trends could be observed even in as remote a district as Morioka in Tōhoku,[7] but the growth of trade and commercial markets was most marked in the areas along the Tōkaidō, the route along the Inland Sea coast followed by most of the *daimyō* on their way to Tokyo and by much of the merchandise en route for Ōsaka and the rest of the Kinai. Rozman argues that urbanisation was heavily concentrated along this line, with 22−24% of the populations of the Kinki and Kantō regions (containing Ōsaka and Tokyo respectively) living in towns in the Tokugawa period, compared with 12−14% in all other regions, and that large shipments of goods from most regions were brought in to help support these urban concentrations.[8]

The agricultural sector was drawn into this process of commercialisation in two ways. Firstly, the markets provided by the cities were the stimulus to the development of commercial agricultural production. Cultivation of rice and vegetables for the market became common in the regions around the big cities, and rice and particular local specialities began to be shipped into the commercial centres from further afield.

Northern Kyūshū, for instance, was a substantial supplier of rice to the Ōsaka market. In some areas, specialised production of particular com-mercial crops became widespread, most notably the growing of cotton in the Kinai, but also silk-raising in the environmentally suitable areas of central Honshū, vegetable growing around Tokyo, and so on. The use of commercial inputs was also expanding in the more advanced areas, especially in the cotton-growing parts of the Kinai, and by the early Meiji period there was an established pattern of trade in fish-based fertilisers.[9]

However, there was a second way in which farm households were drawn into the world of commerce and money, and this brings us to the charac-teristics of the early forms of industrial production in Japan. From very early times, the castle towns and cities had been centres for the manu-facture of luxury products for the urban rich, such as metal-work and high-class textiles. These highly-skilled urban craft industries were con-trolled by monopolistic guilds, similar to their mediaeval European counterparts. As urbanisation and trade grew, however, the increasing demand for commercial consumption goods created an incentive for entrepreneurs to try to develop industrial production outside the restric-tive guild system, and they turned to the countryside for sources of labour which would be cheaper and more abundant than the available urban workers. What emerged were highly developed systems of putting-out and of rural by-employment which tapped the spare labour time of households primarily engaged in agriculture. In the textile industries, for example, middle-men supplied agricultural households with raw materials of silk or cotton, loans to buy necessary equipment, and so on, and took away the finished or semi-finished product. Patterns of seaso-nal migration to manufacturing employment also became well estab-lished.[10] Thus, although urbanisation was significant, the growth of manufacturing had a much wider impact through the spread of by-employment of various kinds among rural households, and although it is impossible to say exactly how far this influence spread, it seems likely that a large proportion of farm households in the more advanced dis-tricts at least were engaged in commercial manufacturing in some form.[d]

The impact on agricultural technology and economic organisation of

---

[d] The survey of the county in the extreme south of Honshū (in Chōshū fief) in 1843, on which Smith bases his article 'Farm Family By-Employments in Pre-Industrial Japan' (7), found that farm families were so heavily engaged in by-employments that 32% of the county's food (amounting to a quantity sufficient to feed 10,000 people for a year) had to be brought in from outside, probably mostly from the rice surplus regions of northern Kyūshū.

these two kinds of commercialising force will be summarised later and is beautifully described by Smith in *The Agrarian Origins of Modern Japan*.[11] Here I just want to emphasise that the form which industrial development took meant that it provided households with ways of increasing the utilisation of their family labour forces and earning extra income, while at the same time maintaining the labour supply necessary for peak agricultural operations and for adopting new agricultural techniques. This improved income-earning potential of the family labour force on small agricultural holdings was reflected in rising wages for, and shortages of, hired agricultural labour in the more commercialised regions, the implications of which for the agricultural sector were, as we shall see later, highly significant.[e]

The system of industrial production which developed during the Tokugawa period has been set out in detail because, in essence, the same system continued to underlie industrial development until the end of the century. The scale of industrial production expanded greatly under the stimulus of the changes brought about by the Meiji Restoration, but the form which it took was not substantially different, at least as far as its impact on agriculture was concerned, from what had preceded it. The new Meiji government abolished the restrictions whereby the Tokugawa rulers and the feudal nobility had sought to control trade and industry, and it opened up the country to foreign trade. It initiated a policy of actively promoting industrial development, setting up model factories, encouraging the introduction of Western technology, developing railways, shipping and so on. Nevertheless, until at least the 1890s, it remained the traditional industries, particularly textiles, which responded most to these changes, and these industries largely retained their small-scale rural character. The chief growth industries of this second half of the nineteenth century, silk reeling and weaving and cotton spinning and weaving, continued to be carried on for the most part in farm households or in small rural workshops.[12] The weight of the textile industries in Meiji industrialisation, and the predominantly rural and small-scale nature of all industry at the time, are shown in Table 3.1, which is taken from Yamaguchi's compilation of the available statistics of establishments recorded as 'factories'.

Most of the labour required for the increase in manufacturing output in the second half of the nineteenth century was thus provided as before

[e] Cf. Hanley and Yamamura: 'What stimulated the improvement in agricultural methods (in the Kinai after 1700) more than anything else was the shortage of labour that resulted from the continued growth of both commercial agriculture and a variety of manufacturing and commercial activities in rural Kinai.' *Economic and Demographic Change in Pre-Industrial Japan* (110), p.103.

Table 3.1: *Distribution of Manufacturing Establishments[1] by Location and by Number of Employees[2] in 1884* (Data assembled from that available for 43 prefectures)

	All establishments	Spinning & weaving	Food industries	Ceramics & building materials	Chemicals	Metal work	Machinery	Other
Number of establishments	1981	1206	184	238	91	159	38	65
% in towns	19·2	19·1	5·4	8·8	56·0	10·1	47·4	52·3
% in villages	62·4	71·4	10·3	76·5	26·4	81·8	15·8	23·1
% unknown	18·4	9·5	84·2	14·7	17·6	8·2	36·8	24·6
% with less than 20 employees	72·1	66·7	93·4	88·2	52·8	84·3	60·5	55·4
% with less than 30 employees	83·4	82·5	95·6	90·7	58·3	91·8	65·8	63·1

Source: Yamaguchi, K., *Meiji Zenki Keizai* (64), p.111 and p.118.

1. In Japanese, Kōjō—generally taken in the sources Yamaguchi uses (prefectural yearbooks) to mean establishments employing wage labour. See Footnote 2 to his p.105.

2. Original data are in man-days. Here converted into number of employees assuming 300 work-days per man, as Yamaguchi suggests, pp.116–17.

through the re-allocation or increased utilisation of family labour time within the household, as the scope for by-employment continued to expand. Even where production took place in a factory or workshop, the labour force was commonly made up of the daughters of farm households who went to live and work in the textile spinning and weaving factories, but who never went far enough away from their homes to be prevented from returning temporarily at peak times in the agricultural cycle and permanently when they married.[f]

In regional terms too, the pattern of the Tokugawa period was maintained. Although Meiji-period industry was scattered through the rural areas to which its labour force and its water-power sources were tied and was not an urbanising force, it still tended to be located in the Inland Sea coastal regions which were the traditional areas of commerce and industry, and in the regions to the north-west of Tokyo well suited environmentally to silk production. Towns continued to be essential, though, to the co-ordination, marketing and financing of the complex putting-out systems and went on growing as centres of trade and finance. The fastest-growing towns and cities were those engaged in the vital movements of rice from the less advanced, predominantly agricultural areas of Kyūshū and Tōhoku to the centres of manufacturing industry, and of manufactured goods and exports from those centres. The most important of these were Ōsaka, Kōbe, Nagoya and Yokohama serving the Inland Sea and Tokyo manufacturing areas, and Nagasaki dealing with the rice trade from Kyūshū.

To summarise, then, the nature of the changes in the non-agricultural sector which affected agriculture. First, from well back in Tokugawa times, the development of towns as the centres of trade, administration and culture for the feudal upper classes created increasing demand for the products of rural labour, and this increase was intensified by the

---

[f] In 1882, women made up 58·2% of the labour force over 15 years old in private manufacturing establishments and 74·3% of the total of all ages. Yamaguchi, K., *Meiji Zenki Keizai* (64), p.45. Cole and Tominaga in 'Japan's Changing Occupational Structure' (109) present data showing that even in 1930 over half of all manual workers in Japanese factory industry were female, and they argue that this heavy reliance on an unstable workforce of young women during the industrialisation of Japan is highly unusual, when compared with the experience of other now-developed countries (pp.60–1). They attribute it to the fact that labour in agriculture was sufficiently productive for farm households to wish to retain their central male labour force on the farm. While I would, as will emerge later, take one step further round the circle to argue that agricultural productivity was high in some respects precisely because industry and commerce themselves were developing, Cole and Tominaga's article in effect describes the industrial side of the institutional and technical adaptation of industry and agriculture to each other, the agricultural side of which is the subject of much of this chapter.

extension of industry and trade after the Meiji Restoration. Secondly, these developments resulted in the increasing commercialisation of agricultural production, as the demand for marketed output grew and as the farm household's need and incentive to buy more commercial inputs and consumption goods grew with its increasing involvement in the market economy. This process was accelerated by the conversion of the land tax into a money tax at the time of the Meiji Restoration, which forced even farmers in remote, uncommercialised areas to market at least some of their output. Thirdly, the growth of industrial production began to offer alternative employment to rural workers, but, since industry both before and after 1868 remained predominantly rural and based either on the farm household itself or on small-scale local factories, it drew off only the surplus labour time which family plots of land could not adequately utilise throughout the year, so that its effect was to increase the income-earning potential of the rural family labour force, rather than cause migration and urbanisation. Given the pattern of the communication system, itself the result of many geographic, administrative, political, military and economic influences, and the level of its development in the pre-railway period, the impact of the above three effects tended to be concentrated in those areas of south-western Japan which possessed relatively easy means of communication with the cities of central Honshū.

(2)   THE EVOLUTION OF NEW AGRICULTURAL TECHNOLOGY

We saw in chapter 2 how, from the macro-economic point of view, during phase 1 the agricultural sector succeeded in responding to and furthering the growth of industry and commerce described in the last section, meeting the growth in demand for food and supplying inputs and foreign exchange until at least the turn of the century. It is generally accepted that agriculture's ability to do this depended on the emergence and spread of a set of improved techniques and inputs whose overall features are by now well established. In this section, in line with the approach suggested in chapter 1, I want to examine how this set of techniques was developed with the particular characteristics which it had, and I shall argue that, in its nature and in the pattern of its spread, it was a response to the commercial and industrial developments described in the last section. I shall leave the related changes in the economic organisation of agriculture until the next section.

The set of complementary techniques and inputs which lay behind the growth of agricultural output in phase 1, and whose emergence and characteristics we are seeking to explain, is often referred to as the *Meiji Nōhō* (Meiji agricultural methods). Some parts of it were in fact in use in some areas well before the Meiji period and some were not adopted in others until after it, but I shall henceforth use the term for convenience. The techniques which made up the *Meiji Nōhō* have been extensively described and analysed and here I shall only summarise them and bring out one or two particularly important features of them.[13]

Central to the *Meiji Nōhō* was the use of what we would now call high-yielding seed varieties of rice, that is to say, plants with genetic charac-teristics such that they are able effectively to absorb large quantities of fertiliser, thereby producing a larger amount of grain per unit area. In general, the necessary characteristics have been found to be a relatively short stem, so that the plant will not overbalance under the weight of its yield of grain, and the ability to produce a large number of ears of grain per plant. The high-yielding rice varieties developed in Japan during phase 1, like modern Green Revolution varieties, had these characteris-tics, differentiating them from traditional varieties which were taller and tended to produce fewer heads of grain. *Meiji Nōhō* seed varieties were also designed to be planted late in the rice-growing season, matur-ing relatively quickly in response to the regular changes in day-length, whereas traditional varieties were adapted to the varying lengths of growing season and amounts of sunshine in different parts of the coun-try. They therefore enhanced the possibilities for double-cropping. The most famous and widely diffused of the new varieties in Japan was called *Shinriki* (power of the gods), and was selected by a farmer in Hyōgo prefecture in 1877.

Like Green Revolution varieties today, the new seeds of the Meiji period outperformed traditional types only under high levels of fertiliser input. The traditional, self-supplied sources of fertiliser (grass, leaves, excrement) were inadequate for this, both because local supplies of them were limited and because they required such large amounts of labour to collect and transport them. The *Meiji Nōhō* therefore also included the use of relatively large quantities of commercial fertiliser. In turn, the absorption of large amounts of fertiliser required deep ploughing. This meant, in the Japanese context, the use of draught animals and new designs of plough, in place of traditional methods of land preparation using human labour power. The use of draught animals required the growing of fodder crops on upland fields or on paddies in the winter.

Various other improvements in cultivation practices were also inclu-ded in the *Meiji Nōhō* package, some directly connected with the use of the other new techniques, others indirectly through the fact that the pot-ential for higher yields made the labour that the new practices involved worthwhile. Such practices included the soaking of rice seeds in salt water solution in order to select the best seeds to plant; improvements in the preparation of seed-beds; transplanting seedlings into the paddy in straight lines, facilitating pest control and the use of a rotary weeding tool; and advances in the control of pests, including planting later in the season.

The overall effect of the adoption of this package was, as we saw in chapter 2, to raise rice yields and total agricultural output through increased inputs of variable capital (commercial fertiliser) and probably also of labour. But the increase in labour input took the form of an increase in the number of days worked in a year by a basic family labour force, so that it raised the productivity of the family labour force on its land without hindering the ability of younger sons and daughters to take up by-employment or work away from home. It was therefore the means whereby agriculture was able to provide the industrial sector with both increased marketed food output and labour time, as well as the housing and long-term support of quite a large section of industry's work force.

How was this successful package of techniques developed in late Tokugawa and early Meiji Japan? In chapter 1 I argued that the characteristics of new techniques are strongly influenced by the economic and institutional forces prevailing at the time when they emerge or are developed. A convenient starting-point in the search for these forces in the case of the *Meiji Nōhō* is with the institutional mechanisms whereby new techniques were discovered and diffused in mid-nineteenth-century Japan. At the time of the discovery and initial diffusion of almost all of the techniques described above, there was no official local or national system for developing agricultural methods, and the vast majority of *Meiji Nōhō* techniques were developed by individual farmers out of their own experience and experiments. Quite a large number of the techniques (including substantial use of commercial fertiliser, selection of the most suitable seed varieties for local conditions, straight-line transplanting, seed selection in salt water, etc.) were commonly used in some places during the Tokugawa period.[14] Knowledge of them spread by word of mouth, sometimes through books about agriculture, sometimes by travellers' observations, and as communications improved with expanding trade, they spread further from their places of origin. After the Meiji Restoration, more organised attempts to diffuse improved methods began with the inauguration of a system of itinerant agricultural lecturers and with the spread of agricultural discussion groups, seed exchange societies, and so on. Towards the end of the century, state and local government became more involved in the dissemination of improved methods with the establishment of nationally-organised agricultural societies and the setting up of prefectural experiment stations, but before that the spread of new techniques relied on the efforts of enthusiasts; particularly among the resident cultivating landlord class, to demonstrate their profitability in local environments.[g] The development of the techniques making up the *Meiji Nōhō* therefore depended on the nature of individual farmers' responses to their particular problems and incentives, and their diffusion depended on the existence of communications with other areas and on the feasibility and profitability of employing methods developed elsewhere in particular local environments.[h]

It follows, then, that we must look for clues to the forces conditioning the characteristics of the *Meiji Nōhō* in the environments and incentives under which the farmers who invented and developed it operated. Some idea of what these were like can be gathered from a closer look at the nature of the *Meiji Nōhō* techniques themselves, since this reveals that they could only be adopted (and hence, presumably, invented) in areas where two pre-conditions prevailed. These were, on the one hand, the existence of adequate and controllable supplies of irrigation water and, on the other, access to or involvement with the commercial market economy.

In chapter 2 I pointed out the association observed, in Japan and in today's developing countries, between the adoption of high-yielding rice technology and the extent and quality of supplies of irrigation water. In the context of the *Meiji Nōhō*, the crucial aspect of irrigation control was the ability to drain the paddy field when required. Only if the field could be drained could it be ploughed by a draught animal and the

[g] See Dore, R., 'Agricultural Improvement' (26), e.g. pp.77–9. Chambliss gives a pre-Meiji example of such an enthusiast, who came across improved methods of sericulture on his travels and 'in 1855, after having adapted these practices to local conditions through experimentation, he compiled the results into a sixteen-page pamphlet for distribution among his friends'. *Chiarajima Village* (42), p. 19. For examples in Saga, see later.

[h] Kee Il Choi, in an interesting article which examines the relationship between commercialisation and the diffusion of new techniques in the Tokugawa period, develops the argument that the Tokugawa government system did not, as is frequently suggested, hinder the regional spread of new methods, and makes the obvious but significant point that many elements of the *Meiji Nōhō* technology would have been hard to keep secret from interested travellers. His paper argues that 'the Bakuhan (Tokugawa) system diffused rather than obstructed technology and accelerated agricultural development, thereby setting the stage for further acceleration of farm output during the early Meiji period, and that regional differences during the Tokugawa period can be better explained on the basis of crop specialisation and exchange associated with regional commercial development rather than discrepancies in farming technology among regions'. Kee Il Choi, 'Technological Diffusion in Agriculture under the Bakuhan System' (31), p.750. The rest of this section will try to show *why* there was a connection between regional commercial development and the pattern of diffusion of new techniques.

water level be matched to the requirements of varieties which matured in a shorter but less flexible time period. And more fundamentally, only a drainable field could be double-cropped, and the *Meiji Nōhō*, with its late-planted, faster-maturing varieties, was above all a package designed to fit into a double-cropping rotation within which fodder for draught animals and additional subsistence or market crops could be produced.

The second pre-condition, access to commercial markets, was essential because the use of the *Meiji Nōhō* depended on the application of commercial fertiliser. This implied that at least some of the additional output produced had to be marketed in order to meet the money cost, and that farmers who adopted the new techniques needed to be involved in commercial dealings at least for this reason, if not also because of the incentive provided by market demand for the increased output which the *Meiji Nōhō* made possible.

Now, these two pre-conditions for the use of the *Meiji Nōhō* were not unrelated to each other. The link between them lay in the incentives to make the investment necessary to convert an undrained field into a drainable one. It is likely that originally all fields were undrained and kept flooded throughout the year, as a means of preserving water supplies and because there was no reason to do otherwise. The *cost* of converting an undrained field into a drainable one depended on two things: (1) the technical difficulties involved in doing so, which depended on the location and the nature of the irrigation system in question (e.g. drainage was very difficult on the flat coastal plains); and (2) whether or not an adequate supply of water could be assured for the summer if winter drainage took place. The *incentive* to carry out the investment depended on the technical possibilities opened up by conversion to drainable fields. That these were very different from those of an undrained field is indicated by the existence of different words for the two types of field, *kanden* for a drainable field, *shitsuden* for an undrained one. The major possibility opened up was that of double-cropping, which was impossible on *shitsuden*, and the incentive for this depended essentially on access to commercial markets, because double-cropping more or less necessitated the use of purchased fertiliser and because it created the scope for producing saleable output in excess of food needs.[15] Suitable climate was, of course, also a pre-condition for double-cropping, and in the north of Japan the weather thus deprived farmers of the main initial incentive to invest in conversion to *kanden*. But elsewhere the extent of investment in such land improvement must have depended on the balance between the technical difficulties of weather, water shortage or drainage in particular natural environments, hence the investment cost, and the incentives provided by the

possibilities of commercial production.[i] It follows that we would expect
to find areas in which the pre-conditions for the development and adoption of *Meiji Nōhō* techniques were met to be concentrated for the most
part in those parts of the country where agriculture was most affected by
the spread of commerce and industry, where the incentives to invest to
create those pre-conditions would have been strongest.

Data by which to test this contention are hard to come by. What we
do have, however, is Arashi's compilation of a large amount of scattered
information on the regional distribution of double-cropping during the
Tokugawa and Meiji periods.[16] From what has gone before, it is clear
that the extent of double-cropping can be taken as an indicator of the
existence of *kanden* and in general of the more commercial approach to
agriculture into which the *Meiji Nōhō* techniques fitted. Arashi's data[17]
show that the earliest areas in which double-cropping became common
were to be found in central Honshū, especially the Kinai and its surrounding areas. His data for 1884 show that by then there were substantial
areas of double-cropping, but that these were highly concentrated in
the south and west of Japan.[18] In the areas along the Inland Sea coast of
Honshū and Shikoku and in parts of northern and western Kyūshū, at
least half the paddy area no longer lay fallow in the winter, but in all the
northern and eastern regions and in southern Shikoku and Kyūshū,
there was very little double-cropping.

By comparing Arashi's data on double-cropping for 1884 with those
for 1907, we can also gain some indication of the spread of the pre-
conditions for the use of the *Meiji Nōhō* during phase 1. Table 3.2 shows
that the spread of double-cropping continued to be concentrated in the
south and west. The proportional change in the double-cropping rate
was also quite high along the southern part of the Japan Sea coast, and
there was a slight eastward shift into Gifu, Shizuoka and Aichi (Tōkai),
but north and east of this very little.

We have seen so far, then, that the characteristics of the *Meiji Nōhō*
were such that it enabled farmers to respond to the pressures and incentives created by the particular forms of commercial and industrial
development occurring in phase 1, and that the pre-conditions for its
adoption tended to be found only in the areas of south-western Japan
which we have seen were most affected by the growth and spread of the
non-agricultural sector. We would therefore expect to find, given the
mechanisms which then existed for the development and diffusion of
new agricultural methods, that the *Meiji Nōhō* techniques were developed by farmers in these south-western areas in response to the particular

---

[i] Incentives not necessarily to farmers themselves, but also to landlords or commercial
investors thinking of putting money into land improvement schemes.

Table 3.2: *Regional Estimates of the Proportion of Paddy Area Single-Cropped (%)*

		1884	1907	1933
Kyūshū		55	30	26
Shikoku		61	29	32
Chūgoku:	Inland Sea side	55	32	50
	Japan Sea side	73	51	53
Kinki		54	31	44
Tōkai		74	47	56
Kantō		84	64	64
Hokuriku		92	75	71
Tōhoku		100	99	96
Average		73	53	55

Source: Arashi, K., *Kinsei Inasaku Gijitsu Shi* (50), p.45.

incentives and conditions there. We do not know a great deal about when and where particular *Meiji Nōhō* techniques were discovered, but Arashi was also able to assemble data from which he could trace back the development of Shinriki, through its immediate parent, a variety called Odoroshi, from which it was bred in Hyōgo (adjoining Ōsaka) in 1877.[19] He shows that Shinriki's ancestors possessed the characteristics of short stem, small grain size and good response to dense planting and heavy fertiliser application, which were essential to high yield. Most significantly he shows that the areas in which they were developed and grown were the plain areas of Kinki and the Inland Sea coastal regions, areas of well-developed irrigation and commercial agriculture, and that they were characteristically late-planted, quick-maturing varieties suitable for inclusion in double-cropping rotations on *kanden*. Shinriki was highest-yielding in this line and could be planted still later in the season, but for the advanced areas of the south-west, it did not represent a revolutionary innovation, just a later stage in the continuing development of technology for such regions. Arashi argues that the significance of Shinriki was that, compared with other high-yielding varieties, it was comparatively adaptable to varying environments, and that it emerged just when official and unofficial extension services were greatly improving communications between agricultural regions.[20] What is most important here is that Shinriki can be seen to have emerged as part of the process of developing a higher-yielding technology in and for the areas of commercial double-cropping in the south-west, most affected by the growth of the non-agricultural sector.

Finally it would follow that, since the *Meiji Nōhō* arose in and was adapted to the conditions of the commercialised south-western regions, its diffusion would be expected to be much more rapid and widespread there than elsewhere. Of the individual items of the *Meiji Nōhō*, the only one for which measurable data could really be collected is the use of improved varieties. Hayami and Yamada have assembled data on this, based on the very rough division of the country into Eastern and Western prefectures.[j] By 1900, 19·1% of the area planted to rice in the Western prefectures was growing varieties classed as improved (almost all of it Shinriki), compared with 7·7% in the East. By 1907, these percentages had risen to 42·1 in the West and 28·3 in the East. Arashi's prefectural-level data on the spread of Shinriki around 1910 show that it was planted on the highest proportions of the paddy area (as much as 60% or more) in Ōsaka and northern Shikoku, and in the traditional rice-trading areas of northern Kyūshū (Fukuoka and Kumamoto).[21]

Perhaps the clearest indication, however, of the regional pattern of adoption of *Meiji Nōhō* techniques lies in the variation in rice yields. This is obviously not an exact measure of regional differences in production techniques, but, given that the *Meiji Nōhō* was primarily a set of yield-increasing innovations, it is highly suggestive of the regional pattern of adoption. Arashi has assembled available county-level official data on yields for as early as 1877, which show that the counties in the Kinki region, especially those in Ōsaka, Nara and Hyōgo, consistently recorded the highest yields in the country, followed by one or two areas of northern Kyūshū, while the records for counties in Tōhoku and southern Kyūshū show consistently low yields.[22] This is the situation revealed by the earliest official prefectural-level figures for the 1880s. Taking average officially-recorded yields for 1881−5, all the prefectures in the Kinki region except Wakayama (i.e. Shiga, Kyōto, Ōsaka, Hyōgo and Nara), and the nearby northern Shikoku prefecture of Kagawa, were achieving yields of over 200 kg/10 ares, some considerably more than this (e.g. 246 in Shiga), while in the whole of the rest of the country only two other prefectures exceeded 200 kg (Yamanashi and Toyama), and much of Tōhoku and southern Kyūshū had yields of less than 150 kg. Although there had been some narrowing of the gap, much the same pattern still prevailed in 1903−7, when only the up-and-coming Saga could match the yields of over 300 kg/10 ares averaged by Kagawa and the prefectures of Kinki.

---

[j] Hayami, Y. and Yamada, S., 'Agricultural Productivity at the Beginning of Industrialisation' (6), and see Table 3.4.

Eastern prefectures = Tōhoku, Kantō + Niigata.

Western prefectures = Hokuriku (−Niigata), Tōkai, Kinki, Shikoku, Chūgoku, Kyūshū.

Finally, the contention of this section, that this regional pattern of success with the *Meiji Nōhō* had much to do with the varying regional impact of industrial and commercial development, is confirmed by Sawada's finding that a significant correlation can be found at the prefectural level between the rice yield in 1903–7 and the date at which the number of farm households began to decline.[23] If we take the decline in farm household numbers as an indicator of the impact of industrialisation on a prefecture which takes into account especially the impact on employment and labour utilisation, then the implication of this correlation is that the greater the overall impact of the development of the non-agricultural sector on a prefecture, the higher its rice yields would be expected to be.

The conclusion which follows from all this is that the *Meiji Nōhō* was the culminating form of a process of technical development taking place in and for the areas of central and south-western Japan where, since Tokugawa times, the impact of the development of commerce had been felt most strongly, and where, as a result, investment in the improvement of the irrigation system was most advanced. In other words, the *Meiji Nōhō* techniques represent perhaps the ultimate form of a process of response by farmers to the growth of commerce and markets, a response which includes the switch from *shitsuden* to *kanden* and the adoption of double-cropping, and works through to deep ploughing, straight-line transplanting and so on, eventually to the emergence of Shinriki. In this section we have regarded this as a purely technical progression. In the next section we can go on to see how it fitted into the economic changes resulting from the spreading impact of commercial and industrial development.

(3)   CHANGES IN THE ECONOMIC ORGANISATION OF AGRICULTURE

In the last section I argued that the technical changes of the late Tokugawa and Meiji periods, culminating in the *Meiji Nōhō*, represented the technical response to the problem of raising rice output in the areas of Japan in which the impact of commercialisation was most strongly felt. In this section I want to consider the economic effects of increasing commercialisation and of the availability of the new technology which went with it and, to begin with, I will briefly summarise the effects of these forces as they impinged on individual farm households.

Firstly, from the Tokugawa period onwards, in some parts of the country farm households were being drawn into the market economy by expanding opportunities to sell output, to buy inputs and consumption goods, and to find full- or part-time employment in non-agricultural occupations. After 1868, farm households in regions still remote from

these commercialising forces were nevertheless forced into market dealings by the conversion of the land tax into money. Secondly, the period
saw the emergence of a package of newly-available techniques designed
to raise yields by increased application of labour time and purchased
inputs, within a double-cropping rotation on reasonably well-irrigated
land. These new techniques were almost certainly neutral to scale,[k] and
they were relatively simple to learn and apply. However they required as
pre-conditions (1) a relatively high level of irrigation control, (2) access
to commercial markets for inputs and output, and (3) in the absence at
this stage of any very highly organised national extension system, access
to sources of information outside the village.

What forms of economic organisation, what types of farm household,
would benefit most from and develop in response to this kind of technical change and the commercialisation which stimulated it and which
was encouraged and permitted by it? In what follows, I shall describe
what we know about changes in such features of the structure of Japanese agriculture as the distribution of land-ownership, tenancy and so on
in this period, and try to see how far they can be explained by the picture of technical change and commercialisation I have been drawing.

It seems clear from the available evidence that the kind of economic
unit which could *not* benefit from these changes was the large-scale,
extended farm organisation which had dominated village structures
from early times throughout Japan. Its decline began in the advanced
regions in the eighteenth century, and continued through the late
Tokugawa and Meiji periods. The mechanisms of this process were
summarised in chapter 2 and are vividly described by Smith, who shows
how traditional family holdings were split up as land was gradually
given to branch households and let out to former farm servants as
tenants. Smith sees the causes of this as lying in the inability of the
larger-scale holding to exploit the economic and technical changes
resulting from increasing commercialisation.[24] The intensive cultivation of commercial crops and of multiple rotations including rice
required large amounts of meticulous labour, which were both hard to
manage on a large scale and increasingly difficult to find as non-agricultural employment opportunities expanded. The solution for the traditional large-scale holdings was, as described in chapter 2, to shed land
by giving or renting it out to the family's former dependents, while
retaining a workable holding of the best land for itself. This would still

---

[k] At least to the extent that (1) the quantity and quality of water supply to individual
holdings was not strongly correlated with size of farm, and (2) arrangements existed
whereby small farmers could gain access to draught animals through *honke/bunke*,
patron/client relationships or through hiring.

be a relatively substantial holding, as the main household would continue to be able to draw to some extent on the labour of its tenants and dependants, who remained tied to it both socially and by the need to make use of the capital assets and livestock which the main household kept. The new smaller units relied for the most part on family labour which was better suited to the new kinds of careful cultivation technique, and were able to take advantage, as household units, of the increasing scope for non-agricultural by-employment as a means of making use of surplus family labour time.

The progress of this trend in the later Tokugawa period meant that by the time of the Meiji Restoration, as we saw in chapter 2, the agricultural structure in many areas was already made up of family labour units differentiated by size of holding and nature of tenure.[25] Tenancy had arisen through the processes described above, both directly, as farm workers became tenants, and indirectly, as those given land lost it through mortgaging, debt, etc. Hired workers continued to exist, though it is difficult to say how widely since there was no clear dividing line between landless agricultural workers and cultivators.[1] At any rate, the more advanced the region the more predominant was the farm unit based on, though not necessarily relying solely on, the family labour force.

This did not, however, mean that there was not substantial economic differentiation among farm households, even in more advanced areas, or that all were in an equal position as regards gaining or losing from the economic and technical trends of the late Tokugawa or Meiji periods and the aftermath of the Land Tax Revision. That they were not is indicated by such data as are available. There are estimates that the proportion of owner-farmer households fell from $37 \cdot 3\%$ to $33 \cdot 3\%$ between 1883/4 and 1908, while the proportion of pure tenant households rose from $20 \cdot 9\%$ to $27 \cdot 6\%$.[26] The proportion of tenanted land is thought to have risen from 29% in 1872 to 45% in 1908.[m] This suggests that increasing numbers of households were losing their land and falling into tenancy in the period after the Land Tax Revision, and it is generally thought that the period saw what Japanese scholars call a bi-polarisation of the agricultural structure, as smaller-scale owner farmers who failed to cope with the prevailing economic conditions lost land and fell into the category of

---

[1] Ishikawa and Ohkawa estimate that there were around a million hired agricultural workers out of a total labour force of 14−15 million in the mid-Meiji period. 'Significance of Japan's Experience' (29), pp.168−9

[m] Ishikawa, S. and Ohkawa, K., 'Significance of Japan's Experience' (29), p.167; Wataya, T., 'Shihonshugi no Hatten' (62), p.192. There are no systematic data on tenancy or scale of owned or cultivated holdings before 1908.

small-scale tenants or part-tenants, while those who were in a position to gain from the changes going on increased the amount of land they owned (though not necessarily cultivated). Wataya, on the basis of his analysis of the available data, summarises the 1880−1910 period as one which saw the decline of the full-time, middle-scale owner farmer and the rise of the part-time tenant farmer.[27]

Can we explain the difference between those households who were able and those who were not able to benefit from the changes of this period in terms of the process of commercialisation and technical change described above? The fact of bi-polarisation−in effect, the rich getting richer and the poor getting poorer−suggests that initial economic position, particularly the scale of land-ownership, was a significant factor in determining the difference, and, as we shall see later, it did indeed seem to be, in general, the households retaining the largest and best plots to cultivate, and ownership or control over the land of branch households and tenants, who were in the forefront of economic development in the villages in this period.[28] This kind of household is called *tezukuri jinushi* (cultivating landlord) in Japanese, and typically in each village there would have been one or two households of this kind, emerging out of the break-up of the old extended families and central to the kinship and social structure of the village. These were the households which, in this phase, performed the role of the initial innovating group in the framework of chapter 1, and it is interesting to ask why it was they who did so.

The answer to the question of why these households made most of the economic change of this period is not a simple one. But it can be said that, although they did tend to cultivate larger holdings than other households, the answer does not lie in technical economies of scale. The initial policy of the Meiji government towards technical change in agriculture had been to try to develop relatively large-scale cultivation techniques, such as then prevailed in more developed Western countries. But it quite soon became clear that such techniques were not feasible within the constraints imposed by the Japanese environment, irrigation system, and infrastructure, and policy shifted towards encouraging the development of indigenous techniques such as those making up the *Meiji Nōhō*, which were, as we have seen, divisible and largely neutral to scale.

I would, therefore, argue that the answer lies in two other characteristics of the *tezukuri jinushi* class *vis-à-vis* the economic and technical changes of this period. The first is their superior access to the kind of information needed. This was partly a question of superior education and literacy, but also a function of their role as village leaders, hence their contact with the outside world and their participation in and leadership of agricultural societies, discussion groups, and so on. I suggested earlier that the need for access to such non-market information sources was a characteristic of the new technology of this period, and there is evidence to suggest that it was the *tezukuri jinushi* class who were most active in these kinds of institution and who were therefore first to adopt innovations.[n]

The second significant characteristic of this class was its superior ability to cope with the spread of the commercial and money economy, a spread forced down to the small-scale farmers by the Land Tax Revision. In a simple way, the more land a household owned, the more rice it had to· market, from both its own production and rents, hence the greater its capacity to withstand and gain from market fluctuations. So, larger-scale farmers could store rice and sell when the price was highest, whereas the small landowner often had to sell at whatever price he could get to meet his tax and other obligations. But beyond this, households of the *tezukuri jinushi* type would traditionally have been running whatever money lending, trading and marketing activities were carried on within the village and with the outside world, so that they had experience in dealing with the market economy which the small farmer initially lacked. With the demand for agricultural output, especially rice, rising as the industrial sector grew, and with the price of rice high for much of the period, such farmers who had rice to sell and access to markets were therefore the first to feel the incentive to produce more to sell and therefore the most likely to adopt the techniques and make the investments required by this.

From the point of view of the smaller-scale farmer, the small-scale owners, tenants and part-tenants who made up the mass of farm households, the picture was more complex. In a number of respects, such small-scale cultivators had advantages over the larger-scale landowners under the changed economic and technical conditions. Their family labour forces were adequate for the cultivation of their holdings even under the new technology, and they therefore faced fewer problems as regards labour supply and supervision. Where opportunities existed for non-agricultural employment, they were able to increase household income through by-employment or through sending family members out to industrial employment, e.g. sending farm daughters to work in textile factories. There is also evidence to suggest that the *tezukuri jinushi* households had economic and social reasons for helping their tenants and dependents to follow their example and adopt new

---

[n] See e.g. Wataya's data on the scales of cultivation of those attending meetings of the National Agricultural Discussion Group, which show that almost all were middle- or large-scale *tezukuri jinushi*. 'Shihonshugi no Hatten' (62), p.211.

techniques. These reasons ranged from the desire to carry out land improvement projects (to which everyone had to agree) to permit the adoption of new commercial techniques, through possibilities opened up by new techniques for raising and stabilising rents, to the feeling of moral responsibility of paternalistic village leaders.°

However, these trends took time to take effect, and, in the meantime, small-scale farmers were being forced to come to terms with the money economy through the permeation of commercial dealings into the village economy, and through the new taxation system. Being inexperienced in market transactions and in general in a weak bargaining position, with their land as their only asset, price and harvest fluctuations threw them into debt and led to their loss of land. The period of the so-called Matsukata deflation in the 1880s was particularly severe in this respect and it is thought that the increase in tenancy was especially marked at that time.[29] As we shall see when considering phase 2, after the turn of the century the smaller-scale farmer seems to have overcome the institutional obstacles in the way of his adoption of new commercial technology, partly through the efforts of the *tezukuri jinushi* class itself, and to have begun to prove in fact better able to utilise it than the larger-scale cultivator.

The contention that it was the larger-scale landowner's commercial advantages, rather than the characteristics of the new technology, which led to the observed concentration of landownership is supported by such evidence as we have of the regional pattern of changes in landownership in this period. This suggests that in the north, despite the fact that, as we have seen, conditions were unsuitable for the adoption of the new technology, land concentration was quite marked after the Land Tax Revision, as small farmers were forced to come to terms with market dealings by the need to find cash for the tax, without the benefits of increasing yields or income from non-agricultural work. While small-scale owner farmers declined everywhere, such regional evidence as exists suggests that this tendency was especially strong in Tōhoku, and that larger-scale landowner/cultivators there were able to increase

---

° Waswo, A., *Japanese Landlords* (36), chapter 3, pp.35–65. Cf. the character called Uncle Noda in the novel *Footprints in the Snow* (133), first published in 1901. He came from a samurai family but gave up work in the bureaucracy to return to his native village. There he bought a house and some land and 'his idea was to lead the local notables in a campaign for the development of agriculture in the district'. He launched various schemes for such things as breeding goats, pigs, cows and poultry, and producing silk which his daughter reeled, and he lectured the villagers on eating meat, keeping poultry and so on. None of his schemes achieved very much, but his son obtained a degree from Hokkaidō Agricultural College and came back to make a success of it all.

their holdings and strengthen their position further than in the more advanced south-western regions (see Table 3.3).[P]

Table 3.3:   Regional Variations in the Distribution of Owner-Farmer Households by Area Cultivated, 1899–1909
(Units: average number of owner-farmer households per village (*mura*) in each size-category)

	AREA CULTIVATED (ha.)				
	0·5−1	1−2	2−3	Over 3	Total
Tōhoku (6 villages)					
1899	60·5	98·1	52·0	26·0	236·6
1909	61·2	66·6	45·5	28·5	201·8
Change	+0·7	−31·5	−6·5	+2·5	−34·8
Kinki (18 villages)					
1899	66·5	56·0	6·3	2·0	130·8
1909	63·1	48·5	7·5	2·0	121·1
Change	−3·4	−7·5	+1·2	0·0	−9·7
Kyūshū (14 villages)					
1899	90·0	77·4	26·7	5·5	199·6
1909	85·7	77·7	28·0	5·8	197·2
Change	−4·3	+0·3	+1·3	+0·3	−2·4

Source: Wataya, T., 'Shihonshugi no Hatten' (62), p.196, from surveys by the Imperial Agricultural Association.

To summarise this phase, the substantial growth in agricultural output which was occurring in the second half of the nineteenth century, and possibly earlier, was the result of the spread of certain interconnected, labour-using, land-saving techniques and commercial inputs. The adoption of these techniques was feasible only in areas where environment, infrastructure, and economic conditions were well developed, since they had emerged in response to the economic change experienced in such places. These areas were concentrated along the Inland Sea coast and in northern Kyūshū, in the neighbourhood of the main areas of urban development in Tokugawa and early Meiji Japan. Although the new methods were technically probably neutral to scale, it

[P] Wataya, T., 'Shihonshugi no Hatten' (62), p.195. See also p.217, where Wataya shows that there appears to be a correlation between the level of a prefecture's rice yield (1903–12) and the proportion of households farming more than 3 hectares, such that the higher the yield the lower the proportion of large farmers.

was initially larger-scale cultivator/landlords who were able to adopt them most easily and to adapt best to the commercialisation forced on farmers in all areas by the conversion of the land tax into money. As a result, and especially in the more remote areas where farmers were forced into money dealings without the assistance of rising yields and non-agricultural income, there occurred the so-called bi-polarisation of the landholding structure as landownership became more concentrated in the hands of large-scale landowners.

2.   Phase 2

(1)   INDUSTRIAL DEVELOPMENT AFTER 1900

We saw earlier (e.g. Table 3.1) how, in the 1880s, the vast majority of factories were rural and small-scale. By 1892, however, Yamaguchi's estimates show that the proportion of urban factories had more than doubled to reach almost 50% of manufacturing establishments, and the proportion of factories employing more than 20 people had risen from 28% in 1884 to 50% in 1892.[30] This growth in urban factory employment was still concentrated in the textile industries, using the same kinds of labour supply as before, and household production remained central to the industrial structure. However, these figures suggest the beginnings of the shift towards urban factory industry, using more modern machine technology, upon which twentieth-century Japanese industrialisation was based. The precise dating of the turning-point is not important for present purposes — it is enough to say that the end of the nineteenth century saw an increasing trend towards factory employment in established industry and, after the turn of the century, expansion in other industries brought with it increasing concentration in large-scale urban factories. This is not to say that small-scale industry did not remain particularly important in the Japanese industrial structure, supported by institutional mechanisms such as sub-contracting, only that industry after 1900 began to break out of its symbiotic relationship with agriculture and to grow under its own momentum.

To mention briefly the causes of this shift — in the textile industries the close of the nineteenth century saw quite rapid progress in the changeover to modern machine techniques as the fruit of earlier efforts by the government and by individuals to bring in Western technology and powered machinery, together with the use of steam and electricity. The growing familiarity of entrepreneurs with this kind of technology, and of the labour force with the requirements of full-time industrial work, made this possible. Exports of manufactured textiles began to take the place of raw silk and tea. The number of cotton spindles rose from 77,000 in 1887 to 2,414,000 in 1913 as the number of cotton-spinning mills increased and the size of the mills expanded.[31]

The significance of the turn of the century period also lay, however, in the beginning of the growth of new industries, especially heavy ones. The Sino-Japanese and Russo-Japanese Wars (1894−5 and 1904−5) were a major stimulus to this, with government military demand rising sharply. Coal output began to rise rapidly after 1894, as steam-powered industrialisation sped up. In 1901, the government-owned Yawata Iron Works in northern Kyūshū began production, and output of pig-iron rose from 26,000 tons in 1896 to 243,000 tons by 1913.[32] In 1896 the government began subsidising ship-building, and a number of new yards were opened. Annual average gross tonnage of steamships launched rose from under 10,000 tons in the mid-1890s to over 50,000 tons in 1909−13.[33] After 1900 the use of electricity for lighting and for factory power increased markedly and the manufacture of electrical equipment became a growing industry. Many other modern industries — cement-making, glass manufacture, fertiliser production, etc. — had their beginnings in the 1890s and 1900s.

The 1890s and 1900s were also a period of rapid expansion of the railway network. Railway mileage tripled between 1893 and 1913.[34] By 1900 it was possible to travel by rail from Tokyo to Shimonoseki, the south-western tip of Honshū, and by 1905 all the way from Kagoshima, the southernmost point of Kyūshū, to Aomori at the very north of Honshū.[35] Rail freight traffic increased enormously, as did the volume of shipping.

I do not want to over-emphasise the stage of modern industrialisation which was reached in Japan by the time of World War I; the modern sector was still small, with imports still supplying much of the heavy industrial output required. Agricultural output still bulked large in total production. The important point to note is the shift taking place in the industrial structure and its consequences for the nature of labour demand. The number of private factories employing more than ten people increased from 5,985 in 1894 to 17,062 in 1914, and their operatives from 381,000 to 854,000.[q] The proportion of the industrial labour force employed in the group of heavy industries (chemicals, metals, machines), in which plant size was largest, stood at 12·4% in 1909, 15·7% in 1914, and 24·3% by 1919.[36] In general, the period 1900−20 saw the first steps in the shift from manufacturing industry based on the

[q] Lockwood, W., *The Economic Development of Japan* (115), p.113. These are not strictly comparable figures since the 1914 figure includes plants employing 10 or more operatives and 'labourers', while the 1894 one is restricted to operatives.

rural household to modern industry based on the urban factory or work-shop.

Japan's comparative non-involvement in World War I gave her further opportunity for the capture of export markets in India and China, as did her acquisition of colonies. Although the collapse of the war boom in the early 1920s and the Great Depression of 1930–1 were setbacks, the stim-ulus continued to work through to the heavy industrial sector, and the increasing demand for military output in the 1930s intensified this. Again using Ohkawa and Rosovsky's categorisation of industrial sectors, the 12·4% of the industrial labour force employed in heavy industry in 1909 produced 19·7% of total industrial output. By 1940 these proportions had risen to 56·8% and 62·6% respectively. Meanwhile, employment in traditional industries fell from 24·8% to 18·8%, and in textiles from 62·8% to 24·4%, of total industrial employment.[37]

The shift to modern heavy industry of necessity brought with it the shift from urban to rural locations. Between 1889 and 1940 the percentage of the population living in cities of more than 20,000 people rose from 9·7 to 37·5.[38] This growth of industrial urbanisation did not fundamentally alter the pattern of population concentration in the south-western part of Japan—the fifteen prefectures on the line from Tokyo to northern Kyushu contained 75·4% of the population of incorporated cities in 1892 and 76·7% in 1940.[39] However, it did change this pattern as regards two areas, by intensifying the demand for mining resources, so that the areas around the two major coalfields in Japan showed quite rapid expansion. These areas were Hokkaidō and the northern part of Fukuoka prefecture containing the North Kyūshū coalfield. Hokkaidō is exceptional, being an area of new settlement, and this leaves northern Kyūshū as more or less the only area to become highly urbanised in res-ponse to the growth of modern heavy industry alone. The population of the Kita-Kyūshū conurbation (Yawata, Kokura, Moji, Wakamatsu, Nogata and Tōbata) rose from 308,000 in 1920 to 794,000 in 1940.[40]

The impact of the changes in the nature of industrialisation on agri-culture will be examined in the next section. The main point to carry forward is that the growth of heavy industry after the turn of the cen-tury, and the consequent growth of urban factory employment, broke the relationship between agriculture and industry within the rural household. Industrial workers increasingly came to move and set up their own households in urban areas, and, although they retained many links with their rural roots, could no longer be expected to contribute their labour and income to the farm household to the extent that they had done previously.

Nevertheless, the pattern which migration took meant that the major impact was still felt in areas within relatively easy communication with the main urban centres. To quote Taeuber: 'It is apparent that the majority of migrants to the majority of cities moved to areas that were known directly or through personal contacts. These were generally areas of easy access for the initial movement and they were also areas in which maintenance of contacts with the family and village was simple.'[r] As a result, the amount of movement from a prefecture tended to be inversely related to its distance from the urban centres, and depended on the balance between access to information and channels of communication and relative income levels between agricultural and industrial occupations. 'While the exodus of the native-born from the prefectures of Japan was primarily a movement away from agriculture, the amount of migration was proportionate neither to the limitations of agricultural land nor to the pressure in the local economies. The decision to migrate involved the pressures in the areas of origin, the awareness of opportunities elsewhere, the possibilities of movement, and the personal factors of qualifications, responsibilities and motivations.'[41]

In general terms, then, the change in the nature of industrialisation after 1900 meant that industry began to grow under its own momentum, no longer constrained by the need to fit its labour demands into those of agriculture or, as we shall see in the next section, by the growth of supplies of food and raw materials from agriculture. The change in the structure of its output meant that industry increasingly came to rely on its own internal markets or on exports for the demand for its output. As industry's growth continued, the gap between industrial and agricultural incomes and productivities increased. Real product per worker in agriculture, which had been $40-50\%$ of that in industry throughout the period 1886–1917, had fallen to $22·8\%$ by 1938.[42] In the next section I shall look in more detail at the impact of this on supply and demand in the markets through which agriculture and industry were now related, before going on to examine its technological and structural dimensions.

---

[r] Taeuber, I., *The Population of Japan* (131), p.127. Cf. 'Even in the eighteenth century the growth of industry in the midlands and north [of England] influenced the supply of agricultural labour and the wages paid. There developed the division between the semi-industrialised high-wage counties of the northern half of the country and the agricultural low-wage counties of the south. In this period and down to the middle nineteenth century English farm labour was normally mobile only over fairly short distances. The working population of large towns like Manchester and Leeds was recruited predominantly from the neighbouring counties. Consequently, the effects of higher wages and greater variety of employment were felt most strongly near the centres of growing industry, and weakened as distance increased.' Chambers, J. and Mingay, G., *The Agricultural Revolution* (139), p.120.

(2) INDUSTRIALISATION AND THE MARKET FOR AGRICULTURAL OUTPUT

The standard accounts of agriculture's role in economic development state that chief among agriculture's functions in the growth process are those of supplying labour and food to the expanding industrial sector. The Japanese agricultural sector is often used as an example of agriculture fulfilling its standard role, and we saw it in the last section indeed supplying labour to the industrial sector. In this section, I shall turn to considering how successful it was in meeting the industrial sector's demand for agricultural output. I shall concentrate on rice, this being by far the most important product of the Japanese agricultural sector from the points of view of both producers and consumers. We need to look at trends in the price of rice relative to other products and at the extent to which demand for it could be met by domestically produced supplies.

To slip back for a moment into phase 1, domestic rice production before about 1900 was in general adequate to meet home demand on a slowly rising relative price trend.[43] This was made possible by the growth in output (either pre-existent in 1868, or occurring between then and 1900) and by the increasing commercialisation of agriculture, including the effects of the substitution of the land tax for the payment of feudal dues in kind. Quite widespread trading in rice between surplus and deficit areas was taking place before 1868,[44] and the national rice market continued to grow after then. But the rural nature of the industrial and commercial development of this period and the continued close links between agriculture and industry within households must have lessened the problems of developing rice marketing to meet industry's needs. The local rice trade was in the hands of the larger landowners who doubled up as rice dealers, money-lenders, etc., and who provided a link, through their personal connections and in many cases their own industrial investments, between farmers and their rice markets. Thus an adequate supply could be channelled towards its demand.

The industrial spurt of 1900–20, and the changes in the nature of industrialisation which it brought, had their implications for the rice market as well. Around the turn of the century, domestic demand for rice began to exceed domestic supply, and Japan became an importer of rice. The amounts were at first small, but quite a large proportion of the urban demand for rice must have been met by imports from quite early on. But in addition, the rise in the relative price of rice began to speed up.[45] As the rice trade became more centralised with the growth of urban industrial concentrations, speculation became more common, and this helped to intensify the price rise caused by excess demand. The rising price of food culminated in the Rice Riots (*Kome Sōdō*) of 1918, which represented the protests of urban workers against the increasing cost of essential consumption goods.

The price of rice was rising relative to both the general price level and the prices of farm inputs, and the 1900–20 period was something of a golden age for farmers. The new technology was now being widely adopted in suitable areas and the rate of growth of output was fast. The high levels of industrial demand for labour meant either higher household income through outside wages or fewer mouths to feed, and more land was becoming available as people left.

However, from the non-agricultural viewpoint, the rising price and increasing imports of rice were disturbing indicators that domestic agricultural expansion was no longer adequate to meet industry's demands, and the panic of the Rice Riots precipitated the government into action. It launched a full-scale policy to encourage the cultivation of Japanese-type rice in Taiwan and Korea for export to Japan. The policy was a great success and imports of Korean and Taiwanese rice rose from 183,000 metric tons in 1915 to 1,917,000 metric tons in 1935, and as a result imported rice rose from 5 to 20% of domestic production.[46]

The collapse of the World War I boom after 1920 also represented the end of the golden age for farmers. The price of rice dropped sharply from its very high 1919 level, below the level of the general price index. It began to recover its relative position as the 1920s wore on, only to be hit again by the impact of the Great Depression. The collapse of the American silk market was a great blow to many farmers, and the rice price tended to fall more sharply than the general price index in the troughs of the two depressions. The decline in the opportunities for industrial employment and the return of unemployed workers to their villages in the depressions also hit agricultural households. Nevertheless, it is difficult to argue that, taking the inter-war period as a whole, the terms of trade for rice turned all that badly against agriculture, despite the increase in imported rice which consistently sold at 20–30% less than home-produced rice (see Table 6.4). The prices of inputs, especially fertilisers, continued their relative decline as the capacity to produce them grew, and farmers continued to increase their use of them. While not denying that many farm households, with their relatively heavy fixed costs and vulnerability to sharp price fluctuations, were hard hit when the depressions struck, I would argue that the problem was less one of low prices than one of inability to continue to expand output through increases in inputs at the same rate as before. Costs per unit of output could not therefore continue to fall fast enough to make domestic rice competitive with imports. This is more or less the argument of Hayami and Ruttan, who attribute the slow-down in growth to 'the exhaustion of potential' of available technology.[47] The next section will be devoted to examining the nature of this phenomenon.

(3)   TECHNICAL CHANGE AND THE ROLE OF THE STATE

We saw in the last section how, just as in the previous phase technical and economic change in agriculture responded to the pattern of industrial development, so in this phase booms and set-backs in industrialisation had their repercussions on agriculture. But we also saw that industry was beginning to draw away from agriculture, both in the structure of the inter-relationships between the two sectors, and in terms of rates of growth of output and income. Underlying this divorce were, on one side, the changing nature of industrialisation, and, on the other, the emergence of supply constraints slowing up the rate of growth of output in agriculture. In this section I shall look in more detail at the nature of these supply constraints and at the measures being taken to overcome them. This will show that significant changes were taking place beneath the macro picture of stagnation, and that these changes required the increasing participation of public institutions—ranging from the government at the national level to farmers' organisations at the village level—in the development and diffusion of new techniques.

There were two dimensions to the problem of supply constraints which had led to the rise in the price of rice, the Rice Riots and the decision to encourage imports. By 1920, the *Meiji Nōhō* package was widely used within the advanced areas of the south-west to which, as I argued earlier, its characteristics were suited. Further advance in the direction of *Meiji Nōhō*-type techniques meant controlling and assuring the production of yet higher-yielding varieties—in effect the scientific breeding of seeds. It also meant further improvements in cultivation methods, fertiliser use, pest control, etc., but there were constraints imposed on this. In advanced areas affected by industrialisation it was no longer possible to assume that family labour supply posed no constraint on the substitution of labour for land to raise yields. As the industrial labour force grew, the supply of labour to the agricultural household at peak times would begin to limit the labour-using characteristics of new techniques and the amount of land the household could farm. Labour saving was beginning to be a desirable characteristic of new techniques. Furthermore, with rising urban incomes changing the pattern of food demand, and with imports meeting the demand for the cheapest rice, Japanese farmers would need increasingly to grow crops other than rice, or to produce higher quality rice. This would require knowledge and training on a large scale.

The second dimension to the problem lay in the 'backward' regions of the East to which the *Meiji Nōhō* was in general not well suited. Advance here meant either adapting the *Meiji Nōhō* to these colder areas, and/ or adapting the infrastructure there to the *Meiji Nōhō*. The first line required adaptation to seed varieties and cultivation practices, which could only be assured through scientific research and experiment. The other required large-scale investment in land improvement, especially drainage, to facilitate deep ploughing, heavy fertiliser use, and so on.

In tracing the development of various aspects of rice-growing technology, we shall see how these lines were followed and what was required by them in terms of resources and institutional innovations.

1. Seed Varieties and Fertilisers

The fertiliser-responsive seed varieties of phase 1 were developed, as we saw earlier, by farmers themselves. The most famous of these varieties was Shinriki and, as can be seen from Table 3.4, this variety was extremely widely grown in the west of Japan, spreading especially in the 1900−20 period. After 1920, however, the area planted to it began to drop sharply. According to Arashi, Shinriki did not respond well to the switch from organic to chemical fertiliser which became pronounced in the inter-war period, and it became very susceptible to blight.[48] In addition, although its yield was as high as any alternative variety,[49] the rice it produced was of low quality, putting it into competition with the cheap imported rice. It was replaced in the west mainly by varieties called Asahi, which were more disease-resistant and produced higher quality rice, though not necessarily higher yields.

As Table 3.4 shows, Shinriki was never widely grown in the east, and the area under improved varieties was small until the emergence in the 1900s of two varieties, Kameno-o and Aikoku, which were better suited to conditions in the north-east. Both were cold-resistant but relatively early-maturing and high-yielding. Aikoku was not a high quality rice, but was a very reliable, less risky variety under poor environmental conditions and was grown chiefly in Kantō. Kameno-o was of high quality and made rice from Tōhoku much more marketable in Tokyo.[50]

All these varieties were developed at the farm level. However, after the turn of the century their diffusion became a much more highly organised process than it had been earlier. This was because there now existed a network of farming organisations through which information could be transmitted, and alongside that a network of experiment stations to analyse and select the information for transmission. In 1899, all the various local-level farm groups which had come into being in the previous years were reorganised into the pyramidal structure of the Imperial Agricultural Association. Large numbers of agricultural co-operatives came into being under new legislation (the Industrial

Table 3.4: Areas Planted to Rice by Varieties
(Units: ha.)

	1875	1880	1885	1890	1895	1900	1907	1910	1919	1928	1932	1936	1939
Western Prefectures:													
Varieties developed by farmers													
Shinriki		1	10	28	72	211	440	441	500	318	171	68	49
Aikoku									21	54	86	86	79
Asahi									12	81	296	435	481
Ōmachi	1	3	5	7	12	41	122	113	96	40	28	17	9
Others			1	4	10	35	84	80	100	98	137	128	98
Experiment station varieties												42	80
Major improved varieties Total	1	4	16	39	94	287	646	634	729	591	718	776	796
Traditional varieties	1338	1378	1364	1442	1390	1213	888	918	836	953	824	734	679
Total	1339	1382	1380	1481	1484	1500	1534	1552	1565	1544	1542	1510	1475
Eastern Prefectures:													
Varieties developed by farmers													
Shinriki					2	27	80	82	110	63	34	28	22
Aikoku					4	23	143	142	176	253	249	221	197
Asahi									1	38	73	95	111
Kameno-o							17	52	133	121	70	21	12
Ōmachi							1	3					
Others				3	11	46	123	116	96	185	290	304	231
Experiment station varieties											137	300	444
Major improved varieties Total			1	3	17	96	364	395	516	660	853	969	1017
Traditional varieties	1150	1187	1192	1228	1224	1152	922	923	858	826	696	558	436
Total	1150	1187	1193	1231	1241	1248	1286	1318	1374	1486	1549	1527	1453

Source: Hayami, Y. and Rutton, V., *Agricultural Development* (152), Appendix D, pp.350–1. (For areas covered under Western and Eastern prefectures see footnote j of this chapter.)

Co-operative Association Law of 1900). The first national experiment station had been set up in 1886, but in 1899 the government passed the law for the subsidisation of prefectural experiment stations, and these were soon being established throughout the country. To some extent, these developments were the work of enthusiasts, but government support for, and involvement in, agriculture was clearly increasing, as we shall see later as well. After the Rice Riots, this became a conscious policy of support and subsidy for agriculture, aimed at encouraging higher output and, within limits, improving the lot of farmers.

The first result of the increasing national organisaton of agriculture was the emergence of a much more sophisticated system for diffusing information—for instance, information about seed varieties. Local organisations could be informed about the availability of improved varieties, and they could test them under local conditions and advise local farmers of their relative merits. Arashi argues that this lies behind the widespread diffusion of Shinriki in the 1900s and 1910s,[51] and it must certainly have facilitated the spread of the later varieties developed by farmers.

Beyond this, however, the local experiment stations were developing the capacity to carry out original work of their own, in particular the cross-breeding of seed varieties, begun at the Kinai station in 1904.[52] The first major result of this was the appearance at the end of the 1920s of much better high-yielding varieties for the north-east, specifically Riku-u 132, developed at the Riku-u experiment station in 1922 for the Tōhoku region, and Nōrin No. 1, bred by the Ministry of Agriculture for the Hokuriku region. These were high-yielding, fertiliser-responsive, good quality varieties which would mature under cold conditions. They provided the real basis for the spread of high-yielding rice cultivation in the north-east.

The necessary concomitant of the increasing use of high-yielding varieties was greater application of fertiliser, and this implied the use of commercial fertiliser. At first the increase was mainly concentrated in organic fertiliser, the most important source being soy-bean cake fertiliser from Manchuria, the importing of which increased sharply after the Russo-Japanese War (1904—5), along with the spread of Shinriki. By 1930, the domestic chemical fertiliser industry was established and domestically produced ammonium sulphate began to take the place of imported organic and inorganic fertiliser. As a result of the development of fertiliser production at home, its relative price continued to fall throughout the period, encouraging its use, as did the spread of the use of high-yielding varieties. Growth in the use of fertilisers was maintained throughout the 1900—39 period, and it is often pointed out as evidence of the exhaustion of technological potential in the inter-war period that during that time, unlike the earlier 1900–20 period, the growth of inputs was faster than the growth of output.[53] For Arashi, it illustrates the lag in the development of seed-breeding behind that of chemical fertiliser production as agriculture waited for the emergence of seed varieties adapted to chemical fertilisers.

2.   Land Improvement

In analysing the *Meiji Nōhō* we saw how heavily it depended on the ability to control the supply of irrigation water sufficiently to be able to drain paddy fields for ploughing and for winter crops. We also saw that the regional distribution of good irrigation facilities was heavily biased in favour of the Inland Sea coastal regions, where investment in improvements to water systems had been going on since well back into the Tokugawa period. Investment in land improvement must have been continuing through the Meiji period, but there are no firm data. Arashi's figures suggest that the double-cropped proportion of paddy land rose on average by about 20% between 1884 and 1907,[54] though this also reflects changes in other factors (demand, fertiliser availability, etc.) besides land improvement. The regional distribution of advanced land infrastructure facilities does not seem to have altered substantially.

What we can say is that most of the projects carried out during phase 1 must have been small-scale, since the abolition of the feudal nobility had destroyed the main institutional means for mobilising resources on a large scale. Arashi's data (see Table 3.2) also suggest that the rate of increase in the proportion of the paddy area double-cropped slowed up around 1907, and that the 1910s and 1920s were a somewhat stagnant period from this point of view. Put together, these ideas would lead to the conclusion that areas in which irrigation and drainage facilities had not by the 1900s been improved to the point at which intensive *Meiji Nōhō*-type cultivation was possible either had no incentive to do so, because the *Meiji Nōhō* was not suited to them environmentally or economically, or faced obstacles too great to be overcome without outside help. These obstacles could be financial—high costs due to particular engineering difficulties—or organisational—problems arising where a large area was covered by an inter-connected irrigation system.

We saw in the last section how the problem of the technical incentive was being dealt with. The organisational and financial obstacles to land improvement required state initiative in just the same way, and the government did indeed respond to the emerging domestic food shortage by introducing measures to try to overcome these obstacles. In 1899, the Arable Land Replotment Law was passed. This made participation in land improvement schemes compulsory if two-thirds of the landowners involved agreed to it, provided that they owned two-thirds of the land to be covered. It applied at first only to schemes for reorganising and consolidating holdings, but was amended in 1905 and 1909 to cover a wider range of projects including irrigation and drainage.[55] It also made provision for the supply of cheap credit to finance the schemes, with loans to be made to the organisations of farmers which had to be formed to carry out the projects (land improvement associations). The scope of the projects which such village organisations could deal with was still not very large, however, and the largest proportion of schemes carried out under the law in the early years of its operation concerned the laying of underground drainage pipes. Next came conversion of upland fields into paddy.[56] Government promotion of larger-scale projects began with the introduction in 1923 of rules for the subsidisation of irrigation and drainage projects, which authorised central government to provide 50% subsidies to prefectural governments undertaking projects covering more than 500 hectares.

The area of land improved under these pieces of legislation steadily mounted during the inter-war period. According to Hayami's data, 1,419,000 hectares of land were improved between 1900 and 1940, out of a total cultivated area of just over 6 million hectares in 1940.[57] That this represented the state involvement required to adapt the infrastructure of areas previously unsuited to intensive agriculture is strikingly illustrated by the regional distribution of projects. Of the area covered by land reorganisation schemes between 1900 and 1935, 22·6% was in the six prefectures of Tōhoku, and 15·8% was in Kyūshū. By contrast, only 6·8% was in the advanced Kinki region and 8·3% in the Chūgoku region along the Inland Sea coast.[58] This trend is also indicated by the rising cost of projects as more and more difficult areas were tackled. So, schemes were costing ¥10−30 per 10 ares in the 1910s and 1920s, but ¥30−90 per 10 ares by the 1930s.[59]

To summarise, under the pressure of the domestic food supply shortage, the government became increasingly involved in promoting and subsidising investment in land improvement. Large areas were made suitable for intensive cultivation through improvement to their drainage and/or irrigation, and the major impact of this fell on the previously backward areas of the north-east and extreme south.

3. Mechanisation and Diversification

While the previously backward regions were beginning to be permitted to intensify their rice cultivation as their infrastructures were improved and as suitable seed varieties were being developed, how did the advanced south-western areas deal with the economic changes of this phase—increasing urban industrial demand for food and for labour and growing foreign competition in the rice market? We saw earlier their switch into higher-quality rice varieties, but higher yields were increasingly hard to obtain, despite heavier fertiliser application, in the absence of any outstanding new varieties or techniques. Moreover, as urban incomes rose, the demand for products with higher income elasticities than rice was beginning to expand. Although rice remained the predominant crop, even in advanced areas, the output of other products began perceptibly to increase as farmers grew steadily more and more of a wide range of fruit and vegetables and kept more and more livestock and poultry, replacing the various miscellaneous low-quality grain crops and also silk production after the disastrous collapse in the American demand for silk.[5]

The change to a more diversified output pattern, while helping to meet changes in market demand, also met the requirements of the other constraint affecting agriculture—the growing shift of workers out of agriculture. It did this by spreading out labour demand for farm operations throughout the year, so that the labour force remaining on the farm maintained their output by working more fully throughout the year on fruit and vegetable crops and on livestock. But in addition, they began to make efforts to maintain the area under rice by mechanising the peak operations, thus making up for the loss of the family members now working permanently in industry, and the most striking technical changes in the advanced regions were in the development of machinery to meet the needs of small-scale family farms. To some extent this trend was inter-connected with the increasing number of organised land improvement schemes, through the use of machines for pumping and draining, but this led on to the development of machine power in other operations for which stationary machines were suitable.

There are examples of the use of steam engines for irrigation and drainage from the 1890s, but only in scattered and very large-scale projects. The period of World War I saw steam power superseded in Japanese industry to be replaced by oil and electricity, and the expansion in industry at this time, with its effects on the supply of agricultural labour, was the stimulus for the first attempts to adapt oil and electric motors for agricultural uses. In industry, oil-driven motors were generally replaced by electric ones as the electricity supply industry developed

---

[5] For example, using *Chōki Keizai Tōkei* (66) figures for the value of crop production at constant 1934−6 prices and comparing 1915 with 1940, the value of output of vegetables rose from ¥164 million to ¥229 million, that of fruit and nuts from ¥46 million to ¥99 million, and that of livestock and poultry from ¥69 million to ¥221 million. The value of rice output changed proportionally much less, rising from ¥1,537 million to ¥1,673 million, but still clearly represented by far the largest item in total agricultural output.

in the 1910s and 1920s, but their use in agriculture was expanded. They were quite widely used as a power source for processing tea in Shizuoka, and in the 1920s they were beginning to be adapted for use in irrigation, chiefly in Okayama, an area which pioneered the use of small-scale oil-driven motors in agriculture. Initially the motors were all imported and not very suitable for small-scale irrigation use, but the domestic industry grew up during the 1920s. In 1935, there were 20 small firms in Okayama producing about 15,000 machines a year, and big companies like Kubota had started to produce on a national scale.[60] The use of electric motors in agriculture began to develop as the electricity supply network expanded into rural areas in the 1920s. Again the only motors initially available were imported and not very suitable, but in the late 1920s domestically-produced motors of more satisfactory design began to be produced.

Table 3.5: Numbers of Agricultural Machines in Use, 1920–39
(whole country)

	Electric motors	Oil motors	Power-tillers	Pumps	Power-threshers	Powered hullers
1920	683	1,785				
1923	2,033	9,265				
1925	4,690	24,849				
1927	11,603	39,406		17,413	29,820	
1931	28,306	63,459	98	26,940	55,954	88,637
1933	37,861	80,491	120	31,858	67,259	106,754
1935	47,138	96,353	211	32,586	91,735	118,247
1937	66,718	125,583	537	44,189	128,620	117,738
1939	91,053	202,046	2,819	83,115	210,579	145,966

Source: Kayō, N., *Nihon Nōgyō Kiso Tōkei* (68), pp.180–1, from surveys by the Ministry of Agriculture.

In the early 1920s, both electric and oil-driven motors were chiefly used in irrigation and drainage, but in the 1930s the use of motor power in other operations began to spread, as can be seen from Table 3.5. This was part of a general process of improving the efficiency of agricultural tools, in terms of both labour productivity and output quality, which was concentrated mainly in the operations of grain preparation. Earliest to be developed was a power-driven huller, which came to be widely used in the 1930s. Its *raison d'être* however was the desire to improve rice quality, and the first efforts to develop it had begun in the 1910s under the stimulus of increasing commercialisation and the concern of landlords and commercial farmers for the marketability of their rice. These were quite large, stationary machines, nearly always owned by groups of farmers, and their use had little impact on cultivation operations, since hulling can be carried out at any time of the year.

Threshing, however, was an operation which could cause a bottleneck within a double-cropping rotation, if adequate labour was not available. The World War I period saw the widespread diffusion of a pedal-driven rotary thresher, which was substantially quicker than the old comb-like threshing tools.[61] This was quite easily connected to a motor, but powered threshing tools also became available around 1920. The use of power-threshers was largely confined to the largest-scale farmers until the 1930s. The government was actively encouraging the growing of wheat at that time, in its efforts to promote self-sufficiency in grain production, and threshers spread particularly in Kantō and Hokuriku and on the Japan Sea coast where the clash between wheat-threshing and rice-transplanting was severe. Where wheat was not grown, either because double-cropping was still not possible (e.g. Tōhoku) or because a more diversified range of second crops was grown (e.g. Kinki), threshers were less common.

Field operations, however, were not mechanised at all. There were great advances in the design of ploughs to facilitate deep-ploughing, and the use of draught animals became the rule. The power-tiller was in the process of development in Okayama, but very few were actually in use before World War II. The rotary weeder spread widely, but chemical insecticides and weed-killers were rarely used before the war. Transplanting remained a manual job until the 1970s.

The pattern of mechanisation was a reflection of the interaction between farmers' needs and the technical problems involved. Irrigation/drainage and threshing were technically simpler to mechanise because the motors could be static (especially in the north-east, where threshing was done indoors, not in the field). The use of machines in irrigation was in general desirable as part of the effort towards land improvements in more difficult areas, though in places, as we shall see, also for saving labour and for assuring water supplies exactly when transplanting labour was available. In threshing, it helped ease the most significant peak in labour demand at the time of threshing/transplanting while transplanting continued to prove technically very difficult to mechanise. Ploughing was not mechanised before the war both because family labour forces were still in general adequate for this less confined operation and because the large tractors which could have been imported were impractical in Japanese conditions (unless a very large-scale substitution of capital for labour had been called for), so that mechanisation had to wait until the technology of the power-tiller had been developed.

The family labour force still had enough time for tasks like weeding which could be more flexibly timed.

If one were to look for the best-practice technical package of the 1930s to correspond to the *Meiji Nōhō*, it would be difficult to find.[t] Agricultural technology was in a transitional phase, with progress at different stages in different operations. Fertiliser use was well developed but seed-breeding less so; grain preparation was mechanised, field operations were not. Hayami and Ruttan's dynamic sequences were still working themselves out. But the main feature which had emerged was that the development of new technology could no longer be left in the hands of the farmers. Hybridisation of seeds, the organisation of irrigation and drainage improvements, the development of powered machinery, and so on, could only be carried out by institutions in the public or private sector who could invest modern resources on a large scale for the achievement of social or private returns.

(4)   The Economic Organisation of Agriculture

Just as with the previous phase, I shall begin by summarising the economic and technical forces operating on the agricultural sector in this period and then consider what kind of farm unit would be best able to cope with these forces. For this period there is substantially more statistical data from which to show that the predicted trend, an increasing proportion of middle-scale farmers, did in fact occur and was most marked in the areas most strongly affected by these forces.

Three kinds of force can be seen as operating on the agricultural sector in this period:

1. Changes in the relationship between agriculture and industry. The intimate relationship between the two sectors, based on by-employment and the nature of the exchange of other inputs and output, began to disintegrate with the growth of urban heavy industry. The declining relative position of agriculture was reflected in its generally depressed state, as industry came increasingly to rely for its markets and its sources of input supply on external trade or on its own internal demand and supply. The increasing divorce of industrial labour from its rural base, as industry came to demand a permanent urban labour force, also deprived agricultural households of their source of outside income and deprived them of the labour of all but the resident family workers. The industrial depressions of this period sent workers back to rural areas, complicating the picture of rural/urban migration, and urban industrial expansion never drew off more, in national terms, than the increase

[t] The nearest thing is the technology of Saga. See later.

in the rural population. But this conceals considerable regional variation in the impact of out-migration to industry on the agricultural structure, as we shall see below.

2. Land improvement and technical change. The pace of technical
change slowed down in this period, but what was occurring could be
summarised as investment in land improvement in previously less well
developed areas, the gradual development of techniques and inputs
suitable for such areas, and the beginnings of mechanisation and diversification in the initially advanced areas.

3. The relationship between farmers and authorities. We saw in the
previous section evidence of the increasing involvement of local and
central government in establishing the institutional means of promoting
agricultural development. These institutions facilitated more direct
contact between the authorities and the mass of farm households, which
was in itself a reflection of the social and political changes taking place
in Japan at the time. Social changes within the villages were in part the
result of economic change which, as we shall see, altered the relative
position of larger landowners and village leaders. But they also reflected
changes in Japanese society as a whole, in particular the spread of compulsory education and the extension of the franchise. The disputes
between landlords and groups of tenants which became increasingly
common in this period are also an indication of the change taking place
in the nature of traditional village hierarchies and social relationships.

What would be the effects of these trends on farm households of
different types? First of all, it can be seen that they constituted a considerable incentive for those at both extremes of the size distribution of
landownership and cultivated holdings to abandon agriculture if they
could. Taking first those at the bottom of the scale, for the mass of farm
households — who owned little land, rented in what they could and
acquired what outside employment they could — urban industrial expansion provided both the pull of new permanent job opportunities in the
cities and the push of the decline in the kinds of work they had
previously been able to combine with agriculture. The periods of heavy
industrial growth, especially in the 1910s, parts of the 1920s, and the
late 1930s, and the development of the colonies, gave such farmers the
chance to leave the agricultural work that had never been able to guarantee them much of a living, and lessened the need to set up small
branch households for younger sons. The possibilities for out-migration
were not evenly distributed either regionally or through time, but we
shall see that, at certain times and in certain parts of the country, these
small-scale cultivators demonstrated that they saw their prospects, or at
least those of their sons and daughters, as far better in urban industry
than in the agriculture of the time.

The forces which gave those at the other end of the scale their incentives to abandon direct involvement in agriculture have been described in detail by Waswo.[62] It was becoming increasingly hard to combine the running of industrial and agricultural enterprises, and as the tying up of capital in agriculture became less attractive,[63] so the incentive to shift capital, time and eventually residence into the urban sector increased. Direct cultivation of larger holdings, using hired labourers, became more and more difficult in areas affected by the pull of urban job opportunities, as the younger sons and daughters of poorer rural households, who had previously hired out their spare labour time, left for the cities. The depressed state of agricultural prices in the inter-war period also made it less profitable. It was still not hard to find tenants who would rent the land that the *tezukuri jinushi* no longer wanted to farm themselves, but as larger landlords withdrew from direct involvement in agriculture, there was less and less reason for remaining in the village and many attractions to leaving it. There was the pull of the glamour and convenience of urban life itself, and the push of the changes in the social role of the large landowning families, epitomised by tenancy disputes, which made the landlord's life in the village a less gratifying one. We would therefore expect a trend towards absentee landownership among the former leading landowner families.

The next step is to suggest that, while those at both extremes of the land distribution were under pressure to move away from agriculture, those in the middle were better able to cope with the changing economic conditions and less drawn to try to leave their traditional occupation. This middle group was made up of those who cultivated a holding of somewhere between a half and two hectares, i.e. a holding for which the average family labour force was adequate under the technical and environmental conditions of given regions. Some may have started with holdings of this size, but others came to acquire them, through additions to a previously smaller holding as both larger- and smaller-scale cultivators gave up agriculture. It may well have been ownership of the original holding that discouraged migration. As a result, a high proportion of cultivators in this middle scale were likely both to own and to rent in land and to fall into the owner/tenant category.

The advantages of this type of small-to-medium-scale family farm holding were basically technical. I argued earlier that techniques of the *Meiji Nōhō* type were neutral to scale and could be most effectively used by a family labour force which had incentives to work carefully and conscientiously. The diffusion of *Meiji Nōhō* techniques to smaller-scale farmers had begun in the previous period as *tezukuri jinushi* had led their villages into adopting the innovations, and this spread continued under the impact of the high prices and boom conditions of the 1900s and 1910s. What was occurring after the turn of the century was the breakdown of the advantages larger-scale cultivators had initially had through their greater access to information and their market experience. With education, with experience, with the increasing role of government in extension work and of group organisations in mobilising investment resources (e.g. for land reorganisation), the smaller-scale farmer was able to overcome the institutional problems that had prevented his technical superiority over the larger-scale farmer from taking effect. And at the same time labour shortage was making large-scale cultivation more and more difficult.

Furthermore, the direction which technical change took as the next stage after the *Meiji Nōhō* did nothing to alter this. On the one hand, it began to extend intensive cultivation techniques over a wider range of areas. And on the other, in areas going beyond the *Meiji Nōhō*, it resulted in the development of forms of mechanisation and diversification which helped to deal with the problems of the medium- or small-scale farm, but which could not permit the re-establishment of large-scale cultivation. For instance, mechanisation took the form of the development of small machinery designed to relieve the peak labour demands which prevented family labour forces from expanding the area they could cultivate or from releasing family members for full-time urban employment. This trend was epitomised in this period by the development of mechanised threshers, and subsequently by that of the power-tiller which made part-time farming universally possible after World War II. Diversification meant individual small farms growing a larger number of crops or acquiring a few cattle. But none of these kinds of innovation produced a sufficient saving of labour to permit larger-scale cultivation, paying an adequate wage to hired labour.[u]

It was in the boom years of the 1900s and 1910s that the advantages of the small-to-medium-scale farm household under *Meiji Nōhō*-type technology really began to make themselves felt on the agricultural structure. In the depressed years of the 1920s and 1930s, it was rather the middle-scale farmers' greater ability to withstand falling prices and incomes, in the given technical conditions, that sustained the concentration in the centre of the size distribution. For the larger-scale landowner,

---

[u] This is in sharp contrast to, for example, experience in Pakistan, as analysed by Gotsch. There, the option of large-scale mechanisation was open, and the response of larger landowners to the rising yields produced by Green Revolution techniques was to acquire the machines which enabled them to evict tenants and appropriate a larger share of the rising productivity of the land. See Gotsch, C., 'Tractor Mechanisation and Rural Development in Pakistan' (148).

the depression intensified the relative unprofitability of investment in land, and the small-scale cultivator struggled under the burden of rents and taxes and falling prices, at times when escape into the non-agricultural sector was impossible. It was the middle-scale owner/tenant farm household who had the little bit of scope necessary for reducing family living standards to make way for returning unemployed urban workers and for the increased inputs of fertiliser and labour which would produce just a little more output or bring about a little diversification.

Table 3.6 brings together the main statistical evidence that the forces operating on farmers in this period did have the effects suggested, and attempts to illustrate the regional variation in the strength of these forces. Data for Saga Prefecture are added for comparison later. The national-level figures clearly show the trend towards concentration in the 0·5−2 hectare range, on the basis of an almost constant number of farm households, taking the period as a whole. The proportion of owner/tenant households was also rising.[64] The technical superiority of middle-scale farmers is suggested by survey data assembled by Wataya, which indicate that they obtained both higher output per man and higher output per hectare than larger- or smaller-scale farmers, through higher double-cropping rates and greater investment in inputs per man and per hectare.[65]

However, Table 3.6 suggests that the effect of this technical superiority in leading to concentration in the centre of the distribution was much stronger in the advanced Kinki region (and also in Saga), where the impact of industrialisation, as reflected in the drop in the total number of farm households, was greatest.[66] This confirms the importance of urban industrial influences in drawing away those at the top and the bottom of the size distribution, thus facilitating the emergence of the middle-scale owner/tenant group who were then able to influence the direction taken by the later stages of technical change.[v]

*

To summarise the story presented in this chapter in terms of the framework of chapter 1: we saw first of all how a new set of intensive techniques emerged out of agriculture's response to the growth of industry

---

[v] Another aspect of urban industrial influences on social and structural change in rural areas is described by Totten, who shows that agrarian disputes (e.g. landlord/tenant conflict) were linked to industrial ones through the spread of knowledge about them, influences on leaders, and so on, and that there exists a correlation between the degree of industrialisation of an area and the number of agrarian disputes. See Totten, G., 'Labour and Agrarian Disputes in Japan' (22).

Table 3.6:   *Regional Variation in Changes in the Distribution of Households by Area
Cultivated. 1912–1937*
(thousands of households)

1.   Whole country

AREA (ha.)	1912 A	Change 1912–22 B	Change 1922–32 C	Change 1912–37 D	D as % of A
0–0·5	1,998	− 107	− 37	− 198	− 9·9
0·5–1	1,792	+ 18	+ 84	+ 72	+ 4·0
1–2	1,045	+ 95	+ 75	+ 191	+ 14.0
2–3	297	+ 2	− 2	− 5	− 1·7
Over 3	146	− 20	− 32	− 57	− 39·0
Total	5,278	− 12	+ 88	+ 3	− 0·01

2.   Tōhoku

0–0·5	154	+ 6	+ 7	+ 22	+ 14·3
0·5–1	138	+ 10	+ 22	+ 42	+ 30·4
1–2	132	+ 18	+ 24	+ 50	+ 37·9
2–3	71	+ 11	+ 1	+ 6	+ 8·4
Over 3	47	− 3	− 10	− 15	− 32·0
Total	542	+ 42	+ 44	+ 105	+ 19·4

3.   Kinki

0–0·5	268	− 17	− 8	− 42	− 15·7
0·5–1	237	+ 3	− 3	− 8	− 3·4
1–2	88	+ 2	+ 5	+ 10	+ 11·4
2–3	10	− 4	0	− 4	− 40·0
Over 3	3	− 2	0	− 2	− 66·7
Total	606	− 18	− 6	− 46	− 7·6

4.   Saga Prefecture

0–0·5	23	− 5	− 1	− 6	− 26·1
0·5–1	27	− 4	0	− 5	− 18·5
1–2	15	+ 5	+ 2	+ 6	+ 40·0
2–3	4	0	0	+ 1	+ 25·0
Over 3	1	0	0	0	0
Total	70	− 4	+ 1	− 4	− 5·7

Source: Calculated from data given in Wataya, T., 'Shihonshugi no Hatten' (62),
p.220 and p.223, and *Saga-Ken Tōkeisho* (101).
Tōhoku = Aomori, Akita, Iwate, Miyagi, Yamagata, Fukushima.
Kinki = Ōsaka, Kyōto, Shiga, Hyōgo, Nara, Wakayama.

and commerce in the nineteenth century, a set of techniques with characteristics such that it facilitated that response in the areas most affected by industrial and commercial developments. We saw also the factors

determining the emergence of the innovator group from within the prevailing agricultural structure. As phase 1 gave way to phase 2, we saw
how the emergence of urban factory industry after the turn of the century led, on the one hand, through outmigration of labour from the
regions nearest the growing industrial centres, to structural changes
(the growing preponderance of small-to-medium-scale family farms),
and, on the other, to the appearance of divergences between what
industry demanded and what agriculture could supply which could only
be narrowed by increasing government involvement in the process of
technical development in agriculture and in the diffusion of improved
methods to previously backward areas. The new techniques sought
through the mechanisms of this government involvement were, in turn,
conditioned by the nature of the agricultural structure based on the
small-to-medium-scale family farm, which had emerged from the earlier phases of economic and technical change.

How does the case-study which now follows fit into this framework?
As we shall see in detail later, its location and its natural environment
made the Saga Plain an area on the periphery of the regions of agricultural development in phase 1. Because of its location, however, it was
profoundly influenced by the early stages of modern industrial development after 1900. As a result of this influence, it had to overcome the
technical and environmental problems which prevented it from responding fully to the growth of industry, developing mechanised methods of
improving its irrigation technology and adapting *Meiji Nōhō* practices
and inputs to its own conditions. In doing this it became a pioneer in the
development of agricultural methods for areas with difficult environments affected by the second stage in the development of Japanese
industry. The technical system in operation on the Saga Plain in the
1930s perhaps comes nearest to representing the best-practice technology of the inter-war period. Japanese writers talk of the mid-to-late
1930s as the 'Saga stage' (*Saga dankai*) of Japanese agricultural development.

Table 3.7 illustrates this by bringing together the main macro-level
ways in which Saga differed from the national average. It was always a
fertile area with high yields (part 5), specialising in rice cultivation (part
6), but it managed to maintain its growth rate in the inter-war period
much better than was typical (part 2). The causes of this were, as we
shall see, embedded in its relationship with the industrial sector, whose
impact on Saga Plain agriculture is revealed by the drastic rise in cultivated area per farm worker in the 1900−20 period (part 3).

What Saga therefore shows us is an area, not initially well suited to
available advanced technology, adapting to it under the stimulus of the
development of the non-agricultural sector. The study will consider the

Table 3.7: *Macro-Economic Trends in Saga Compared with the Whole of Japan*

Part 1: Growth rates (% per annum) of the total value of all agricultural output, valued at 1934−6 prices.
(Calculations based on 5-yearly averages for years shown)

	Japan	Saga Prefecture
1880−1900	1·6	
1900−1920	1·8	
1920−1935	0·8	1·2
Source:	(66)	(67)

Part 2: Growth in rice output.
(% per annum between 5-yearly averages for years shown)

	Japan	Saga County
1890−1900	0·8	− 1·8
1900−1920	1·6	2·3
1920−1935	0·4	1·3
Source:	(66)	(101)

Part 3: Cultivated area per worker.
(Ha./worker, male and female)

	Japan	Saga County
1890	0·34	0·22
1900	0·36	0·23
1920	0·42	0·43
1935	0·44	0·46
Source:	(66)	(101)

Part 4: Rice output per worker.
(Kg, 5-yearly averages)

	Japan	Saga County
1890	409	583
1900	448	504
1920	638	1,405
1935	684	1,842
Source:	(66)	(101)

Part 5: Rice yields.
(Kg/10 ares, 5-yearly averages)

	Japan*		Saga County
1890	215	211	294
1900	226	222	246
1920	286	282	378
1935	297	294	444
Source:	(66)	(65)	(101)

Table 3.7:   Macro-Economic Trends in Saga Compared with the Whole of Japan (cont.)

Part 6:   Rice as a proportion of the total value of agricultural production. (%)

	Japan	Saga Prefecture
1880	62·8	
1900	55·9	
1920	56·7	70·81
1935	50·2	66·38
Source:	(66)	(101)

Source: *Chōki Keizai Tōkei* (66); *Saga-Ken Tōkei Sho* (101); *Nōgyō Keijōzaitō* (67); *Nōrinshō Ruinen Tōkeihyō* (65).

* *Chōki Keizai Tōkei* does not give figures for areas planted to individual crops. Yield figures have therefore been calculated using *Chōki Keizai Tōkei* production figures and official crop areas. *Chōki Keizai Tōkei* figures are not strictly comparable with the unadjusted prefectural yearbook figures, so in the crucial area of yields, official national data have also been included for comparison.

ways in which the impact of industrialisation conditioned this adaptation, and will examine in detail the mechanisms by which public authorities were induced to develop techniques with appropriate characteristics. This chapter has shown how the *Meiji Nōhō* emerged, mainly through the efforts of individual farmers, out of agriculture's response to the growth of a predominantly small-scale, rural, industrial and commercial sector, a process which would be hard to repeat elsewhere today, at least through conscious government effort. But the subsequent adaptation and diffusion of this set of techniques had much more to do with government policy and with the actions of local research and extension authorities, and it is with these policies and actions, the influences on them and the factors which made them successful, that much of the case-study is concerned.

CHAPTER FOUR

Land, Water and Work: Agriculture on the Saga Plain in the Mid-Nineteenth Century

1. Introduction

At this point the time has come to shift the focus down to the micro-economic level and to introduce the land, the water and the farmers with whom this study is chiefly concerned. In this chapter, I shall attempt to piece together a picture of agricultural life, in its technical, economic and social aspects, in the area known as the Saga Plain in the late Tokugawa and early Meiji period, around 1850–80. The choice of such a period as a starting-point, covering as it does a time of great political upheaval and substantial institutional change in the agricultural sector, may seem at first sight odd. The rationale lies in the fact that, although this period was not static in terms of technical and institutional change, it represents a time before the commercialising and industrialising forces of Japanese economic development came to exert a significant impact over the lives of farm households in this area, and it therefore presents the opportunity to analyse the interlocking technical, economic and institutional system whereby production was carried on and consumption sustained in an agricultural society as yet only on the margin of commercialisation. A glimpse of the way in which technology and economic and social institutions were adapted in this period to the needs of agricultural production, within the constraints of the particular environmental conditions of the area, is essential to an understanding of the way in which the system responded to the subsequent opening up of new technical and economic possibilities as the outside economy developed. But first a little geographical and historical background is required.

The Saga Plain is part of present-day Saga Prefecture and lies in the north-west corner of Kyūshū, in the south-west of the Japanese archipelago (see Map 2). The prefecture is sandwiched between the prefectures of Fukuoka, to the east and north, and Nagasaki, to the west, with

Map 2: Kyūshū

Map 3:   The Saga Plain

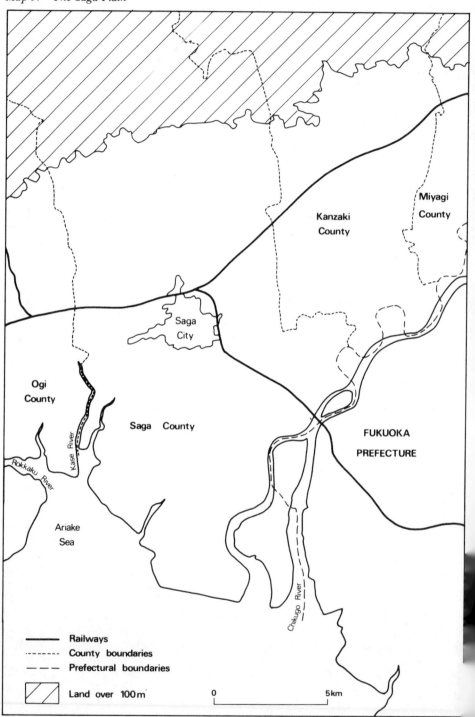

Miyagi
County

Kanzaki
County

Saga
City

Ogi
County

Kase River

Saga   County

Rokkaku River

FUKUOKA

PREFECTURE

Ariake
Sea

Chikugo River

——— Railways
- - - - - County boundaries
— — — Prefectural boundaries

Land over 100 m

0   5km

its eastern and southern boundaries formed by the river Chikugo and the Ariake Sea. The north and west of the prefecture are mountainous, with a rocky coastline around the fishing port of Karatsu and the famous ceramic-producing towns of Arita and Imari. But the south and west are made up by the alluvial plains of the major rivers which flow out of the mountains into the Ariake Sea, the Chikugo in the east and the Kasegawa and Rokkakugawa in the west (see Map 3). It is about 20 km from the mountains to the sea, passing through Saga City in the centre of this plain area, and about 15 km from the Chikugo in the east to the Kasegawa in the west. The whole area contains about 27,000 cultivated hectares, and is generally thought of as falling into three separate plains, distinguished by their environments and their main sources of irrigation water. These are: (1) the area at the northern end of the Chikugo basin, which relies on water from the Chikugo itself, supplemented by ponds; (2) the area in the west dependent on water from the Rokkakugawa, on the whole an area of recent reclamation; and (3) the Saga Plain proper, centering on Saga City, covering the main part of the whole plain, and dependent chiefly on water from the Kasegawa.[a] The first two of these areas take up a little over a third of the cultivated area of the whole plain, but it is with the remaining 16,000 or so cultivated hectares, known as the Saga Plain, that this book is chiefly concerned.

The first and most remarkable feature of the landscape of the Saga Plain is its flatness. The 5-metre contour line is not reached until the line of Saga City itself, some 10 km from the sea, and the overall slope of the land is very slight. The naturally marshy alluvial plain merges into great coastal mud flats, creating a natural environment beloved of frogs and snakes and the *mutsugorō*, which lives buried in the mud until dug out, cooked in soy sauce, and eaten as a local delicacy. Approaching the coast, the lines of the successive generations of sea walls attest to the relative ease with which the muddy coastline can be reclaimed from the sea.

The Saga Plain is thus one of the rather few Japanese examples of a wide, flat, more or less uniformly cultivated area, a distinct contrast to the terraced river valleys and coastal strips, with the ever-present mountains looming behind them, which make up the typical Japanese landscape. Because of this uniform flatness, very little land is too high or inaccessible to be reached, potentially, by the supply of irrigation water. As a result, 90% or more of the land in most villages is irrigated paddy land; and unirrigated fields (*hatake*), which typically make up about half of the cultivated area in most parts of Japan, are quite rare on the Saga Plain. In the winter, the golden-brown stubble fields, dotted

[a] See Map 4 and section 2 (1) for more on the structure of the irrigation network.

with stacks of drying straw, stretching away unbroken into the distance, look not entirely unfamiliar to a native of Eastern England, and in summer the sea-like appearance of the flooded plain belies the investments of generations controlling the movement of that water.

The natural environment of the Saga Plain is therefore well suited to the cultivation of grain in general and paddy rice in particular, and the alluvial soil is highly fertile. The climate is also suitable, with long sunny summers, when temperatures of 20−30 degrees are maintained, and relatively mild winters, when the temperature rarely falls below zero.[1] As in the rest of Japan, there is a concentrated rainy period (*tsuyu*) in June or July. Typhoons sometimes strike the area in late summer, but apart from this climatic conditions favour rice cultivation.

Historically, the central part of the Plain was naturally drained and in existence as cultivable land before 800, but a substantial strip, covering much of the land of the Kawazoe villages below Saga City, was reclaimed after this, and it has been estimated that the cultivable area expanded on average 21·9 hectares a year during the Tokugawa period.[2] In addition, there was a good deal of investment in improving the river system for irrigation purposes. The main outlines of the irrigation network on the Saga Plain, as it existed at least until the post-war construction of the large dam on the Kasegawa which today controls the Plain's water supply, were laid down in the early seventeenth century. At that time, the feudal rulers (*han*) of the area employed an engineer called Narutomi Hyōgo, who constructed the major dams and sluices controlling the flow of the Kasegawa and thus made possible a more secure water supply and an extension of the cultivated area.

The dominant *han* of the Saga Plain, whose family name was Nabeshima, in general exerted quite a strong influence over the economic life of the area, an influence characterised by a mixture of traditional values and progressive leadership. The Nabeshima were famous for their strict upholding of the samurai ethic and way of life,[b] which manifested itself in the economic field in strong efforts to maintain the division of society into estates of soldiers, farmers and tradesmen, and in a firm belief in the duties, responsibilities and authority of government officials. Former samurai of the Nabeshima *han* were responsible for staging the Saga Rebellion of 1874, during which they expressed their opposition to the modernising policies of the new Meiji government in attacks on banks in Saga City.[c] However, the Nabeshima themselves encouraged

[b] For example, the *Hagakure*, the famous eighteenth-century work of moral and practical instruction for samurai, was written for, and preserved by, the Saga *han*.

[c] See Iwata, M., *Ōkubo Toshimichi* (112), p.180, where the author remarks that 'over 90% of the officials of the prefectural government were sympathetic with these elements'.

not only the development of agriculture but also local industries such as iron-smelting and the production of cannon.[d]

After the Restoration, most of the Saga Plain fell under the jurisdiction of the local governments of Saga City (*shi*), Saga County (*gun*) and Kanzaki County, with small areas reaching into Ogi and Miyagi counties. In what follows, data for Saga County, the bulk of whose cultivated area is located on the Plain, will frequently be used as typical of the Plain area. Coastal reclamation continued at much the same rate as before and a further wide strip of new cultivable land was in existence by the outbreak of World War II. With the end of the Nabeshima *han* and the final crushing of the opposition to the Meiji government, which had been strong in the south-west, Saga slipped into the background of historical developments in Japan, concentrating on the agriculture to which it is environmentally so well suited.

Although the important Chikuhi coalfield reaches into Saga Prefecture and coal was for long the second most important product of the area, agriculture, and rice production in particular, has always been the major source of income and employment in Saga. Early Meiji Saga fits Yamaguchi's picture of the less economically and commercially advanced areas of Japan at that time,[3] exporting primary produce (mainly rice) and importing basic consumer goods manufactured in other areas. According to Yamaguchi's analysis of the 1884 official data, rice provided about half of the value of goods sent out of the prefecture. Coal generated about half of the value of rice exports, and pottery was also significant. The remaining 20% of export value was made up by various agricultural and fishery products. A very wide range of goods was imported in return, mostly finished consumer goods, the largest item on the import side being the category of dry goods and draperies. Other items included products such as sugar, tobacco, indigo, oil and wood which were not widely produced in Saga. This picture of Saga as essentially a specialist primary-product-producing area remained true throughout the period with which this book is concerned, and indeed beyond it. In 1888 69·2% of the prefecture's population were employed in agriculture;[4] in 1940 primary industry still provided employment for 56%.[5] The Chikugo/Kasegawa plain is the centre of this agriculture, covering about half of the prefecture's paddy area, and in the pre-war period Saga County alone produced about a quarter of the prefecture's rice output.

Thus the Saga Plain remains to this day a quiet but relatively prosperous agricultural area, and Saga City a large-scale market-town, off the beaten tracks of Japan's industrial and cultural history. Its one claim

[d] For which, interestingly, they used water-wheel power. See Minami, R., *Water Wheels in the Pre-Industrial Economy of Japan* (119), p.4.

to fame in the period between the Restoration and World War II lay in its successful development of techniques of rice cultivation, to the origins of which we now turn. I shall try to build up a picture of the technical and economic conditions of Saga Plain agriculture around 1850−80, beginning with a picture of the technology in use, and going on to analyse the way in which the economic organisation of production was adapted to the requirements of this technology and environment.

2. Technology

(1) THE SUPPLY OF IRRIGATION WATER

In this section I want to look at the technical factors conditioning the supply of irrigation water, the first pre-requisite for the cultivation of paddy rice, to the individual field in this period. This involves looking at the way in which a particular irrigation system developed as a response to the problems of rice cultivation in a particular environment. The economic consequences of this irrigation technology and the institutional organisation of the allocation of water and the maintenance of the system will be considered in later sections.

In chapter 2 we saw how typical irrigation systems in Japan were constructed so as to channel a down-flow of water by gravity into individual fields. The Saga Plain is a wide, flat, marshy, alluvial plain, very different, from the point of view of irrigation possibilities, from the more typical narrow coastal strips and river sides of the rest of Japan, and closer in some ways to the great plains elsewhere in Asia. Cultivation was made possible on the Saga Plain by the construction of ditches which drained the marshy fields and carried off flood water from the rivers. As reclamation and cultivation expanded over the generations, the Plain became covered with an intricate, interlocking network of such ditches, naturally filling as the water came down in the spring, and carrying it further and further away from the rivers. Every paddy field on the Plain was adjacent to a ditch in the network and through it ultimately connected to a distant river (see Frontispiece). These ditches could clearly provide not only the means of draining fields, but also that of carrying and storing water for irrigation purposes, and gradually sluices were constructed whereby the level of water in individual sections of the network could be controlled. What made these ditches fundamentally different, though, from irrigation channels elsewhere in Japan was the fact that water was stored in the ditch itself at or below the level of the field. This meant that, instead of gravity, some artificial power source had to be used to transfer the water into the paddy. Because of this crucial

Map 4:   The Irrigation System of the Saga Plain

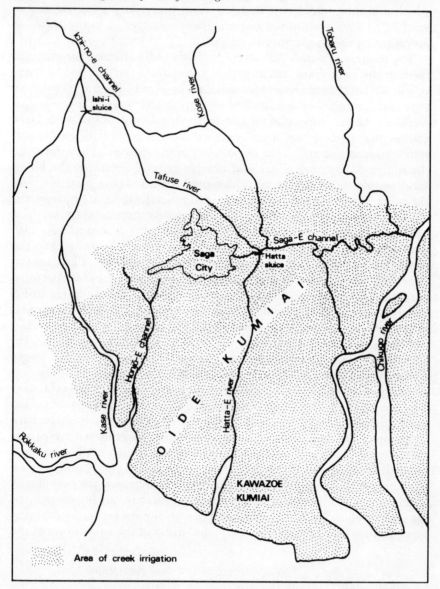

difference in their functions, irrigation ditches such as those in Saga, which are to be found only in a few other places in Japan,[e] are distinguished by their own name and are always referred to in the Japanese literature by the English word 'creek'.

The existence of the creek network profoundly affected the environment of the Saga Plain. Because they had to fulfil the function of reservoir as well as that of feeder channel, creeks were in general larger than typical irrigation channels, six feet or more in width, and they took up a relatively large proportion of the cultivable land.[f] Many were large enough to carry boat traffic and were the most important means of communication in the area until the coming of the railway. They were also the source of drinking water and were in general central to the life of farm people. Farm houses were designed to surround a platform over the creek, with steps leading down to it on which food could be prepared, washing done, and so on. The waste food that accumulated round these platforms served as groundbait for fishermen, and, less sportingly, fish stranded as the water level fell, in specially created depressions in the creek bottoms, provided an important source of protein.[6] The banks of the creeks provided reeds and rushes for fuel,[7] and spaces for vegetable gardens, and the creeks themselves a place to grow the water chestnuts which became a local speciality.[8] And the sounds of the birds and insects in the reeds in the summer provided the inspiration for Saga poets.[9]

The main source of water for the creek network was the Kasegawa. Although creeks had been constructed for irrigation and drainage[g] from early on, the basis for the consolidation and expansion of the network lay in the substantial improvements to the head-works on the river and the main feeder canals, carried out in the mid-Tokugawa period under the auspices of the Nabeshima family. These involved the construction of the Oide Dam and the Ishi-i Sluice, together with improvements to the Tafuse River and other channels, which made possible a controlled flow of water out into the eastern part of the Plain (see Map 4). The possibility of expanding the network increased the complexity and inter-connectedness of it, so that more and more areas were opened up which relied for their water supplies on the excess water draining away from creeks further upstream, and areas at the extremities of the

[e] Notably on the opposite bank of the Chikugo in Fukuoka prefecture.
[f] A survey made in 1953 found that on average the creeks took up an area equal to 6·9% of the cultivated area they covered (the highest recorded level being 17%), and they could hold at any one time an average 8·3% of total water requirements. Kyūshū Nōsei Kyoku, *Saga Heiya* (76), pp.98−9.
[g] And for other purposes, including as moats to defend the houses of powerful families. *Kasegawa Nōgyō Suiri Shi* (77), p.27.

network were always liable to water shortage. In the south-eastern corner of the Plain an interesting supplementary source of water was developed through the construction of special sluices designed to cream off the fresh water carried back up the Chikugo River by the tide, feeding it into the creek network in the opposite direction. Rainwater also collected in the creeks, of course, and since the irrigation water from the fields drained back into the creeks, it could be stored and used over and over again, either on the same fields or on those further downstream. In general the creek network represented the means of making maximum use of a given water supply over a wide and flat area.

Although creek irrigation made drainage and cultivation possible on the Plain, it had, however, the one great disadvantage that it required an external source of power to lift water into the field. The simplest method for this was to lift water manually from the creek in some sort of bucket and tip it out on to the field, and this was the method used in early times on the Saga Plain. However, in the second half of the eighteenth century, pedal-driven, man-powered water wheels began to appear.[h] They consisted of wooden wheels about five feet in diameter, criss-crossed with wooden spokes, which held angled slats or paddles to carry the water. The wheel was turned by a person treading the slats, balancing himself on long poles stuck in the ground on either side of the wheel (see Illustration 2, p.223). Construction of such wheels required quite a high level of carpentry skill, and the first ones were crude and difficult to use. In 1781 a local feudal lord (the *daimyō* of Kurume) instructed a *rōnin* (masterless samurai) to begin making them, but the first farmers to use them petitioned the lord to be allowed to go back to the old bucket method.[10] Construction techniques soon improved, however, and by the end of the eighteenth century, use of the water wheel was more or less universal on the Saga Plain. This continued to be so until the events of 1922–3 to be described in chapter 7.

Water wheels like those used in Saga were not unique to creek irrigation areas. Pictures of them, or similar devices, appear in some of the Tokugawa period books on agriculture,[11] but, as Kitamura points out, this probably attests to their rarity and novelty, since they were generally used only as a supplement to gravity power in times of

---

[h] There seems to be no straightforward reason why bullock power was not used and nothing like the Persian wheel ever developed. The problems of growing fodder crops in addition to food crops may be at the back of this. In Japanese agriculture in general, until at least the Meiji period, animal power was a luxury to be used only where human power could not be used instead. Wind power was apparently not used because of the frequency of typhoons. See Minami, R., *Water Wheels in the Pre-Industrial Economy of Japan* (119), pp.19–20.

shortage.[i] Complete reliance on water wheels as the means of transfer-
ring water into the fields was found only in creek areas. In addition, the
distances through which water had to be raised, given the relative positions of creek and field, were in general much greater than in more typical regions, and in many cases required the use of two or three wheels
operated in sequence to lift water the necessary distance.

Since it was human power which was used to provide irrigation water
to the field, it is obvious that the labour requirements per cultivated
hectare would be much higher than in areas where the power of gravity
needed only occasional supplementation. The economic implications of
this, as of the heavy capital requirements entailed by the necessity of
acquiring two or three wheels, will be considered later, but the implications for the life of Saga farmers were severe. To keep the fields supplied
with the necessary amount of water required almost continual labour
under the hot sun throughout the spring and early summer, but even a
strong man probably could not do more than an hour at a stretch.[12] The
labour, the heat, the wear on legs and feet, are said to have so racked the
bodies of Saga people that they needed the winter, and a huge array of
patent medicines, to recover their strength again.[13] It is now over fifty
years since the water wheels went out of use on the Saga Plain, but they
are still to be found preserved — as the equivalent of a pub sign over a
restaurant in Saga City, as decoration for the foyer of a smart hotel in a
mountain resort — as symbols of what Saga farmers lived through. Creek
irrigation in general, and the use of water wheels in particular,
conditioned not only, as we shall see later, the technical and economic
character of Saga Plain agriculture, but also very many aspects of the
life and attitudes of Saga Plain people, in ways which made the area
significantly different from places with other irrigation methods.

(2)   LAND PREPARATION

The alluvial soil of the Saga Plain is potentially very fertile and yields
obtained from rice cultivation there in normal years have always been
above the national average. However, the nature of the soil has not
made it easy to obtain these yields. Saga Plain earth is heavy and muddy
when wet, but dries very hard, so that it is difficult to break up. In addition, the existence of the creek network meant that there was a relatively
deep ditch next to every field into which water could drain, and it was
difficult to hold water in the fields when it was required for the growing

---

[i] Kitamura, T., *Nihon Kangai Suiri Kankō* (52), p.106. They seem to have been quite
heavily used in the plain area of Okayama which was the subject of Beardsley, Hall and
Ward's study. See *Village Japan* (41), pp.130–1.

plants. This was especially problematic given the amount of gruelling labour required to lift water into the fields in the first place. In response to these problems, Saga Plain farmers had, by the early Meiji period, developed a system of land preparation which, though it required long hours of work by men and draught animals, helped to overcome the difficulties of cultivation in their particular environment.

The purpose of this land preparation system was to break up the heavy soil and prepare the field in such a way as to minimise the rate of water leakage. The system depended on the use of draught animals, and Saga farmers were relying on the power of draught horses before animal power came to be widely used in Japanese agriculture in general. The development of ploughing with draught animals, in place of the traditional methods of preparing land with a hoe and human labour, was pioneered in the north Kyūshū area, and gradually spread through the country as part of the package of intensive techniques which was raising output in the late Tokugawa and Meiji periods. Deep ploughing with a horse or ox was necessary for the absorption of the heavy applications of fertiliser which were part of that package. Saga farmers, however, relied on horses not in order to plough deeply, but for the power to break up the hard, caked soil and carry out the complex set of ploughing operations through which a relatively leak-proof base to the field could be formed. In the late Tokugawa period there were four separate, named operations (by the 1900s five) to be carried out with a horse and two different kinds of plough in order to break up the soil, before any water was raised into the field. A further highly important ploughing operation was then carried out with water in the field. This was called '*tokojime*' (*toko* = floor, *jime* from the verb to close), and involved ploughing several times with another special kind of plough which pressed the mud down to form a kind of sealed base to the field. With the banks round the field also carefully sealed with mud, the paddy came to resemble a 'mud plate', relatively impermeable to water. It was then worked over again with a horse-drawn hoe, before the transplanting of the rice seedlings began.[j]

This set of land preparation operations required a high degree of skill and strength. If the *tokojime* process was carried out badly, the water raised at such cost into the field could drain out overnight and the unhappy farmer become the laughing stock of the village.[14] Unlike

[j] Kyūshū Nōsei Kyoku, *Saga Heiya* (76), p.234, Miyajima, S., *Kome Tsukuri* (72), pp.17–8. In all areas in which fields could be drained it was important to create a good base to the paddy. The difference in Saga lay in the importance which the cost of raising water laid on this operation, hence in the extreme care and thoroughness with which it had to be carried out. Personal letter from Professor Yamada.

pumping, which women and children could do if necessary, ploughing could be carried out only by strong men who had learned the necessary skills and it is estimated that, in the 1880s, one man could manage the ploughing of no more than about a hectare.[15]

The economic significance of the technical necessity of access to a horse, a set of ploughs and the skilled labour required to operate them lay in the ways in which it conditioned the relationships between households, as they sought to overcome the scale problems involved, and we will return to this in a later section.

(3) CROPS AND ROTATIONS

Almost all of the cultivated area of the Saga Plain was, as we have seen, paddy field, so that the crop pattern and rotation centred on the growing of paddy rice. From what has been said already, it will be clear that the cultivation of rice on the Saga Plain required an unusually heavy concentration of labour in preparing the land and supplying the necessary water. This necessitated a number of adaptations to the typical pattern of land use in Japanese rice cultivation and conditioned the cultivation of other crops, especially second crops on the paddy field.

In essence the problem was that the available labour force in Saga Plain villages, from at least the second half of the Tokugawa period onwards, was insufficient, given the techniques which had to be used, to prepare and supply water simultaneously to the whole area on which rice could be grown. This meant, therefore, either leaving land unused, or staggering the growing season so that it was not necessary to prepare and supply water to the whole paddy area at the same time. Staggered cultivation of both early and late varieties was not an uncommon practice, as a means of reducing the risk of crop loss as well as of spreading out peak labour demands, in Japan in the Tokugawa and Meiji periods.[k] But in Saga it had developed to the point of representing an unusual and quite strict form of crop rotation system, into which the growing of a second winter crop could be fitted where conditions permitted.

This rotation system involved each farm household in dividing the land it cultivated into two parts. One part was prepared for cultivation first and was planted early in the rice-growing season with early-maturing rice varieties. The second part was prepared later and planted with late-maturing varieties. The use of this rotation made it possible to fit in the cultivation of a second crop on the early-planted paddy, and the full

---

[k] A similar practice was used by the Vietnamese farmers studied by Sansom, also as a means of spreading out peak labour requirements. *The Economics of Insurgency* (170), p.79.

Fig. 4.1:   The Two-Year Phased Crop Rotation on the Saga Plain

	Section 1	Section 2
April	Rice planting (early varieties)	
May	Transplanting	Rice planting (late varieties)
June		
July		Transplanting
August		
September	Harvesting	
October		
November	Winter crop (eg. wheat, rape-seed, broad beans)	Harvesting
December		
January		Fallow
February		
March		
April		Rice planting (early varieties)
May	Rice planting (late varieties)	Transplanting
June		
July	Transplanting	
August		
September		Harvesting
October		
November	Harvesting	
December		Winter crop
January	Fallow	
February		
March		

Source: Adapted from Isobe, T., 'Iwayuru Saga Dankai' (70), p.12.

rotation is shown in Fig. 4.1. Limits of time, labour and horse power made it impossible to double-crop the late-planted section as well, and this therefore generally remained fallow[1] until the spring, when the rotation was reversed and last year's late-planted area became this year's early-planted area. Any given area could thus grow three crops in two years. A rotation such as this, with two distinct planting periods, separated by the harvesting of the second crop, was almost only found in the Saga creek area.

[1] It was sometimes planted with beans or a green manure crop.

In general, the yield of the late rice crop was higher than that of the early,[m] so that rice output was to some extent sacrificed in order to be able to grow a second crop and to relieve the peak labour demands. The use of this rotation also had serious drawbacks from the point of view of pest damage, as we shall see later. But it enabled a larger area to be kept under cultivation, maintaining the relatively large cultivated area per household which continuous reclamation permitted.

The actual double-cropping rate achieved within this rotation must have varied greatly from village to village and time to time, depending on supplies of labour, fertiliser and, especially, water. The practice of keeping fields flooded over the winter continued to be used in places in Saga as elsewhere, as a means of conserving water supplies. The late Tokugawa villages in the south of the Plain, described by Yamada, were achieving a 60% double-cropping rate, with wheat planted on over half of the second-crop area.[n] However, a survey of Saga County in 1882, reported in the Saga-Shi Shi, shows a 30% rate for all crops, with only 18% of the paddy area planted to a second grain crop.[16] Various pieces of data mentioned by Arashi also suggest that double-cropping rates of no more than 30% were typical of Saga in the 1880s.[17]

Wheat was the chief item grown as a second crop, followed by barley and naked barley. A survey of crops grown in Saga County in 1877 lists in addition a range of small quantities of subsistence crops, including soy beans, millet and buckwheat, sweet potatoes, cotton and flax, tea, tobacco, indigo, honey and wax, rape-seed, and mulberry for making paper, though some of these must have been grown in hill rather than plain areas.[o]

The phased rotation was the means whereby the available labour force on the Plain was able to cultivate rice over a relatively large paddy area, but, at the same time, part of its attraction to farmers lay in its subsistence insurance aspects. By permitting a degree of double-cropping, it made possible the cultivation of a wide range of subsistence crops, and, beyond this, it spread out the risk to the main food crop, with the early crop coming to tide the family over just when the remains of last year's late crop might be running out. Farmers' attachment to the

---

[m] At least by the 1880s. During the Tokugawa period the yields of the early varieties were probably higher. See chapter 5, section 3 (1).

[n] Yamada's description is based on the data given in surviving reports made by *han* officials, who toured round inspecting the harvest. The villages covered are *buraku* in the Kawazoe area south of Saga City. See Yamada, T., 'Saga Heiya ni okeru Bakumatsu-ki' (98).

[o] *Saga-Shi Shi* (81), Vol. 3, p.257. The survey gives some figures for areas planted: 9,772 ha. to rice; 1,436 ha. to wheat; 743 ha. to barley and naked barley; 219 ha. to soy beans.

rotation on these grounds, and their nervousness about giving it up, even when yields had risen to levels high enough to make subsistence insurance unnecessary, were said to have lain behind the strong opposition to efforts to change it in later years.[18]

(4) FERTILISER

In the Tokugawa and early Meiji periods most Japanese villages communally maintained areas of non-cultivable hill and woodland from which grass and leaves could be collected, and these served as the main source of fertiliser for the fields in most regions, supplemented by the use of human excrement, compost, and other forms of natural fertiliser supplied within the village. In more advanced areas, commercially-marketed, fish-based fertilisers were being used well before 1868, but in most areas the laborious collection and transportation of large quantities of greenstuff remained the chief means of supplementing soil nutrients.

Saga Plain farmers, however, quite simply had no hill or woodland to use in this way. So much of the flat, fertile land was cultivable that there was no waste ground to provide such leaves and grass. Instead, Saga farmers made use of the peculiarities of their environment to provide an alternative source of fertiliser. This was the mud or silt, brought down through the creek network, which collected in the bed of every creek. It was essential in any case to dredge this mud from the creeks in order to stop them from silting up, but by developing methods for depositing mud on to the fields, Saga farmers found a substitute for the natural fertiliser sources which their area lacked. The operation of lifting the mud on to the fields had to be carried out in the winter when the creeks could be drained, and the fallow period in the rotation therefore provided an essential opportunity for applying this form of fertiliser to the paddy.

The job of lifting mud on to the fields was another extremely hard and unpleasant one. The creek network could be drained by the closing of the various sluices which connected it to its sources of water. These sluices were shut at agreed times every autumn, and by February or March the creeks contained only a little water covering the mud, debris and stranded fish. The operation of lifting the mud required a team of eighteen men: eight stood knee-deep in the icy mud at the bottom of the creek collecting the mud in buckets; four stood on the bank of the creek and lifted the buckets full of mud; two or three collected up the mud coming out of the buckets; and another three or four meanwhile operated water wheels to help drain out the remaining water.[19] The mud could either be dried and saved for later use, or spread on the field to fertilise it for the forthcoming rice crop. The teams were communally organised (though, as we shall see later, mud-raising rights were privately owned) and the completion of the job was the occasion of celebration and feasting on the fish caught.

Mud was supplemented as a fertiliser by the use of night-soil, for which a considerable amount of labour was required for transportation and preparation. A little dried fish fertiliser was also being used in the late Tokugawa Kawazoe villages.[20] But mud remained the most important source of fertiliser, and mud-raising a vital operation in the farming year, as well as a significant basis, as we shall see, of village cohesion.

(5)   PESTS AND CROP DAMAGE

Agriculture on the Saga Plain in the nineteenth century involved both the risks that were common to all of Japanese agriculture at that time and risks peculiar to the particular environment of the area. Whenever possible, technology was adapted to lessen or spread out these risks, but output still remained subject to severe fluctuations as a result of natural causes.

The existence in many parts of Japan of a relatively sophisticated irrigation system lessened the risk inherent in dependence upon the timing and quantity of rainfall experienced in many rice-growing areas of Asia. However, crop loss through drought or flooding was common in many areas, including the Saga Plain. The parts of the Plain nearest the sea, at the extremities of the creek network, were particularly prone to water shortage, necessitating leaving land fallow or keeping water in the fields over the winter. On the other hand, flooding was also a danger, especially given the temptation to keep the water-level in the creeks as high as possible, which meant that sudden heavy rainfall could overflow them. Typhoons and storms were also a danger, as were the crop diseases common to most areas.

The greatest cause of crop loss on the Saga Plain, however, was one which was rather peculiar to the particular conditions there. This was loss due to the ravages of an insect pest called the *san-ka meichū* or three-brooded rice-borer. This was a type of rice-stem borer (*Schoenobius*) which in its two-brooded form, the *ni-ka meichū*, was prevalent in many parts of south-western Japan. In its adult form it was a moth, the Pearl Moth, which deposited its eggs in the rice fields. The grubs hatched and bored into the stems of the growing rice plants, causing them to turn white and die. The *ni-ka meichū* could go through two life-cycles in the course of a rice season, but the *san-ka miechū* could go through three, and flourished on the Saga Plain because of the particularly long period during which rice was growing there under the phased rotation. It could inflict considerably greater loss than its two-brooded relative, and destruction of 20 – 30% of the crop was by no means uncommon. A survey of estimated losses from rice-borer damage in Saga Prefecture in 1880 found an average loss of 20%, and losses of 27% and 30% in Saga and Kanzaki counties respectively.[21] In the disastrous year of 1893, Saga Prefecture's harvest, which usually averaged about 120,000 tonnes at that time, was reduced to 51,000 tonnes by rice-borer damage,[22] and famine conditions were said to have prevailed at times in the past as a result of the rice-borer.

Research carried out during the Meiji period was to make clear the connection between the use of the phased rotation and the prevalence of the *san-ka meichū*. The timing of the rotation meant that there was always rice in the fields at the right stage of growth to provide a suitable environment for each of the three broods. The moths of the first brood hatched from the chrysalises which had wintered in the straw of last year's crop. Their peak hatching period occurred around the time of the transplanting of the early crop, on whose stems their offspring lived. This second brood emerged as moths around the time of the transplanting of the late crop and laid their eggs on it. The third brood moths appeared in late August and left their offspring to winter in the straw of the late crop.[23] This was not, however, understood by farmers in the Tokugawa and Meiji periods and, indeed, the phased rotation was seen as a way of spreading out the risk of loss — with rice at different stages of growth in the fields at any one time, the chances of losing the whole crop were that much less. The only other ways known to farmers before the 1870s and 1880s for dealing with the damage were the luring of the moths with lamps or processions of torches, drawing them away from the fields. Sutras were said, and stone monuments erected, for the souls of the insects so killed,[24] but they always returned, confirming farmers in their belief that the incidence of crop loss was an act of the gods, against which human actions were by and large useless.

As a result, farming on the Saga Plain was not only harder work than farming elsewhere, but also more risk-prone. The combination of the two conditioned not only the traditional technical system, but also, as we shall see later, the ability to respond to new technical opportunities, and even when it was known that the phased rotation created the environment for the rice-borer, it could not easily be abandoned, embedded as it was in the complete technical system of Saga Plain agriculture.

(6) THE AGRICULTURAL YEAR

The easiest way to bring together the various elements of Saga Plain agricultural technology around 1850 – 80 described here, and to see how they altered, or were added to, the typical pattern of cultivation methods in Japanese agriculture, is to piece together the sequence of operations over the course of a year.

To begin in the spring. In March the weather would start to turn warmer. In some fields, second-crop wheat would be showing, by now quite tall and green. In others, beans and rape-seed would be coming into flower. But the landscape would still have been dominated by the fallow fields, some perhaps still waterlogged, others spread with mud fertiliser. At this time, second crops had to be kept weeded with a hoe, and there was always work to be done in vegetable plots and at home, but the early spring was, as it were, the calm before the storm, a time for celebrating the weddings arranged over the winter, or for taking a trip to a local shrine or park to view the blossom.[25]

In the early spring the downstream sluices in the creek network would be closed, and the creeks would gradually begin to fill. The farmers could only watch and wait, and hope that there would be enough water to fill them by transplanting time. Meanwhile, in April the seed-beds were prepared and the seed for the early crop sown, and the great operation of ploughing begun. The soil which had lain fallow all winter was broken up with a sharp tool and then ploughed several times until it was level. Water was raised into the fields and the meticulous process of *tokojïme* ploughing begun. When the base of the fields and the banks around them were smooth 'as mirrors', and the soil was hoed and ready, the operation of raising water could begin in earnest.

The fields for the early crop had to be ready for transplanting, with adequate water in them, by late May or early June, when the village organised itself into gangs to begin transplanting. At about the same time, the seeds for the late crop were sown in the seed-beds. While they were growing, the land had to be prepared for them, first by harvesting the second crops, and then ploughing and irrigating as with the early-crop fields. In late June or early July, the late crop was finally transplanted.

Throughout this time the young men of the labour force were working with the horses, moving on from field to field as man and horse time became available. When transplanting was complete, there were feasts and festivities for everyone who had helped, and then pumping was resumed in earnest in order to keep up the level of water in the fields, with the whole family taking their turn at working the wheels in the heat of the summer sun. Meanwhile, the early crop began to need weeding almost as soon as the late was transplanted, and the operation of weeding with the hoe or by hand continued throughout the summer.

The summer was a difficult time. There was the worry that there would not be enough water in the creeks and the hours of pumping with two or three wheels in sequence would not raise sufficient water for a reasonable crop. There was the worry also that the period of heavy rain in June might cause the creeks to overflow. In addition there was the wait for the first signs of rice-borer damage in the young rice plants. But as the landscape turned from being a sea of water to a sea of green rice plants, as the vegetation grew thick along the banks of the creeks, there was time, in the intervals between weedings, to sit and fish amidst the sound of frogs and insects.

The early rice crop was ready to harvest around the beginning of September, and it was cut with a sickle and left to dry until it was time, in October, to plough up the stubble and prepare the field for a winter crop if possible. Once the winter crop was planted, the late rice had to be harvested, and then began the long process of threshing. With the comb-like threshing tool, a group of three to five people, working very hard, could thresh the grain from 10 ares in a day.

The threshed rice was put into straw bags ready for disposal or storing. Some of it had to be used to make various payments, as we shall see later. What was left was stored, for consumption during the year or perhaps for sale later on. Those with plenty to store had store-rooms, others partitioned off part of the earth-floored work area in their houses. The bags were stacked in a standard way, and the number of these stacks was a visible measure of a household's wealth.[26]

In December the frosts begin, and it was cold work planting winter crops or threshing rice, but there were the New Year celebrations to brighten up the mid-winter. By this time, the inlet sluices to the creek network would have been closed, and the creeks gradually drained. By February or March they were dry enough to permit mud-raising, and meanwhile there was always work, both private and communal, to be done, repairing and clearing banks, dykes, sluices, field paths and so on. In addition, there was the work of feeding and caring for the horse. Tools and buildings had to be repaired and maintained, and any other spare time could be spent making bags, ropes, shoes and so forth from straw, hulling rice, pickling vegetables, making soy sauce and sake. But when there was no outside work to be done, or when, as occasionally, snow lay on the ground, there was time to rest a little and recuperate, ready for another year.

*

Altogether, the agricultural techniques in use on the Saga Plain in the mid-nineteenth century were adapted to one another to form a complex and integrated technical system whose object was to overcome the difficulties posed by a peculiar natural environment and a highly labour-using method of irrigation. Although few of the elements of the system, or the ideas behind them, were unique to Saga, the highly developed combination of them was Saga's own. Thus from the starting-point of the irrigation technology there followed the intensive method of land preparation, and from that the phased rotation which made it possible to meet the labour requirements of ploughing and pumping. The rotation made double-cropping feasible, creating the capacity to grow fodder for the draught horses essential for ploughing, and yet allowing for the fallow period required for the use of creek mud as fertiliser. And although it was in large part the cause of the rice-borer problem, the rotation spread out the risks involved and contributed towards ensuring a supply of subsistence crops. The crucial point arising from this interconnectedness of the technical system was its dependence on the irrigation technology, which we shall see made it very difficult to bring in new techniques as long as that technology was in operation, but brought a string of 'dynamic sequences' in the train of changes in irrigation methods. For the time being, we shall go on to look at the economic organisation through which production, using this technical system, was carried out.

3. The Economic Organisation of Production

In chapters 2 and 3[27] we saw how, by the early Meiji period, Japanese village society had come to be made up of a mass of very small holdings, rarely more than a few hectares, each composed of a number of scattered plots and cultivated by farmer households of every gradation of tenure status, from pure tenants through all degrees of part-owner/part-tenant farmers to pure owner-cultivators and landlords, with no very exact fit between different types of tenure status and different scales of cultivation. This pattern had emerged from the break-up of larger holdings farmed with extended family labour, which had begun to take place under the influence of spreading commercialisation, and which left the former large landowners as cultivator/landlords, farming holdings of two or three hectares, but retaining strong economic influence over other households through their ownership of capital equipment, their position as landlords, and their lineage relationships as main households. In remote areas such as Tōhoku, this process had advanced less far than elsewhere, and large-scale cultivators and landowning families retained and even increased their importance. In the advanced commercialised areas of the south-west it had progressed much further, leaving village societies composed of much more equal farm households, cultivating holdings of a hectare or less, where the influence of main-household, cultivating landlords was much smaller. These variations corresponded to variations in the degree to which commercialised market relationships had begun to take over from personal and community relationships in determining the supply of inputs to individual households. In what follows, I shall examine how the Saga Plain fits into this picture in terms of both the structure of village communities and the institutional organisation of the supply of inputs. I will begin the discussion by considering the distribution of land, since the area of land a household owned or cultivated was the most significant determinant of its economic position and of its access to other inputs, and will go on from there to look at the allocation of other resources and the organisation of the village economy as a whole.

(1)   THE SUPPLY OF INPUTS

1.   Land

In Saga, as elsewhere, village society was made up of a mass of small-scale, scattered holdings dominated by a relatively limited group of old main families, who owned more land than they cultivated and were central to the village lineage structure. But while in its main outlines Saga Plain land distribution resembled that of the rest of the country, there were certain influences on it which made it different from the typical patterns, both of the north, where large-scale landowners still remained, and of the advanced south-west. The effects of these influences are very important in explaining the structure of the village community in Saga and its conditioning of the path of technical change followed, and I will describe the three which stand out.

i. Land reclamation. Firstly, and most straightforwardly, the Saga Plain area is one which has been undergoing a continual process of land reclamation since early Tokugawa times. The frontier of cultivation has been moving continually out into the coastal region, stretching out the creek network into newly drained areas of the coastal mud flats. Thus although the central plain area of Saga City and Saga County, and the areas upstream from there, had been drained by the mid-Tokugawa period, the possibilities for moving out on to new land, albeit risky land with an unreliable water supply, remained to lessen the pressure on the land area experienced in the areas of older settlement. There was always the possibility that younger sons could be established on new land, thus avoiding the necessity of dividing a holding. In addition, investment in land reclamation provided an outlet for the accumulated funds of traders, money-lenders and so on, which might otherwise have gone into building up holdings of existing land to be let out to tenants. The possibility of land reclamation would thus have lessened the pressure towards subdivision of family holdings and the drift into tenancy experienced in other areas.

ii. *Han* policy in the Tokugawa period. The Nabeshima *han*, the dominant *han* in the Saga Plain area, provided a government which combined enlightened leadership with a strict upholding of traditional samurai ethics. It was also a *han* faced with considerable problems, especially towards the end of the Tokugawa period, in raising revenue: ruling over almost exclusively agricultural areas, not as yet very greatly commercialised, it was forced to rely heavily on taxation of the ordinary farmer, having little of the scope for taxing or borrowing from the commercial sector enjoyed by *han* in economically more advanced areas. These characteristics combined to lead the Nabeshima *han* into a policy designed to try to help the ordinary peasant farmer and to preserve him from impoverishment at the hands of merchants, moneylenders and their like. This policy approach appealed both on ideological grounds, embodying the traditional division between pure cultivators and the (socially inferior) commercial classes, and on revenue-raising grounds, since the *han* income depended on the ability to tax what remained to the cultivator after he had met his expenses.

This approach led in general to a high level of official concern with and involvement in agricultural matters, including, for instance, considerable encouragement for land reclamation and irrigation development, and to a generally discouraging stance towards commercial influences in rural areas, but its most dramatic manifestation was in what can only be described as a land reform carried out in the closing decades of the Tokugawa period.[28] In 1842 the Nabeshima authorities proclaimed a moratorium, to last ten years, on all payments of interest or pseudo-rent by cultivators, in an effort to preserve farmers' incomes, and their tax-paying capacity, from the inroads of rental payments especially to non-resident, commercial landowners. The order was renewed in 1852, but by 1862 the need for a permanent settlement became overwhelming and the Nabeshima rulers made a law, proclaiming the virtues of the separation of agriculture from commerce, which in effect set a ceiling of 6 hectares on land holdings and confiscated the land of non-resident landlords above this ceiling. The confiscated land was to be farmed by the former tenants, who were to pay their taxes direct to the Nabeshima treasury. The areas affected were chiefly those around the ports located in Saga, especially those connected with the pottery trade like Imari, but the high ceiling, combined with certain exceptions allowed for newly-reclaimed land, meant that the total area handed over to cultivators was only about 3% of the cultivated land of present-day Saga Prefecture. The whole process, however, was overtaken by the events of the Meiji Restoration and the new government tried to reach a permanent settlement as part of the land tax revision. Proposals to return a proportion of the cultivated land to the original landlords met with fierce opposition from the cultivators, but the final settlement of 1877 saw half the confiscated land returned to its original owners and the other half made imperial property, to be farmed by the former tenants, with the government paying some compensation to the former landlords.

Although the amount of land actually involved in these proceedings was small, Kamagata and other authorities argue that, as an expression of official attitudes, the land reform did significantly inhibit the accumulation of larger holdings, especially by non-resident landlords, and that it did help to preserve the position of the type of resident cultivating household owning around a hectare or perhaps more, which elsewhere was tending to fall into tenancy under the influences of commercialisation.[29]

iii. Technology. The third, and perhaps most important, influence on the structure of landholding on the Saga Plain was the nature of the technology necessitated by the peculiar characteristics of the environment. In the previous section we saw how these characteristics included particularly heavy and concentrated capital and labour demands in the form of, on the one hand, horses, ploughs and treadle wheels, and, on the other, skilled ploughing and pumping labour. These demands distorted the size distribution of cultivated holdings by creating barriers which limited upward movement along the scale of holding size.

As we shall see in more detail later, the nature of the labour requirements of the technology of Saga Plain agriculture placed strict limits on the area which a family could farm with its own labour. While it was true that everywhere in Japan, because of the difficulties of supervising the careful labour required in rice-growing, cultivation of larger holdings using non-family labour became increasingly difficult as the scale of farm increased, the point at which the labour force became unmanageably large was reached at a smaller scale in Saga than elsewhere. Thus cultivated holdings of more than two or three hectares were very rare in Saga. At the other end of the scale, however, there were also considerable barriers in the way of the small landholder trying to rise into the class of medium- or large-scale cultivators farming more than about a hectare. These barriers were reached at the scale at which it became impossible to farm a holding without owning the capital equipment and horse power necessary. At small scales, by means of arrangements to be described later, it was possible for a household to rent, borrow or share the horse and equipment it needed to farm its holding. But to go beyond that scale a household needed its own horse and equipment if it was to have adequate access to these essential capital inputs. As we shall see when we come to consider the economic situation of small-scale cultivators around the early Meiji period, the scope for accumulating the funds necessary to buy these capital inputs was very limited, and there was therefore a tendency for those at the lower end of the size distribution to be held back behind the line of around a half to one hectare above which ownership of horses, ploughs, wheels and so on was essential.

*

These influences would lead to a prediction that the land distribution pattern in Saga Plain villages in the early Meiji period would show a relatively large average size of cultivated holding, few very large-scale owners or cultivators, a fairly marked distinction between the group of small-scale farmers and the group of medium-to-large cultivators owning most of the capital equipment, and a tendency for tenancy to be restricted to intra-village arrangements between households. There is not a great deal of data available against which to test this prediction. The various authorities agree that the average size of holding on the Plain has always been relatively large, with a relatively large proportion of farms over 1·5 hectares or so.[30] Some data showing the distribution of cultivated area owned in a number of Plain villages in the 1870s and 1880s are shown in Table 4.1. This reveals at least half of village households owning very small areas of less than half a hectare, with a high proportion owning less than 0·3 hectares. Above this there is an intermediate group owning 0·5−1·5 hectares, and then a relatively large group of 10% or more of households owning 1·5−3·0 hectares, with a few owning more than that. For one village we have figures on area cultivated for 1879.[31]

Area (ha.)	0−0·5	0·5−1·0	1·0−2·0	2·0−3·0	Over 3·0	Total
Number of households:						
Owning	23	7	2	2	1	35
Cultivating	30	7	5	2	−	44

These reveal the existence of a certain amount of renting in by the intermediate group and of a number of small-scale pure tenant households, but suggest that in general the distribution of cultivated holdings showed the same kind of pattern as that of owned holdings. Although it is not possible to go much further than this statistically, and comparable figures for other areas or the country as a whole are hard to come by, we shall find this picture of the relatively marked division of Saga village communities into a mass of very small-scale cultivators and a group of upper-medium-scale cultivating households confirmed in other aspects of Saga Plain social and economic structure, contrasting it, on the one hand, with the structure of backward regions, like Tōhoku, based on

Table 4.1:   The Size Distribution of Owned Holdings in Saga Plain Villages in the 1860s and 1870s

	Under 0·3	0·3 to 0·5	0·5 to 1·0	1·0 to 1·5	1·5 to 2·0	2·0 to 3·0	Over 3·0	Total
				HECTARES				

A.   12 villages in Kanzaki County, 1867–1870

	Under 0·3	0·3 to 0·5	0·5 to 1·0	1·0 to 1·5	1·5 to 2·0	2·0 to 3·0	Over 3·0	Total
No. of households	49	75	91	52	23	18	3	411
Percentage	36·2	18·2	22·1	12·6	5·9	4·3	0·7	100

B.   2 villages in Kanzaki County, 1881

No. of households	150	18	38	37	27	13	5	288
Percentage	52·0	6·3	13·2	12·9	9·4	4·5	1·7	100

C.   Wakamiya village
1873:

No. of households	39	11	21	11	9	3	2	96
Percentage	40·6	11·4	21·9	11·4	9·4	3·1	2·1	100

1876:

No. of households	28	9	16	11	10	4	3	81
Percentage	34·6	11·1	19·8	13·6	12·3	4·9	3·7	100

Sources: A. Yamada, T. and Ōta, R., *Saga-Ken Nōgyō Shi* (73), p.273.
B. Yamada, T., and Ōta, R., *Saga-Ken Nōgyō Shi* (73), p.288.
C. *Saga-Shi Shi* (81), vol. 3, p.691.

the large-scale cultivator/landowner with his traditional extended family and household servants, and, on the other, with the structure of advanced regions where much more land was farmed by small-scale, family-sized units, often renting in part of their land.

On tenancy at this time, there exists one estimate of the proportion of tenanted land in Saga County in the early Meiji period which puts it at 33% in 1878, somewhat below the probable national average of 36%, and figures for subsequent years suggest that the proportion of land rented out in this Plain area remained below the prefectural and national averages.[32] The Saga-Ken Shi quotes an estimate that 26·8% of the cultivated area of the prefecture was farmed by tenants in 1873,[33] and this would also confirm that the influences described above did to some extent retard the drift of smaller owner-farmers into tenancy, as compared with other areas.

There is some evidence that, despite official discouragement, there were, however, some large-scale, non-resident landowners buying up or reclaiming land as an investment. The household owning more than 3 hectares (actually 9·5 hectares) in the above table was one such, being that of a Mr. Tanaka, who had accumulated a considerable amount of land in Saga by the 1890s, but subsequently appears to have lost it.[34] The rice-trading, money-lending families described later acquired pieces of land here and there which they managed as part of their various business activities.[35] But such families were clearly far from being the great landowners of Tōhoku who owned whole villages, and with their scattered holdings and their primary interest in trade and finance, their significance in the agricultural scene was probably not very great. The nature of the prevailing tenancy customs described below suggests that most landlords were still resident in or near the villages in which they leased out land and that they had personal dealings with their tenants.

It is difficult to find evidence about rents and tenancy conditions in this period. By 1908, when the first prefectural yearbook figures appear, rental rates in Saga Plain areas ranged from about 35% to 45% of the crop,[36] always paid in rice.[37] For 1888 we have the figures given in the large-scale survey of agricultural conditions in Saga called the Saga-Ken Nōji Chōsa (Survey of Agricultural Matters in Saga Prefecture),[P] which gives a rate of about 42% for Saga County.[38] In 1912 there was a survey of tenancy conditions in Saga and there is no reason to suppose that these had changed greatly since earlier times. According to this survey,[39] the tenant had very little formal security of tenure: the length of tenancy was generally not specified and the landlord confirmed the tenancy each year and could evict if he wanted to. In practice, tenancies were perpetual, however, in the absence of trouble or special circumstances. Rent was paid in December, when the tenant had to transport his rent rice, properly hulled and bagged, to the landlord's house, where the landlord would inspect it for weight and quality in the presence of the tenant. The rent paid was generally less than the contracted rent, confirming the common practice of rent reduction related to the state of the harvest. Typical practice over rent reduction seems to have been as follows:

No reduction up to 20% crop loss
30% crop loss led to 20% rent reduction
40% ”   ”   ”   ” 35% ”   ”
50% ”   ”   ”   ” 50% ”   ”
60% ”   ”   ”   ” 70% ”   ”
Over 70% ”   ”   ”   ” 80% ”   ”   or no rent at all.[40]

P The Saga-Ken Nōji Chōsa was one of a number of prefectural surveys of agricultural conditions undertaken in the 1880s. It covers quite a wide range of topics, including such things as crop acreages, output, landownership and so on, often giving data down to the county level. Its main findings have been conveniently summarised by Ōta. See 'Meiji Zenki ni okeru Saga Nōgyō no Jōtai' (91).

This kind of sliding scale clearly indicates the subsistence-insurance nature of the rent reduction system.[q]

Landlords would generally pay for large-scale land improvements or repairs, paying the tenant a daily wage for any work he did, though the tenant would be expected to do small repairs himself, with the landlord supplying materials. That the landlord had certain obligations towards the tenant, suggested by the practice of adjusting rents according to the state of the harvest, is confirmed by the survey's evidence that landlords would lend tenants equipment and sources of fertiliser, and in bad years would make interest-free loans of seed and of money to buy rice, and no doubt loans at interest at other times. It is unlikely, at least in the early Meiji period, if much if any of the content of the relationship between landlord and tenant was ever put down in writing. However, given the field structure in Japan and the way in which tenancy developed, it would be unusual for a farmer to rent all his land from one landlord, and this, along with the obligations imposed on the landlord by society, placed some limits on the landlord's power over the tenant.

In conclusion, the conditions of land distribution and tenancy on the Saga Plain in the late Tokugawa and early Meiji period indicate the existence of, on the one hand, a relatively large group of 10-20% of households farming holdings of between one and three hectares, with very few really large-scale holdings, and, on the other, a mass of very small-scale cultivators, owning and farming areas of half a hectare or less. We can now go on to see how the supply of other inputs was organised on the basis of this structure.

2.   Capital Inputs

i. Horses. To the majority of small-scale farmers of Meiji Japan, draught animals were large-scale, expensive inputs, whose use only began to spread in conjunction with the shift to deep ploughing and heavy fertiliser application towards the end of the nineteenth century. But to Saga Plain farmers, the use of a draught animal was essential for the series of elaborate land preparation operations necessitated by the technology of cultivation on the Plain, and all farmers, large and small, had required access to a horse for ploughing since some time before 1868. Horses were expensive both to buy and maintain, and therefore created the need for institutional arrangements to overcome the scale problems caused by their physical indivisibility.

[q] Cf. Scott, J., *The Moral Economy of the Peasant* (172), pp.44–52. It should be noted also, for future reference, that rent reductions were granted only in cases of loss through natural causes, not for loss caused by price fluctuations. *Saga-Ken Nōchi Kaikaku Shi* (79), p.396.

For the farmers in the Kawazoe villages in the south of the Plain, the purchase price of a work-horse at the end of the Tokugawa period was equivalent to the value of just under 750 kg of rice, which represented the annual yield of about a third of a hectare of paddy, or the subsistence rice of four to five people for one year.[41] Its fodder cost these farmers the equivalent of another 225 kg of rice per horse, and it was said to be necessary to farm at least 1½ hectares to have sufficient capacity to grow fodder for a horse.[42] On the other hand, one horse could cope with the ploughing of about 3 hectares.[43]

In the Kawazoe villages there were six horses for every ten households,[44] and in Wakamiya village, towards the end of the Meiji period, there were twenty-five horses serving thirty-six farming households.[45] So clearly not everyone owned a horse, and it follows from the economics of horse-ownership that only the group of medium-to-large cultivators would have been likely to be able to raise the purchase price of a horse, or to have had the capacity to maintain and utilise fully a horse of their own. Even in 1939, in a village surveyed by Isobe, every household owning a horse farmed more than one hectare (and only five out of those twenty-six farmed less than 1½ hectares), while of the eleven households not owning a horse, only one farmed more than a hectare.[46]

How, then, did smaller-scale farmers gain access to the horses they could not afford to keep for themselves? One common way of lessening the burden of keeping a horse was to send it away to be boarded out for the summer in mountain areas where pasture existed. Farmers in mountain areas would supplement their incomes by keeping and feeding horses in return for a fee and the manure they produced. Shared ownership of horses (*moyai-uma*) was also quite commonly practised. Households without horses at all could rent the use of them (sometimes with the ploughing labour of their owners), or borrow the horses of richer households with whom they had ties, in return for labour services. By such means, the indivisibility of the horses could be overcome, but it remained true that the division of village society into the middle-to-large-scale cultivating group and the mass of small cultivators was reflected in the division between those who had all the advantages of owning their own horse and those who had to make use of one of these types of institutional arrangement, with all the problems of timing that that implied, in order to gain access to horse power.

ii. Tools. The biggest item of capital equipment, after a horse, required by a Saga Plain household was its set of treadle wheels. In the Kawazoe villages at the end of the Tokugawa period, a household farming one hectare would have needed two wheels, costing the equivalent of a little over 150 kg of rice for a set of one new and one second-hand.[47] Other evidence suggests that more wheels than this would have been necessary,[48] but clearly it depended on the height of individual fields relative to the creeks. Wheels lasted about ten years.[49] In addition, the one-hectare farm in the late Tokugawa period needed a set of ploughs, a hoe, two sickles, tools for threshing, winnowing, hulling and so on. The mass of small farmers cultivating less than half a hectare would have managed with borrowing and sharing expensive equipment, like their equivalents in other areas, and owning perhaps one wheel, but clearly the need to buy more equipment was a barrier to expanding the scale of cultivation to the half-to-one hectare level which represented the family farm elsewhere.

iii. Fertiliser. In the late Tokugawa and early Meiji periods, the mud lifted from the bottoms of the creeks remained the main source of fertiliser, substituting for the grass and leaves used elsewhere in areas owning communal grassland and woods. The mud was supplemented to some extent by commercially-acquired fertiliser of two kinds: one was night soil, either collected in the towns and sold by traders, or bought from other villagers, who would be paid in rice, a certain amount for each member of the supplying household;[50] the other was the commercial dried fish and bean fertilisers widely used, by these times, in regions of commercialised agriculture. Late Tokugawa Kawazoe farmers relied quite heavily on night soil to support their 60% double-cropping rate, with a small supplement of dried fish fertiliser, and the value of purchased fertiliser worked out at about 10% of the rice yield.[51]

Howevever, it was access to mud that really determined a household's ability to maintain the fertility of its land. Whereas, in other areas, grass for fertiliser was communally owned but privately collected, creek mud was privately owned but communally collected. The right to the mud from particular creeks attached to particular fields according to village custom. In some places, for instance, the right attached to the largest field adjoining a particular creek; in others, fields on the north banks of creeks owned the rights, and in some, creeks were clearly divided down the middle with markers.[52] Fields with rights to creek mud were obviously more valuable than those without, and it would seem likely that the larger-scale landowning households, when forming *bunke*, for instance, would retain for the main family the fields with such rights.

However, no family could carry out the operation of mud-raising on its own, and large numbers of people had to be organised to do it. The village as a community needed to ensure that mud-raising was carried out in order to prevent the creeks from silting up, and mud-raising was a community operation. The relationship between the owner of the mud and those who made up the group lifting it varied, as did the form of payment they received. The owner could simply call on the services of his *bunke* or other dependent households for no very specific payment;

he could pay a share of the mud, either lifted direct on to other adjoining fields or dried and transported; or he could pay a rice wage supplemented by meals and the feast of fish and eels at the end.[53]

Thus the mud-raising operation was an important aspect of the interrelationships between households, both between mud-owners and those dependent on them for their supply of fertiliser, and as a basis for group solidarity within the village as a whole.

3.   Labour

Throughout Japanese agriculture in the late Tokugawa and early Meiji periods (and indeed ever since), the family managing a holding provided the basic labour force to cultivate it. Even on relatively large holdings the family provided the nucleus of the labour force. There might sometimes be a need to hire labour for a few days or weeks where the size of the family happened to be inadequate for its holding, or where the labour of branch households or that exchanged with other households could not be drawn in to fill the gap, but typically only the two or three largest landowners in the village would have needed permanent additions to their labour forces. Such additions would still often take the form of adopting into the household a poor relation or servant, and labour hiring which was not either a casual day-to-day matter or part of a more complex relationship between main and dependent households or exchange-labour groups was relatively rare in most regions.

It will by now be very clear that labour requirements per hectare on Saga Plain farms were exceptionally heavy. Appendix Table 1 brings together the available scattered data on changes in the pattern of labour use in Saga Plain agriculture. From the information for the late Tokugawa and early Meiji period, it would seem that Saga Plain farmers had to find something in the order of 30–40 labour days per 10 ares of rice cultivated, and this was concentrated into two periods: one, the three-to-four-month period from March or April to July or August, when the land had to be ploughed and irrigated, the seedlings transplanted and the fields kept weeded and supplied with water; the other, the period from late September to December, when rice had to be harvested and prepared and any second crop planted. Well over half the total labour requirement was concentrated in the first of these periods and much of this labour was either very hard (pumping) or needed special skill and strength (ploughing). A family farming a hectare with, for instance, the labour of a father and son with their wives and children would therefore be very pressed to find the 200 or more labour days required in a strictly limited time in the spring and summer. The estimates of the time were that one man could not manage the pumping for more than about 0·4 hectares, a couple perhaps 0·8,[54] and that most households farming more than about a hectare would not have enough family labour to meet requirements.[55] Furthermore, the pattern of labour requirements meant that additional labour would be required for a relatively long period, from perhaps March to the New Year, to meet the needs of both periods of labour concentration. All this, combined with the relatively large size of holding and the rather large numbers of households with medium-to-large-scale farms, meant that on the Saga Plain resort to non-family labour was considerably more widespread than elsewhere, involving not just the one or two largest cultivators but also a substantial group of middle-scale cultivators.

Smith's work has shown that, in the late Tokugawa period, large-scale cultivators were finding the cost of supporting the traditional living-in agricultural worker and his family increasingly hard to bear and were shifting to arrangements which both reduced the labour they needed to bring in and gave the worker sufficient land to work to make him responsible for his own and his family's subsistence. For the not very large-scale farm on the Saga Plain which needed to bring in extra labour, the burden of the traditional way of expanding a labour force was even harder to bear, and at least by late Tokugawa times the system of hiring labour from families with small independent holdings of their own was well established on the Plain. We shall see when we come to consider the economic circumstances of small-scale cultivating households that many of them must have relied heavily on outside employment as almost full-time agricultural labourers to provide work and income for family members whom their holdings could barely support, and it was not uncommon for two or more members of such families to be going out to work for different employers.[56] It is difficult to say how many of these workers there must have been, but there are data showing that in one village of 36 households (Wakamiya village) in the late Meiji period, 19 men, 8 women and 4 childminders were employed for wages.[57] On the demand side, it is clear that most of the 20–30% of village households farming more than a hectare needed to employ at least one annual employee, and those at the top of the scale needed more than one, as well as temporary, seasonally-hired labour. Because of the relatively long terms of their employment, the major part of the hired labour force on the Saga Plain fell into a category known as *nenko* (annually hired employees) which typically made up a relatively small proportion of the hired workers in existence in early Meiji Japan, and they were skilled and experienced as 'professional' agricultural labourers, specialising in the difficult task of *tokojime* ploughing. Thus the division of village society into the group of upper middle-scale cultivators and the mass of very small-scale cultivators, which we have seen reflected also in the ownership of capital assets, is here seen as the division between employer households and labour-supplying households.

The relatively unusual circumstance of outside hired labour being required for about nine months of the year necessitated the development of particular institutional arrangements for the supply of labour which place the employment system of the Saga Plain somewhere in between casual wage employment and the traditional system of adoption into the employer's household. At the beginning of the year, a household wishing to employ an annual worker would arrange a contract with the worker or his family, or an intermediary. A surviving example of such a contract shows that it took the traditional form of a document selling the person of the worker to the employer, but that it actually specified that he should work a fixed number of days during the year, at so many days per month, and clearly implied that he would not live in but would commute to his work.[58] The employer would advance wages to the worker or his family, the rate being originally calculated in rice terms, but increasingly converted, at the rice price, into cash.[59] However, the worker would be given meals by his employer while he was at work, and, as we shall see, the relationship between employer and employee might often have non-market aspects, making it part of a wider patron/client relationship between the two households.

Since most agricultural workers commuted from households farming holdings of their own, they must have worked for employers within their own or neighbouring villages. All the *nenko* employed by the two families whose records for the early 1900s will be discussed later came from the local area, and some at least had been employed by the same family for many years.[60] However, recruitment of annual labour on the scale required was clearly not always easy to organise, and there is evidence of the existence of agents or foremen (*kogashira*) who acted as go-betweens, bringing together employers and employees. Yamada suggests that in the late Tokugawa and early Meiji period the position of *kogashira* took on almost the character of an official post, financed by village funds,[61] and the negotiations over the wage rate for the year, which took place in mid-January, were something of an annual village event.[62] At any rate, employment relationships between households were a vital part of the structure of the village community and, as we shall see shortly when we turn to the economic operations of the village as a whole, they served to bind together the two groups of households, the larger-scale cultivator/employer households and the small-scale cultivator/agricultural labourer households, whose existence we have seen emerging from the discussion of input supply.

4. Water

The organisation of the distribution and management of irrigation water is a much-neglected topic of great significance for the understanding of

the economics of rice-growing communities.[63] The peculiarities of the
irrigation system on the Saga Plain make its organisation to some extent
atypical, and Saga is in some ways a less useful example than those of
other areas for understanding how intra-village water allocation was
determined, how disputes were dealt with, and so on. Nevertheless, in
its basic principles, especially above the level of the village unit, irrigation organisation in Saga resembled that elsewhere in Japan and
provides an additional historical example of how these principles were
applied in determining the allocation of a crucial resource in the Japanese context.[64]

As we have seen, water was carried to the edge of each field by the
creek network, which provided the irrigation supply to all Plain farms,
but from that point the quantity of water supplied to any individual
paddy depended, by and large, on the amount of labour put into pumping. As a result, a larger area of control over the individual farmer's
access to water lay in his own hands than was the case under the more
typical, gravity-driven irrigation systems. There were differences
between fields in the ease with which water could be pumped into them,
depending mainly on their height relative to the creek water level, and
keen farmers could steal a march on their more easy-going neighbours
by getting up early and creeping off to the fields to begin pumping while
the water level in the creeks was at its highest.[65] But these were individual matters, and the village group as a whole had much less influence on
the distribution of water to the fields than in areas where this depended
on the opening and closing of communally-controlled sluices within the
village.

Nevertheless, there were areas of water allocation on the Plain which
required communal control, and these were managed in most respects
along the same lines as other, more typical, irrigation systems. These
areas mostly concerned the maintenance of communally-used parts of
the creek system, of the main channels, sluices and outlets which carried
water to and from different parts of the network. Within the village
also, the mud-raising operation described earlier was in part an aspect
of the routine maintenance of the village creek network and was to some
extent organised as a community task.

Within the overall irrigation network serving the Saga Plain, there
were, first of all, several major sluices controlling the flow of water into
the main supply channels and out into the chief drainage channels. The
most important of the former was the Ishi-i Sluice, on the Kasegawa itself,
and examples of the latter were the Hatta Sluice, controlling the outflow
along the Hatta channel, and other sluices, along the Saga-e channel,
controlling the outflow into the Chikugo (see Map 4). Secondly, at the
lower level, there were many points at which the flow of water into and

out of particular sections of the creek network could be controlled, i.e. some creeks were not only feeder channels to individual fields and reservoirs for those fields, but were also feeder channels carrying water to other parts of the network. These control points ranged from proper sluices to sandbag dams which could be used to block the outflow until the water level in that particular section was high enough. In addition, at the southern end of the network, there were sluices to control the reverse flow of tidal fresh water. All these sluice points, and the interconnecting channels which they controlled, had to be managed and maintained.

Throughout the Tokugawa period, the feudal government of the Nabeshima *han* provided the ultimate authority through which the task of maintaining and managing the irrigation system was carried out. The *han*'s objective in this was to ensure a steady flow of revenue from the rice harvest, and they managed the allocation of water accordingly, with some tendency to give priority to the areas most likely to be able to provide consistently high tax payments.[r] They could decide on the timing of the opening and closing of sluices and they could ensure that villages provided the labour necessary for the routine dredging of channels and re-building of dams, sluices and dykes, in addition to labour for the substantial investment projects which were undertaken under their rule. The day-to-day and year-to-year practice which emerged developed into a body of customary rules, balancing production needs against the relative strengths of upstream and downstream villages and enforced in cases of dispute, for instance during floods or droughts, by the power of the feudal rulers.

After the abolition of the feudal *han*, this body of customary rules was all that farmers had left by which to administer the irrigation system, since the new Meiji government, preoccupied with the question of assigning private property rights over land, made no attempt to legislate over water rights until the 1890s. By that time farmers had succeeded, through 'disputing using old books, agreements, actual practice, morality and law as their shields,'[s] in imposing some sort of order on the system. The customary rules for such things as the timing of the opening and closing of sluices, the dimensions of diversionary devices and the provision of labour for the maintenance of jointly-used facilities which became fixed during this time remained the basis for the administration of the irrigation network on the Saga Plain, at least until the post-war

[r] Kyūshū Nōsei Kyoku, *Saga Heiya* (76), p.353. An early example of 'progressive farmer bias'.

[s] 'Kobunsho, keiyaku, jijitsujō no hanko, dōtoku, okite nado o tate to shite arasoinagara...' Kyūshū Nōsei Kyoku, *Saga Heiya* (76), p.353.

construction of the dam which has substantially altered the shape of Saga's irrigation. Little is known about how, institutionally, the system was administered at this time, before the legislation of the 1890s required records to be kept, but villages appear to have continued to provide labour for maintenance work according to the practice of pre-Meiji times — for instance, 136 people were required every spring from the villages served by the Kawazoe River to clear the channel and rebuild the sluice to dimensions strictly laid down by custom.[66] Water-guards continued to be provided by the families who had traditionally done so.[67] Disputes which occurred[68] were solved, as elsewhere, by argument, violence and negotiation over the interpretation of customary practice, but in the last resort, in bad times, areas better endowed with water would be customarily and morally bound to respond to suitably humble appeals from drought-stricken areas,[69] especially since downstream areas controlled the drainage sluices and could thereby ensure, by keeping them closed, that upstream areas received the brunt of the damage in times of flood.[70]

To summarise: inter-village and inter-area water allocation, along with routine maintenance of jointly-used parts of the system, was administered according to customs built up over the generations, the ultimate aim of which had been to ensure the stability of the region's harvest, supplemented from time to time by more or less violent negotiation. Intra-village water allocation was by and large determined by the labour input of individual households. The maintenance of facilities within the village was the village's collective responsibility, and the most important part of it — the dredging of mud from the creeks — was organised by communal groups within the village.

(2)   THE ECONOMIC OPERATION OF THE VILLAGE COMMUNITY

From the previous section has emerged the picture of Saga Plain village societies as made up of, on the one hand, a relatively large group, by national standards, of upper-middle scale cultivators, farming around 1–3 hectares, owning horses and essential capital equipment of their own, and relying to some extent on hired labour, and, on the other hand, the remaining majority of small-scale cultivators, owning and farming less than half a hectare, borrowing equipment and horses, and depending on income earned as workers on other holdings. It has also emerged that to a large extent the allocation of production inputs among households was organised on the basis of personal intra-village relationships rather than external market ones. Impersonal market relationships were perhaps beginning to appear in some fields — for instance in fertiliser supply — but nowhere near to the extent that they already pervaded the more commercial areas of central Honshū. This was no doubt the result of Saga's relative remoteness from the main centres of commercial development, strengthened by official discouragement of such commercialising forces as were arising. Although in Saga the supply of water was, for technical reasons, more an individual matter than it was elsewhere, we have seen that, in the content of tenancy relations, in relationships between employers and employees, in arrangements for the supply of fertiliser, horses and equipment, the supply of inputs was still heavily conditioned by personal ties between households.

What was it that gave this strength and content to intra-village relationships in Saga Plain villages at this time? In most Japanese villages, the economic basis for community functions lay in the need for communal control of the water supply and communal ownership of the land supplying fertiliser.[71] While some aspects of Saga's irrigation involved these kinds of community functions—for instance in ensuring that the mud-raising operation was properly carried out—these bases were much less strong for Saga Plain villages. The basis for their intra-community relationships lay in those aspects of the technology, rather than of the irrigation system, which made it impossible for an individual household to operate on its own without being linked to other households. This was the case for other areas also, but the peculiarities of the technology required in Saga made this basis particularly strong. The exchange of labour for land and the use of capital inputs was ultimately crucial both to the larger-scale landowner, who could not operate without extra labour, and to the small-scale cultivator who relied on extra income and the use of borrowed equipment and rented land. Relationships between larger-scale cultivators and smaller were thus often not simply arrangements between employer and employee, but also between landlord and tenant, main household and branch household, patron and client, and so on,[72] whose basis lay in the need to ensure the mutual survival of both households. Relationships between more equal households were similarly mutual arrangements to try to make secure the supply of vital inputs. The implications of this are many, but from the purely technical point of view it meant that everyone had to operate more or less the same technical system in order to fit in with the capital equipment, labour skills and time of other households on which they relied.

In essence, therefore, despite the difference in emphasis in the basis of intra-village co-operation, community relations in Saga as elsewhere arose from the fact that the survival of the individual household to a considerable extent depended on the survival of the group. We saw in chapter 2 evidence of how households in Japanese villages tended to see their individual prosperity as bound up with the prosperity of the village group as a whole, and the Saga-Ken Shi remarks that this kind of approach, whereby the village as a whole sees itself as collectively responsible for ensuring that all its members are able to operate the technical system, was 'a way of thinking' in Tokugawa and early Meiji villages.[73] It describes the *kogashira* system for organising the annual employment of *nenko* as 'a scheme whereby the village as a whole supported the *nenko* class'.[t] A clear example of the approach in operation is in transplanting customs, where, in Saga as elsewhere, it was the practice for those who finished transplanting first to help those who had still to complete it. It was not considered necessary, in Saga, to return the help received in this way, although the recipient was expected to provide meals for his helpers, and the price he paid was simply a degree of scorn for being last to finish.[74]

As we shall see in later chapters, the development of commerce and industry and the permeation of market relationships into the village economy disrupted the basis for this approach to resource allocation, in the case of Saga in a rather dramatic way. However, the influence of this attitude remained profound, and it conditioned in many ways the methods of dealing with the problems, especially the technical ones, raised for Saga Plain farmers by the growth of the modern industrial sector.

4. Output and its Distribution

We can now turn to considering what Saga Plain farmers produced as a result of the technical and economic organisation described in the previous sections, and what happened to that output once produced.

Rice was, of course, the major item in the total output produced, and the survey mentioned earlier of the crops grown in Saga County in 1882 shows that every one of the 9,930 irrigated hectares covered was planted to it.[75] Yields were in the region of 250–300 kg/10 ares, as were the yields achieved by the late Tokugawa Kawazoe farmers.[76] Surviving records of two individual Plain households in the late Tokugawa period show them obtaining yields of between 300 and 350 kg/10 ares in most years.[77] The Nōji Chōsa gives a yield of 216 kg/10 ares for the prefecture as a whole in 1884.[78] These yields are substantially higher than the national average level, officially recorded as reaching about 180 kg/10 ares at that time. Not too much should be made of the actual quantities here, given the doubts concerning yield data in Japan, and output must have varied substantially from year to year, depending on weather and,

[t] 'Mura zentai to shite nenko-sō o ijisuru shikumi' *Saga-Ken Shi* (80), p.598.

especially, pest damage, but Saga was clearly a productive rice-growing area. In addition to rice, wheat and various vegetable crops, notably beans, were grown on the quarter or more of the paddy land which was double-cropped, and wheat, barley and naked barley were the main crops grown on the small area of unirrigated land which existed.

What happened to this output? The types of non-rice crop grown, and the wide range and small quantities of such crops, indicate that they were essentially subsistence crops. The vegetables and pulses, along with the grain, produced by each household provided almost all its food requirements, and heating, clothing, lighting, tools and so on could also have been provided by home-grown, home-made products. Even the relatively rich families to be described in the next section, as late as the 1910s, were growing and preparing their own food, making their own clothes from home-grown cotton, and so on. Wheat and barley were chiefly used as fodder and as a supplement to rice as a food grain, although some was sold to make the noodles which were a local speciality. The area planted to specifically commercial or industrial crops was negligible.[79]

Turning to rice, the Nōji Chōsa data make it possible to estimate that if each member of the agricultural population of the prefectue (70% of the total) consumed the 150 kg of rice per annum which was generally taken to represent a normal basic rice consumption, then roughly half of the prefecture's rice output in 1888 would have been consumed on the farm.[80] The surplus must either have been siphoned out of the village economy as tax or rental payments to support the non-cultivating population and provide the basis for the prefecture's trade with other areas, or traded by producers for other inputs or consumption goods. It will become clear that, in the period with which we are dealing, the former remained the major route by which Saga rice found its way out of the village economy, although there was probably also substantial movement of rice within the village itself. To see this it is useful to begin by tracing the development of the system for marketing rice in the late Tokugawa and early Meiji periods.[81]

By far the largest part of the rice not consumed within the village, before 1868, was the tax rice of the feudal lords — the *han* taxes and the stipends of individual samurai — which Beasley's figures suggest accounted for 30% of the assessed rice output of Saga *han* at the time of the Restoration.[u] The marketing system at this time was geared to dealing

[u] See Beasley, W., 'Feudal Revenue in Japan at the time of the Meiji Restoration' (106), p.270. 30% is quite a low proportion compared with most other *han* areas in Kyūshū covered by the above data, though similar to those of nearby *han* such as Kurume and Ogi. The Saga-Shi Shi (81), p.221, maintains that *han* taxes took a higher percentage of the crop than the 35% of the Meiji land tax.

with this rice, and the rice trade in Saga was in the hands of the group of households who managed the dealings whereby the *han* tax rice was shipped to Ōsaka and sold on the rice market there. These merchant households were located in Saga castle-town or in the ports along the Chikugo, and they chartered the ships to carry the rice out to the *han* storehouse in Ōsaka. These households also lent money to the *daimyō* and to individual samurai and some were beginning to accumulate land, despite the official discouragement of tenancy. There was also clearly some retail selling of rice in the castle-town itself, but there are no records, for the big merchant houses at least, of any buying from middlemen dealing in the surplus rice of cultivators, so it would seem that, if larger-scale cultivators or village landlords were selling rice outside the village before 1868, it was not on a very large scale. This points out Saga as a rather backward region by comparison with the areas of advanced commercial agriculture already developed in south-western Honshū.

After the Restoration and the Land Tax Revision, the *han* rice taxes were converted into national taxes payable in cash. The Saga-Shi Shi estimates that Saga farmers after 1868 were paying about 35% of their output in tax.[v] By 1873 about half of the taxes paid in the area of the former Saga *han* were being paid in cash.[82] However, the marketing of the rice concerned was through an official company, set up by the national government to ease the transition to money taxes by acting as an agent to convert taxes paid in rice into cash to pay to the government. So there was at that stage little change from the point of view of the cultivator. The local merchant households were anxious to break into this trade in rice. Those who had relied exclusively on their position with the feudal lords disappeared with the abolition of the *han*, but others who had begun to build a base of their own by accumulating land and contacts in the countryside were beginning, by the late 1870s, to develop channels for marketing cultivators' rice directly. The records of the trading house which Yamada has described show it beginning, after 1877, to buy rice from agents who were trading direct with the villagers, at this stage only in small amounts from each agent and only within a relatively small radius, but still marking a change of direction. The agents from whom rice was bought were either particular larger-scale cultivators within the villages, such as those acting as the house's representatives in the villages where it owned land, or smaller-scale cultivators who had some reason to travel about—horse-dealers, for instance.

[v] Ogura calculates that, for the country as a whole, the land tax took about 35% of officially recorded rice output immediately after the Land Tax Revision. *Can Japanese Agriculture Survive?* (24), p.110.

It follows from the above that, until the beginning of the 1880s at least, the mass of cultivators on the Plain were probably only marginally involved in commercial market dealings in rice. Tax rice and rental rice were finding their way out of the local village economy and, according to the Nōji Chōsa, in 1888 18% of Saga Prefecture's rice harvest was being sent out to other prefectures.[83] Some rice sales for the purchase of commercial fertiliser or occasional consumption goods were beginning to be made. But in general most of the needs of most farm families were still at this time being met from their own output. This does not mean, however, that there was not substantial redistribution of produced rice within the local economy. Rental payments, amounting to 40% or so of the output of 30–40% of the cultivated area, were obviously a major part of this. Wages paid to *nenko* in rice were another important item. But in addition many payments for locally provided goods and services would have been made in the form of rice or meals — ranging from interest on loans and payments for the use of horses or equipment, to fees paid to priests or fortune-tellers or geisha.

Finally, were there any flows of income from outside into the village economy? Most *nenko* worked for farmers within their own village or nearby. But they were not all employed for the whole year and some probably did find seasonal work away from the village, for instance in mining.[84] A survey of wage rates in Saga City in 1883 gives a wage for migrant rural workers.[85] The *kogashira* system was used to recruit gangs of workers for outside work. However, given the generally low level of industrial development in Saga, the scope for this kind of work was probably not great. Alternatively, there was the possibility of producing goods for sale in spare hours at home, the most important being production of goods made from straw. The Nōji Chōsa lists the following as side occupations of small-scale farmers in Nishi-Matsuura County: salt-boiling, day labouring, carting, logging, charcoal-making, basket-weaving, rope-making, manufacture of straw sandals, spinning, fishing, paper-making, collecting firewood.[86] But a number of these occupations, especially those dependent on access to the sea or to woodland, were not open to inhabitants of the central Plain area, who were therefore forced to rely most heavily on employment as agricultural labourers in their own or neighbouring villages.

*

The picture we have, then, of the Saga village economy in the 1870s and 1880s is of the farmers of a productive, and largely specialist, rice-growing area just beginning to be drawn into market dealings in rice, as the old system for drawing off the surplus in feudal taxes and rents was giving way. Within the village, though, the traditional inter-household exchanges of rice for goods and services remained the basis of the economy, and although there might have been a slight widening of the labour market taking place, there was none of the scope for household manufacturing and by-employment which was bringing market dealings into the villages of the advanced areas of central Japan.

5. The Economies of Farm Households—Some Examples

In this section I want to consider the economies of individual farm households, using the production and consumption patterns described earlier, in order to provide a framework within which to analyse households' responses to the economic and technical changes appearing in later chapters, and to give some idea of how and at what standard typical families lived in the late Tokugawa and early Meiji period. What has gone before will, I hope, justify the approach to this in terms of two types of Saga Plain household: the upper-middle-scale cultivator/labour employer, one of the group of a quarter or so of leading village households; and the small-scale cultivator/agricultural labourer, one of the 50% or more of village households farming a small plot and supplementing its output with income earned as *nenko* on larger holdings. In what follows, I will describe the little that is known about particular households and make some back-of-envelope calculations of typical income and expenditure patterns.

First, though, it is perhaps worth repeating here that the differences in economic operation between the two sorts of household did not, for the most part, arise because of differences in the technology employed. Because of their shared use of capital equipment, irrigation facilities and labour skills, large- and small-scale farmers were constrained to use similar, compatible techniques. Larger-scale farmers who owned horses and the best-drained fields, and had better access to sources of fertiliser, stood more chance of being able to grow a second crop, but in most respects the cultivation techniques employed were the same on all holdings. The cause of the difference between the economic operations of the two types of household lay in differences in the factor proportions available to them, differences between households with little land and more than adequate family labour forces and households with more land than the family could work on its own.

(1) THE LARGER-SCALE EMPLOYER/CULTIVATOR

For this type of household we have, first of all, the information contained in the records of their economic operations kept by two families in this category.[87] In both cases, the information refers to periods after the beginning of this century, by which time outside forces had begun to affect the economic organisation of Saga Plain farmers. Nevertheless, the basic structure of their household economies retained many of the features of this type of farm in the late Tokugawa and early Meiji period.

The information about one family, referred to as Family S, comes from a record book kept during the period 1907–12. Family S farmed 1·89 hectares on the Saga Plain. Its holding consisted of eighteen separate plots. At the beginning of the period it owned 0·74 hectares of this. By the end it had come to own another 0·65 hectares of it. The rest was rented. Family S was thus essentially a medium-scale, owner/tenant household.

Family N, on the other hand, was a very large-scale landowning household. It owned 17 hectares, of which the family farmed 5·2 and rented out the rest. It therefore represents very much the upper level of resident cultivating landlord. During 1917 it kept a record of the labour days worked on its farm, and it is from this that Yamada and Ōta draw their information.

The economies of both households retained many elements of self-sufficiency. Even the members of the wealthy family N grew cotton and mulberry to make their own clothes, vegetables for their own consumption and so on. Both sets of records were kept at a time when Saga Plain farmers were beginning to market increasing quantities of rice and to buy increasing amounts of commercial fertiliser. Nevertheless, the economic operations of even these relatively large-scale farmers were still subsistence-oriented.

We know something of the labour forces with which these holdings were farmed. Household S consisted of the house head and his wife, his eldest son with his wife and three babies, and his two daughters. In addition, two *nenko* were employed. Although the individuals employed varied each year, they always came from within the local area (*mura*). The head of household N was an official of the local cooperative, so the farm was run by the next eldest brother. Another younger brother also worked on the farm and they employed three *nenko* and some other temporary hired labour. The labour of the temporary workers and of the women members of the household is not recorded. Household N had employed the same three men as *nenko* for some years and all three came from the local area. Neither household's *nenko* lived with their employer's families, even in the case of one *nenko* who had no holding of his own to farm.

Family N's records tell us something about the way these labour forces were used. One *nenko* did 73% of the horse-ploughing, this being 66%

of his work in grain production and 40% of his total working days. He was clearly a specialised ploughman. Family members did most of the pumping. The acting house head did the largest amount, although the women probably also did a good deal. Despite their wealth, the members of family N worked as hard and as long as their hired workers. Grain cultivation was the main occupation of the male members of the household and of employed workers, as is shown in Table 4.2, but mixed in with this were all kinds of other operations concerned with the household as well as the farm, and production activity is not clearly separated from the running of the household. This would be even clearer had family N recorded the labour of its women members in the house and on the farm.

From this and other scattered pieces of information,[88] we can try to piece together something of the income and expenditure position of a household in this category. In these calculations I shall work in terms of the Japanese measure of capacity, the *koku*, which is equivalent to 150 kg of brown (unpolished) rice, because one *koku* of rice is roughly equivalent to what was taken to be the basic food requirement for one person for a year,[w] and calculations made in *koku* therefore give a much better and more vivid picture of what particular levels of income and expenditure meant in a still largely self-subsistent economy. A household cultivating about two hectares would probably represent the typical farm of this type. Such a household might be renting in some land (like household S), or it might be renting some out, if its family circumstances required, or it might be doing both. It is therefore easiest to take the middle point and assume that it owns all the land it farms, and also that all its land is paddy.

Income: rice yields on the Saga Plain in, say, the 1870s, probably averaged somewhere between 1·5 and 2 *koku* (225 − 300 kg) per 10 ares (see earlier). Two hectares would therefore produce 30 − 40 *koku* of rice. In addition, such a household would probably have been able to grow a second crop of wheat on perhaps 20 − 30% of its paddy land, yielding about 8½ *koku* of wheat for fodder, etc.,[89] and other second crops of vegetables and pulses for home use. It is unlikely that at this time any members of a household with an adequate holding of this size would be working away from the farm, so its only other possible sources of income would be interest on any loans it might make, payments for the use of its horse or any equipment it lent out, and meals received when doing communal work or helping out neighbours.

---

[w] See Smith, T., *The Agrarian Origins of Modern Japan* (8), p.25 and p.125. Also Ōta, R., 'Meiji Zenki' (91), p.220, quoting Max Fesca, who estimated the average food consumption in early Meiji Japan as 1·26 *koku* per person per annum, of which 0·71 *koku* was rice.

Table 4.2: The Distribution of Labour Time in Household N
(Units = days)

	Acting Househead	His brother	Nenko 1	Nenko 2	Nenko 3
Grain cultivation	129·2	125·1	122·55	129·75	166·85
Ancillary to grain cultivation	71·25	98·35	86·3	89·1	73·8
Miscellaneous	26·8	10·75	24·55	22·55	12·15
Household activities	27·0	14·4	21·6	24·55	18·2
Help given to neighbours	4·5	4·0	5·0	3·0	9·0
Public work	—	5·5	1·5	6·25	—
Other	16·25	1·9	7·75	7·0	5·5
Holidays	39·0	74·0	23·0	22·5	22·0
Missed days	—	—	41·75	29·5	26·5
Total days worked	275·0	260·0	269·25	282·0	285·5

The period covered is February to December 1917.
Source: Yamada, T. and Ōta, R., *Saga-Ken Nōgyō Shi* (73), p.303.

Expenses: after the consumption needs of the family itself, a household of this type next had to pay its taxes. The Saga-Shi Shi's estimate of the tax burden on farmers after the Restoration put it at 35% of the rice crop, but by the time of the Nōji Chōsa in 1888, the proportion was put at 20%, and we know that inflation did reduce the land tax burden on farmers in the years after the Restoration. Measured in this way as a proportion of the rice crop, the fixed money burden of the tax obviously varied according to the price of rice and the year's harvest, but as a very rough estimate for, say, the 1870s, we could say that it took about 25% of the crop, i.e. 7½ – 10 *koku*.

The largest item of production expenses would have been wages paid for hired labour. Although family S employed two *nenko*, in general other data suggest that a two-hectare farm could manage with one full-time *nenko*, and the rule of thumb seems to have been that it was necessary to employ one *nenko* for every hectare cultivated above the one hectare or so that the average family could farm with its own labour.[90] In 1888 *nenko* wages were recorded as ranging from ¥30 p.a. for a skilled strong man of 25 – 30, to somewhere between ¥7 and ¥15 for men of 15 – 20, and ¥4 – 10 for women workers. The top rates were enough to bring in 6 – 7 *koku* of rice at the rice price of that year.[91] This accords with Yagi's finding that in the late Tokugawa village he studied, *nenko* received on average 5·4 *koku* p.a.[92] In addition, workers had to be provided with meals. So the two-hectare farmer would probably have to pay out at least 6 *koku* for its hired labour expenses, and probably more for temporary labour as well.

There also exist some estimates of farm household expenditure on purchased fertilisers. The late Tokugawa Kawazoe farmers were paying out approximately 10% of their rice yield for bought fertilisers (mostly night soil), to support their high double-cropping rate. In the Plain villages for which we have some data for 1880, farmers were spending about 0·2 *koku* of rice per 10 ares on purchased fertilisers, still mainly night soil, but supplemented by oil-cake, dried fish and lime fertilisers, and this again works out at roughly 10% of the rice yield.[93]

Deducting taxes, wages and fertiliser expenses from the rice yield produces the result that the two-hectare farm would have something like 15–20 *koku* p.a. in an average year to meet its other expenses and its own consumption requirements. A family of four adults and five children, like family S, would need about 7 *koku* for their basic food consumption. A holding of this size would be able to produce enough fodder for its horse and would produce enough non-rice crops to meet its requirements for clothing, heating and so on if it wished to — it could be extravagant and buy things if it chose. The remaining surplus had to meet the farm's capital requirements — depreciation of equipment, the capital cost of a horse, repairs to buildings and so on.[x] There then remained weddings, funerals, visits to shrines, socially required feast- and party-giving, and so on. In average and good years, such a family clearly had some scope for saving if it chose, but, on the other hand, as we shall see in comparison with other incomes, neither was it able to sustain a standard of living markedly different from that of many other rural and urban dwellers at the time.

(2)   THE SMALL-SCALE CULTIVATOR/AGRICULTURAL LABOURER

Income: the basic income of such households consisted in the rice they grew, supplemented by other crops of vegetables and perhaps wheat or other grains. A half-hectare holding, for instance, would have produced about 7½ – 10 *koku* of rice p.a. Such a household might well not have had the resources to double-crop much of its holding, but if it could plant wheat on, say, 10 ares, it could have produced a further 1½ *koku* or so of additional grain or fodder, perhaps for a shared horse. It would also have been able to grow pulses and vegetables to meet much of its subsistence food requirement.

In addition, depending on the size and structure of the family, there

---

[x] A horse cost 5 *koku* and two wheels cost about 1 *koku* and lasted for 10 years. Yamada, T., 'Saga Heiya ni okeru Bakumatsu-ki' (98), p.47.

was the possibility of earning income from outside employment. If a household could send out a strong young man to work as a *nenko*, he could bring in a further 6 *koku*, as well as having some of his food provided. There might also be the possibility of doing seasonal work outside the village, or some kind of by-employment at home. A survey of wages and salaries in Saga City in 1883[94] records that unskilled rural migrant workers received 9−11 *sen* per day (¥1 = 100 *sen*), i.e. approximately 50 days' work would bring in a *koku* of rice. Workers making Japanese-style socks at home received 3½ *sen* per 10 pairs and could make about 25 pairs in a day, i.e. 8·75 *sen* per day, or about 60 days to earn a *koku* of rice.

Expenses: a household such as this might well have been renting in some of the land it farmed and therefore paying about 40% of the yield of such land as rent. It would also have had to pay taxes on the land it owned. Production expenses for such a household are almost impossible to estimate since there were so many ways in which it might have acquired access to the tools, draught animals and fertiliser it required, and all we can do is see what surplus was left after known expenses and basic consumption needs had been met.

If we imagine a household farming half a hectare, of which 20 ares are rented, then it would have a rice income of 7½ − 10 *koku*, plus other subsistence crops. It would be paying 1·2−1·6 *koku* as rent on 20 ares, and 0·9−1·2 *koku* as tax on 30 ares.[y] If we assume it also spent 10% of its rice yield on purchased fertiliser, then it would be left with altogether 5−6 *koku* to meet its subsistence needs and its other production expenses. This would be adequate for an average-sized family (e.g. 4·6 people per household in the late Tokugawa Kawazoe villages[95]), but a larger family or a smaller holding would put such a household on to the subsistence margin, unless it could send one or more of its members out to work. A household which could release a son to work as a *nenko* could raise its income very substantially while that son was young and fit. As he grew older, however, as he acquired a wife and children, and as his father also grew older and less able to work, such a household would become increasingly burdened by the mouths it had to feed relative to its income-earning capacity. In the short term, the decision to rent in land rather than send someone out to work as a *nenko*, which the half-hectare

[y] In general, landlords seem to have been responsible for paying taxes on tenanted land. This being so, it would appear that, immediately after the Restoration, landlords were not making a great profit on land they rented out. However, as the tax rate was reduced (in response to landowners' protests), and as the price of rice increased, reducing the quantity of rice it was necessary to sell to meet the fixed cash tax payment, landlords' profits grew much larger. See Waswo, A., *Japanese Landlords* (36), pp.18−19.

household above is assumed to have taken, looks unprofitable. However, over the longer term, cultivating a larger area of land offered greater security (including the security of rent reductions in bad years and of the ability to grow subsistence crops) as well as higher status.

The scant details of the lives of two *nenko* families, which can be gleaned from the cases, discussed by Isobe,[96] of two *nenko* who later became cultivators of reclaimed land, confirm the above picture. One was born in 1873 and his family worked 0·7 hectares on the Saga Plain. He worked as a *nenko* and day labourer until he was thirty, i.e. while he was physically at his peak, and then became a tenant farmer for a time before moving to Korea and eventually returning to settle on the reclaimed land. The other was born into a family which cultivated 0·4 hectares (0·2 owned, 0·2 rented) on the Plain. He had four brothers and all five worked as *nenko*. These men were lucky enough to live to see a time when alternative employment opportunities had greatly increased. For the generation before them, there remained little choice but to rely as they grew older on less and less remunerative outside employment to supply the subsistence which the family holding was too small to provide.

*

The survey of wages and salaries in Saga City in 1883[97] makes possible some very rough comparisons between the incomes of our typical farm households and people in other occupations. The money value of farm incomes of course depended on the price of rice, which varied substantially from year to year and over the year. In 1883 it stood at around ¥4−5 per *koku*, though this represented a drop over the previous few years.[98] Our two-hectare farmer's 15−20 *koku* was therefore worth ¥60−100. This is about the same as the salaries of lower-level white-collar workers in the survey — the low-level managers, local government workers, school teachers and journalists, who are recorded as earning ¥60−80 p.a. Our small-scale farmer's on-farm income of 5−6 *koku* was equivalent to ¥20−30 p.a. Manual workers are recorded as earning 12−13 *sen* per day, which would be equivalent to ¥36−40 p.a. if they were able to work 300 days in the year. Male household servants received ¥1−1·5 per month plus food, clothing and housing.[z]

---

[z] The prefectural governor earned ¥1,200 p.a., a bank president ¥600, a primary school headmaster ¥170. *Saga-Shi Shi* (81), Vol. 3, p.619. Chūbachi and Taira record that the public relief level in the 1880s was the equivalent of 1·8 *koku*, and the minimum per capita consumption among the lower, but not the lowest, strata of urban society was a little less than this. The average per capita ghetto income in Tokyo in 1886 was about 1·5 *koku*. See 'Poverty in Modern Japan' (108), pp.392−4 and p.408. N.B. the estimates of Saga farm incomes in the text cover income from rice cultivation only and are not total incomes as in Chūbachi and Taira's data.

These comparisons leave out so many factors as to be, perhaps, dangerous. They ignore for instance: non-rice subsistence crops grown by farm households; the large-scale fluctuations in farm incomes with variations in the harvest; the scope for earning extra income in the slack periods of the farm year, and so on. Nevertheless, they leave the conclusion (which is also that of the Saga-Shi survey) that farmers at the upper end of the land distribution lived at roughly the level of lower-grade white-collar workers. The mass of small-scale farmers, meanwhile, earned from their operations on their own holdings at best no more than regularly-employed manual workers, and for those with smaller holdings, or with large families, or in years of bad harvests, the margin above bare subsistence was slight.

*

To summarise what has been covered in this chapter: the technology in use in Saga Plain agriculture around 1850 – 80 represented a set of interconnected adaptations to the basic techniques of rice cultivation in Japan, in response to the potentials and problems arising from the peculiarities of the natural environment. To be specific, the flat terrain necessitated the use of a method of irrigation which greatly increased labour requirements per hectare over what was typical in Japan at the time. This led to technical adaptations which helped to increase the efficiency of the use of irrigation water (*tokojime* ploughing) and to spread out the labour demands thus created (the phased rotation), hence making it possible to grow a second crop on the paddy land to provide fodder for the essential draught horses. The rotation itself caused the greatly increased risk of pest damage but, as long as this causal connection was not understood, justified itself also as a means of spreading this risk. In addition, it permitted a measure of double-cropping, while at the same time including the fallow period necessary for the use of the mud-fertiliser which served as a substitute for the natural fertiliser sources the area lacked. The interconnections between the various aspects of the technology meant, as we shall see, that it was hard to make any fundamental changes to the technical system as long as the irrigation technology on which it was based remained unchanged.

On the basis of this technology there grew up a system of social and economic relationships between households within the village, which helped to make production and survival feasible and as secure as possible within the limits of the environment. These arrangements ensured for larger cultivators the supply of hired labour without which they could not carry on production, and for small-scale cultivators access to the capital inputs and draught power which they lacked, as well as a guarantee of the outside income without which they could hardly survive.

Although individual villages had some contact with the outside world before 1868 through officials of the feudal government, and, after the Restoration, through contact with other villages over irrigation matters, occasional employment away from home, the need to pay taxes and so on, yet at this stage Saga villages were only on the very edge of the market economy, selling and buying their output and labour for cash only where unavoidable or for occasional luxuries. It is to the impact on Saga villages of, on the one hand, the gradually increasing penetration of the market economy and, on the other, the policies and administration of the new government that we turn in the next chapter.

CHAPTER FIVE

Commercialisation, Technical Change and the Role of the State, 1880–1910

This chapter will deal with the period from approximately the 1880s to the 1900s when Japanese agriculture is generally said to have made its greatest contribution to the development of the economy. This is the period of the spread of the *Meiji Nōhō*, under the stimulus of the opening up of new commercial opportunities for farmers, and of the increasing efforts to diffuse information about improved techniques. This chapter will examine how these forces affected the Saga Plain, an area with considerable rice-growing potential but with environmental conditions and prevailing technology somewhat different from those of the regions where the *Meiji Nōhō* developed, and as yet still quite remote from the main centres of commercial and industrial growth. The aim is to show the problems encountered in Saga in responding to industrial and commercial change in other parts of the country and in introducing techniques developed in and for other areas, and to describe the preliminary stages of the institutional development and adaptation required to overcome these problems. I shall look first at the impact on Saga Plain farmers of the spread of the money economy, and then at the means by which efforts were made to introduce the new techniques developing elsewhere. This will lead on to an examination of the extent of technical change in this period and the developing role of the new research and extension institutions.

1. The Spread of the Money Economy

(1) Commercialisation in the Markets for Goods

We saw in the last chapter that in the 1870s and 1880s Saga Plain farmers were just beginning to find themselves drawn into selling a proportion of their rice crop. Direct evidence of changes in the amounts which they marketed is hard to come by. From 1892 onwards we have prefectural figures for the quantity of rice shipped out to other prefectures (see Chart 5.1). For a predominantly agricultural prefecture like Saga, with no substantial centres of trade or industry, internal sources of demand for marketed rice would not be great, and changes in the quantity of rice shipped out would reflect quite closely changes in the amount of rice marketed. These figures show that around 1892 about 25,000 tonnes of rice were being shipped out annually, and this accords with the figure of 24,150 tonnes for 1888 in the Nōji Chōsa. In the course of the 1890s this rose to about 55,000 tonnes, representing an increase in the proportion of the total crop shipped out from about 20% to around 40%. This would clearly suggest that Saga farmers were marketing an increasing proportion of their rice crop, and there are indeed a number of indirect reasons why they would be expected to do this.

Chart 5.1:   Rice Shipped out of Saga Prefecture, 1892–1935

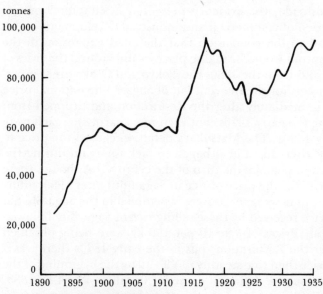

Source: *Saga-Ken Tōkei Sho* (101).

First and foremost was the farmer's increasing need for cash income. The most significant cause of this increase was the conversion of the land tax into a money tax; farmers were by the 1880s finding the cash for this themselves. This required the marketing of perhaps 20% of the crop for owner farmers. In the last chapter we saw farmers also beginning to use commercially purchased fertilisers. As we shall see later, this use of bought fertiliser was increasing quite rapidly towards the end of the century and providing another reason for needing to acquire cash. In addition, there is some evidence that an increasing range of bought consumer goods was becoming available in the villages.[1] These included textiles—cotton cloth purchased instead of made at home, woollen goods, and so on—sugar, coal, oil lamps, matches, etc. In addition government controls put an end to the production of *sake* (rice wine) and tobacco at home. School fees were another increasing cash demand, as educational facilities spread (see later). While the farm continued to provide most of its own food requirements, and rent for paddy fields continued to be paid in rice, the number of necessary items which had to be paid for in cash was clearly increasing. This would account also for the increasing tendency for *nenko* wages to be paid in cash. The effects of the technical changes to be described later, in raising rice yields, were also beginning by the later 1880s and the 1890s, as we shall see, to provide farmers with increasing surpluses to sell to meet their requirements.

On the demand side, the evidence presented in chapter 3 on the regional distribution of commercial and industrial development in this period would lead to the conclusion that the chief expansion in the market for food output would be taking place in and around the cities of central Honshū, and from the 1880s the Tokyo and Ōsaka areas provided the main markets for the rice sent out of Saga.[2] The national price of rice was high immediately after the Restoration and dropped from these levels during the early 1870s, but then rose sharply to reach peak levels in the early 1880s. The Matsukata deflation caused the price to fall quite sharply after this, but it began to pick up again during the 1890s to reach a new peak by the turn of the century.[3] Although there are no official series for the price of rice in Saga until after 1900, information, mainly from newspaper sources, assembled in the Saga-Shi Shi shows that the price received by those selling rice in Saga City followed the national trend. Prices of ¥9−10 per 150 kg were being obtained immediately after the Restoration, but in the early 1870s there was a sharp fall. The price then rose steadily to ¥9−10 by the beginning of the 1880s, but the Matsukata deflation caused it to fall to ¥3−4 by 1883. After that it gradually recovered to reach ¥11 by the time the prefectural yearbook data appear in 1900.[4] Thus, in general, although there were sharp price fluctuations, demand conditions were quite favourable for those Saga farmers with rice to sell.

Furthermore, the ability to market rice from Saga, especially to the distant but expanding Honshū markets, was greatly facilitated by the development of railway communications during the 1890s. In Tokugawa times, and in the 1870s and 1880s, Saga's marketed and exported rice was shipped out along the creek network to the ports on the Chikugo and thence to Nagasaki and on round Kyūshū to Ōsaka.[5] In 1891 the railway between Saga and Tosu was completed, opening up the possibility of travelling, or sending freight, from Saga to Fukuoka or to the port of Moji, and thence on to the commercial centres of Honshū. During the 1890s, the line was extended on to Sasebo and Nagasaki, its primary function being the transport of troops to and from the naval ports there.[a] The coming of the railway is clearly reflected in the big rise in the proportion of the harvest going out of the prefecture during the 1890s, with the waterways continuing to provide a convenient means of getting rice to the stations, from which it was transported away to Ōsaka and Tokyo.

Further indirect evidence of the spread of trading in rice is provided by the fact that the quality of the rice being shipped out was definitely declining. During the Tokugawa period, rice from Saga had been highly regarded in the national rice markets. *Han* officials had strictly inspected the rice they received as tax and had kept firm control over the quality of rice shipped out. With the abolition of the *han*, this control was lost, and as the rice trade spread into many more hands, much less care was taken over the preparation of the rice for sale.[b] As a result, the reputation and hence the relative price of Saga rice fell. In 1882 a group of prominent Saga citizens[c] set up the Saga Rice Improvement Company to try to combat this trend, and in 1885 this company was taken over by the prefectural government. Facilities for rice inspection, at first voluntary and later compulsory, were set up throughout the prefecture, but while landlords and traders accepted the need for improvement, the campaign seems to have made little headway with the actual producers, who continued, for instance, to refuse to pack their rice in the nationally-standardised size of bag.[6] The important point for present purposes is that by this time the farmers selling rice on the market were sufficiently numerous and widespread that their activities could not be effectively regulated and they could have a substantial influence over the quality of marketed rice.

The trend towards more widespread marketing of rice can be seen reflected in the records of the dealings of one rice-trader/money-lender, described in the Saga-Shi Shi.[7] He owned 40 hectares of paddy and 20

[a] *Saga Shinbun 75−nen Shi* (86), pp.25−6. It cost 20 sen to travel from Fukuoka to Saga at the time of the opening of the railway.
[b] Rice merchants were said to use practices such as the adding of water to rice to increase its weight. *Saga-Shi Shi* (81), vol. 3, p.639.
[c] Mostly from ex-samurai families who felt the loss of Saga rice's reputation was due to greedy tradesmen. *Saga-Shi Shi* (81), vol. 3, p.641.

houses as well as substantial financial assets, but his records for 1886 show that the majority of the rice he acquired was bought through brokers, rather than received as rent, and his brokers were by now buying over quite a large area to the south of Saga City, often in small amounts from many villages. Up until 1880 he sold his rice mainly to Nagasaki and Kagoshima, but after that he began to send it further afield, chiefly to Ōsaka, and to specialise in improved quality rice. It will be of interest later to note that he continued to accumulate land, owning 214 hectares in 1924, but that most of his income continued to come from his money-lending and other financial activities.

The 1880s and 1890s thus saw Saga farmers drawn into marketing not only more rice, as their output grew, but also an increasing proportion of their rice crop, under the influence of expanding cash requirements, improving communications and, in general, favourable demand conditions. However, because the markets to which Saga farmers sent their rice were far away, they provided few of the reciprocal influences on employment opportunities, input supplies and so on which we saw were an important aspect of the process of commercialisation in rural areas closer to the centres of industrial and commercial expansion. For Saga farmers, commercialisation meant simply selling rice in order to pay taxes and buy fertiliser or perhaps some purchased consumer goods. As yet, in Saga, it lacked the characteristics required to alter the economic and technical structure of village society in the ways in which it had in other areas.

(2) LANDOWNERSHIP

We saw earlier how the second half of the nineteenth century saw a trend towards what Japanese writers have called the bi-polarisation of the structure of land holdings, as farmers struggled to cope with the spread of the money economy. As the previous section has suggested, despite generally favourable demand conditions, Saga farmers were not spared from the difficulties of adjusting to market fluctuations, particularly those consequent on the Matsukata deflation in the 1880s. The Nōji Chōsa of 1888 clearly blames the spread of the money economy for the increasing number of bankruptcies among farmers which it records, and for the high level of debts per household,[8] and other evidence supports the idea that farmers in general were hard hit by the Matsukata deflation. In Saga County, 1,949·2 hectares, about 15% of the cultivated area, were mortgaged and 266·2 hectares sold during 1882, the first year of the price fall.[9] In addition 1884 was a very bad harvest,[10] and in 1889 there was serious flooding in the lower reaches of the Chikugo.[11] To what extent in Saga did these price and harvest fluctuations lead to the same kind of bi-polarisation as observed nationally?[d]

There are no systematic data on the size distribution of owned or cultivated holdings in Saga until 1908. However, between 1885 and 1892, for the prefecture as a whole, there was a 20% decline in the number of landowners eligible to pay between ¥5 and ¥10 in land tax (roughly corresponding to the category owning 0·7−1·5 hectares of paddy), indicative of the difficulties suffered by smaller-scale owner-farmers,[12] and there is other scattered evidence to suggest that, as would be expected from the evidence of land sales and mortgaging described above, some concentration of landownership was taking place. For the prefecture as a whole, the proportion of the cultivated area farmed by tenants, which the Saga-Ken Shi estimates to have stood at 26·8% in 1873,[13] had risen to 36·7% by the time the first prefectural yearbook figures become available in 1884. Thereafter, it gradually rose to a peak of 44·6% in 1891. A picture of landownership trends in one village over quite a long period of time can be gained from the Saga-Shi Shi's data on Wakamiya village.[14] Up to 1887, there were three landowners owning more than three hectares of village land, one from outside the village and two village residents, one of whom was said to have acquired his land through foreclosing on those to whom he had lent money. In the period between 1888 and 1908, four more landowners with more than three hectares appeared, three rising from the class of 2−3 hectare owners, and one previously owning less than two hectares. They acquired their extra land mainly from the small landowners in the village, and the proportion of village land owned by those owning more than two hectares rose to a peak in 1898 when eleven households owned 50·2% of the land.[e] The figures from land registers of villages in Kanzaki County, shown earlier as Table 4.1, also reveal definite bi-polarisation in landownership taking place in the period up to 1881. From this very patchy evidence we can probably say no more than that there is no reason to suppose that trends in landownership and tenancy in Saga were very different from the national trends, as farmers tried to adapt to the same kinds of force.[f]

---

[d] The discussion here concentrates on landownership, hence on owner or part-owner farmers. From the point of view of the ability of tenant farmers to cope with the spread of the money economy, it is worth recalling that it was not customary to reduce rents in response to price falls as it was in response to bad harvests.

[e] At this time no outsider owned more than 2 hectares of village land, though.

[f] Rental rates seem to have remained at the level of 40−50% of the rice crop as in the early Meiji period. For example, the prefectural yearbook gives rates of 43·9% for Saga County and 41·7% for Saga Prefecture in 1908.

We have no data on any changes in the scale of cultivation before 1908, nor on any changes in intra-village economic relationships in general. However, since the irrigation technology, which ultimately conditioned most of the other technical and economic relationships within Saga Plain villages, remained unchanged, there is no reason to suppose that village economic organisation changed significantly. Employment relationships between households remained essential to both large- and small-scale cultivators, and the labour and capital requirements of the technology continued to place barriers on movement up and down the scale of cultivation. Where villages in other areas had relied on fertiliser collected from communally-owned land, the increasing use of commercial fertiliser lessened the basis for community activity and produced pressure to give up communally-owned land. But on the Saga Plain, mud-raising had to be carried out in order to keep the irrigation channels clear, and so the spread of commercialisation produced no such weakening of the ties between village households. Thus while landownership may have become more concentrated, as elsewhere, as small farmers lost ownership of their land to larger farmers better able to deal with the money economy, the structure of land use and the pattern of economic ties between households, apart from an increasing amount of tenancy within the village, were probably little changed before the 1900s.

2. The Organisation of the Diffusion of New Technology

While the permeation of the money economy and of commercial transactions was the first and perhaps greatest force operating on Saga farmers in the early years after the Restoration, towards the end of the century they also came to feel the impact of a second force: the growth of organisations designed to promote the spread of new production techniques. I shall leave consideration of the extent to which new techniques did in fact spread in Saga at this time until the next section, concentrating here on describing the development of the institutional organisations for promoting technical change through which, for the most part, new technology became available.

(1) Farmers' Organisations

The origins of the system of farmers' organisations which grew up in Saga can be traced back to 1878 when the central government began to set up local committees whose function was to report to and advise the government on matters of trade and industry at the local level. These committees were called 'Encouragement of Industry Committees' (*Kan-gyō Iinkai*) and one was set up in each county. It was the Saga County Encouragement of Industry Committee which set up the first organisation in Saga aimed at promoting improvement in agriculture. This was a discussion group, which was to consider agricultural matters in the county and advise the committee, and it was similar to agricultural discussion groups in other parts of the country. It began work in 1881 and some of the records of its meetings still survive.[15] Its favourite topic for discussion seems to have been the promotion of silk-worm production, which did not develop much in Saga compared with other areas.[g] After that came the problem of the rice-borer and methods to try to deal with it. The group was also concerned with the rationalisation of the rice trade and improvements in rice quality, and it discussed a wide range of innovations and new products which might be introduced in the area. Its membership was made up of important local people concerned with agriculture, landlords and *tezukuri jinushi*, and former samurai turned *tezukuri jinushi*, and the kinds of topic discussed reveal their main concern in agriculture as a commercial business.[16]

The establishment of the Encouragement of Industry Agricultural Discussion Group was followed by the setting up of other groups whose aim was the promotion of agricultural improvements. These groups at first tended to reflect, like the original group, their bureaucratic origins, and to be imposed from above as intermediaries between local government and farm interests. However, whether as a result of the example of these groups or of ordinary farmers' increasing interest in trying to grow more under the stimulus of the spread of the market economy, agricultural groups with genuine roots among the mass of practising farmers began to grow up over the 1880s and 1890s. Seed exchange societies were a common example of this sort of group, and the first one in Saga was founded in 1884.[17] In addition there were ploughing societies which held ploughing competitions, organisations to run experimental plots, and simple local-level discussion groups.[18] Village-level agricultural groups began to be formed in the mid-1890s.[19]

It was these more or less spontaneous private local groups that formed the basis for the system of official agricultural organisations which was set up in the late 1890s and the 1900s. These official organisations (henceforth referred to as *nōkai* — agricultural associations) were established, with government financial assistance, as the organs through which technical and economic improvements were to be introduced to farmers, taking over from the private groups which had been performing these

[g] Perhaps because of lack of space for growing mulberry, lack of idle periods in the farm year into which silk-worm raising could fit, etc.

kinds of function. In Saga, between 1891 and the outbreak of World War I, the complete system of *nōkai* was set up, providing a means of communication from the national-level Teikoku Nōkai (Imperial Agricultural Association) through the prefectural and county *nōkai* to the level of the administrative village (*mura* or *shi*) and finally to the village or hamlet itself. In 1892 the official Saga Prefecture Nōkai was set up. Its first leaders came from the old samurai families who provided it with respectability, but its subsequent leadership came from the group of more advanced, modernising landowner/businessmen.[20] It published and disseminated information and acted as co-ordinator for local agricultural groups. In 1893 the organisation which became Saga County Nōkai was set up. During the later 1890s and the early 1900s, there was a considerable amount of legislation about, and re-organisation of, the *nōkai* system. During this time the *nōkai* began to take on the role of technical leadership in local agricultural matters, and those with technical training in agriculture[h] began to predominate in their management.[21] Finally, in 1914, village (*buraku*) level *nōkai* (called Agricultural Practice Unions—*Jikkō Kumiai*) were set up. All cultivators (owners and tenants) had to belong to their village *nōkai* and help meet the cost of it.

The basic aim of the *nōkai* system was to give technical guidance and leadership. It was therefore involved in Saga in such things as the distribution of salt to encourage salt-water seed selection, the holding of ploughing competitions and the distribution of improved seed varieties, as well as the publishing and distributing of written material, and it received subsidies from the prefectural government for a number of its operations.[22] *Nōkai* in Saga were more heavily involved in the marketing and distribution of fertiliser than *nōkai* elsewhere,[23] and, most significantly, the *nōkai* were, as we shall see later, of great importance in spreading improved methods of controlling the rice-borer. The size of the *nōkai* technical staff increased gradually as the number of qualified graduates grew. By the 1920s there were technicians as far down the network as the administrative village (*mura*) level, with two or three technicians per administrative village *nōkai*, responsible for perhaps ten village agricultural practice unions between them.[i]

The importance of the *nōkai* in the marketing of fertiliser in Saga may account for the rather slow growth of co-operatives, the other main local-level agricultural organisation to emerge in most areas from the

[h] In Saga, graduates of the new Saga Agricultural College. See later.
[i] Conversation with Professor Yamada, 26 December 1980. A description of the work of village-level technicians (or, as he calls them, agricultural advisers) in pre-war Kumamoto Prefecture is to be found in Embree's *Suye Mura* (44).

village groups of the 1890s and 1900s. Fertiliser marketing was often an important function of local co-operatives, although under the law passed in 1900 they could also be set up to provide credit, to market agricultural output, to acquire communally-used facilities, or any combination of these. By 1907, 21 had been set up in Saga Prefecture of which 17 were still in existence, but they were mostly very small, with only 20–30 members. The number of co-operatives grew quite fast during the 1910s, but memberships remained generally small.[24]

(2) AGRICULTURAL EDUCATION

The agricultural groups which emerged in Saga as elsewhere in Japan after 1868 provided an institutional means through which information about improved techniques could be disseminated to farmers. If technical change was actually to take place through this means, there had to be, of course, an input of suitable new techniques to disseminate, and the provision of this input will be considered in the next section. But in addition there had to be, on the one hand, a supply of adequately trained personnel able to transmit the input to the farmers, and, on the other, a capacity on the part of the farmers to understand the information transmitted. Both of these were, to a considerable extent, dependent on the provision of education — technical training in agriculture on the one hand, and basic literacy and numeracy on the other.

Official technical education in agriculture began in Japan in 1877 when the Emperor opened the Komaba Agricultural School in Tokyo. This school offered two- and three-year courses in agriculture, and its graduates became the staff first of the Ministry of Agriculture and gradually of prefectural government agricultural departments and experiment stations.[25] There were also private agricultural schools, one of the most influential of which was that of Enzo Hayashi in Fukuoka.[j]

In 1885 the central government inaugurated the scheme under which itinerant lecturers travelled around talking to local agricultural groups. The idea was also taken up at the prefectural level and in 1890 Saga Prefecture appointed its first itinerant lecturer, a graduate of the Komaba School (of whom more later). His successor as itinerant lecturer, also a graduate of the Komaba School, became the first head of the Saga Agricultural College which was set up in 1895 in Saga City. Its courses were open to farmers, or the sons of farmers, who owned 50 ares or more in the prefecture. In its first year it took 45 students on its main

[j] Hayashi was a great advocate of deep ploughing, and he had a number of followers in Saga, including some who, in 1886, set up an experimental plot to try out his methods under Saga conditions. *Saga-Shi Shi* (81), vol. 3, p.647.

two-year course and 10 on special courses, though only 6 got as far as taking the exam in the next year.[26] In 1898 it started running three-year courses based on Wesern agricultural science. At times it had more than 50 students, though its drop-out rate was always fairly high. After graduating, its students either returned to work on their family farms or became the technicians and officials who staffed the expanding *nōkai* system, the experiment station and the local government agricultural departments.[27] Thus those initially trained at the national level moved out to train those who would eventually provide the technical expertise necessary to diffuse new technology at the local level.

In the villages to which the graduates of the Agricultural College returned, the education system was gradually expanding through the 1880s and 1890s. Village schools grew out of the old temple schools of the Tokugawa period, in which village children had been taught the first steps in reading, writing and arithmetic. In the Kawazoe villages there was more or less a temple school in each natural village (*buraku*).[k] After 1868 the temple schools were converted into state primary schools and gradually more and more new schools were built. In 1883 there were 59 primary schools in Saga Prefecture,[28] and four years' school attendance became compulsory in 1886.[l] Although there are no data to prove it, it would thus seem likely that basic reading and writing skills were quite widespread in Saga villages by the turn of the century.

(3)   AGRICULTURAL RESEARCH AND EXTENSION

The basic ideas underlying the techniques which formed the *Meiji Nōhō* came, as we saw in an earlier chapter, from the experience and experimentation of practising farmers and agricultural enthusiasts in various parts of Japan. They were not the result, at that stage, of an organised research effort. The early stages of agricultural research in Saga were similarly efforts by enthusiasts to try to apply new knowledge and new techniques to conditions in Saga. Among these enthusiasts were the followers of Enzo Hayashi mentioned earlier and the local farmers who carried out the research on the rice-borer, to be covered in more detail

---

[k] *Kawazoe-Chō Shi* (75), p.681. This conforms with the probable national distribution of temple schools. See Levine, S., and Kawada, H., *Human Resources in Japanese Industrial Development* (114), p.42. It cost about 18 kg of rice per annum, plus various money gifts at New Year and *Bon*, for a child to attend one of the temple schools in Kawazoe. *Kawazoe-Chō Shi* (75), p.680.

[l] The *Kawazoe-Chō Shi* (75), p.684, quotes figures showing 60–70% of boys and about 50% of girls attending school in the Kawazoe villages in 1895, though it does not state the age-group concerned.

later, which produced the basis for the control methods subsequently practised.

However, as with the agricultural groups described earlier, the local government became increasingly involved in encouraging, subsidising and co-ordinating the work of local enthusiasts. From the second half of the 1880s, local government in Saga began to provide subsidies for experimental plots at the county offices and later at lower levels in the administrative hierarchy. These plots were used to try out seed varieties in local conditions and were managed by committees of local enthusiasts.[29] An experimental plot, set up in 1877, in which various new plants and varieties were tried out, under the auspices of the Saga Silk Producers' Association, was taken over by the prefecture in 1885.[30] In 1890 the prefecture allocated some land within the grounds of the government offices to be used as an experimental plot in which to try out new types of plant. These facilities were later improved, and their management given over to the prefecture's itinerant lecturer.[31] Also in 1890, the agriculture department of the prefectural government was set up.[32] However, most of the technical information used by this growing research and extension organisation was still coming from the central national experiment stations until, in 1900, with the passing of the law for the subsidisation of prefectural experiment stations, the gradual process of increasing local government involvement in research and its application in Saga culminated in the establishment of the Saga Experiment Station on its own site in a village just north of Saga City.

At the time of its establishment the experiment station had a staff of five, made up of one technical officer, two technicians and two secretaries.[33] Its initial projects included testing varieties of rice and other grains, trying out agricultural practices, working out the best fertiliser combinations to use, and, most importantly, testing the conclusions about the rice-borer reached by earlier independent researchers.[34] The nature of these projects reveals the experiment station at this stage simply centralising and systematising the kind of applied research which had been going on before. In addition, since there was not at this stage, or indeed until after World War II, a separate official extension service in Japan, the experiment station worked in co-ordination with local government officers and with the *nōkai* to publicise and diffuse its own results. It was thus not, in its origins, in the kind of work it did, or in the methods it used, a separate, isolated research institution, and it was, as we shall see later, closely involved in the problems of actually operating new techniques in the particular conditions of the area.

Finally, the character of official attitudes to agricultural development in Saga at this time can be summarised in the career of someone closely involved in it: the prefecture's first itinerant lecturer, whose name was Kusuhara.[35] He was born in a village in Kumamoto Prefecture in 1863 and studied English in Kumamoto City before going to Tokyo in 1881 to become a student at the Komaba School. He was apparently not rich and had to work hard to support himself, but he was a good student and eventually graduated satisfactorily in 1886. For the next four years he worked as an ordinary schoolteacher until his appointment in 1890 as Saga's first itinerant agricultural lecturer. His job was to travel about the prefecture giving instruction, and this he did, going to stay with each of the local enthusiast farmers in succession, organising lectures and touring round the villages giving farmers highly detailed instructions. He is said to have been a somewhat unconventional person, credited, for instance, with composing and reciting exhortatory poems at lecture meetings,[m] but he succeeded in building up close contacts with local farmers, combining the knowledge he thus gained with the Western science he had learnt in Tokyo. In addition he is said to have conducted research in his own house, assisted by his wife, and he clearly became more and more interested in the experimental side of agricultural promotion, becoming in 1894 head of the experimental plot in the grounds of the government offices.

Kusuhara's career reveals the lack of separation between experiment and extension, the mixture of formal scientific training with practical experience, and the close links between agricultural officials and practising farmers, which characterised the institutions developed to promote technical change at this time. We shall see these characteristics further revealed when we look at these institutions actually in operation later on in this chapter and subsequently.

(4) THE DEVELOPMENT OF IRRIGATION ORGANISATIONS

In the last chapter we saw how Saga Plain farmers, one way or another, devised a means of running their irrigation network after the abolition of feudal rule. This was done on the basis of customary practice, and government regulation was little involved. However, such a system was liable to increasing strain as the incentive for farmers to try to improve their irrigation facilities grew with the spread of the market economy and the widening of the technical possibilities for expanding production. In 1890, the central government finally entered the field of irrigation

---

[m] For example the following, which is in the form of a *dodoitsu*, a fixed-syllable poem for less lofty subjects: 'Hiroi yoi ta ni hie no ho miyuru, Are wa dannō no hatajirushi.' This means, roughly, 'the sight of a weed in a nice big rice-field is the sign of a lazy farmer'. *Saga-Shi Shi* (81), vol. 3, p.650. My thanks to Ikuko Kiyokawa for explaining this poem to me.

administration with the passing of the Irrigation Association Law (Suiri Kumiai Hō). This was complemented by other legislation which completed the framework for the establishment of legally recognised bodies for the management of irrigation facilities.[n]

This legislation had two important characteristics for the understanding of irrigation administration in Japan. Firstly, the irrigation associations (*suiri kumiai*) formed under it were based on the management of particular facilities, not on particular geographical areas, and, secondly, they were the organs through which subsidies for irrigation and land improvement could be obtained. As a result, legally recognised associations tended to be formed only for the management of large-scale facilities on which many villages depended and which had to be run by some kind of outside body, or for the purpose of obtaining subsidies. Facilities within the villages, for instance, could remain untouched by the law and managed as always by the village as a unit. An individual farmer might therefore have to belong to a number of different irrigation organisations: his own village organisation, associations formed to obtain subsidies for particular new or improved facilities, and associations managing large-scale works controlling any sources of water on which he might depend.

How did this system work on the Saga Plain? Mainly as a result of the large-scale work carried out on the irrigation system during the Tokugawa period, there were certain crucial facilities on which a large number of Saga Plain farmers depended. The most important of these were the Oide Dam, the Ishi-i Sluice and the Tafuse Channel (see Map 4). Until the passing of the new legislation, these had been run according to the practice of Tokugawa times, under the nominal control of the local government. In 1892 they were handed over to a newly-formed irrigation association called the Oide Suiri Kumiai, which became responsible for maintaining them and for opening and closing the sluices. The command area of these facilities included much of Saga County and all of Saga City. In the same year another legal *kumiai*, the Kawazoe Irrigation Association, was formed to manage the facilities controlling the water draining out of the main creek network and the sluices taking the tidal fresh water from the Chikugo, on which farmers in the south-east of Saga County depended. Later in the 1890s, a number of other, smaller, legal *kumiai* were formed to manage specific facilities, for instance one for the Hatta Sluice and Channel.[36] Many farmers must have belonged to one of these smaller *kumiai* and to the Oide Association as well. Facilities below the level of these relatively major works, however, remained the concern of the groups of farmers dependent on

[n] The Kōchi Seiri Kumiai Law of 1899 and the Futsū Suiri Kumiai Law of 1908.

them, just as they had always done, often with no special formal organisation but with the management of irrigation work seen as part of the
general function of village leaders, and irrigation expenses part of
general village expenses.[37]

Under the new legislation, official *kumiai* had to draw up rules and
keep records of what they did. One surviving document setting out the
rules and regulations of one of the smaller legal *kumiai* shows it trying to
set down and codify existing water-use practice, but occasionally resorting to vague expressions like 'according to custom'.[38] The expenditure
of this *kumiai* grew fast over the period for which we have records
(1899–1908), as it found its feet and began to branch out into new
activities, for instance, setting up committees to examine proposals for
improvements to the facilities.[39]

In 1908 the legislation covering irrigation *kumiai* was revised under
the Irrigation Law of that year, and there exists more information
about how *kumiai* were run after that. The headship of the *kumiai* in
Saga formally went with one or other of the major local government
posts. For instance, the head of Saga County was head of the Oide
Kumiai. Below that, though, there was provision for election of the
kumiai leadership, and in the Oide Kumiai every man over twenty-five
paying more than ¥2 p.a. in land tax was eligible to vote.[o] In practice,
especially in smaller *kumiai*, elections were a formality, and headship of
the *kumiai* was a sort of honorary position held by an eminent local
personage.[40] In the Oide Kumiai, which was a large *kumiai* with many
functions, the *kumiai* meeting chose two managers, from amongst those
nominated by the County head, who ran day-to-day matters. They
could employ a secretary and technicians, water guards and so on, if
they chose, but they could also call on the County secretarial staff.
Thus, in the case of a large *kumiai* like the Oide, the line between the
local government bureaucracy and the *kumiai* management was not
very clearly drawn.

Kumiai had to meet the cost of their operations through levies on
members. Initially these levies were paid in labour. As a typical
example, in 1908 in one of the smaller *kumiai* 1,494 people from the
1,835 member households were involved in dredging operations.[41] However, by this time, especially in larger *kumiai*, more and more of the
work had to be paid for in cash. The size of the *kumiai* staff was increasing,
and, especially for larger-scale work, with the growth of labour markets, it
was becoming easier to hire the necessary labour at the market wage

---

[o] The *kumiai* was divided into sixteen divisions, each of which elected one member of the
management committee, except for Saga City, which elected three. Those elected held
office for four years. *Kasegawa Nōgyō Suiri Shi* (77), p.68.

rather than try to mobilise members' labour, so increasingly members of larger *kumiai* came to pay their dues in money. Dues were usually levied first on the village unit, and varied from place to place depending on how much the individual area received from the *kumiai*. The village then either paid the dues as part of its budget or allocated them amongst village members, as a rule according to area cultivated.[P] Within lower-level irrigation groups, and especially within the village, however, management and maintenance through communal labour remained the rule. At the extreme, mud-raising from the creeks continued to be carried out communally by small groups throughout the pre-World-War-II period.

The system for administering the irrigation network on the Saga Plain was thus a complicated, unsystematic, historical creation, and the question of exactly who was responsible for a particular channel or sluice or dyke was often not easy to answer. The system seems, however, to have worked quite efficiently as a means of ensuring the routine running and maintenance of the network. It could mobilise large amounts of labour when required and seems to have been able to achieve a peaceable and reasonably equitable distribution of the available water. Where it might be expected to be less effective was in making changes or improvements to the system, and indeed this does seem to have been a problem.[42] The smallest change in the dimensions of a channel, for instance, had to be passed by numerous committees and meetings, and there was much scope for obstruction and delay, resulting in unsatisfactory compromises. However, when a change in irrigation technology was seen as urgently necessary, the *kumiai* organisation was capable of promoting and achieving it both efficiently and equitably, bringing the benefits of improved techniques speedily to all farmers, as we shall see more dramatically in later chapters.

*

To summarise: by the 1900s the Saga Plain area possessed a system of more or less official organisations which together constituted a research and extension network. These organisations had grown up in a somewhat haphazard, pragmatic way, born from the union of private farmers' groups with national legislation and regulation. From the central, prefectural institutions of the experiment station, the prefectural *nōkai* and the prefectural government agricultural department, which themselves had links with their regional and national counterparts, there spread out the network of lower-level organisations: the county,

[P] In the Oide Kumiai at least, dues were generally paid by the cultivator rather than the landlord. Kyūshū Nōsei Kyoku, *Saga Heiya* (76), p.69.

administrative village and village agricultural associations concerned with the diffusion of largely technical advice and information; the scattered co-operatives providing economic assistance; and the irrigation associations running the water allocation system. The circumstances through which this network was born and grew up meant that it was not simply imposed from above, but had to some extent its own roots within the area, which gave it the capacity to reflect and respond to local conditions and prevented technical staff from becoming divorced from farmers' practical problems. We shall see this characteristic more clearly as we turn now to consideration of the system in action in efforts to promote the spread of new techniques.

3. The Adoption of New Techniques

In 1904 the agricultural department of the prefectural government in Saga issued what it called 'Seven Major Points for Agricultural Improvement'. These summarised the chief aspects of the new techniques then being promoted throughout the country, as they applied to Saga. They were:

1. Unification and improvement of seed varieties
2. Improved use of fertiliser
3. Use of deep ploughing
4. The cultivation of better seedlings
5. The use of check-row transplanting
6. Seed selection using brine
7. More attention to pest control.

These seven points represented the standard *Meiji Nōhō* package, developed for the most part outside Saga, with added emphasis on insect control, and it was this package which the various organisations described in the last section were trying to diffuse in Saga in the late nineteenth and early twentieth century. They therefore provide a convenient framework within which to examine the extent to which the standard *Meiji Nōhō* techniques did spread in Saga under the stimulus of the expansion of the money economy and the growth of research and extension organisations. After that we can examine their impact on output and yields.

(1) SEED VARIETIES

It is very difficult to say what was happening to the pattern of seed varieties in use in the earlier years of the period, when the naming of varieties as still very inconsistent. However, there is some evidence that substantial experimentation and change were going on. Yamada and Ōta have assembled data from a number of sources on the names of the varieties grown in seven Saga villages in the later Tokugawa period.[43] Of the 107 varieties recorded there, only one was still in common use in the 1880s and 1890s.[44] It would seem, then, that, under the influence of the seed exchange societies and the increasing availability of commercial fertiliser, farmers were trying out new varieties on quite a large scale.

What changes in the pattern of seed varieties resulted from their experimentation? In the absence of systematic naming of varieties this is difficult to assess, but we can judge something from the distribution between early- and late-planted varieties. As was argued in chapter 3, the improved varieties which were central to the *Meiji Nōhō* package were late-planted varieties, and progress in the development of higher-yielding types of seed was concentrated on late-planted varieties. In the Tokugawa period the evidence suggests that in general the yields of early and middle rice were higher than those of late,[45] and that only 20–30% of the paddy area was planted with late varieties.[q] By the time of the Nōji Chōsa in 1888, however, late varieties had considerably higher yields and the proportion of late-planted area was steadily increasing, reaching over 40% by the 1900s.[46]

However, the first major survey of seed varieties planted in Saga, carried out in 1911, reveals that, while Saga Plain farmers were growing a number of improved varieties, on an increasing proportion of their land, they continued to grow a wide range of traditional varieties as well, and there was not the same consistent shift towards uniform new varieties as observed elsewhere. The survey recorded 61 different varieties being grown in Saga County, of which 21 were early varieties, 10 middle varieties and 30 late.[47] 90% of the early-planted area was given over to two variants of an old variety,[r] and on the remaining 10% there were 19 other varieties. Shinriki, which was first distributed by the experiment station in 1902, covered 23% of the late acreage, being much less uniformly grown than in other places, including the non-creek Plain areas of Saga. 7 other late varieties were grown on areas of more than 100 hectares each, taking up a further 68%, and 22 other varieties were grown on the remaining 9%.[48] The seed varieties grown by Family S, who kept records of what they planted in each of their plots

---

[q] Though higher proportions were late-planted in the Kawazoe villages. See Yamada, T., 'Saga Heiya ni okeru Bakumatsu-ki' (98), p.49.

[r] One of these was a 'red' variety, i.e. an Indica-type rice grown because of its ability to withstand poor water conditions and low levels of fertiliser application. It was gradually replaced by a 'white' Japonica version as irrigation conditions improved and fertiliser application rose. *Saga-Shi Shi* (81), vol. 3, pp. 662–3 and cf. *Nihon Nōgyō Hattatsu Shi* (55), vol. 6, pp.615–29.

between 1907 and 1911, conform to this picture of non-uniformity. They grew a wide range of varieties, some improved, some traditional, and rarely grew the same variety on more than two or three of their plots, or on the same plot two years running.[49]

Can this picture be explained? Saga Plain farmers, like farmers everywhere, needed to plant the improved fertiliser-responsive late varieties to complement their increasing application of fertiliser, and the evidence suggests that they were gradually shifting in this direction. In this they were encouraged by the seed-exchange societies and by the extension work of the authorities. It is interesting that the varieties recommended by the prefecture in 1908 were the main varieties being grown on the Plain in 1911.[50] But why, then, did Saga farmers not wholeheartedly and uniformly grow improved varieties? One obvious reason is that they were obliged by their technical system and their irrigation methods to plant a substantial proportion of their paddy area with early varieties, and the major improved varieties available were late-maturing. A second reason may lie in the fact that, as we shall see later, some of the other techniques, most notably deep ploughing, which complemented the use of improved varieties and heavy fertiliser application, were difficult to use within the technical system. However, the most frequently cited cause of Saga Plain farmers' reluctance to use improved varieties uniformly and consistently was the rice-borer. Saga Plain farmers believed that improved varieties were less resistant to the rice-borer than traditional ones.[s] The Saga County Memoirs (Saga-Gun Shi) of 1915, reporting that eighty different varieties were grown in the county, of which only a few were improved, blamed the susceptibility of the new varieties to the rice-borer and hoped that, as pest control methods improved, so better seeds would be used.[51] The Saga-Shi Shi similarly argues that systematic diffusion of improved varieties could not take place as long as the rice-borer problem remained unsolved, and notes that farmers would not grow a variety, however high-yielding, if its resistance to the rice-borer was low.[52] Thus the growing of an assortment of varieties, some improved, some not, can be seen as a way of not putting all the eggs in one basket—improved varieties could be grown on some fields but not on all, in case they proved susceptible to the rice-borer, and if they did, then it was worth trying another variety next year, as long as some traditional resistant varieties were also grown.

To summarise, while Saga Plain farmers were gradually shifting towards the cultivation of improved varieties, they were doing so in a

---

[s] See e.g. Kyūshū Nōsei Kyoku, *Saga Heiya* (76), p.309. I do not know of any evidence as to whether or not they were justified in this belief.

sporadic and hesitant way, and the Plain did not see the widespread, uniform growing of Shinriki which typified the advanced areas of the *Meiji Nōhō*.

(2) FERTILISER USE

In the period before 1900, there seems little doubt that, while mud and other self-supplied fertiliser continued to provide for basic fertiliser requirements, farmers were beginning to supplement this with commercially purchased fertilisers. This was so even in the late Tokugawa period,[53] and by the time of the Nōji Chōsa, quite substantial amounts of purchased fertiliser seem to have been in use. However, in Saga as elsewhere, it was after the turn of the century and the Russo-Japanese War that the use of commercial fertiliser began to grow really fast, with the import of cheap soy-bean fertiliser from Manchuria. This can clearly be seen in the first series on fertiliser consumption to appear in the prefectural yearbook (see Table 5.1), and by 1917 approximately half of the value of the fertiliser consumed in Saga Prefecture came from commercially-purchased sources. There is no evidence of any noticeable decline in the input of self-supplied fertilisers,[54] so that this must have represented substantial growth in the total amount of fertiliser applied.

Relatively sophisticated techniques for the application of different kinds of purchased fertilisers were clearly known, even, according to Yagi,[55] in Tokugawa times, and the winner of the 5 *koku/tan* (150 kg/10

Table 5.1:   The Growth of Purchased Inputs—Saga Prefecture

	Fertilisers (tonnes)					Inputs of non-agricultural origin. (million ¥ — 1934—6 prices)
	Oil-seed cakes	Dried sardines	Herring meal	Soy-bean cake	Man-made chemicals	
1905	1,110	1,428	514	1,654	176	1·56
1906	866	1,669	810	1,961	645	1·63
1907	626	1,920	450	3,015	1,421	1·90
1908	495	1,470	416	4,747	1,065	2·13
1909	604	2,700	551	9,184	930	2·89

Sources: Fertilisers—*Saga-Ken Tōkei Sho* (101), Yamada, T. and Ōta, R., *Saga-Ken Nōgyō Shi* (73), p.283.

Non-agricultural inputs—Hitotsubashi Daigaku Keizai Kenkyū Jo, *Nōgyō Keijōzai* (67).

ares) prize in 1913 (of whom more later) used night soil, fish meal, bone meal, lime and compound fertiliser, all applied at different stages to the seed bed and the paddy.[56] Family S's records for 1907–12 show it buying small quantities of various types of fertiliser, including some inorganic compound fertiliser, in defiance of the general trend towards Manchurian soy-bean cake.[t] How widely sophisticated methods were used is difficult to say, but technicians from the local government, the *nōkai* and the experiment station were engaged in a system of regular lectures on fertiliser use in the villages in an effort to raise the general level of knowledge.[57]

The ability of farmers to acquire and learn to use fertilisers was also promoted by falling fertiliser prices and improvements in fertiliser marketing. One of the unusual features of this in Saga was the extent to which fertilisers were marketed by the *nōkai*. In general at this time, fertilisers were marketed by relatively small fertiliser merchants, and Saga was one of the first places in which co-operative marketing of the main farm inputs became common. Over the period 1908–17 the *nōkai* in Saga acquried almost a quarter of the market in compound fertilisers and substantial shares of those for other inorganic fertilisers.[58] Fertiliser marketing by the *nōkai* was originally encouraged by the prefectural government as a way of helping farmers avoid being cheated by fertiliser merchants, who took advantage of their ignorance and sold them substandard products. It was also a means of disseminating information about fertilisers, and of helping to keep the price down, and, as domestic production of inorganic fertiliser increased, prices fell by a third over the ten years between 1908 and 1917.[59]

In conclusion, falling prices, increasing availability, growing knowledge and the spread of fertiliser-responsive seed varieties encouraged Saga farmers to expand their use of fertiliser rapidly, and none of the complaints voiced about Saga farmers' reluctance to adopt new techniques are heard in connection with fertiliser use. The technical system on the Plain presented no obstacles to increased fertiliser application, and an efficient and widespread system of distribution and instruction made sure that farmers learnt to apply fertiliser in the quantities recommended by the experiment station. As we shall see in the next chapter, the price of rice was beginning to rise steadily after the turn of the century and this, combined with the falling price of fertilisers, ensured that most farmers had the cash they needed for fertiliser purchases. The problem lay in the failure to use that fertiliser as effectively as possible

[t] Yamada, T., and Ōta, R., *Saga-Ken Nōgyō Shi* (73), pp.310–11. This was probably because the farm was situated in a port to which dried sardine fertiliser had traditionally been shipped, probably from Hokkaidō.

by adopting the techniques which complemented it. We have already seen this to some extent in the case of seed varieties, and we turn now to the other major example of the problem, that of deep ploughing.

(3) DEEP PLOUGHING

Deep ploughing was essential for the absorption and efficient use of heavy applications of fertiliser. In general it required the use of a draught animal and one of the improved types of plough being developed at this time. Saga Plain farmers had been familiar with the use of horses for ploughing since before the Meiji Restoration. But as we have seen, they had developed a system of land preparation designed to meet the needs of their particular environment, in which the criterion for good ploughing was not depth but the creation of a leak-proof base to the field. It proved very difficult for Saga farmers, however much they were encouraged to do so, to build deep ploughing into their land preparation system.

The clearest evidence of Saga Plain farmers' failure to adopt deep ploughing comes in the Memoirs of Saga County (Saga-Gun Shi), written in 1915, which is in general very optimistic about the technical progress going on on the Plain, but which cannot conceal the lack of success in promoting deep ploughing. Ploughing competitions were first held in Saga County in 1901 and subequently took place in each village. The young men of the village had to plough a field and were judged by a member of the county technical staff and leading local farmers. Deep ploughing was also taught at short courses held every year from 1906 in ten different places in the county. However, the Memoirs record that few of the participants in these promotional efforts actually used deep ploughing when they got back to their villages.[60] The authorities' response was to try to tailor the criteria for judging in the competitions more closely to local conditions, and to hold them in fields typical of particular localities. They also tried to encourage the purchase of better horses.[61] But the basic problem was that deep ploughing was not compatible with *tokojime* ploughing and was therefore unlikely to be adopted as long as water-wheel irrigation prevailed.[u]

---

[u] Tanaka also notes that improved, short-sole ploughs were very difficult to use within the phased rotation of Saga Plain agriculture. Ploughing for the second crop took place before the harvesting of the late rice crop, so that the water level in the fields was still quite high. Short-sole ploughs could not be used on insufficiently drained ground and so could not in general be adopted on the Plain while the phased rotation prevailed. Tanaka, Y., 'Suiden Urasaku' (96), p.333n.

(4)   SEED SELECTION, SEED-BEDS AND TRANSPLANTING

The *Meiji Nōhō* package included a number of techniques for the preparation of seeds and seedlings which, although they tended to require extra work, encouraged the growth of strong, healthy seedlings and facilitated the control of weeds and pests. These included the soaking of seeds in salt water to separate the good seed from the bad; the use of thinly-planted, oblong-shaped seed-beds, which facilitated the removal of pests and allowed the sun to get to the plants to produce strong seedlings; and the transplanting of seedlings in regular straight lines, making it possible to use the rotary weeder and to check more easily for pests and diseases.

The use of salt-water seed selection was first tested in Saga County on the experimental plots run by the Encouragement of Industry Committee around 1880. It was found to make a noticeable difference both to yields and quality and began to be enthusiastically promoted.[62] The county government gave the *kumiai* a subsidy to buy brine to distribute to the villages under the supervision of technicians and officials.[63] In general, Saga Plain farmers seem to have adopted this new practice gladly, since it quite simply raised the yield from a given amount of seed, and it was widely used from the mid-1880s.[64]

It was not, however, so easy to persuade farmers to use improved seed-beds. Full-scale promotion of thinly-planted seed-beds was taken up by the authorities and each year the recommended quantity of seed was reduced.[65] However, farmers believed that thickly-planted seed and weak seedlings helped to deter the rice-borer and there was therefore much more resistance to seed-bed improvements than was found elsewhere.[66] The use of improved seed-beds was not general until around 1910.[67]

There were similar problems with the diffusion of straight-line transplanting. The common method of transplanting on the Plain was called *mawari-ue* (circular planting). With this method, a line of seedlings was first planted down the middle of the field and this served as a guide-line round which the rest of the seedlings were planted. The planting of the first line was very difficult and only a few people knew how to do it well. But the method meant that, once the guide-line was laid, the rest of the field could be planted very quickly.[68] The Saga County Memoirs say that farmers objected to the extra work involved in straight-line transplanting,[69] and the Saga-Shi Shi records that, since they had this very efficient method of transplanting, farmers felt that there was no need to bother with all the measuring involved in the straight-line method.[70] Underlying these explanations is the fact that speed was crucial to the transplanting operation, given the large areas to be covered and the strict time limits imposed by the phased rotation. Thus while some farmers on the Plain were using straight-line transplanting around the turn of the century, it was not in general use until the time of the outbreak of World War I.[71] This meant that the spread of the rotary weeder, which could not be used on irregularly-planted fields, was also slow, and Saga Plain farmers continued to use the traditional hoe, which damaged the early growth of the plant, long after it had been abandoned in the more advanced regions.

From the above it can be seen that the diffusion of some parts of the *Meiji Nōhō* package posed particular problems on the Saga Plain. The fact that these techniques were eventually adopted is some measure of the effort put in by the government and *kumiai* officials whose job it was to try to induce farmers to use them. We can see this effort in operation most clearly in the case of the work of the authorities on the most important problem facing Saga Plain agriculture at this time — the control of the rice-borer.

(5)   THE CONTROL OF THE RICE-BORER

The Chikugo basin had for generations been subject to frequent and often severe crop loss through the withering and dying of a substantial proportion of the rice plants. This loss was considerably more consistent and large-scale than that suffered through pests and diseases in other areas. The cause of the loss was not fully understood until the 1870s, and then, as we shall see, only by a limited number of people, and the mass of farmers in Saga and Fukuoka who suffered from it continued to believe that whatever caused the loss was brought on the east wind in the spring and could not be stopped by human intervention.

In the 1860s and 1870s a number of local agricultural enthusiasts (*rōnō*) were conducting their own research on the cause of crop loss in the Chikugo area. Perhaps the most significant of them was a farmer called Ekita, who was based in Fukuoka Prefecture though he was also commissioned by Saga Prefecture to do research work in Saga.[v] Ekita recorded the results of his work in his 'Record of Experiments on Rice Pests'.[72] In this he described how he had discovered that an insect was the cause of the loss, and how he had distinguished the two-brooded and three-brooded varieties of rice-borer. He followed the insect's development, through egg, grub, chrysalis and moth, and set out the timing of its three life-cycles. He also described possible prevention techniques. These included collecting the eggs from straw and seedlings; killing the

[v] Kyūshū Nōsei Kyoku, *Saga Heiya* (76), p.245. Ekita's work and the trouble it caused are also described by Waswo, *Japanese Landlords* (36), pp.35−7.

grubs; cutting stubble very short and burning the straw in which the eggs of the third-brood moths were carried over into the next year; using luring lamps to kill the moths; and, if possible, stopping the staggering of rice-planting so as to plant everything either early or late and break the cycle of the three broods.

The problem of pest damage in the Chikugo area was considered sufficiently serious for the central government in 1878 to dispatch an official of the agriculture department (then a part of the Ministry of the Interior), who was trained in Western scientific methods, on a tour of the area to study the problem and make recommendations. This visit, and the fact that the expert's results confirmed the research of the local enthusiasts, provided moral support for people like Ekita,[73] but failed to make any great impact on ordinary farmers.[74] The expert made his headquarters in a village in Fukuoka and toured around surveying the rice-borer problem in Fukuoka and Saga and talking to local people. It is recorded that the assembled villagers of one of the worst-affected places were speechless at being shown the rice-borer grub inside the stem of the plant.[75]

Before returning to Tokyo the expert set out the main principles of the control measures which he advocated and which were essentially the same as those of Ekita. These provided the basis for the methods which local government officials, now fired with enthusiasm for rice-borer control, set about trying to persuade farmers to use. In 1880 the Saga Prefecture government sent a circular to every household containing instructions on insect prevention measures and followed it up the next year with another publicising the successful reduction in crop loss in villages which had carefully applied the measures.[76]

The mass of farmers, however, seems to have been unimpressed by this propaganda. The records of the Encouragement of Industry Committee contain the report of a meeting in 1882 at which a visiting agriculture department official explained how thinly-planted seed-beds, facilitating the collection of rice-borer eggs, were essential to reducing crop loss. Committee member number 8 said these eggs had never been seen and changing the type of seed-bed was useless. Others said that the farmers in their local areas certainly did not know of the existence of the eggs.[77] This was the time of the Saga and Satsuma rebellions, a period of strong opposition in Kyūshū to the new government, and in Fukuoka attempts to enforce insect control measures led to quite widespread violence. Local governments at this time relied heavily on the advice of the local enthusiasts, and in Fukuoka the influence of Ekita, who put strong emphasis on the need to cut and burn stubble, had led to the issuing of regulations to this effect. Attempts to enforce them caused rioting over quite a wide area and attacks on the houses of those who advocated stubble-cutting.[78] The authorities in Saga at this stage therefore steered clear of any direct attempts to force farmers to use the measures and relied on publicity and persuasion, to little effect.

Then in 1886 orders came from the central government to the Prefecture to issue regulations about insect control with penalties of fines or imprisonment for those who disobeyed.[79] In fact this made little difference, since it was not possible to threaten people into putting in all the extra work involved. Farmers accepted 10−20% losses as inevitable and a few years of good harvests made them think control measures unnecessary.[80]

Then came the disastrous year of 1893, when over half the crop was lost through rice-borer damage. This shocked the authorities into a more positive attitude.[81] In 1896 new regulations were issued, and when the Saga Prefecture Nōkai was set up in that year, the first task it undertook was the enforcement of these regulations.[82] In 1904 more detailed regulations were issued, requiring the setting up of insect prevention committees composed of local experts, policemen, officials and so on, at each local government level down to the administrative village, to supervise the enforcement of the new rules, which specified even such things as how many luring lamps there were to be per hectare. The prefectural chief of police would ride round the countryside at night, at the head of a party of ten policemen, and arrest those who were not using the correct number of luring lamps.[83]

This authoritarian phase was succeeded around 1908 by a shift to policies of persuasion and subsidy, with village-level organisations being given grants to help them carry out the measures.[84] All along, the basic problem had been to persuade farmers that the laborious jobs of collecting eggs and searching out damaged plants were worthwhile, and this was ultimately only achieved by a long process of education and example, carried out on the spot by local government officials and later *nōkai* technicians. The Saga experiment station possesses photographs of officials and technicians, incongruously dressed in straw boaters and stiff collars, working in the fields with the farmers at rice-borer control measures and lecturing to groups of villagers. They withstood considerable hostility and opposition, and there are reports of them having to hide to escape pursuing crowds of angry farmers.[85] Nevertheless, they did in the end succeed in convincing farmers of the value of the methods. The Saga County Memoirs of 1915 regard the belief that the damage was caused in some way by the weather as a thing of the past, although there were still farmers who thought this 'up to recent times'.[86]

However, these measures attacked the symptoms not the cause, and their introduction required a considerable increase in labour input at a time when, as we shall see in the next chapter, the supply of labour to

Saga farms was beginning to decline. The real solution, as Ekita had pointed out in the 1880s, lay in changing the rotation and planting the whole crop at one time, either early or late in the season. As yet, no-one knew how this could be achieved or enforced over an entire area as large as the Saga Plain, but in 1912 the head of the Saga Prefecture Nōkai resolved to try an experiment with it.[87] He persuaded the farmers in the village where he lived, and of which he was head, and those in another village of which a friend and fellow agricultural enthusiast was head, the following year to plant their entire rice crop late. Great hopes were placed on the experiment and it proved a dismal failure. Insect damage was not reduced and the farmers found it almost impossible to cope with planting the whole crop at once because of the labour needed for pumping. Disappointment ensued, but two things were learnt: that late-planting on a limited scale was not effective because insects from other areas simply spread over into the late-planted villages, and that unified planting of the whole paddy area at once was impossible with the present irrigation technology. Despite the setback, though, the achievement of unified late-planting remained a dream in the backs of the minds of officials and technicians concerned with the Saga Plain which was significantly to influence subsequent events.[88]

*

The teaching and enforcement of rice-borer control measures provides a focus for the picture of the methods and work of local-level technical and extension staff. But it was only part, though perhaps the most important part, of the wider range of extension activities, covering the diffusion of all the new techniques described here. The important point is the extent to which, perhaps precisely because of the difficulty of spreading insect control measures, this involved particularly close supervision and contact between officials and farmers. According to Dr. Miyajima, pre-war local government officers concerned with agriculture in Saga were said to appear in their offices only once a month to collect their salaries, spending the rest of the time touring round from village to village holding meetings, giving demonstrations and so on.[89] Professor Yamada recalls that the technicians based at the administrative village level knew all the farmers within their responsibility by sight and could chat to them about the births, marriages and deaths in their families.[90] Eguchi describes how the winner of the 5 *koku/tan* prize in 1913 received a great deal of help from a technician from the Saga County Nōkai in achieving this phenomenal yield. The technician thus earned much respect from local farmers, but Eguchi notes that he was still remembered, not just because he understood the theory of achieving high yields, but because he was a practical man as well, and was prepared to go out and spread fertiliser or wade around in the paddy field investigating the way the plants were growing.[w] To some extent, the officials' attitude to farmers retained elements of the kind of authoritarian paternalism which had characterised the feudal rulers of the area, but from the point of view especially of subsequent technical changes, it had the result that technicians and officials carried back with them to their offices and to the experiment station detailed knowledge of local conditions and problems, and that they created for themselves a position from which to organise the development and diffusion of the more far-reaching changes to be described in later chapters.

(6)   GROWTH IN OUTPUT

It is not at all an easy matter to assess the impact of the changes described in this chapter on output and productivity. Although the prefectural yearbook began to give county-level figures for crop output and area from 1888, it is not possible to rely on this data in the light of Nakamura's questioning of official government statistics.[91] All that can be done is to piece together various scattered items of data, which mostly concern rice yields, to see what picture emerges. Rice yields are probably the best indicator of agricultural growth, given the general lack of scope for expansion of the cultivated area and the predominance of rice as a crop. Even in Saga, where the prospects for land reclamation were especially good, the cultivated area of Saga County rose only 3% between 1888 and 1920.[92] Various records of rice yields exist for early years on the Plain, and I will consider these first before going on to look at labour productivity and what is known of the output of non-rice crops.

As we saw in the last chapter, there are no comprehensive figures for yields in Saga in the late Tokugawa and early Meiji period, but it seems safe to assume that many farmers were achieving yields of over 300 kg/10 ares at that time. For the 1890s, we have the first prefectural yearbook figures, shown in chart 5.2, but it is dangerous to compare these with the scattered data for the early period, both because of doubts about under-recording in official rice statistics and because the early 1890s and also the early 1900s contained two spells of bad harvests. These facts might explain why the average official figures for this time rarely show yields of over 300 kg/10 ares. However, by the mid-1900s, officially recorded yields had risen to levels of 360−70 kg/10 ares. This is confirmed by a report made for the prefectural government in 1909,

[w] Eguchi, M., *Saga Nōgyō Oboegaki* (82), pp.142−6. The widow of the prize-winner recalled that the technician always wore a suit with a stand-up collar and always spoke to everyone in a friendly, familiar way.

Chart 5.2:   *Rice Yields, 1890−1935*
(5-yearly averages)

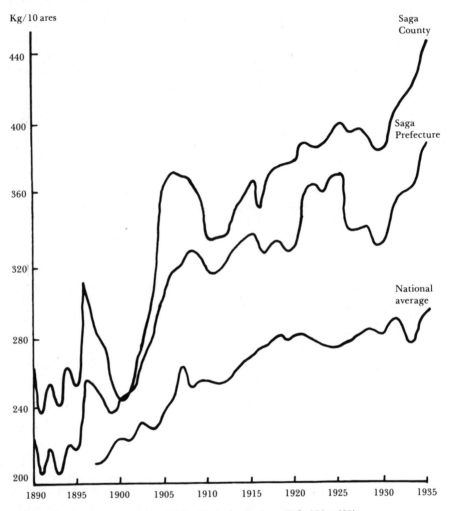

Sources: *Saga-Ken Tōkei Sho* (101); *Nōrinshō Ruinen Tōkei Hyō* (65).
Data for Saga as in Appendix Table 3.

which gives a yield for Saga County of 370·5 kg/10 ares,[93] and it would seem reasonable to conclude from this that yields were rising to some extent between the Tokugawa period and the 1900s. Thereafter, stagnation seems to have set in, with little difference between yields in the mid-1900s and the yields of 1915−20. This contrasts both with other parts of Saga Prefecture,[94] and with the national average shown on the chart.

This picture of some steady growth between the 1880s and about 1905, followed by stagnation, can be seen as a reflection of the experience described in earlier sections. With the growth of the market and increasing efforts at spreading technical improvements, Saga Plain farmers achieved a steady rise in rice yields, mainly through increased use of fertiliser and gradually through the adoption of some of the new techniques to complement it. By 1905 or so, however, the limitations on the use of the new Meiji technology posed by the existing technical system and the prevalence of the rice-borer, combined, as we shall see in the next chapter, with increasing problems of labour supply, brought this growth to a halt. By this time Saga Plain farmers had mostly adopted those parts of the *Meiji Nōhō* package which were compatible with their initial technology, but could go no further without fundamental change in the method of irrigation which underlay that technology.

Other crops were much less important to Saga Plain farmers than was rice. However the double-cropping rate was probably rising during this period, reaching proportions of 50% or more by 1910, with the area planted to second-crop wheat and barley rising substantially.[95] Thereafter, as we shall see in the next chapter, problems set in as they did with rice cultivation. Meanwhile, though, the prefecture's output of wheat, which was largely grown as a second crop in Plain areas, much of it for export to other areas or for sale to noodle manufacturers, rose by about a quarter between 1891 and 1911,[96] and the output of the various kinds of beans also rose relatively fast over this period.[97]

Finally, what happened to labour input and productivity? The data assembled in Appendix Table 1 show that there was probably some reduction in labour input per hectare in rice cultivation over the period between the end of the Tokugawa era and the 1900s. Labour days per 10 ares seem to have declined from about forty in the 1850s to about thirty by 1909. The source of this reduction which can be most easily explained is the drop in labour days spent on grain preparation, which can be seen as resulting from the relaxing of the strict Tokugawa rules on preparing and packing grain.[98] There is a decline in the labour input for pumping for which there is no obvious explanation. It may simply be that pumping was especially hard under the conditions of the villages on which the 1857 data were based. There is also some decline in labour input in land preparation which may be due to improvements in the design of ploughs or in the techniques of horse-ploughing. On the other hand, there is a slight increase in labour input for seed-bed preparation and transplanting, presumably due to the use of new methods, and in harvesting, perhaps because of bigger harvests.

How was such labour time as was saved used? The agricultural labour force in Saga County changed very little before 1900, but after that it began to fall quite fast, as we shall see in the next chapter. To some extent, therefore, reductions in labour input per hectare were beginning to become necessary to offset a declining labour force. But some of the saved labour must also have gone into expanding the cultivation of second crops, along the lines of Ishikawa's finding of an association between a decline in labour input in rice cultivation and an increase in labour input in agricultural operations as a whole.[99]

All in all there must have been some increase both in rice output per worker and total output per worker in the period between the 1880s and 1900. That at least some of this was siphoned off in the form of rent on the increasing proportion of land which was tenanted must be clear from the data presented earlier.

From the evidence of this section, we can conclude that the efforts of the research and extension system to diffuse *Meiji Nōhō* techniques were meeting with some success by the 1890s and early 1900s and that yields were probably rising. However, we have also seen that, by the mid-1900s, these efforts were beginning to run up against barriers imposed ultimately by the peculiar irrigation technology of the Saga Plain and that, in contrast to the rest of the country, growth was beginning to stagnate. The significance of this will be considered in the concluding section which follows.

4. Conclusions

What, then, can be learnt from the experience of Saga Plain farmers in the face of the spread of the money economy and of the availability of a package of new techniques?

The Saga Plain at this time differed from the central areas of the *Meiji Nōhō* in two main respects. Firstly, although it had become increasingly easy to ship goods to and from Saga, the markets to and from which these goods travelled were far away and the influence they exerted on Saga farmers was simply that of the prices and quantities of the goods they supplied and demanded. In particular, they exerted little influence over labour markets in Saga, providing none of the opportunities for side-employment or for part-time or full-time industrial work which the centres of trade and industry at this time provided for the farmers of Kinki, Northern Shikoku, and so on. Secondly, although in some respects environmental conditions on the Saga Plain were, from the point of view of rice cultivation, as good as or better than those in technically more advanced areas, irrigation technology was significantly different from that common in the areas of the *Meiji Nōhō*, posing its own particular problems including that of the rice-borer, and necessitating an initial technical structure which differed in important respects from that into which the *Meiji Nōhō* was designed to fit.

The first difference led to the development of a limited kind of commercialisation, a sort of commercialisation for outlying areas. That is to say, it led to increased marketing of the staple grain crops but to little of the diversification — the cultivation of a wider range of second crops, the movement into new activities such as silk-worm raising, and the growth of industrial side-employment — which increasing contact with the commercial sector brought about in areas closer to the centres of industrial and commercial activity. The second difference meant that Saga Plain farmers found it much harder to adopt the package of newly-available techniques than farmers cultivating under the environment and the infrastructure for which it was designed, and they therefore tended to use only those parts of the package which were compatible with their existing technical system. Some kind of change in the underlying irrigation technology was a pre-condition for adopting the package in its entirety, and without this there could be only a limited transfer of technology from the advanced areas to outlying ones like Saga. Hence, when such changes as could be adopted had been, stagnation in growth in yields set in.

These limitations to the spread of commercialisation and technical change were in their turn important factors conditioning the way in which the research and extension services developed in Saga in this period. The earliest agricultural organisations in Saga, as elsewhere, tended to be dominated by the agricultural enthusiasts, landlords, former samurai, and so on who had traditionally provided village leadership, and who, it is often argued, were typically one of the main engines of technical progress in villages at this time. But as it became clear that these leaders were unable to bridge the gap between the requirements of the new technology and the actual conditions under which Saga Plain farmers worked, official, bureaucratic organisations increasingly came to act as intermediaries between the sources of new techniques and the farmers. Thus it was officers and technicians of the local government, of the experiment station and the *nōkai* who eventually set about the task of persuading and ordering farmers to adopt *Meiji Nōhō* techniques and pest control measures. In the same way, bureaucracy came to enter the field of irrigation administration. Official local organisations thus came to try to supply, as it were, the 'missing prerequisite' which an area like Saga lacked in comparison with more advanced regions, and this role, which government and the extension services were at this stage just beginning to play in the development and diffusion of new techniques, in some ways puts Saga closer to the experience of present-day developing countries than the areas of more 'spontaneous' technical development elsewhere in Japan. But what is perhaps most significant in this respect is the extent to which officials built up a relationship (often an authoritarian one) with the mass of cultivators, through constant contact with them. This was significantly to condition their ability to develop appropriate new technology in later years.

Finally, we saw how the spread of commercialisation and of new techniques in Saga probably led to the same kind of structural bi-polarisation as observed elsewhere, and to the siphoning off of at least part of the increase in land and labour productivity in the form of rents on an increasing area of tenanted land. Because of the limited scope for diversification within the rural economy of the Saga Plain, however, the landlords who received this increasing surplus were either village landlords, essentially farmers like their tenants, with little interest in using their increased income to diversify into new forms of investment in the manner of village landlords in advanced regions, or absentee landlords whose main interests lay in the rice trade or in money-lending and banking, and who saw land as a financial investment. The internal structure of the village economy on the Saga Plain thus remained largely unchanged, witnessing little of the break-up of community ties formerly based on communal ownership of woodland, or the splitting up of extended holdings into family units better able to take advantage of new economic opportunities, observed elsewhere. These changes, like the changes in the infrastructural pre-conditions needed to achieve further technical change, awaited a greater impact from the outside economy, and this is the subject of the next chapter.

CHAPTER SIX

The Impact of Industrialisation, 1900–20

In chapter 1 I argued that the process of technical change in agriculture was inextricably bound up with the impact on it of the development of the non-agricultural sector. We have since seen how the first stage of Japanese industrialisation, centring on the growth of the small-scale textile industries, influenced the pattern and characteristics of technical change in agriculture in the Meiji period; and how Saga, still on the edge of the sphere of influence of the main industrial centres, was experiencing problems in adopting techniques designed for more highly commercialised regions — problems whose solution demanded state intervention in the form of the development of local research and extension organisations. We have also seen how, after the turn of the century, the second stage of Japanese industrialisation, centring on the growth of urban heavy industry, remained for the most part concentrated in the traditional commercial and industrial regions, with one exception, that of the area around the coal-fields and ports of northern Kyūshū, 50–100 miles distant from the Saga Plain. The aim of this chapter is therefore to describe how the impact of this new form of industrialisation fell on the Saga Plain farm economy, producing the structural changes which were to generate the pressure for, and condition the characteristics of, the technical changes to be described in subsequent chapters. I shall look first at the product and labour market influences on Saga Plain agriculture of full-scale urban industrialisation, and then go on to a detailed analysis of the consequent technical and economic responses of different types of farm household.

1. **Saga Plain Agriculture and the Industrial Development of Northern Kyūshū**

(1) THE CHARACTERISTICS OF INDUSTRIALISATION IN NORTHERN KYŪSHŪ

The Sino-Japanese and Russo-Japanese wars (1894–5 and 1904–5) marked Japan's entry into the warring world of the Western industrial powers. The requirements of war made it clear to her leaders that Japan needed a heavy industrial base beyond her present export-oriented textile industries if she was to fulfil her military and economic aims. Central to this was the development of an iron and steel industry out of which could grow the machine-making industries necessary to provide the capital equipment for independent industrialisation. The government therefore decided to take the initiative in creating the capacity to produce iron and steel, and to encourage the establishment of domestic heavy industry in other fields, such as shipbuilding.

As we have seen, the industrial development of the second half of the nineteenth century had taken place largely in and around the commercial and industrial centres of the Tokugawa period, i.e. in the Ōsaka/Kōbe and Tokyo/Yokohama regions. What these areas lacked, however, from the point of view of the initial development of heavy industry, was easy access to the one major coalfield then developed in Japan, the Chikuhi field which stretches from Fukuoka into the mountains of Saga. The only other important coalfield was in Hokkaidō, but the northern island was as yet only beginning to develop and it lacked the other great asset of the northern Kyūshū area, a good system of ports and communications, with a tradition of trade with the outside world, into which imported iron ore and other raw materials could be fed. For these reasons the government chose to locate the state-owned ironworks, which it set up in 1901, at Yawata on the north Kyūshū coast, to the east of Fukuoka in what is now the Kita-Kyūshū conurbation. In addition, the new military and economic demand focused also on the traditional shipbuilding centres of northern Kyūshū, leading to the development of the naval dockyard at Sasebo and the Mitsubishi Shipbuilding Company's yard at Nagasaki.

The industries central to northern Kyūshū's development were thus more or less artificial creations, brought into existence by the demands of war and of government policy, and they required a type of industrial structure rather different from that of the industries so far developed in Japan. With the exception of mining, they had to be carried on in relatively large-scale factories, drawing on urban concentrations of labour. There was much less scope for the small-scale input supplier, the rural

workshop employing farm girls, or the putting-out work of farm households, which characterised industry elsewhere. This also continued to
be the case over the whole period up to World War II, since the development of the machine-building industries which used the inputs produced in northern Kyūshū, and supplied much of the equipment
needed, for the most part took place in the traditional industrial areas
of Honshū, and northern Kyūshū remained a supplier of basic inputs
processed from imported raw materials and coal.[a]

This kind of industry required a certain kind of labour force. The
work was mostly heavy and manual and required a large, unskilled,
urban male labour force. As the industries grew, therefore, under the
stimulus of the World War I boom in the Japanese economy, their
demand for this kind of labour expanded fast. By 1922 the Yawata Iron
Works was producing 73% of Japan's output of pig-iron and 84% of her
rolled steel,[1] and Odaka's data, collected from the company's records,
show that the number of permanent production workers employed had
risen from 1,763 in 1902 to 17,190 in 1920, while the temporary workforce rose from 3,073 in 1905 to 6,185 in 1920.[b] In 1893 the Mitsubishi
Company enlarged its existing dockyard at Nagasaki and began construction of a second one. In 1905 a third was built and in 1907 further
enlargements were carried out.[2] The permanent workforce rose from
3,376 in 1899 to 17,061 in 1920.[3] Mining production also grew fast, with
the Chikuhi field providing about half of Japan's coal through the 1900s
and 1910s.[4] In Fukuoka Prefecture the number of permanent workers in
mining rose from 5,588 in 1904 to 69,866 in 1916, while the number of
daily workers rose from 18,614 to 60,616.[c]

The urbanisation consequent on industrialisation of this type was also
rapid. The population of Sasebo, site of the expanding naval dockyard,
rose from 50,968 in 1902 to 114,167 in 1918.[5] That of Fukuoka City rose
from 63,422 in 1898 to 105,267 in 1921, and Yawata itself, which was

[a] Matoba, T., *Kyūshū ni okeru Keizai to Nōgyō* (90), pp.65—6, where northern Kyūshū's
industry is described as 'Alsace-Lorraine type'.
[b] Odaka, K., 'History of Money Wages' (121), Table A8, p.98. Japanese companies
have customarily employed both permanent workers with rights to long-term employment and temporary workers with no such rights.
[c] Odaka, K., 'History of Money Wages' (121), Table A3, p.94. While mining resembled
the other expanding heavy industries in requiring full-time, male, manual workers,
mines were mostly small and employment was less stable than in other industries, so that
miners, unlike the workers in the steel mills and dockyards, did tend to retain a rural
base to which to return when they grew too old for the hard and dangerous work.
Matoba, T., *Kyūshū ni okeru Keizai to Nōgyō* (90), p.32, and see also Mathias, R., 'The
Recruitment and Organisation of Labour' (117) and Hazama, H., 'Historical Changes
in the Life-Style of Workers' (111), especially pp.32—3.

not significant enough to be recorded as a town in the prefectural year-book in 1892, had a population of 112,470 by 1921.[6]

Thus the industrialisation of northern Kyūshū, unlike the industrial development which preceded it in other areas, in many ways resembled the standard picture of modern industrialisation, involving the large-scale movement of full-time male workers into urban factory employment, setting up new homes and breaking their ties with agriculture. The standard picture portrays this kind of industrialisation as affecting the agricultural areas with which it had communications in two ways, on the one hand creating a demand for the food supplies needed by the expanding urban population, and on the other drawing in labour from the surrounding countryside. With this in mind, we can now turn to considering how the industrial development of the cities 50–100 miles away affected the villages of the Saga Plain.

(2)   THE DEMAND FOR RICE

The expanding populations of the cities of northern Kyūshū represented a rapidly growing potential demand for marketed foodstuffs, and especially for rice, the staple food. This increase in demand could be expected to cause an increase in price, and indeed, in the country as a whole, rising demand for rice in this period of rapid industrial growth, fuelled by speculation, led to the sharp increase in prices which culminated in the Rice Riots of 1918. The figures for the price of rice marketed in Saga City (Table 6.1) show that Saga farmers experienced the increase in demand through rising prices like their counterparts elsewhere, with the price of a *koku* (150 kg) or rice rising from about ¥12 in the early 1900s to nearly ¥20 in 1912 and 1913, then dropping a little only to rise again to over ¥40 by 1920.[d]

How did Saga Plain farmers respond to the increase in demand represented by the rising rice price? In the first place, it is clear that increased demand induced them to increase quite sharply the amount of rice they were marketing. Using the quantity of rice shipped out of the prefecture as an indication of the amount of rice marketed, we saw in chapter 5 how the coming of the railway in the 1890s had raised both the quantity of rice and the proportion of the crop which Saga farmers sold to other prefectures to levels of about 55,000 tonnes and 40% respectively. As Chart 5.1 showed, these levels remained roughly stable during the 1900s, but after 1910 the amount of rice shipped out rose dramatically

---

[d] This follows the same pattern as the national average price, at a level a little below it (see Kayō, N., *Nihon Nōgyō Kiso Tōkei* (68), Table Q.b.3). On the difference between the price of rice in Saga and the national average, see later.

Table 6.1:   The Price of Rice in Saga City, 1899–1937
(Yen per *Koku* = 150 kg)

1899	9·2	1919	42·7
1900	11·0	1920	41·8
1901	12·3	1921	27·0
1902	11·8	1922	31·2
1903	13·2	1923	28·4
1904	13·1	1924	34·9
1905	12·0	1925	37·0
1906	14·3	1926	34·4
1907	14·3	1927	30·2
1908	14·3	1928	26·2
1909	12·2	1929	26·2
1910	13·0	1930	16·1
1911	17·5	1931	16·0
1912	19·5	1932	20·5
1913	19·8	1933	20·5
1914	14·4	1934	20·8
1915	11·9	1935	28·7
1916	*	1936	30·1
1917	17·8	1937	31·6
1918	30·7		

* not available.
Source: *Saga-Ken Tōkei Sho* (101).

to reach a level of over 90,000 tonnes by the middle of the decade. The growth in output recorded in the last chapter must have accounted for some of this increase, but the proportion of the harvest shipped out, which had declined somewhat to around 35% during the 1900s, had risen to over 50% by the late 1910s.

For Saga Plain farmers, for whom rice was the major commercial crop as well as a subsistence crop, the impact of the increased demand and rising price could be expected to be greater than that for the prefecture as a whole, including as it did farmers in more remote and hilly areas growing a more diversified range of crops and less subject to commercial forces. That this was so is revealed by the results of a survey on 'Levels of Rice Production and Consumption' carried out by the prefectural government in 1917, some figures from which are set out in Table 6.2. These show that by then Saga Plain cultivators were marketing 74% of the rice they retained after paying rent, as compared with 51% for the prefecture as a whole. Altogether, 83% of Saga Plain rice output was being marketed, compared with 68% for the prefecture as a whole.

Table 6.2: The Proportion of Produced Rice Marketed in 1917
(Tonnes)

	Saga City & County	Saga Prefecture	
A. Output	37,500	166,950	
B. Rent	13,200	55,050	
C. Retained by farmers	24,300	111,900	(A−B)
D. Consumed by farm households	6,300	54,300	
E. Sold by farmers	18,000	57,600	(C−D approx.)
F. Sold by landlords	13,200	55,050	(B approx.)
G. Total sold	31,200	112,650	(E+F)
% of retained output sold by farmers	74	51	(E/C)
% of total output sold	83	68	(G/A)
% of marketed output sold by cultivators	58	51	(E/G)

Source: Isobe, T., 'Iwayuru Saga Dankai' (70), p.28.

By making the assumption that all rental rice was sold, it can be calculated that almost 60% of the rice marketed was sold by actual cultivators, indicating that the expansion of demand was drawing a wider and wider range of farmers into commercial rice dealings.

The second response which Saga rice producers made to the growth of demand in the north Kyūshū area was to switch the destinations to which they sent their rice. Nagasaki had always provided one important market for Saga rice, but, as we saw in the last chapter, much of the rice shipped out of Saga in the late nineteenth and early twentieth centuries was going to Ōsaka and Kōbe and even as far as Tokyo. The extent to which this had changed by 1920 is revealed by the results of two national surveys of rice-trading, carried out by the Ministry of Agriculture, which are shown in Table 6.3. By 1919/21, 75% of the rice shipped out of Saga was going to other prefectures in Kyūshū, almost all of it to Nagasaki and Fukuoka. By 1934/8, this had risen to over 80%. Looked at from the point of view of the receiving prefectures, the table shows that Saga was a highly significant source of supply for the industrialising areas, providing 80% of Nagasaki's imported rice and 28% of Fukuoka's. Thus it is clear that the market for Saga rice had come to be found almost entirely in the two industrialising prefectures of northern Kyūshū, and Saga farmers had, by 1920, become specialist suppliers of rice to the industrial workers of the area.

Table 6.3:   The Market for Saga Rice

Destination	Total imported from other prefectures (tonnes)	Quantity coming from Saga (tonnes)	Percentage coming from Saga	Percentage of total sent out of Saga
	Average 1919–21			
Fukuoka Prefecture	77,850	22,050	28·3	30·2
Nagasaki Prefecture	40,950	32,700	79·8	44·8
Kyūshū total	150,150	54,900	36·6	75·2
Kyōto, Kōbe, Ōsaka	361,200	9,300	2·6	12·7
Tokyo, Yokohama	806,550	4,350	0·5	6·0
Non-Kyūshū total	1,686,300	18,150	1·1	24·8
Total	1,836,450	73,050	4·0	100·0
	Average 1934–38			
Fukuoka Prefecture	138,000	38,100	27·6	38·9
Nagasaki Prefecture	51,750	41,250	79·7	42·1
Kyūshū total	214,350	79,500	37·2	81·2
Kyōto, Kōbe, Ōsaka	438,900	10,050	2·3	10·3
Tokyo, Yokohama	981,300	6,750	0·7	6·9
Non-Kyūshū total	1,986,000	18,450	0·9	18·8
Total	2,200,350	97,950	4·1	100·0

Source: Isobe, T., 'Iwayuru Saga Dankai' (70), p.24.

There are obvious reasons of geography and communications to explain why Saga farmers were able to respond so rapidly to the increase in demand and create for themselves this role as specialist suppliers to the urban industrial markets. However, equally significant was the nature of the product which Saga farmers had to sell. Saga rice was low quality rice. It was low quality partly because, as we saw in the last chapter, the rice-borer and the technical system worked against the adoption of the practices and the seed varieties which would have raised quality, and partly because it was, as it were, mass-produced rice, grown on larger-than-average holdings by farmers who had less-than-average time to spend in caring for and preparing their rice. It was notably cheaper than rice from most of the other main rice-producing areas of Kyūshū, including Kumamoto and Fukuoka;[7] and, perhaps most importantly, during the 1920s and 1930s, although it was more expensive than imported Taiwanese rice (which was of a significantly different type from Japanese rice varieties), it sold for very little more than Korean rice, as shown in Table 6.4. It was therefore precisely the kind of rice

Table 6.4:   Prices of Domestic and Imported Rice
(Yen per 150 kg)

	Domestic	Korean	Taiwanese*	Saga
1919	45·0	42·4	33·6	42·7
1920	44·6	40·5	33·0	41·8
1921	30·8	26·9	19·0	27·0
1922	35·1	31·6	17·1	31·2
1923	32·5	29·4	18·2	28·4
1924	38·6	35·3	22·2	34·9
1925	41·6	39·8	26·2	37·0
1926	37·6	36·4	23·9	34·4
1927	37·8	34·0	20·2	30·2

* traditional varieties
Source: Kajinishi, M., Nihon Shihonshugi no Botsuraku (113), vol. 1, p.253; *Saga-Ken Tōkei Sho* (101).

demanded by the mass of new industrial workers. So while officials wrung their hands at the low reputation of Saga rice, Saga farmers proceeded to sell it in large quantities, ignoring all the efforts to improve its quality and packaging and so on. They thus created for themselves a market position which was much more protected from the inroads of imported colonial rice than that of farmers in other areas. If Hayami and Ruttan are right in ascribing a significant part of the stagnation in rice yields in inter-war Japanese agriculture to the depressing effect on the demand for home-produced rice of the large-scale imports from the colonies,[8] then the high and stable level of demand for Saga rice, created by its easy access to a large source of demand and its suitability to that demand, is an important fact to be borne in mind when considering the progress of technical change in Saga agriculture in the 1920s and 1930s.

(3)   THE DEMAND FOR LABOUR

As the industries of northern Kyūshū expanded, especially during the boom years of 1900–20, they required increasing numbers of employees to work full-time on the heavy manual tasks which their production involved. Where was this labour to be found? As was argued in chapter 3, Japanese industries as a rule drew their initial labour forces from the countryside of the neighbouring prefectures. In some industries, labour could be recruited in gangs who travelled quite long distances from their native places and made no permanent homes at the places of their employment. But in the heavy industries of northern Kyūshū, permanent, all-the-year-round labour was required, from workers who made their homes in the urban industrial centres. Such workers were generally recruited through personal contacts, coming to the cities initially to live with relatives or friends who opened up the channels through which to find work.[9] When work was found, brides or families could be brought from the villages.

The farmers of Saga Prefecture were therefore likely to be among the first to feel the pull of expanding employment opportunities in neighbouring Fukuoka and Nagasaki Prefectures, and Saga Plain workers were for a number of reasons especially well placed to take up these opportunities. Since the building of the railway, communications between Saga City and the chief urban centres had become comparatively easy, helping to open up and maintain the channels between rural families and friends and relatives in the cities. In addition, among Saga Plain farm families, there was the tradition whereby younger sons went out to find work outside the parental household rather than be absorbed within it. For the most part, these younger sons had worked as *nenko* within the village, but some, at least during the slacker periods in the farm year, had gone away to work in the mines or in the towns, and were in a position to compare wages and opportunities outside the village with those within it. At any rate, the tradition of employment outside the family meant that it came more easily to the younger sons of Saga Plain households to leave for the cities, and the family holding represented less of a tie to them than to the younger sons of other areas.

Table 6.5 shows that by 1930 substantial numbers of Saga people had indeed made their way to all the main urban centres of northern Kyūshū,

Table 6.5: Populations of Fukuoka and Nagasaki Prefectures by Place of Origin, 1930

	Total population	Of which born outside Prefecture A	Of which born in Saga B	B/A × 100	Position of Saga among labour-supplying Prefectures
Fukuoka Prefecture	2,527,119	539,052	71,554	13·2	3
Fukuoka City	228,289	60,785	13,226	21·8	1
Nagasaki Prefecture	1,233,362	174,500	57,775	33·1	1
Nagasaki City	204,626	42,150	9,932	23·6	1
Sasebo City	133,174	66,760	27,223	40·8	1

Source: Isobe, T., 'Iwayuru Saga Dankai' (70), p.31, from census data.

providing over a fifth of the migrants into both Nagasaki and Fukuoka Cities. Sasebo City, however, was the destination of the largest single group of Saga migrants, and 40% of Sasebo's migrants came from Saga.[e] Among employees of the major companies, whose permanent labour forces probably represented the cream of industrial workers, we find that in 1925, 30% of the 10,652 workers at the naval dockyard at Sasebo came from Saga, as did 8% of the 8,978 working at the Mitsubishi Shipyard in Nagasaki.[10] 7·4% of the workers at the Yawata Iron-works in 1924 also came from Saga.[11] Thus it is clear that channels existed along which large numbers of those born in Saga Prefecture passed into industrial employment, especially in Sasebo, in the 1900s and 1910s.

As a result of the outflow of labour, the growth of the total population of Saga Prefecture began to slow up, declining from over 1% p.a. in the 1880s to 0·5 p.a. in the early 1910s, and stopping altogether after 1920, when the prefecture's population reached a peak and began to decline.[12] That it was the rural areas of Saga that supplied most of the outflow is clear from the dramatic decline in the numbers of agricultural workers, shown in Chart 6.1. According to these prefectural yearbook data, the number of agricultural workers in the prefecture as a whole fell by approximately 40% between the 1890s and the 1930s, and the number of farm households also declined by about 10%. These figures (and those for Saga County to be discussed shortly) should be viewed with some caution in the light of the problems, mentioned in chapter 2, concerning the definition of agricultural and non-agricultural workers. They may well overestimate the change in the relative amounts of agricultural and non-agricultural work actually done. However, this and subsequent pieces of data do point to the fact that there was a very significant migration of agricultural workers from Saga Prefecture into industrial employment, some into mining within Saga Prefecture, but most into the heavy industries of Fukuoka and Nagasaki. The fact that the number of households, as well as the number of workers, declined also provides evidence that this outflow represented the permanent migration of families, rather than the temporary migration of individual workers who might subsequently return to the villages.

Chart 6.1 also shows that, as would be expected from what was said earlier, the outflow of agricultural workers from the Plain areas, represented by Saga County, was faster and more drastic than that from other parts of the prefecture. According to these data, the number of farm workers in Saga County declined by a half between 1892 and 1921. Table

---

[e] Among them, for example, Mr. Hayashida, whom we will meet in the next chapter, and whose family left their 20 ares of rented land on the Plain to migrate to Sasebo in 1904.

Chart 6.1:   Agricultural Workers and Households, 1890–1935
(Indices of 5-yearly averages, 1890 = 100)

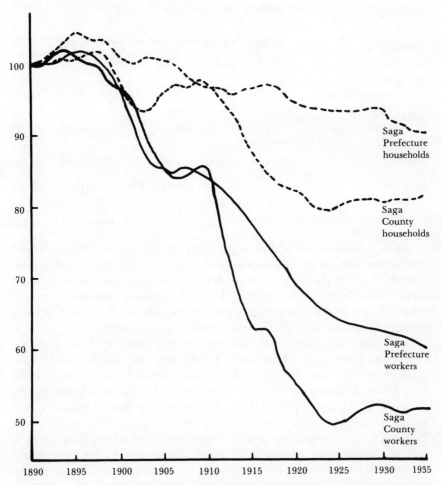

Source: Calculated from data in *Saga-Ken Tōkei Sho* (101), as in Appendix Table 4.

6.6 compares the changes in the male agricultural labour force in the various parts of the prefecture, and confirms that the outflow of the core of the labour force began earlier and was substantially greater on the Plain than in other types of area. A survey into wages and employment in each county, carried out by the prefectural Interior Department in February 1918,[13] blamed rising wages in the Plain areas on the fact that so many people were leaving to work in the cities, whereas for the other

Table 6.6:   *Changes in the Male Agricultural Labour Force in the Counties of Saga Prefecture, 1908–34*

	1908	1912	1918	1922	1929	1934
Saga (plain)	21,099	19,274	16,528	15,181	14,721	14,738
Kanzaki (mainly plain)	10,757	10,941	9,038	9,509	8,770	8,021
Miyagi and Ogi (bordering on the plain)	22,551	20,522	23,932	21,656	19,006	19,222
Higashi and Nishi Matsuura (mountain)	26,758	24,768	25,949	25,504	24,557	24,444
Kishima and Fujitsu (non-creek plain)	28,538	29,337	30,084	29,763	27,587	26,459
Total	109,703	104,842	105,531	101,613	94,641	92,884

Source: *Saga-Ken Shi* (80), p.596.

counties it blamed increasing opportunities for side-employment and temporary work away from home (*dekasegi*). All this points to the conclusion that, as the industries of northern Kyūshū sought to expand their labour forces in the 1900s and 1910s, it was the potentially mobile farm workers of the Plain areas who first responded to the pull, leaving in large numbers to establish new homes in the cities.

We would obviously expect that those most likely to be drawn away from Saga Plain agriculture would be the sons and daughters of small-scale cultivators who had previously made up the hired labour force available to larger-scale Plain farmers. That this was so is borne out by evidence of the sharp rise in wages for hired agricultural labour which would be the predicted result of such a fall in supply. This is clear from Table 6.7, which shows the available prefectural yearbook data on agricultural wages; and alternative surveys carried out by the prefectural agricultural department show annual wages for male *nenko* rising from ¥75 in 1909 to ¥140 in 1918 and daily wages rising from 40 to 100 sen over the same period.[14] However, although the Saga figures are rather too erratic to permit close comparison with other data, these wage rises appear to have been little if any greater than those of consumer prices,[f] and until about 1920 they were more or less matched by the increase in the price of rice. This can be seen in Chart 6.2, which shows the relationship

[f] The consumer price index for farm households (1934–6 = 100) rose from 56·98 in 1909 to 106·66 in 1918 and 151·15 at its peak in 1920. *Chōki Keizai Tōkei* (66), vol. 1, Table 2.

Table 6.7:   Wages of Male Agricultural Labourers in Saga (Yen)

	Nenko per year	Day workers per day
1906	91	·37
1907	156	·58
1908	156	·58
1909	113	·55
1910	100	·50
1911	100	·50
1912	100	·55
1913	100	·55
1914	95	·55
1915	80	·45
1916	*	*
1917	100	·70
1918	130	·70
1919	200	1·27
1920	275	1·50
1921	250	1·20
1922	275	1·85
1923	250	1·60
1924	252	1·65
1925	*	1·90
1926	*	1·20
1927	250	1·50
1928	275	1·25
1929	275	1·25
1930	230	1·25
1931	200	1·20
1932	250	1·00
1933	175	1·10
1934	150	1·20
1935	150	1·20
1936	150	1·20
1937	180	1·55

* not available
Source: Saga-Ken Tōkei Sho (101).

between agricultural prices and wages in Saga. Moreover, up to about 1920, the rise in agricultural wages in Saga does not seem to have been much sharper than the national average, despite the fact that the decline in the total number of agricultural workers in the country as a

Chart 6.2:   *Indices of Wages and Prices in Saga Prefecture (1910–14 = 100)*

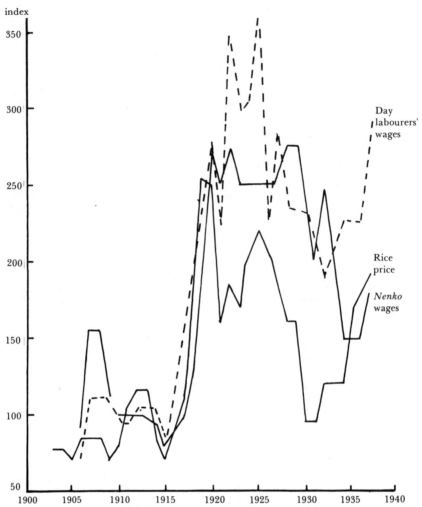

Sources: Rice price and wages indices calculated from data in *Saga-Ken Tōkei Sho* (101).

whole was much less marked than that in Saga.[g] It is not therefore surprising that the rise failed to halt the outflow of labour.

This failure becomes even less surprising on consideration of Table

[g] According to *Chōki Keizai Tōkei* (66), vol. 9, Table 34, annual wages for male *nenko* for the country as a whole rose from ¥69 in 1909 to ¥141 in 1918 and ¥221 in 1920. Daily wages for men rose from ¥0·41 in 1909 to ¥1·00 in 1918 and ¥1·64 in 1920.

Table 6.8: Comparisons of Industrial and Agricultural Wage Rates for Male Workers, 1906–22
Units: Yen per day.

	Agricultural day labourers in Saga	Employees of the Nagasaki Shipbuilding Yard	Employees of the Yawata Iron Company	Mining in Fukuoka Prefecture		Averages for North Kyūshū cities	
				Production workers	Day labourers	Carpenter	Machinist
1906	0·37	0·54	0·57	0·55	0·51	0·67	0·72
1907	0·58	0·56	0·59	0·56	0·55	0·77	0·82
1908	0·58	0·60	0·64	0·61	0·60	0·79	0·87
1909	0·55	0·63	0·65	0·59	0·59	0·89	0·90
1910	0·50	0·64	0·66	0·57	0·47	0·90	1·00
1911	0·50	0·63	0·69	0·58	0·58	0·86	0·97
1912	0·55	0·64	0·68	0·62	0·59	0·89	0·97
1913	0·55	0·66	0·67	0·65	0·64	0·82	0·96
1914	0·55	0·68	0·66*	0·62	0·68	0·82	0·94
1915	0·45	0·68	0·65*	0·61		0·81	0·94
1916	—	0·66	0·65	0·68		0·85	1·01
1917	0·70	0·85	0·69			0·96	1·12
1918	0·70	1·06	0·78			1·45	1·66
1919	1·27	1·39	1·45			1·98	1·94
1920	1·50	1·78	2·18			2·54	2·20
1921	1·20	1·92	2·40			2·59	2·12
1922	1·85	2·05	2·48			2·68	1·94

* Including female workers

Sources: Agricultural wages: *Saga-Ken Tōkei Sho* (101).
Industrial wages: Statistical Appendix (pp.90–100) of Odaka, K., 'History of Money Wages' (121)

6.8, which uses Odaka's compilation of data on wages paid in various north Kyūshū industries to compare agricultural and industrial wages at this time. Average wages in, for instance, the Nagasaki Shipbuilding Company, remained substantially above those paid to agricultural day-labourers despite the rapid rise in agricultural wage rates.[h] In practice, a worker would have had to take into account various other factors when comparing industrial and agricultural wage rates. Living costs would have been higher in the towns; agricultural workers received food and other income in kind from their employers; the migrant agricultural labourer might well not have been able to enter immediately into employment with a big company like the Nagasaki Shipbuilding Company, and day-labourers in mining, for instance, earned little more than agricultural labourers. Nevertheless, the gap between agricultural wages and the incomes to which migrant agricultural workers could at least aspire in the towns remained wide enough to maintain the outflow of labour.[i]

In summary, the Saga Plain was particularly strongly affected by the impact of industrialisation in northern Kyūshū, both because of its location and communications with the main industrial areas, and because of particular features of its agricultural structure and production system. It was the home of relatively large numbers of agricultural workers who were both used to working for wages and relatively untied to family holdings, and it was capable of marketing large quantities of the cheap, low quality rice demanded by the new urban workers. Industrialisation therefore affected Saga Plain agriculture in very much the text-book manner, drawing off agricultural workers to the town and providing a growing market for agricultural output. How this affected the structure of Saga Plain agriculture itself is the subject of the following sections.

2. The Impact of Industrialisation on the Agricultural Structure

(1) THE DISRUPTION OF THE TECHNICAL SYSTEM

In a relatively short space of time, the industrial development of northern Kyūshū drew off an undoubtedly substantial part of the labour force in Saga Plain agriculture. In other words, it caused a rather abrupt change in the relative factor supplies available to farms. In this section I

[h] A *nenko* who worked 200–250 days in a year (contracts for 20 days' work per month were common) would have earned less per day than a daily agricultural worker.
[i] For more on this choice between agriculture and industry and on why agricultural employers did not raise wages further, see section 2 (2).

will consider the extent to which, within the confines of the existing technology, Saga Plain farmers were able to adapt technically to this change, i.e. how far they were able to substitute other inputs for the hired labour which had become relatively much more expensive and difficult to find.

We have already seen that, under the technology of Saga Plain agriculture, in the spring and summer when the land had to be prepared and water pumped, the pressure on the labour force was severe even before the labour outflow. As a very rough indication of what the change in labour availability meant, the operations of seed-bed preparation, transplanting, pumping and weeding, which had to be carried out during the approximately four-month period between May and September, required in the 1900s and 1910s about 18 man/days per 10 ares altogether, of which 7 were for pumping.[15] The paddy area of Saga County was roughly 11,000 hectares at this time, so that in total 1,980,000 man/days had to be found for these operations.[j] In 1908 this meant about 95 man/days per male agricultural worker in the county, to be found over a period of about 120 days. By 1920 the labour force had fallen to the extent that it meant 125 man/days per male worker.

One obvious solution to this kind of problem would be the mechanisation of some of the operations concerned. However, since the abandonment of the Meiji government's early experiments with Western agricultural technology, there had been, virtually speaking, no development of mechanised techniques suitable for agricultural use in Japan. At this stage, therefore, there existed no machines which could be readily bought and utilised by Saga Plain farmers, and the option of mechanisation was, as yet, effectively ruled out. What responses could farmers then make, given that the basic structure of the irrigation technology had to remain unchanged?

Without giving up double-cropping, there was little that could be done to lengthen the period over which the operations could be performed. The first recourse, therefore, was to try to substitute other kinds of labour for the *nenko* and other local hired workers who were becoming so much more scarce and expensive. This meant chiefly greater and greater use of family labour, and the literature abounds with descriptions of the burden of work, chiefly pumping, imposed on the women and children and old people of the Saga Plain at this time. Children returning from school had to go straight out to help their mothers with the pumping.[16] It was said that fathers would not let daughters they cared for

j Strictly speaking, not absolutely all of Saga County's paddy area used creek irrigation, so that, since labour requirements in creek areas were higher than elsewhere, this total overestimates slightly.

marry into even quite rich Saga Plain families, if the prospective son-in-law's land was of a height to need several wheels.[17] But there was little alternative to such increasing pressure on the family labour force. One possible compromise expedient was to hire labour just for the peak months, from spring until 15 August, when weeding was over, and then to hire again at harvest time, if things got bad.[18] But this still could not open up to Saga farmers sources of labour from outside the immediate area, such as transplanting labour hired from areas where transplanting was completed. The relatively long period over which labour demand was at its peak meant that the bulk of the labour force must of necessity be resident for much of the year, and the only real substitute for local hired labour was family labour.

A further step was to try to reduce the amount of labour required, especially for pumping. One way was to raise the levels of the wheels a little, so that the paddles only half filled with water but one less wheel was needed to lift the water from creek level to field. The work was harder and longer but it reduced the number of workers needed simultaneously.[19] Beyond this, though, there was no way of reducing pumping labour requirements further without having deleterious effects on the efficiency of the technology. The next step, for instance, was to seek to lower the level of the field by removing soil from it. This made pumping easier, but also made the field harder to drain and was, in effect, a move back towards *shitsuden* farming, with fields permanently flooded and no double-cropping. Beyond this there was nothing but to begin to cut out operations or to perform them less thoroughly, to weed less often, to spend less time on insect control, so as to free more time for pumping. The ultimate step was to give up double-cropping. This postponed the deadline by which other operations had to be completed and saved labour at the autumn peak so that workers hired just for the spring and summer would be enough.

There are, of course, no direct measures of the extent to which Saga farmers used these technical expedients, but it is reflected in two indirect forms, firstly, in the relative stagnation in yield growth, and secondly in the reduction in double-cropping. As we saw in the last chapter, rice yields on the Plain in the late 1910s were little if any higher than those of the mid-1900s. This stagnation occurred at a time when the price of rice was rising fast and there was every incentive to try to produce and sell more. Its causes lie, as was argued earlier, in Saga Plain farmers' difficulties in adopting yield-increasing techniques, but labour shortage clearly intensified these difficulties, making the use of improved labour-using methods less likely, offsetting the effects of the use of better seeds and more fertiliser by encouraging the neglect of weeding, and so on. The effect of labour shortage on double-cropping can be seen in the quite sudden decline in the late 1910s in the paddy area planted with a second grain crop, which for the prefecture as a whole fell from around 30,000 hectares in 1916 to 23,000 hectares in 1919 and had fallen below 20,000 by 1923.[20] For the Plain area, Chart 6.3 shows changes in the area planted to non-rice grain crops in Saga County. Since the major part of this area was taken up by wheat grown as a second crop on paddy land,[k] the figures are a clear reflection of the sharp decline in double-cropping after the mid-1900s.

It will be clear from this that the scope for substituting other inputs or other kinds of labour for hired labour without reducing yields was not very great. The attempt to do so led to extreme pressure on the remaining labour force and ultimately there was little option but to abandon the effort to adopt the more intensive techniques whch would have provided a way of producing more to meet the growing demand for marketed grain. Given, therefore, that the possibilities for technical response to the changed factor supply situation were, in the present state of knowledge, rather limited, it was upon the economic organisation of production that the burden of response would have to fall, and it is to this economic response that we now turn.

(2)   THE IMPACT ON FARM HOUSEHOLD ECONOMIES

What kinds of economic or structural response were the farmers of the Saga Plain forced to make to the changes brought about by industrialisation? While the technology operated by Saga Plain farmers was much the same for all types and scales of farm, the economic structure of farm households varied, and to answer this question it is necessary to look at the problem from the points of view of the two basic types of farm household which, as we saw earlier, made up the Saga village community. The differential effect of industrialisation on farm households of different types can then be seen to explain the changes in the structure of agricultural communities to be examined in the next section.

1.   The Small-Scale Cultivator/Agricultural Labourer Household
Those households at the bottom of the size distribution of cultivated holdings, who owned or rented in areas of, say, less than half a hectare, and

---

[k] For some years, the prefectural yearbook figures are broken down into paddy and non-paddy areas, revealing the predominance of second-crop wheat on the Plain. For example, the breakdown for 1910–14 averages out as follows:

	Barley		Wheat		Naked Barley	
	Upland	Paddy	Upland	Paddy	Upland	Paddy
Hectares	47·5	265·6	621·8	2,913·5	311·3	786·0

Chart 6.3: *Area Planted to Non-Rice Grain Crops (wheat, barley and naked barley) in Saga County, 1893–1939*

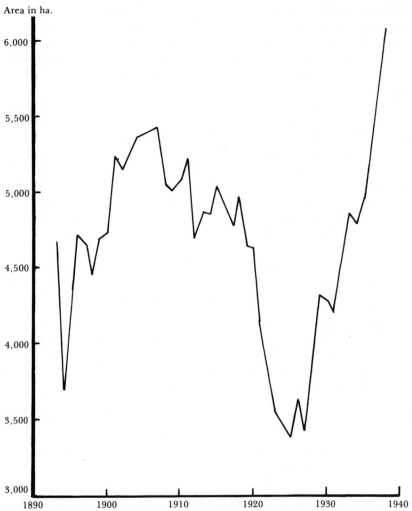

Area in ha.

Source: *Saga-Ken Tōkei Sho* (101), data as in Appendix Table 2.

who relied on wages earned as agricultural labourers to provide an essential part of household income, were faced with a new choice as a result of the expansion of employment opportunities. This choice was, by and large, a fairly straight one, between remaining a farming household, possibly earning higher wages for outside labour and perhaps with the chance of acquiring more land, or moving sons and daughters, or even the whole household, to the city to become urban industrial workers. The kinds of intermediate choice, such as commuting from the farm to industrial work or engaging in industrial side-employment on the farm, which were open to farm households in some areas, were not really feasible for Saga Plain farmers.

What considerations were operative on the farm household faced with this choice? On the side of moving to the cities, there seems little doubt that the differential between agricultural wages and the money income which the migrant could potentially earn in industrial employment was significant (see e.g. Table 6.8). Given the rapid expansion of employment by the major companies of northern Kyūshū, the individual worker's chance of eventually obtaining a good job in such a company must have been quite high. This had to be offset to some extent by the fact that living costs for urban dwellers would certainly have been higher than those for the partially self-sufficient small-scale cultivator, and were rising fast in the period leading up to the Rice Riots. Industrial employment was in some respects more regular and stable than agricultural labouring, but perhaps what it offered above all to the increasingly educated sons and daughters of rural families was the prospect of improving income and status which agricultural employment could not provide. In addition, it should not be forgotten that agricultural labour on the Saga Plain was physically extremely hard and any opportunity to escape might be welcomed by those facing the long summer months spent pumping water.

What the migrant to industrial employment lost was the security and insurance of subsistence that membership of the village community brought with it. However, the insurance of subsistence was valuable to the small-scale farmer only on the assumption that the opportunities for alternative employment were very limited. The expansion of industrial employment thus took away much of the basis for the inter-household relationships which had provided subsistence insurance. The expansion of outside employment opportunities offered the farm worker the chance to opt for employment based on market relationships rather than community ones, and it is clear from what we have seen already that many Saga Plain farm workers found the choice of market-based outside employment more attractive.

The expansion of outside employment opportunities, however, also opened up the possibility of improved conditions for those who chose to remain. The wages they could earn for their work as hired agricultural workers were being steadily pulled up by labour shortage. In addition, in order to match the attractions of industrial work, employers found themselves having to raise the status of their *nenko*, and to accept that the relationship between employer and employee was becoming a market rather than a social one. Written contracts became more common, farm workers were called 'farm managers' or 'salaryman farmers', and they took to bringing their own lunches with them rather than be provided with food by their employer, a gesture indicative of the increased independence of the worker.[21]

In addition to higher wages and status, the labour outflow opened up increasing possibilities for those who remained to acquire more land to farm. This land included, as we shall see shortly, both that of those leaving agriculture and that released by larger-scale cultivators forced to reduce the area they farmed. Rising wages and the rising price of rice provided sources of savings to use to buy this land and the capital equipment needed to farm a larger area. In general, therefore, just as higher industrial wages pulled up agricultural wages, so the opportunity provided by industrial work for improved status and prospects pulled up the status and prospects of agricultural workers.

2. The Medium-Scale Cultivator/Labour-Employer Household

As we saw in chapter 4, households cultivating over about 1½ hectares rarely had enough family labour, given the technical system in use, to cultivate without the use of hired labour employed for relatively long periods of the year to do relatively skilled and heavy work. The expansion of industrial employment opportunities and the consequent outflow of agricultural workers presented such households with severe problems. As we saw earlier, the scope for technical adaptation and factor substitution was limited. Those with holdings of around 1−2 hectares could try to substitute more family labour for hired labour, but for those farming holdings larger than this there was no technical expedient whereby they could manage without hired labour. What choices, then, were open to such households as means of responding to the changed situation?

It was, of course, open to farmers of this sort to leave agriculture, just as it was to their farm workers. However, the more land a household owned and the more capital it had invested in the means of production necessary to farm a larger area, the less sure could it be of earning an equivalent income or status outside agriculture. The richest landowners with capital to spare did, like their counterparts elsewhere, begin to invest outside the agricultural sector in industry and banking,[22] but the medium-scale village cultivator class, having no particular skills away from agriculture, had more to lose and only very uncertain prospects of improvement from abandoning agriculture. They might well invest in the education of their younger children, and send them out to white-collar work in the cities, but they were less likely to want to abandon agriculture than those either above or below them in the size distribution of holdings. In addition, the high demand for, and rising price of, rice made farming potentially very profitable if the labour supply problem could be dealt with.

If such a household was to remain in agriculture and maintain ownership of at least a substantial part of its holding, there were two possible paths to follow. One was to continue cultivating and pay the level of wages necessary to retain the required hired labour, i.e. wages comparable to those which could be earned in industry. The alternative was to reduce the area cultivated to a size manageable with family labour and rent out the remaining land, or possibly sell some and invest the resulting capital elsewhere. The appendix to this chapter contains some very rough calculations of the economic positions of households farming varying sizes of holding during this period to illustrate the choices facing them. These calculations suggest that, in about 1920, the income from rice cultivation of a household owning five hectares would have been greater had it farmed one hectare itself and let out the remaining four than if it had farmed the whole area itself, even at the wage rates then prevailing. These wage rates were in fact well below those earned in industry, and had the household been forced to pay wages comparable to industrial ones in order to obtain a labour force, the gains from renting out land compared with cultivating it directly would have been even greater. For a household owning two hectares, the income obtainable from the two alternatives was almost exactly the same, provided it could manage with only one hired labourer and it was able to find such a worker at the prevailing agricultural wage rate. Attempts to repeat this calculation for an earlier period before the impact of industrialisation was felt are beset with data problems. However the attempts do tend to confirm the conclusion that in the 1880s and 1890s the configuration of rice price, labour supply and yields was still such as to make it worthwhile for households owning larger areas to cultivate most of the land themselves, but that somewhere around 1900 this configuration changed, putting such households under pressure to reduce their scale of cultivation. It was after this that it began to become more profitable for a larger-scale landowner to reduce his scale of cultivation rather than continue farming himself, if he had to pay wage rates comparable to those in industry. This would explain why the labour shortage did not generate the pressure to push wage rates up more sharply than the national average.

*

This analysis of the choices facing farmers suggests that the economic pressures of the 1900–20 period would be leading to a decline in the numbers of households farming very small holdings, as a result of both

Table 6.9: *Changes in the Distribution of Households by Area Cultivated in Saga Prefecture*
(Units = households)

Cultivated area (ha.)	1908	change 1908−18	change 1918−28	change 1928−38	1938	change 1908−38
Under 0·5	25,480	− 4274	− 2837	− 1843	16,526	− 8954
0·5−1	24,892	+ 452	− 405	− 4074	20,875	− 4017
1−2	12,927	+ 3992	+ 1858	+ 2564	21,341	+ 8414
2−3	5,889	− 1362	− 149	+ 688	5,066	− 823
3−5	1,587	− 503	− 335	+ 188	934	− 653
Above 5	323	− 224	− 62	− 11	26	− 297
Total	71,098	− 1909	− 1933	− 2458	64,768	− 6330

Source: Kamagata, I., *Saga Nōgyō* (71), p.180, from data as in Appendix Table 5.

out-migration and the acquisition of more land by the former small-scale cultivators, and a tendency for larger landowners to be reducing their scale of cultivation in response to the reduced availability of hired labour. That this is what did happen will be shown in the next section.

(3)   CHANGES IN THE AGRICULTURAL STRUCTURE

The evidence for the kind of choices which Saga Plain farmers did in fact make in the face of the changed situation caused by the impact of industrialisation is to be found in the data on changes in the agricultural structure, as exemplified in changes in the size distribution of holdings. The prefectural yearbook gives long-term data on holding size only for the prefecture as a whole, but the trends are clearly visible in these figures, as Table 6.9 shows. At the bottom end of the scale, the ten years between 1908 and 1918 saw a 17% decline in the number of households farming less than half a hectare. This decline must have been composed of the movement of some households up into larger-scale categories, and of the abandonment of agriculture by others as part of the much larger outflow of farm labour taking place at this time. At the other end of the scale, 224 out of the 323 households initially farming more than five hectares had given up cultivating areas of this size by 1918, and 32% of those farming 3−5 hectares had similarly reduced their scale of cultivation. Conversely, the number of households farming 0·5−1 and 1−2 hectares rose sharply as the larger farmers reduced their scale of cultivation and smaller farmers picked up the land thus released.

For the Plain area, there exists one set of estimates for the size distribution of cultivated holdings in the early 1920s in Saga County.[23]

Area cultivated (hectares)	0−0·5	·5−1	1−2	2−3	3−5	over 5	total
Percentage of households	20·9	25·8	35·4	14·1	2·7	0·1	100·0

If this is compared with the picture of the structure of holdings on the Plain in the second half of the nineteenth century (see e.g. Table 4.1), the decline in the proportion of households farming both larger and smaller areas is clear. By the beginning of the 1920s over half the households in Saga Plain villages appear to have been farming somewhere between a half and two hectares.

Something of the way in which these changes took place can be gathered from the data on changes in the size distribution of owned holdings and in the ownership status of cultivators. The official prefectural data provide the following picture of changes in the percentage distribution of owned holdings over the 1908−18 period for the prefecture as a whole:[24]

Owned Area (hectares)	0−·5	·5−1	1−3	3−5	5−10	10−50	over 50
Percentage of Households:							
1908	35·98	35·61	20·57	5·21	1·82	0·74	0·07
1918	42·75	31·75	19·36	4·07	1·44	0·58	0·05

This suggests that the land released by larger-scale landowners, was being bought in small parcels by those who had previously owned little or no land, causing a rise in the proportion of very small-scale landowners. The increase in the numbers of medium-scale cultivators was thus not reflected in a rise in the proportion of medium-scale landowners. Nor does there appear to have been any change in the proportion of the cultivated area which was tenanted.[1] Table 6.10 shows that what was in fact taking place was a gradual increase in the proportion of households both owning and renting in land, matched by declines in the proportions of both pure tenant and pure landowner households.[m]

These changes are reflections of the mechanisms through which the rise of the medium-scale cultivator took place. They show how the

---

[1] This remained at around 42−43% for the prefecture as a whole and around 45% for Saga County during the 1910s and 1920s.

[m] The prefectural yearbook gives some data for the distribution of agricultural workers (not households) by tenure status at the county level. These data for Saga County fluctuate rather violently from year to year but show the same trends as those for households at the prefectural level. The proportion of owner/tenants rose from 41·5% in 1905 to 52·6% in 1920, while that of pure owners fell from 38·0% to 27·5% and that of pure tenants from 20·5% to 19·9%. See Isobe, T., 'Iwayuru Saga Dankai' (70), p.30.

Table 6.10: *Changes in the Distribution of Agricultural Households by Tenure Status* (Saga Prefecture, %)

	Owners	Owner/tenants	Tenants
1891	34·7	36·0	29·3
1895	32·5	44·8	22·7
1900	34·9	46·3	18·8
1905	33·4	44·3	22·3
1910	31·3	45·1	23·6
1915	31·1	46·3	22·6
1920	30·6	47·0	22·4
1925	30·3	47·2	22·5
1930	31·4	47·2	21·4
1935	29·0	50·7	20·3
1940	29·0	50·5	20·5

Source: Kayō, N., *Nihon Nōgyō Kiso Tōkei* (68), p.83.

larger-scale landowners reduced their scale of cultivation partly by selling off some land and partly by renting out an increasing proportion. This process would stop when the household had reduced its cultivated area to what it could manage with its family labour force and such labour as it was still able to hire, i.e. to around 1−2 hectares.

Meanwhile, the small-scale owner or tenant cultivator who remained in agriculture would find that rising wages and the rising rice price provided him with the resources to acquire more land. The small-scale owner would begin by renting in some of the land increasingly becoming available as large-scale landowners reduced their area of cultivation. The small-scale tenant could begin to think about buying some of his holding from landlords increasingly willing to sell. This is reflected in evidence of a rising level of land sales, with banks in the Plain area reporting a rush to borrow money to buy land and many groups of villagers coming together to form mutual financing associations (*tanomoshi-kō*) in order to secure loans.[n] Small farmers' demand for land kept its price rising, as Table 6.11

---

[n] *Tanomoshi-kō* were club-like organisations made up of someone who wanted a loan and a group of people who would lend to him. Repayment took place at each meeting of the club, when members bid (or sometimes drew lots) for the sum available at that meeting. It was possible to withdraw the investment made in the club at any time, but the longer a member was able to wait, the bigger the return he would receive. For a full description of the complex way in which the system worked in Japanese villages, see Embree, J., *Suye Mura* (44), pp.138−47, and for exactly the same form of credit club operating in Vietnamese villages, see Sansom, R., *The Economics of Insurgency* (170), pp.114−21.

Table 6.11:   The Price of Land in Saga Prefecture
(Yen/10 ares of middle-grade paddy)

1913	293
1914	286
1915	271
1916	177
1917	347
1918	416
1919	671
1920	677
1921	658
1922	714
1923	614
1924	640
1925	625
1926	613
1927	635
1928	668
1929	645
1930	621
1931	509
1932	511
1933	498
1934	498
1935	519
1936	544
1937	646
1938	710

Source: Isobe, T., 'Iwayuru Saga Dankai' (70), p.33, taken from a survey of land sales made by the Hypothec Bank.

shows. Small-scale owners and tenants would continue to acquire more land, either by buying or by renting in, until they reached the limits of the area they could manage with the labour of those members of the family who stayed in agriculture, probably somewhere between 0·5 and 1·5 hectares, and both sorts would find themselves, in the course of their upward movement, falling into the owner/tenant category.

What was occurring could therefore be summarised as a shift away from the old structure composed of a group of medium-to-large employer/cultivators and the mass of small-scale cultivators/agricultural labourers, towards one in which the majority of households were 1–2 hectare, owner/tenant ones.

*

The data presented above therefore lead to the conclusion that the initial impact on Saga Plain agriculture of the development of industry in northern Kyūshū fell on the agricultural structure, there being little scope for factor substitution or technical adjustment as long as the basic infrastructure conditioning the technology remained unchanged. Increasing demand for industrial labour drove up industrial wage rates and drew off large numbers of agricultural workers, particularly from the Saga Plain which had good communications with the industrialising cities and a tradition of work for wages outside the household. Agricultural wages were pulled up and conditions of work improved, but not by enough to stem the labour outflow, employer farmers finding that, once the technical possibilities for saving labour had been exhausted, it was more profitable to reduce their scale of cultivation than to pay the level of wages required to retain hired workers. Meanwhile, those small-scale farmers who remained were able to increase their holdings towards the 1−2 hectare level which represented the limit to cultivation with family labour alone. But even for such households, the strain on the family labour force remained severe, and labour shortage stood in the way of the adoption of the kinds of intensive technique which would have enabled Saga Plain farmers to respond more fully to the increased demand for their product.

The development of modern heavy industry, with its demand for permanent, full-time, urban labour, had thus brought about a marked change in the agricultural structure by disrupting the intra-village employment system on which the old structure depended. But the new structure and the old technology could only with difficulty be made compatible with one another, and the solution to this disequilibrium could not be achieved without a fundamental change in the basis of the technology which would make it possible to save labour and generate the levels of labour productivity required to give incomes for farm workers comparable to those paid in industry. The development of local industry, however, combined with the structure of extension institutions described in chapter 5, also provided the means of solving this problem. The way in which this happened, and the degree to which the solution adopted was conditioned by the structural changes described here, are the subjects of the next chapter.

Appendix to Chapter 6

In order to give some content to the analysis of the choices facing farmers of different types on the Saga Plain in the 1900−20 period, I have attempted to reconstruct very simplified versions of the economic

Table 6.12:   Calculations of the Relative Income Positions of Saga Plain Households

Area cultivated (ha.)	0·5	1	2	2	5
Averages for 1918–22					
Rice yield (kg/10 ares)	380	380	380	380	380
∴ Output (kg)	1,900	3,800	7,600	7,600	19,000
Price of rice (¥ per 150 kg)	34·7	34·7	34·7	34·7	34·7
∴ Value of output (¥)	439·5	879·1	1,758·1	1,758·1	4,395·3
Hired labour requirement					
(persons per year)	−2	0	1	2	4
Wage rate	226	226	226	226	226
∴ Hired labour cost (¥)	+452	0	−226	−452	−904
Fertiliser cost (¥)	109·9	219·8	439·5	439·5	1,098·8
∴ Income (¥)	781·6	659·3	1,092·6	866·6	2,392·5
Income assuming wage rate =					
¥400 (¥)	1,129·6	659·3	918·6	518·6	1,696·5
Averages for 1903–7					
Yield (kg/10 ares)	366	366	366	366	366
Price of rice (¥ per 150 kg)	13·4	13·4	13·4	13·4	13·4
Rice output value (¥)	163·5	327·0	653·9	653·9	1,634·8
Fertiliser cost (¥)	40·9	81·7	163·5	163·5	408·7
Income, with wage = ¥100 (¥)	322·6	245·3	390·4	290·4	826·1
Income, with wage = ¥75 (¥)	272·6	245·3	415·4	340·4	926·1

Sources: see notes overleaf.

positions of households farming varying areas of land. Table 6.12 shows the basic accounting framework used, with the values for 1918–22 and some results of recalculating under different assumptions.

One or two words of caution are necessary. For simplicity the calculations only deal with rice production. They also ignore a number of costs, including rent, taxes and capital depreciation. Thus, although the values used are derived from the relevant statistical data, and some attempt is made to represent the largest non-labour input cost item (fertiliser), the neglect of both additional income from secondary marketed and subsistence crops and additional capital costs, taxes and rent means that the absolute levels of income derived should not be taken as accurate representations of the actual incomes of Saga Plain farmers at this time. The point of the calculations is not to determine absolute income levels but to illustrate the choices confronting different farmers as a result of the labour outflow, and the relative changes in economic position.

Notes to the Table

1. 1918−22: average values for the five-year period are used. This period represents the culmination of the 1900−20 boom for Saga Plain farmers, with the price of rice and the wage rate moving more or less in parallel (see Chart 6.2).

2. Area cultivated: 0·5 hectares represents the farm of a small-scale cultivator/agricultural labourer, 1 hectare a stable, family-sized farm, 2 hectares a medium-scale employer/cultivator like Family S, and 5 hectares a large-scale employer/cultivator such as Family N.

3. Output: rice yields for Saga County have been taken from the prefectural yearbook.[25] There exists no evidence to suggest that yields varied with the scale of cultivation. The technology employed, and much of the capital equipment used, by large-scale and small-scale cultivators was the same, and since members of small-scale cultivating households spent much of their time working on other holdings, there is less reason than for other areas to suppose that they applied more labour to their own holdings than larger-scale farmers. The first survey evidence for Saga Plain farms relating yields to scale, the Rice Economy Survey of 1913−15,[26] shows no systematic variation, although the survey did not cover any very small farms.

4. The price of rice: from the prefectural yearbook.

5. Hired labour requirement: this is very hard to estimate since the available information on individual households shows considerable variation in the sizes of labour forces used. Much would depend on the size of the family and on the extent to which short-term hired labour could be utilised. The calculations for the half-hectare farm are based on the assumption that it could send out two workers at the prevailing male *nenko* wage rate. One couple would have been able to manage the cultivation of 0·5 hectares, so the income from wage employment would depend basically on the number, age and sex of this couple's children. A househead couple with their successor and his wife would have been able to manage a one-hectare farm quite easily, and one hectare is generally taken to be about the size of farm cultivable by family labour alone. As a general rule, one *nenko* was required for every hectare cultivated in excess of one, so that a two-hectare farm would need one *nenko*, and two of the households in the Rice Economy Survey cultivating 2 and 2·5 hectares respectively indeed employed one *nenko* in addition to four family members. However, Family S employed two *nenko* on slightly less than two hectares, and one of the Rice Economy Survey households used a total labour force of six on exactly two hectares. The calculation is therefore repeated for a two-hectare household employing two *nenko* because it reveals the pressure on this sort of household to save labour. By the rule of thumb, the five-hectare holding would need

four *nenko*. Household N, cultivating five hectares, employed three *nenko*, in addition to a family labour force of two couples, but was said to use considerable amounts of temporary labour as well. The six-hectare farm in the Rice Economy Survey employed four *nenko* in addition to a family labour force of five.

6. Wage rate: from the prefectural yearbook, unless otherwise specified.

7. Fertiliser expenses: these are estimated simply by taking 25% of the value of rice output. This accords with the results of the Rice Economy Survey, and with the available data for Saga County in the 1920s in the prefectural yearbook.

ALTERNATIVE ASSUMPTIONS

1. 1918–22 with a wage rate of ¥400: ¥400 is the annual income of an employee of the Nagasaki Shipbuilding Company who worked 250 days in a year during 1918–22 (see Table 6.8). It is taken as a rough estimate of what a Saga Plain employer would have had to pay to be assured of being able to hire a worker. There are instances of farmers actually paying considerably more than this.[27]

2. 1903–7: reliable data do not exist to enable us to make this calculation for a period before the rises in prices and wages set in. For 1903–7, when these rises were just beginning, there are data for the rice price and for yields, but prefectural yearbook wage data only begin in 1906 and, as Chart 6.2 showed, are somewhat erratic for the first few years, rising from ¥91 p.a. in 1906 to ¥156 in 1907 and 1908, then falling to around ¥100 for the next few years. The prefectural government surveys give a rate of ¥75 in 1909 gradually rising to ¥100 by 1913.[28] The table shows the results of the calculations for 1903–7 using alternatively ¥100 and ¥75 as estimates of the wage rate.

3. 1888: the Nōji Chōsa provides the data needed to make a very rough calculation for 1888 for the prefecture as a whole. Its yield figure of 250 kg /10 ares is probably lower than the yields for the Plain area. It gives a rice price of ¥4·25 per 150 kg, and wage rates for men ranging from top rates of ¥30 for skilled *nenko* to between ¥7 and ¥15 for less skilled or strong annual workers.[29] On the basis of previous discussion, fertiliser costs could be estimated at 10% of the value of rice output at this time. The results of this calculation are not shown in the table but are discussed below.

IMPLICATIONS

1. The calculations make clear that, for households farming half a hectare or less who had family members who could earn the going *nenko*

wage, income from outside employment was more significant than income from rice cultivation. This would be even more so for those farming smaller areas and those who rented part of their holding. Non-rice crops offset this a little, but it remains clear that outside employment was not, for these households, just a subsidiary job to supplement profits from cultivation, but a major source of income. In many cases, the maximisation of such income could more than offset the loss of income from cultivation. On the assumptions made here, such households would need to raise their scale of cultivation to something over a hectare before they could earn as much from cultivation as from sending workers out. However, the assumptions are rather favourable to the small-scale farm, ignoring rent, income from second crops and so on, and assuming that two family members could continue to earn the full *nenko* wage rate.

2. What these calculations most help to illustrate is the larger-scale farmer's choice between direct cultivation and renting out land. They show that, for 1918–22, a household owning five hectares would earn slightly more from rice cultivation if it reduced the area it farmed itself to one hectare (thereby avoiding the problem of trying to recruit labour) and let out the remaining four hectares as one-hectare holdings, than it would from farming five hectares directly (i.e. assuming a rental rate of 50% of the rice crop, its new income would be ¥659·3 from direct cultivation + ¥1,758 from rents = ¥2,417). In fact, to obtain the necessary labour it would probably have had to pay more than the recorded wage rate, which was insufficient to stop the labour outflow, in which case the gains from giving up direct cultivation would have been even greater. The two-hectare farm employing one *nenko* would earn almost exactly the same from direct cultivation as from renting out one hectare and farming the other, so that, taking account of further income from second crops, it was still viable in this sense. At a wage rate of ¥400, however, it was not.

3. The calculations for 1903–7 suggest that around that time there occurred the turning-point after which the larger-scale cultivator had more to gain from letting out land than from farming it himself. This is because, at the higher estimate of the wage rate for this period, it pays the five-hectare farmer to let out four hectares as in 1918–22 (income = ¥899·3), but at the lower estimate it does not. At both rates, the decision to rent out one hectare is marginal for the two-hectare farmer with one *nenko* (total income from renting out = ¥408·8).

4. Using the available 1888 data and taking ¥15 as an average *nenko* wage rate, it does not pay either the five-hectare farm or the two-hectare farm with one *nenko* to let out land. The income from farming one hectare and letting out one hectare gives even the two-hectare farm

which has to use two *nenko* a marginal choice (¥99 from renting out, ¥97·5 from direct cultivation). If all labour had to be paid ¥30 it would just pay both the five-hectare and two-hectare farms to let out land, but this is an extreme assumption and ignores second-crop income which would probably tip the balance towards direct cultivation.

CHAPTER SEVEN

The Choice of an Appropriate Technique: the Mechanisation of Irrigation Pumping 1920–23

The object of this chapter is to tell the story of the development and implementation over a large part of the Saga Plain of what would nowadays be called a project for the mechanisation of the irrigation system. In this I shall consider some of the questions raised in chapter 1 as to the forces conditioning the characteristics of new techniques developed, as they apply in the context of Japanese agricultural change. The chapter seeks to show how the institutional environment which we have seen developing in Saga over the preceding years made it possible to produce a highly appropriate new technique and to implement successfully a large-scale scheme for its diffusion. It will also show how the impact of industrialisation was an important factor conditioning both the ability to develop and introduce new agricultural techniques and the particular characteristics of those techniques selected. The longer-term economic effects of the project will be considered in chapter 8.

1. The Nature of the Problem

We saw in the last chapter how the outflow of labour from Saga Plain villages in the 1900s and 1910s had led to severe problems with the operation of the existing technology. More or less the only response which farm households were able to make was to change the structure of holdings so as to be able to make maximum use of family labour forces. Even so, the strain on the labour force was intense, and households were obliged to make what adjustments they could to lessen the amount of labour required, even where this meant lowering yields or abandoning double-cropping. It is clear from the nature of the adjustments which farmers tried to make (e.g. lowering field levels, cutting down the numbers of wheels used, etc.) that the focus of the problem was the amount of labour needed to raise water. It was the need for human power to lift water into the fields that made the Saga Plain different from other areas and caused the effects of the labour outflow to be so severe.

Beyond this, even without the decline in the labour force, it was clear to many of those concerned with Saga Plain agriculture that the irrigation technology was the bottleneck preventing farmers taking full advantage of the advances in agricultural techniques then available. The immediate cause of Saga Plain farmers' problems in using *Meiji Nōhō* techniques, improved seed varieties and so on was the risk of rice-borer damage, but the underlying cause of that, as the experiment with planting one late crop had shown, was the labour requirements of the irrigation technology which made the use of the phased rotation unavoidable. Of course any technical change which helped to reduce labour requirements in the peak spring and summer months would be welcome, but pumping absorbed such a large proportion of the available time that reduction in the amount of work it required was the only way to free enough labour to make it possible to abandon the phased rotation. Pumping was a basic manual task, and a reduction in the amount of time that had to be devoted to it would release the skilled labour of farm families for the more careful work required for intensive farming, and the physically exhausting task of pumping was, above all others, the job which Saga farmers wanted to avoid.

For all these reasons, then, the problems experienced by Saga Plain farmers after about 1900 all tended to focus on the need to reduce the labour required for irrigation, and the search for some way of substituting capital for labour in the pumping process began to gain momentum during the 1910s. Then in 1920 the search was given added urgency by the collapse of the boom in rice prices, causing a sudden divergence in the trends of the rice price and of agricultural wage rates (see Chart 6.2). With wages still rising but the price of rice falling, the pressure to break the barrier which prevented farmers from producing more and reducing their costs became intense and, as we shall see shortly, 1922 and 1923 saw the achievement of the dramatic change in the irrigation technology which made this possible.

Before describing this, however, it is important to consider, given that some form of mechanisation of the pumping process had become essential, the background conditioning the kinds of technique which could be successfully developed and diffused on the Saga Plain of the early 1920s. The mechanisation of water-lifting requires a combination of some kind of mechanical pump, a motor of some sort to drive the pump, and a source of power for the motor. As we shall see, although there were by this time some examples in Japan of the use of mechanical power in irrigation, there existed no ready-made pump and motor sets from which to choose the one which met the requirements of the Saga Plain. It was therefore necessary to devise a combination of pump, motor and power source, and there were a number of ways in which they could be combined, involving different sets of technical characteristics — different scale, different levels of technical sophistication, and so on.[a] The choice of such a set would be conditioned, as argued in chapter 1, by such factors as the prevailing, historically determined state of technical development, the technology presently in use in related production operations, the existing organisation of production, and the selection procedures of decision-makers. I shall examine the determinants of this choice in the case of Saga in terms of three questions facing the decision-makers concerned.

(1) What sorts of machinery could be made available to Saga Plain farmers around 1920?

There are two sides to this question, the first concerning the stage of development of the supply of the relevant machinery by that time in Japan, and the second concerning the possibilities of supplying what was available at a national level in a relatively remote rural area like Saga. The power source was the crucial factor from which most of the other characteristics followed, and there were three possibilities which could be considered available for use in irrigation projects at that time:

1. Steam. The majority of the projects in operation in Japan in 1920 in which motor power was utilised for irrigation or drainage used steam engines, and Table 7.1 shows that, up till the early 1910s, over 90% of the horse-power used for lifting water in agriculture was provided by steam engines. Most of these projects were large-scale irrigation or drainage schemes which required large, static power sources. The average horse-power of the machines in use was 45 in 1908 and 85 in 1926.[1] The engines were heavy and immobile, necessitating the construction of a large number of channels to carry water from the pump/motor to the fields. They required operators and a supply of fuel, and were in general not well suited to producing a constant supply of power over a wide area. Their use reflects the fact that until the 1900s and 1910s steam was the chief power source used in Japanese industry, hence steam engines were virtually the only form of power that was easily available for these early projects. However, while over 75% of the machines used in Japanese industry in 1906 were steam-powered, by 1917 this proportion had fallen to 20% and by 1926 to zero.[2] Hence steam engines were more or

---

[a] The resulting technique can hardly be called an invention, but it represented a set of mechanical devices not used before in Japan in the same combination and for the same purpose.

Table 7.1:   *Motors Used for Lifting Water in Agriculture*
(whole country, schemes over 5 h.p. total)

	1908	1912	1920	1926	1935
Number of schemes					
Electric	2	42	216	738	
Steam	145	251	325	188	
Oil	14	55	181	227	
Other	2	14	178	221	
Total	163	362	900	1,405	2,632
Number of motors					
Electric	2	48		2,299	3,878
Steam	167	294		243	82
Oil	14	52		284	582
Other	3	14		237	104
Total	186	408		3,103	4,903
% of horse power					
Electric	0·3	5·4	22·3	50·2	71·5
Steam	97·0	91·5	65·1	33·8	6·9
Oil	2·7	2·4	3·4	4·7	5·4
Other	—	0·8	9·2	11·3	16·2
Total	100	100	100	100	100

Source: *Nihon Nōgyō Hattatsu Shi* (55), vol. 6, p.225, from surveys of water-lifting machinery made by the Ministry of Agriculture.

less obsolete by 1920, though they were still the most commonly used and best-developed type of power source for irrigation projects.

2. Electricity. It was to electric power that most of Japanese industry was being converted during the 1900s and 1910s.[3] Electricity generating capacity grew very fast and the domestic electrical machinery industry began to develop. The first known use of an electric motor in agriculture was in 1902, and subsequently other isolated cases of the use of electricity were recorded in irrigation and for powering threshers and polishers and tea-processing machines in Shizuoka.[4] However, the use of electricity in agriculture did not develop widely before 1920 because electricity companies were unwilling to bear the costs of laying supply lines to rural areas at a time when much more profitable industrial uses for electricity were easy to find, especially as there existed no suitable small-scale electric motors which could use the same DC supply required for lighting and heating.[5] Potentially, though, electric motors had many advantages for agricultural uses, where what was required were motors which were simple to operate and maintain and which could run

for long periods. Electric motors could also potentially be used both for irrigation or drainage pumping and for powering small machines such as threshers.

What spurred the spread of the use of electricity in agriculture was the collapse, around 1920, of the World War I boom, which left electricity suppliers with considerable spare capacity. This resulted in a competitive war which led to the oligopolisation of the industry and the creation of regional monopolies. Smaller local companies, who found themselves cut out of the urban electricity markets, turned to rural areas in their search for outlets for their excess capacity, and although the cost of laying cables was high, the provision of electricity for agricultural use had its attractions, since the peak demand was in the spring and summer when other sources of demand were at their lowest.[6] The period after 1920 therefore saw a considerable expansion of the electricity supply network into rural areas and a concerted effort by electricity companies and suppliers of electrical equipment to encourage the use of electric motors in agriculture. However, the designs of small-scale motors available in the early 1920s were still those adapted to industrial uses, requiring AC current, and it was not until 1925 that Hitachi successfully developed a suitable small-scale electric motor which could be plugged into the mains supply.[7]

3. Oil. Although there were instances of the use of oil-driven motors in Japan before 1900, domestic production and use of them did not spread until some time later, and from around 1920 industrial use of oil motors declined again as electricity became predominant. Some were used in agriculture before 1920, but mostly in processing operations, especially in tea production.[b] These motors were almost all imported and had a number of characteristics which made them unsuitable for small-scale irrigation use. They were heavy and difficult to move about,[c] and their fuel consumption was high. They were also complex to maintain, noisy and dangerous. Nevertheless, they were used for irrigation purposes in the early 1920s, chiefly in Okayama, the area which pioneered the use of small-scale oil-powered motors, where an industry supplying, maintaining, and eventually producing them grew up. As domestic production of suitable oil-powered motors developed, they came to be quite widely used in agriculture, especially during the 1930s.

*

[b] 1,023 out of the 1,785 oil-driven motors in agricultural use in 1920 were in Shizuoka, a major tea-growing area. *Nihon Nōgyō Hattatsu Shi* (55), vol. 6, p.195.

[c] The lightest imported motor available in the early 1920s weighed 274 kg for a horsepower of 1·5, whereas the Kubota 2·5 h.p. Japanese-made motor available in 1930 weighed 125 kg. *Nihon Nōgyō Hattatsu Shi* (55), vol. 6, p.196.

Around 1920, therefore, the development of motors suitable for use in irrigation schemes was in general still in its early stages and there was no obvious or easily available method to choose. In addition, turning to the second aspect of the problem, there were no specialist, national-level suppliers of machinery suitable for use in agriculture, so that, as in the case of oil motors in Okayama, much would depend on the existence of local-level facilities for bringing together equipment imported or produced elsewhere and not specifically designed for agricultural use. Saga is not, at first sight, the sort of place where such facilities might be expected to have grown up. However, it was an area with a long tradition of involvement in mining, and associated metal-working trades, and with close connections, through Sasebo, with shipping and shipbuilding. These were industries in which the use of pumps and relatively small motors was important. As a result, there did exist in Saga City a company with considerable experience in producing power-driven machinery and its components.

The origins of this company go back to 1877, when a resident of Saga whose name was Masaki set up a factory for the production of machines to make noodles. He developed an improved design of noodle-making machine on whch he held a patent — the first patent granted to anyone in Saga. His machines were sold all over the country and he is said to have employed 70–100 people in his factory around 1910.[8] After 1910, he began to branch out into the manufacture of various electrical machines and high pressure turbine pumps, and in 1916 he became an accredited supplier to the naval arsenal at Sasebo.[9] This side of the business was at this time doing much better than the noodle-making machine side, and in 1918 he separated it off to form a new company called Nihon Denki Tekkō K.K. (Japan Electrical Machinery and Metal-Working Company). A new factory was built in Saga City, employing about 250 people, and the company advertised itself as able to produce electrical machinery, generators, electricity distribution equipment, turbine pumps, mining machinery, etc.[10] In 1919 the company was doing well, with orders pouring in from its main customers, the Sasebo arsenal and the local mining companies.[11] The collapse of the World War I boom, though, put an end to this, and around about 1920, Nihon Denki, like the electricity companies, found itself with spare capacity, searching for ideas for possible orders to remedy the situation.[12]

The company was by this time run by the founder's oldest son. The technical side, however, was the concern of another of his sons, who had graduated in engineering from Kyōto University. The company also at this time employed a German engineer who had formerly worked for

Siemens.[d] Given the growing movement of people between Saga and the North Kyūshū industrial centres, it seems likely that the company was also able to employ shop-floor workers with some experience of industrial work. Mr. Hayashida, for instance, who worked for Nihon Denki at this time, had previously been employed in the mines around Sasebo.[e] In addition, through the earlier success of the noodle-making machine the company had built up contacts in industrial circles in the big cities of Honshū.

What Nihon Denki possessed, then, was the technical capacity, knowledge and connections to be able to put together a set of pumping equipment and supply it to farmers under the conditions of 1920, when there existed no specially designed machinery for agricultural use and no national distribution mechanisms. We can now turn to the second question, which concerns the factors conditioning the sort of machinery this company would need to supply.

(2) What sort of machines could Saga Plain farmers effectively use?
The kinds of machinery available for use in irrigation projects around 1920 varied in many technical respects, but the most significant from the point of view of farmer-users were probably (a) the scale or size of the machine, (b) its mobility, i.e. whether it had to be operated statically or could be moved from field to field, and (c) its technical complexity, determining how easy it was to operate and maintain.

By 1920 it was clear that any irrigation machinery to be used on the Saga Plain would have to be operated by small-to-medium-scale farmers. As we have already seen, by this time the majority of households in Saga Plain villages farmed holdings of ½ −2 hectares, and as we shall

[d] He had been taken as a prisoner-of-war during World War I and held in a prison in Kurume, near Saga. Instead of returning home at the end of the war, he decided to stay in Japan and took up a three-year contract with Nihon Denki. He apparently turned out to be something of a disappointment to the Masakis, who found that his knowledge was of no great use to them, and he parted from them at the end of his contract on less than good terms. *Togami Denki no Arubumu* (a photographic history of the Togami Electric Company, produced by the company in 1973), p.16. I am grateful to Professor Susumu Nagano of Saga University for this reference and for extensive help in finding out about Nihon Denki.

[e] Mr. Hayashida, who is eighty-three at the time of writing, was born on the Saga Plain, where his father farmed twenty ares. The family migrated to Sasebo in 1904 and Mr. Hayashida went to school and began work there. On his retirement Mr. Hayashida Senior wanted to return to Saga, and it was then that his son went to work for Nihon Denki, where he was employed until his own retirement. Mr. Hayashida was kind enough to talk to me for many hours, and his recollections of Nihon Denki's part in the mechanisation project have provided a valuable source of information for this chapter.

see later, it was farmers with holdings of around this size who were most active in pressing for mechanisation in the villages. The Saga Plain therefore no longer possessed the potential for the emergence of the kinds of pioneering large-scale landowner, found in other areas, who had bought steam engines or gone off to investigate and buy large electric motors.[13] It followed that if farmers were to buy and operate irrigation pumps and motors individually, the machinery would have to be very small (for technical and financial reasons) and mobile (i.e. usable on an individual household's scattered plots). If the equipment was acquired and operated by farmers in groups, then it could be larger and, if these groups owned neighbouring plots, static, but the greater the capacity of the individual pump/motor, the further would the water it pumped up have to be carried, and the more channels would therefore have to be constructed, taking up valuable rice-growing land. The choice of scale and mobility therefore hinged on the question of whether — and, if so, how — farmers could share the use of pumps, and on the complex balance between the size and efficiency of the motor and the need to sacrifice land in order to make distribution channels.

On the question of the degree of technical complexity with which Saga Plain farmers could cope, most workers under about forty would have had some years of compulsory education and would probably have been able to read and write. There might have been a few who had spent some time at the agricultural college and returned to their family farms, but most who had obtained any educational qualifications would have used this as a means to find work outside agriculture. The majority of farmers would therefore rely on the local extension staff, and possibly on the enthusiast farmers of the neighbourhood, to teach them anything new they had to learn about farming. As we have seen, considerable efforts were put into teaching in this way, but such a system could not give farmers experience of matters which were not of direct, practical relevance to their existing cultivation methods. Given that most farmers, in their day-to-day lives, would be unlikely to come across any equipment more complex than a bicycle or rotary weeder, their experience with machinery was limited.[f] Those who had worked in the mines,

---

[f] Cf. Embree's list of the machines in existence in the village (*mura*, 285 households) he surveyed in Kumamoto Prefecture, just to the south of Saga, in 1935–6. Bicycles were quite common and had been available for twenty-five years or so. There were also a few sewing machines, dating back as long as thirty years. All households had had pedal-driven threshers for some time, and many had rope-making machines. Petrol-driven motors, threshers and hullers had begun to appear within the ten years prior to the survey, but there was only a scattering of radios, one telephone, one motor-bike and still no cars. *Suye Mura* (44), pp.34–7.

or in some aspect of the shipping industry, or who had been away to work in the cities and had returned, might have more experience of equipment such as pumps and motors, but in many villages the skills necessary to operate and maintain complicated machinery would not exist. It was therefore an important criterion in the choice of technique that machinery should be able to run reliably for long periods and not require a great deal of mechanical knowledge for its operation and maintenance.

(3) How, institutionally, could the diffusion of mechanised irrigation technology be organised?

Given the answers so far obtained to questions 1 and 2, the conclusion follows that it would be difficult for irrigation machinery simply to be marketed by suppliers to individual farmers. The supplying industry was not yet sufficiently well developed to distribute suitable equipment easily, and farmers lacked the knowledge necessary to go out and find what they needed. In addition, given that most purchasers would be farmers of relatively small areas, there was the question of where they could obtain the finance for the purchase of relatively expensive machinery. Also, since the irrigation system was in many ways the communal property of village and supra-village groups, and its use was governed by generations of customary practice, it was difficult for individual farm households to contemplate changes in irrigation technology in isolation from the groups to which they belonged. This was a less significant factor than in other areas, where very often the flow of water to individual fields was communally controlled, but, given the inter-connected structure of labour and capital use in Saga Plain agriculture, it would still have been hard for one farmer by himself to switch to a mechanised pump, abandoning all the traditional practices which went with the use of water-wheel irrigation, and gain the benefits (for instance the possibility of planting the whole crop late and avoiding the rice-borer) which could potentially accrue from the innovation.

However, two features of the institutional organisation of Saga Plain agriculture meant that these problems were not insuperable. The first was the existence of a research and extension system which, by 1920, had developed to the point of possessing both technical training and close contacts with practising farmers. In chapter 5 we saw how the problems of diffusing improved methods on the Saga Plain had forced extension workers to put in a great deal of effort at the level of the individual village, and to develop the facilities and the will to try to find solutions to Saga's peculiar problems. This system therefore stood ready to fill the role of intermediary between farmers and the potential sources of new irrigation techniques, and to provide the technical and organisational abilities which individual farmers of necessity lacked. Combined with this was the second feature: the ability of Saga farmers to act in groups, and the existence already of well-developed group institutions, both within the village and at higher levels in the organisation of the irrigation system. Thus it was feasible to consider both small group action within the village, as a means of acquiring and operating irrigation equipment, and the use of the system of irrigation *kumiai* as a way of administering change from the higher levels downwards. The irrigation *kumiai* provided an organisation through which the extension authorities could exercise their role as intermediaries with suppliers outside the rural economy.

*

These, then, were the main considerations which Saga Plain extension officials and farmers had to take into account in the selection of the characteristics of new irrigation techniques which could be successfully adopted and operated under the conditions of Saga Plain agriculture in the 1920s. We can now turn to the process by which they made this selection.

2.   The Evolution of the Project

It is probable that the agriculture department of the prefectural government, along with the Saga County government, the *nōkai* and the experiment station, first began to try to think of a way of reducing the amount of labour required for pumping after the failure of the 1912 experiment with planting the whole rice crop late. At that time, however, there was no practicable small-scale water-lifting device available, and the first scheme which the prefectural agriculture department is known to have entertained was one, published in 1918, according to which a large 30−40 h.p. pump would be installed on the Chikugo.[14] This pump was to be used to try to raise the water level in the whole creek network, so that the number of wheels needed to raise water into the fields would be reduced. The experiment station was opposed to this kind of scheme though, and was more interested in something along the lines of a scheme then in operation across the Chikugo in Fukuoka Prefecture, using large, electrically-driven, 30−50 h.p. pumps to pump up the irrigation water on an area of reclaimed land.[15] The experiment station took a party of irrigation *kumiai* officials on a trip to see this scheme. The farmers were apparently very impressed, but could not imagine being able to initiate such a scheme themselves.[g]

Around this time, however, the farmers of a village called Kose, where water-raising problems were particularly severe, decided to take the initiative and attempt to mechanise their pumping.[16] The village as a whole bought a 5 h.p. diesel motor and an 8 h.p. pump to use to raise water for fifty hectares of paddy. The capital cost of this scheme worked out at ¥3,687, or ¥7·4 per 10 ares, but the biggest cost the project had to bear was that of compensation for the large amount of land lost in order to dig the distribution channels required. For the fifty hectares to be irrigated, 1·1 hectares of good paddy land were lost, so that the total costs of the project worked out at ¥27·7 per 10 ares. Within a year the project was however given up as a failure. This was largely because the motor did not work well and the farmers were unable to repair and maintain it.[17] Its capacity also turned out to be too small for the area it had to irrigate. So the villagers sold the motor again and waited in the hope of a better technique for making use of the channels they had built.

Among those who watched the failure of this scheme were the various extension authorities and Mr. Masaki of Nihon Denki. Masaki had decided to lay the future of his company on the possibility of supplying the irrigation machinery which he felt sure would soon be demanded on the Saga Plain.[18] The conclusion Masaki drew from the failure of the diesel engine project was that large-scale static motors involved too great a loss of land, and the costs of mechanising could be much reduced by the use of mobile equipment which could be used without the construction of a large number of new channels. He therefore devised the ingenious idea of acquiring small, imported, 3 h.p. oil-driven motors and fitting them, along with the pumps, to small boats which could be moved about the creek network and used wherever required. He manufactured a hundred of these little boats, and tried out some prototype pump-sets on farmers in Kawazoe. But this scheme also ran up against farmers' lack of experience with the use of motors.[19] The Kawazoe farmers found it very difficult to operate the motors on the boats, and they were unable to maintain and repair them. In addition, it proved harder than expected to move the boats to where they were needed because of the obstructions posed by sluices.

It was around this time, with the failure of these two schemes, that

[g] Kamagata, I., *Saga Nōgyō* (71), p.188. They perhaps had some justification for this belief since the pump was installed as part of a reclamation project which presented far fewer problems than the mechanisation of creek agriculture. See Yamada, T. and Ōta, R., *Saga-Ken Nōgyō Shi* (73), p.335.

local government and *nōkai* officials began to grasp the problem of how to achieve the mechanisation of creek irrigation. Contemporary accounts[20] record the local government officials who more or less took over the task of finding a way of achieving mechanisation as being remarkably clear in their objectives. Pumping labour had to be reduced if rice farming was to be profitable at the prevailing wage rate and rice price. Mechanisation of pumping would make it possible to plant the whole crop late, thus doing away with the rice-borer and permitting the use of improved seeds and the production of higher-quality rice. It would also give farmers the time to diversify and take on side-jobs.[21] They saw mechanisation as the means whereby Saga could become like other areas and adopt the kinds of intensive techniques used elsewhere. They were also substantially clear about the requirements of the technique to be selected. Discussions between the technicians of the prefectural agriculture department and the prefectural *nōkai* produced a statement of the requirements of the technique, which for the first time raised the possibility that electric motors might best meet the needs of Saga farmers. They concluded:[22] (a) that the machines must be simple enough to be operated by farmers with no technical knowledge; (b) that the motors should be able to run continuously all day, minimising operation and maintenance costs; (c) that the machines should lift water directly into the fields, not just raise the water level in the creeks; and (d) that although the initial cost of a limited number of big pumps and motors might be less than that of many small motors, the cost of land lost would probably outweigh this.[h]

These discussions among local government technicians were part of a wider process of investigation into what would be the most suitable form of mechanisation. The instigator of much of this was the head of the Saga County government, who was ex officio head of the Oide *kumiai*.[i] He spent much time consulting with enthusiast farmers, 'hammering on the gates of experts', and carrying out his own investigations.[23] In addition, the head of the prefectural agriculture department went on a trip to Ōsaka, Hyōgo and Shiga to look at other projects and to investigate the relative costs of alternative techniques.[24] His findings are set

[h] As Professor Minami has pointed out to me, the avoidance of the high cost of land lost to channel construction is the agricultural equivalent of the benefits to industrial firms of avoiding the 'group drive' arrangements consequent upon use of large steam engines. Thus, where in industry small electric motors did away with the need for the shafts and belts which carried power from large-scale motors (with all their attendant mechanical problems), so in agriculture they lessened the need for new water-carrying channels. See Minami, R., 'The Introduction of Electric Power' (118), pp.307–8.

[i] He was also the author of *Tenmatsu* (85).

Table 7.2: Relative Costs of Alternative Methods of Raising Water, 1920

	h.p. of motor	purchase and installation cost ¥/h.p.	fuel cost sen/h.p.	lubricant sen/h.p.	OPERATORS number	cost sen/h.p.	other inputs sen/h.p.	maintenance sen/h.p.	total running costs sen/h.p.
							FOR 12 HOURS' OPERATION		
Oil	3	160·0	105·0	4·0	1	66·6	13·3	16·6	205·5
Gas induction	15	346·0	30·5	4·3	1	13·3	1·0	13·3	62·9
Steam	50	210·0	42·0	6·0	2	8·0	0·6	8·0	64·6
Steam	300	241·6	12·6	2·0	3	2·0	0·4	5·0	22·0
Electricity	3	113·3	13·3	0·4	0	0	0	5·0	18·7

Source: adapted from data given in Kamagata, I., *Saga Nōgyō* (71), p.189 and pp.190−1.

Illustration 2. A Water Wheel in Operation.

Illustration 3. An Electric Pump in Operation today.

out in Table 7.2, from which it is clear that electric motors represented by far the cheapest way of providing the necessary horse-power.[j] The only alternative small motor, the oil-driven one, was as yet much more expensive, especially from the point of view of fuel and operating costs, than the electric one, and the only form of motor which compared with the electric one in terms of total running costs was the huge 300 h.p. steam one, which was much more expensive to buy and install and would have involved enormous channel-construction expenses. Everything therefore seemed to point towards the use of electrically-powered pumps, and Masaki was commissioned to put together a suitable electric motor and pump.

This was, however, only the beginning of the process of decision-making which determined the ultimate choice of technique. The group of technicians and local government officials, now more or less in the position of advising the Oide Kumiai, next had to take a decision as to the size of what might be called the units of the project, i.e. the areas to be served by an individual pump. This depended, on the one hand, on the horse-power required to lift the necessary amount of water on to a given area, and, on the other, on the exact size of the pumps/motors used. The horse-power required could be calculated on the basis of the average amount of water needed, as derived from observation of water-wheel use.[k] This was estimated to be approximately 1 h.p. per 5 hectares, though this was a very rough calculation, allowing quite a lot of spare capacity, since it was meant to apply to the Plain as a whole and, although evaporation rates and water requirements for plant growth did not vary greatly from place to place, the rate of seepage did.[25] On the basis of previous experience, the advantages of small pumps as already discussed seemed to outweigh the higher initial cost of buying them and of laying the electricity supply lines to them. The decision was therefore taken to aim at units of 10–15 hectares, with some variation to allow for differing land conditions, using pump-sets of two or three horse-power. After experimenting with a number of prototypes, Masaki put together such a set, meeting the technicians' requirements, and it went on show in Saga City in September 1921. The set consisted of a 2 h.p. electric

[j] For the same conclusion reached fifty years later in a very different environment (North Arcot in southern India), see Harriss, B., 'Rural Electrification' (151). The unsubsidised cost of lifting water by electrically-driven pumps worked out at 0·0056–0·0075 rupees per cubic metre lifted one metre, compared with 0·01 rupees for oil engines and 0·009–0·029 for bullock-powered lifting devices. See p.183.

[k] The wheels most commonly used had 17 paddles holding about 10 litres each. 100 turns of the wheel was about enough for 10 ares for 2 days. Kamagata, I., *Saga Nōgyō* (71), p.191.

motor attached to a centrifugal pump by a belt. The pump was static but the motor could be detached from it and put to other uses when required.

Having decided to go for small-scale static electric pumps, the authorities also had to decide how the adoption of their choice of technique by Saga Plain farmers was to be organised. They decided to make use of the institutional organisation of the irrigation *kumiai* and drew up a scheme for converting the whole area under the administration of the Oide Kumiai, in effect most of the central Plain, to mechanised irrigation at one time, as part of one big project. There were a number of obvious practical reasons for this. First and foremost, it was much more efficient to organise the laying of electricity supply cables for the whole area as a unit than to have individual villages, or even households, attempt to arrange their electricity supply independently. Secondly, if the kumiai organised the project, it could negotiate for a low-interest loan from the Hypothec Bank with which to buy the equipment, thus solving the problem of finance. Thirdly, official permission was required for electrification, and this necessitated, as we shall see, a good deal of paper-work, which the bureaucratic organisation of the Kumiai was best able to handle. Personal factors perhaps also played a part, given the influence of the head of the Oide Kumiai and of the group of officials, including the head of Saga County Nōkai, the head of the plant section of the experiment station and the head technicians of both the *nōkai* and the prefectural agricultural department, who had long cherished the hope of bringing about unified late planting on the Plain. The sooner and the more comprehensively mechanisation was achieved, the sooner could this hope be realised. The organisation of the project bore the stamp of Saga officials' traditionally strong sense of their duty and responsibility towards the farmers, combined with their streak of paternal authoritarianism.

It was therefore to a meeting of the Oide Kumiai in December 1920 that the emerging plan was first revealed. At this stage, however, the officials proved unable to carry the farmers' representatives with them. The Oide Kumiai head put this down to the fact that the plan was too novel and large-scale to be appreciated by the 'inexperienced' farmers,[1] although it must be said that the plan itself can have been by no means clear at that time. The authorities therefore began one of the campaigns of promotion and persuasion in which they had had some practice by now, sending technicians out to lecture in all the villages, distributing propaganda, organising trips to inspect the existing project in Fukuoka, and so on.[26] As a result, by the time that Nihon Denki exhibited its pump-set in

[1] 'Keiken naki mono', *Tenmatsu* (85), p.381.

September 1921, several villages were eager to set up schemes and began trying to arrange their own supply of electricity and equipment. By the end of 1921, the Kumiai had the agreement it needed to take over the project and set it in motion.

Before the final implementation could get under way, though, there were still more decisions to take about the organisation of the electricity supply. The original scheme put to the Kumiai in 1920 had included proposals for generating the required electricity within the Kumiai itself, and the officials had costed out the purchase of generators and the inputs required to produce electricity. However, when, towards the end of 1921, the first villages had begun to negotiate with Nihon Denki for the supply of the equipment to generate their own electricity, the Kyūshū Electric Company (Kyūshū Dentō Tetsudō K.K.), which held the monopoly over the Saga area, objected, so the Kumiai officials were forced to give up the idea of self-supplied electricity and settled for buying it from the electric company, which was eager to supply off-peak summer electricity for agricultural use. This still left a further choice though: whether to have the electric company lay all the necessary cable and supply direct to each pump or whether to have the Kumiai lay the cable itself and buy the electricity from the company as a unit. The pros and cons of this choice are carefully set out in the Kumiai head's account of the project.[27] If the Kumiai laid its own cables it would save money on the equipment, which it could buy more cheaply than the Company would supply it, and its electricity charges would be lower. It would own all the facilities, so that it could expand, contract or improve them as it chose and sell them if, for any reason, the project had to be given up. It would also be in a better bargaining position with the Company. On the other hand, the Kumiai would have the work of obtaining all the necessary official permits and it would have to hire the technical staff necessary to plan and maintain the supply system. Much deliberation took place and eventually it was decided that the Kumiai would construct its own supply system.

By the end of 1921, then, with Nihon Denki set to supply the pump-sets and the electrical equipment, with negotiations beginning over the electricity supply and the application being made to the Hypothec Bank, the main decisions which shaped the choice of technique and of institutional organisation had been made. The ultimate choice was in fact compounded, as we have seen, of a number of smaller decisions influenced by a wide variety of technical, institutional and environmental considerations. That this complex process resulted in the development and diffusion of a highly successful innovation will begin to emerge in the next section.

3. The Implementation of the Project

The details of the project which had taken shape by the beginning of 1922 were, in summary, as follows.[28] The project was to be implemented continuously over a period of two years. Villages covering a total of about 2,000 hectares were to be mechanised during 1922, and the remaining villages, covering a further 3,000 hectares, were to be dealt with during 1923. A contract was to be negotiated with the Kyūshū Electric Company, specifying the maximum amount of electricity to be supplied and the price. Nihon Denki was to be contracted first to provide and install the necessary electricity supply facilities, and second to supply the pump-sets and their fittings at a fixed price. If those supplied during 1922 proved satisfactory, those for 1923 would be bought. There was also a ten-year guarantee. Pumps were to be installed to cover units of land area of between five and twenty hectares, depending on land conditions, and the pump-sets would run, as a rule, for thirteen hours a day from 1 June to 15 September. The landowners within each pump unit area were to be responsible for the construction of necessary new water channels and were to provide the labour required. The layout of the cables and the siting of the pumps were all planned by the Kumiai. The Kumiai was to be financially responsible for the cost of the cables, switches and so on, the pump-sets, the electricity charges, and day-to-day management expenses. The households belonging to each pump unit were to be responsible for the labour and material costs of channel construction and for the purchase of any land lost because of this. The Kumiai was to meet its capital expenses (i.e. cables etc. and pump-sets) by means of a low-interest loan, repayable over fifteen years, from the Hypothec Bank. Its annual expenses, including repayment of the loan, were to be charged to individual pump units, who could decide for themselves how to allocate the charges amongst member households.

At the level of the Kumiai administration, the implementation of the project involved eighteen months or so of paper-work and meetings.[29] Official permission for the project and the electricity system had to be obtained from various bodies including the prefectural governor, the Communications Ministry, the Hypothec Bank, and so on. Many Kumiai meetings had to be held to approve the various stages of the project. The loan from the Hypothec Bank was received in instalments and a bridging loan from various local banks had to be negotiated. Each stage of the project consisted, at this administrative level, of the granting of approval by the Kumiai meeting, the receipt of official permission from the relevant authority, the organisation of the necessary finance, and then the commencement of construction work. In October 1922 the electricity work was ready to be inspected by a technical officer from the Communications Ministry. The construction of channels and the installation of the pump-sets then got under way. On 1 June 1923, the Kumiai informed the central authorities that the work was completed and on June 13 the pumps were switched on for the first time.

The construction work required the laying of 184 km of electric cable and the building of two transformer stations and two switch-points.[30] Nihon Denki, which specialised in the production of electrical equipment such as switches and transformers, was responsible for this work. 465 pumps were set up, each with a little platform and a wooden shed to house it. The pumps were all manufactured by Nihon Denki, who may also have made at least some of the electric motors, but some appear to have been imported.[m] The area covered by the initial scheme amounted to 4,225 hectares,[31] and 4,452 households were involved in the project.[32] The area of land lost in the construction of channels was, as hoped, very small, amounting to.88·4 ares in total, or 0·09 ares for every 10 ares irrigated. The costs of the project are set out in Table 7.3.[n]

When the pumps were installed, technicians from Nihon Denki went out to the villages to instruct farmers on how to use them.[o] After this, maintenance became the responsibility of the Oide Kumiai, who employed five or six technical officers to do this. However, there are no reports of any serious problems with the operation of the machinery — all that the farmer had to do was switch on the pump and periodically go round to check the water level, and the table shows that repair costs were minimal.[p]

The degree to which the scheme was judged to be an effective solution

[m] The major works on Saga Plain agriculture do not distinguish between the pumps and the motors and simply state that Nihon Denki made the equipment, and there seems little doubt that Nihon Denki did have the technical capacity to make electric motors. However, *Nihon Nōgyō Hattatsu Shi* (55), vol. 6, p.245, claims that the early motors used were imported, and a survey made in 1948 of the pump-sets then in use on the Saga Plain shows that a number of the oldest ones had foreign brand names (see Saga-Ken Nōrin-bu, *Saga Heitan-bu ni okeru Denryoku ni yoru Yōsuikangai* (92) and Kyūshū Nōsei Kyoku, *Saga Heiya* (76), p.409). According to Mr. Hayashida, Nihon Denki simply did not have the capacity to manufacture enough motors to meet the demand, and some imported German motors were used. He recalls making alterations to the pumps manufactured by Nihon Denki in order to fit them to the imported motors.

[n] For discussion of the returns to the investment, see section 5.

[o] The inhabitants of two or three villages assembled for this instruction. Mr. Hayashida, who was involved in this, recalls the excitement of the villagers at the prospect of no more pumping, and remembers being plied with drink by grateful farmers.

[p] According to Mr. Hayashida, the farmers' only complaint was over the unaccustomed noise made by the motors, and the only mechanical problems were caused by attempts to cover up the machines to reduce their noise.

Table 7.3:   Costs of the Oide Mechanisation Scheme

	Total cost ¥	Cost per 10 ares ¥
Capital costs		
Electric cable: 184 km	266,333	
Pump sets: 465		
(Total h.p. 946)	323,191	
Pump sheds: 465	22,944	
Transformer stations	15,000	
Other electrical (switches etc.)	8,700	
Other general	30,343	
Total construction expenses	666,511	15·77
Water channel construction	210,304	4·86
Average annual costs		
Repayment of capital costs		1·70
Electricity		0·80
Management		0·30
Repairs		0·08
Rent (for land lost to water channels)		0·44
Total		3·32

Source: Yamada, T. and Ōta, R., *Saga-ken Nōgyō Shi* (73), p.337, Kyūshū Nōsei Kyoku, *Saga Heiya* (76), p.264.

to Saga Plain farmers' problems is reflected in the speed and extent to which areas not covered by the Oide scheme followed suit. Table 7.4 shows all the mechanisation schemes in operation in 1928 in areas of Saga which had previously used water-wheels. Areas outside the Oide Kumiai carried out their schemes by forming legal-person Land Re-Organisation Associations (Kōchi Seiri Kumiai).[q] Schemes carried out from 1923 onwards were able to take advantage of an amendment in that year to the Agricultural Land Re-Organisation Law (Kōchi Seiri Hō) which made the subsidisation of communal irrigation projects easier, and they could obtain various government subsidies. The Kawazoe villages in Saga County began their schemes in 1923 as the Oide scheme came into operation. The Plain areas of Miyagi County followed in the next few years and there was also a considerable extension of the

[q] In form these were like irrigation *kumiai* (see chapter 5, section 2 (4)) and they were set up by groups of farmers wanting to carry out projects under the Agricultural Land Re-Organisation Law.

Table 7.4: *Summary of Irrigation Mechanisation Schemes in Areas of Saga Formerly Using Water-Wheels (as of 1928)*

	Area covered (ha.)	Number of pumps	Total h.p.	Date of commencement of project	Total construction costs (¥)
Oide Kumiai					
as of 1923	4,224·6	465	898·5	1922	877,637
as of 1928	5,103·0	569	1,081·0	1922	n.a.
Land Re-Organisation Associations using electricity					
Saga County:					
East Kawazoe	366·2	17	51·0	1922	92,365
North Kawazoe	499·0	23	89·0	1922	109,082
Kanzaki County:					
A. (Sakaino)	192·7	14	34·5	1923	66,238
B.	262·1	22	48·5	1923	178,940
C.	225·0	12	38·5	1923	129,894
D.	393·1	21	62·0	1923	243,519
E.	25·7	3	5·0	1925	12,787
F.	41·7	4	8·0	1928	17,299
Miyagi County:					
A.	38·1	3	11·0	1925	13,666
B.	71·1	3	13·5	1926	25,054
C.	58·9	4	10·5	1924	24,127
D.	28·3	3	6·0	1926	14,836
E.	63·1	6	16·5	1925	28,795
F.	43·5	1	15·0	1925	22,731
Ogi County:					
A.	229·6	14	47·5	1923	105,198
B.	32·8	3	8·0	1922	12,448
C.	42·1	3	7·0	1925	19,203
Land Re-Organisation Associations using other power sources					
Saga County:					
Kose Village, 1926, steam	52·7	1	15·0	1921	18,693
Kose Village, 1928, electricity	52·7	5	12·0		45,335
Miyagi County:					
A. Gas	35·2	1	30·0	1920	64,348
B. Gas	67·3	1	30·0	1922	32,948
C. Steam	73·8	3	46·0	1914	n.a.
D. Steam	208·5	1	32·0	1919	137,888
Total electric (1928)	7,718·7	730	1,564·5		
Total mechanised (1928)	8,103·5	736	1,702·5		

Sources: Compiled from Kyūshū Nōsei Kyoku, *Saga Heiya* (76), pp.266−7 and Taki, T., 'Saga-Ken ni okeru Kikai Kangai Jigyō' (93), pp.145−6.

Oide scheme. By 1928, 7,718·7 hectares of paddy had been converted from water-wheels to electrically-powered irrigation pumps and a further 384·5 hectares to mechanised irrigation using some other power source.[r] Nihon Denki supplied the equipment for most of the schemes carried out in 1922 and 1923 and for other similar schemes in Fukuoka and probably manufactured about a thousand pumps in the course of a year.[33]

We have some information about two of the smaller schemes carried out by Land Re-Organisation Associations, which gives some idea of what the mechanisation process was like at the village level. The Land Re-Organisation Association of Sakaino Village (*mura*)[s] was formed in 1923 and although its regulations and objectives were set out so as to conform with the Land Re-Organisation Law, its real purpose was to mechanise irrigation pumping. Thus, although formally it was composed of the landowners of the village, in practice it was the cultivators of village land who paid its expenses. The association was responsible for the organisation and financing of the project, which involved the installation of fourteen electric pumps to serve 192·7 hectares. During 1923 it paid out a total of ¥57,000, ¥43,000 of which went on buying and installing the pump-sets, with ¥3,000 for the first year's running costs. This expenditure was largely financed by a loan of ¥45,000 from the Hypothec Bank. The association also received small subsidies from the prefectural government (¥6,600), the County Nōkai (¥120) and the village (*mura*) council (¥770), leaving ¥7,500 to be met by the farmers, who paid at the rate of ¥4·33 per 10 ares cultivated. In the second year (1924), there were some further construction costs to be paid, along with the running costs of the pumps and interest payments on the loan. In this year there were no loans or subsidies received, so the members had to meet the expenses at the rate of ¥7·70 per 10 ares. After this they also began to repay the loan, with contributions varying from year to year in the region of ¥5−10 per 10 ares.

The second example concerns East Kawazoe village in the south of Saga County, where a Land Re-Organisation Association was established in 1922 with the aim of carrying out the mechanisation of water-wheel irrigation. The two Kawazoe villages approached Nihon Denki for the supply of electric pump-sets as soon as the finished model was

---

[r] These included Kose village, in which the early failed attempt to use a large diesel motor had taken place. In 1921 the village bought a steam engine which worked much more successfully than the diesel one, although later it too was given up in favour of electric motors.

[s] Kanzaki County A in Table 7.4. Data from Yamada, T. and Ōta, R., *Saga-Ken Nōgyō Shi* (73), pp.339−42.

exhibited and their mechanisation schemes began to be planned earlier than and separately from the Oide scheme. In East Kawazoe village, seventeen pumps were planned to serve an area of at that time 332·2 hectares.[34] The total cost of the project was ¥84,836. The association acquired a subsidy of ¥10,411 from the prefectural government and ¥165 from Saga County. The rest was met by a loan from the Hypothec Bank, with repayments divided half and half between landowners and cultivators.

The method by which the association managed this project is described by Nagata.[35] The association's area was divided into sections which were roughly flat and one or more pumps were set up as required to serve this area. Brick channels were constructed to distribute water from the pump throughout this area. The cultivators of each of the areas formed a pump-users' *kumiai* to manage the day-to-day running of the pump(s) in their unit. Table 7.5 shows how this worked. The members of individual pump *kumiai* did not necessarily all come from the same natural village (*buraku*). Thirty-one of the sixty members of the *kumiai* running pump no. 15, for example, came from one *buraku*, but the remainder were scattered over four other *buraku*. Although the pump *kumiai* ran the use of the pumps, they did not as a rule control the flow of water into individual fields, and cultivators were generally able to open and close the inlets into their fields as they chose.

The water-wheel did not entirely disappear after the mechanisation. There were still areas which were impossible to mechanise because of their location or because it was not worth laying electricity cable to them, and these, as we shall see, were able to do away with the water-wheel only when small-scale oil-driven motors became economic. In all areas the wheels were brought out when water was required out of the season during which the pumps ran. But the gruelling work of pumping through the summer months became a thing of the past and the wheels gradually became antique curiosities, replaced, as the symbols of Saga Plain agriculture, by the little wooden sheds housing the pumps, to be seen dotted about over the landscape of the Plain to this day (see Illustration 3, p.223). Dr. Miyajima recalls Saga farmers telling him that the mechanisation of pumping, which ended the need for the terrible labour of working the water-wheels, was the greatest landmark of their lives before the war.

4. The Implementation of Unified Late Planting

As we saw earlier, a number of the officials involved in the mechanisation project saw it simply as a necessary preliminary to the switch from the phased rotation, under which the rice-borer thrived, to unified late

Table 7.5:   Use of Pump-Sets in East Kawazoe Village

| Pump Number | H.P. | PUMP-USERS' KUMIAI | |
		Number of Member Cultivators	Area Served (ha.)
1.	2·5 }	46	34·4
2.	2·0		
3.	2·5 }	59	27·3
4.	1·5		
5.	1·5		
6.	3·0 }	107	62·0
7.	4·5		
8.	3·5		
9.	3·5 }	64	64·5
10.	3·0		
11.	3·0		
12.	3·0 }	142	79·0
13.	3·5		
14.	3·0		
15.	4·0	60	22·0
16.	5·0	55	29·9
17.	2·0	28	13·1
TOTAL	51·0	561	333·2

Source: Nagata, K., *Nihon Nōgyō no Suiri Kōzo* (54), p.268.

planting, which would eliminate it. The successful completion of the mechanisation scheme was therefore for them just the end of the first stage of the process of technical change through which Saga agriculture could come to rank with other areas. The way in which late planting was achieved provided perhaps the ultimate example of the agricultural extension system on the Saga Plain at work, bringing about what was in many ways a more profound technical change, and one which was much less whole-heartedly welcomed by farmers, than the mechanisation of pumping.

The discovery that the phased rotation was the root cause of the rice-borer problem had, of course, been made as early as the 1870s. Since then much research had been undertaken, at first by individuals and after 1900 by the experiment station. Unified early planting would have solved the problem as well as late planting could, but the experiment station's research brought it firmly down on the side of late planting because of the substantially higher yields obtainable with late-planted varieties. It had also prepared the way for the change by working out the best timing for the new rotation, proving that a second grain crop could still be grown if the right seed varieties were used, assessing the extent of rice-borer losses which would be avoided, and so on.[36] The head of Saga County Nōkai, who had been responsible for the earlier, failed experiment with late planting, continued to work towards it, keeping in touch with the enthusiast farmers who were his contacts in the villages and urging them to impress on farmers the benefits of late planting.[37] Finally, in December 1922, before the Oide scheme was completed, he called a meeting of local government and *nōkai* representatives, to be followed by a big farmers' conference in Saga City, to endorse the issue of prefectural regulations prohibiting the planting of an early crop from 1923 onwards.

The first meeting was attended by the heads of the local government agriculture departments and of the *nōkai* of the five counties and one city whose administrative areas included the Plain. Many brought other technicians with them, and representatives of the experiment station and the prefectural government also attended.[38] The meeting was the occasion of a certain amount of conflict between the experiment station and the influential head of Saga County Nōkai over the selection of the date before which rice-planting was to be prohibited. The experiment station advocated 20 June, which their research showed was the earliest date at which to be absolutely safe from the rice-borer,[t] whereas the Nōkai head proposed 15 June, which would have created fewer practical problems for farmers.[39] Eventually the experiment station carried the day and the meeting agreed that the prefectural government should issue regulations forbidding the planting of rice, throughout the Plain area, before 20 June.

The meeting also agreed on a timetable for procedures to organise the implementation of the regulations at the village level.[40] In January there were to be meetings in each county between the local agricultural technicians and the heads of all the administrative villages and towns (*mura* and *chō*), the heads of village (*buraku*) agricultural practice unions, and anyone else interested. At the beginning of February there were to be meetings of the agricultural discussion groups (*nōdankai*) of each administrative village and town, at which lectures on late planting would be given and details of the implementation could be arranged. In mid-February the village agricultural practice unions were each to hold

---

[t] I.e. the moths were only rarely known to appear from their chrysalises after this date. If all rice were planted after that, the moths would all already have hatched out and died and farmers could be sure there would be none to lay eggs in the crop.

meetings at which the methods of implementation would be explained. Provision was also made for the setting up, if necessary, of committees in each village to oversee the implementation, and for local *nōkai* to supply suitable seed varieties.

The conference which followed was attended by a thousand farmers' representatives from all over the Plain.[41] They were given lectures on the life-cycle of the rice-borer, hence the need for late planting, and on all the benefits which would accrue from adopting it — in fact, on the results of the experiment station's twenty years of research into the problem. There was much airing of views, and a certain amount of opposition to the scheme expressed, but in the end agreement seemed to be reached, and the authorities were so pleased with the conference that they gave everybody a packed lunch.[42] On 18 December the prefectural government issued the necessary regulations and the schedule for implementation got under way.

However, the stirrings of opposition among farmers' leaders, which the conference had helped to still, were reflections of much more widespread feelings among farmers themselves. The shift to late planting was an administrative measure for insect control and the area which the regulations covered was considerably larger than the area which was being converted to mechanised irrigation. The 20,000 hectares over which the regulations applied stretched out fom the creek area of the Saga Plain to the edge of the mountains and into the southern plain regions. They therefore covered some farmers who relied on natural irrigation, and for whom late planting represented only an extra, enforced concentration of labour demand at transplanting time.[43] There were also areas in the south where a second crop of beans had traditionally been grown after the early rice crop and this would be impossible with late planting.[44] The farmers in these areas had always held a festival after the planting of the beans which everyone enjoyed and which punctuated the agricultural year, and they objected strongly to the disruption of the familiar pattern of their lives.[45] Feelings of this sort were widely held in many areas. The phased rotation had been in use since way back in Tokugawa times, and the order of operations which it involved had for generations determined the rhythm of life on the Plain. Most farmers therefore held what the Saga-Shi Shi calls 'feelings of emotional opposition'[u] towards late planting.

The officials who set out on the series of lecture meetings in the villages therefore encountered a great deal of resistance to the idea of late planting, despite their efforts to explain how it would do away with the rice-borer. They were accused of arrogance in suggesting changing the

[u] 'Shinjōteki na teikōkan.' *Saga-Shi Shi* (81), vol. 4, p.359.

practices which had been handed down over the generations and they had to tread very carefully to avoid actual violence.[46] At one meeting the technicians were threatened with swords and were obliged to hide in a shed for several hours until it was safe to leave.[47] Technicians reporting back were therefore not optimistic about the chances of successful widespread implementation of the regulations.

Expecting that there would be non-compliance in some areas, the prefecture set up, at the end of March, five new local agricultural offices at which technicians were stationed permanently to organise and oversee late planting.[48] The original committee, meeting again in April, agreed to set up a central committee, of whose fifty-nine members twenty-two were policemen, and local committees in each administrative town and village, to attempt to enforce the regulations and to keep strict control over non-complying areas. The local committees were to be composed of technicians and officials from the local encouragement-of-industry offices. They were to publish the date at which seed selection, the first operation of the rice-growing calendar, was expected to begin, and were to carry out strict surveillance to try to ensure that it did not begin earlier. If they found areas disobeying the regulations, they were to report the names of offending farmers and the locations and areas planted immediately to the prefectural office, and straight away set up luring lamps, the counts from which were also to be reported back.[49] In addition, the police clearly played a considerable role in the enforcement of the regulations. Police officers were attached to the local committees and patrolled round at all hours, in all weathers, looking for offenders and checking the luring lamps.[50] Anyone caught preparing to plant was summoned and lectured, and in places officials went round pulling up seedlings planted too early.[v]

As a result of this 'agricultural extension by the sabre',[51] in the end only 800 hectares, or 4% of the area covered, were planted with an early crop, and eighteen people were fined for non-compliance.[52] Kamagata describes one example of a village where there was considerable non-compliance.[53] This village was on the Plain and already had mechanised irrigation. All the surrounding villages went over to late planting, but over half the farmers in this village planted an early crop, covering 31% of the paddy area, in 1923. The reason seems to have lain in the strength of feeling in this village for traditional transplanting practices. There they still held to the custom whereby those who finished transplanting first went to help those yet to finish. The concentrated transplanting labour demand necessitated by unified late planting would have made this practice unworkable and the villagers refused to

---

[v] The *Saga-Shi Shi* (81), vol. 4, p.365, remarks that there was probably a certain amount of *toraburu* (trouble) about this.

abandon a custom which ensured that the village as a whole would stand by those who, for whatever reason, might be unable to plant their crop.

In the ten years up to 1923, the experiment station's luring lamps caught an annual average of about 800 moths. In 1923 they caught 40.[54] The only areas to suffer any significant rice-borer damage in that year were areas, such as the village above, where the regulations were disobeyed, and the strict control measures applied to those areas were able to prevent any spread to surrounding complying areas. Without exception, the areas which had disobeyed the regulations in 1923 went over to late planting in 1924. From the point of view of the authorities, late planting, and the measures taken to enforce it, had proved a great success, and, as we shall go on to see now and in chapter 8, the benefits to farmers in terms of reduced crop loss and potential for improved techniques were also great. In the implementation of late planting, the authorities' ability to convert a decision taken at the prefectural level into practical actions at the level of villages and farms was clearly revealed. What the enforcement of late planting lacked was the corresponding village-level organisation and co-operation which was part of the process of achieving mechanised irrigation, and which will be discussed in greater detail in the next section as we go on now to consider the scale and the distribution of the gains from the complete mechanisation and late planting project.

5.   The Gains from the Project

One of the main points which I want to make, in analysing technical change in Saga Plain agriculture, is that the fundamental change in the basic irrigation technology represented by the mechanisation of pumping was an essential pre-requisite for the development of the whole package of new techniques (of which late planting was part) which gave the Saga Plain the high yields and labour productivity it achieved in the 1930s. The reasons for carrying it out did not lie simply in the profitability of substituting capital for labour in pumping, but more broadly in the possibilities opened up by the solution of the problems raised by labour shortage. It follows that the benefits to society from the mechanisation project consisted in the increase in output, per man and per hectare, which resulted from subsequent technical developments. At this point, however, I am concerned only with the immediate profitability of the investment in mechanisation to individual households and with differences in the gains which different types of household might have expected to make from the project. These differential expectations of gains from the particular characteristics of the project can then be seen reflected in the types of household who promoted the innovation in the villages.

The immediate gain to farm households from the mechanisation of irrigation consisted in the reduction in the labour cost of pumping. To evaluate this we have to estimate the cost of pumping-labour under the old water-wheel technology. The amount of labour required for the supply of irrigation water varied considerably from place to place and from year to year, but the most commonly accepted estimate is that pumping required on average seven man-days per ten ares in the 1910s (see Appendix Table 1). After the mechanisation, labour required for irrigation had fallen to about 1·3 man-days per ten ares. The valuation of this labour depends to some extent on what kind of farm is being considered. One approach is to value the 5·7 man-days saved at the pre-vailing wage rate for daily agricultural labourers. At the ¥1·5 per day rate for 1920, this gives a total saving of ¥8·55.[w] This would represent the saving to the smaller-scale farmer, either as the cost of hiring a little labour to deal with peak pumping requirements, or as the opportunity cost of the family labour saved by the household which had not pre-viously needed to hire in labour. Another way of looking at the problem, however, is to say that the mechanisation of irrigation allowed a three-hectare farmer to manage with one less *nenko* than before.[55] He therefore saved something in the region of ¥400 p.a. in wages and food costs over his three hectares, or ¥13·3 per 10 ares. As we shall see later, 1·5–2 hectare farms, although still needing temporary hired labour for transplanting, could, after the mechanisation, manage most operations with family labour alone, and a two-hectare farm which could save a *nenko*'s wages gained correspondingly more than a three-hectare one. In addition, use of prevailing wage rates in these estimates undervalues the gain because, as we saw earlier, much of the problem lay in the unavailability of suitable labour at those wage rates.

To calculate the total costs of wheel irrigation we need to take into account the capital cost of the wheels. At the time of the mechanisation one wheel cost ¥50–60 and lasted about ten years. On average a house-hold needed about 0·4 of a wheel per 10 ares. Repair and maintenance of the wheel cost ¥0·6–0·7 per wheel per year, or ¥0·26 per 10 ares.[56] For simplicity ignoring interest costs, depreciation on the wheel cost on average ¥2·2 p.a. per 10 ares, so that altogether capital maintenance and replacement cost ¥2·46 p.a. per 10 ares.

---

[w] This is the wage rate given in the prefectural yearbook (101). Estimates made at the time (e.g. *Tenmatsu* (85), p.403 and that quoted in Kyūshū Nōsei Kyoku, *Saga Heiya* (76), p.268) work with a slightly higher wage rate of around ¥2 per day.

We can now compare the savings from abandoning the old technology with the costs of the new. For the areas covered by the original Oide scheme, the total capital cost of the project (including water channel construction) came to ¥20·63 per 10 ares. Annual running costs (electricity, maintenance, etc.) amounted to ¥1·62 per 10 ares (see Table 7.3). Considering that savings of labour costs of ¥8−13 per 10 ares were being made, it is clear that, for most households, the project paid for capital costs in two or three years.[x] In terms of the household economy, outlays per 10 ares of around ¥14·5 (about ¥12 for labour, ¥2·46 for expenditure on wheels) were replaced by outlays of ¥3·32 (pump running costs of ¥1·62, interest and capital repayments of ¥1·70, as in Table 7.3). Other schemes were generally more expensive than the Oide scheme, covering smaller and more difficult areas. The survey made by the prefectural agricultural land department in 1928, while not entirely clear about coverage in places, can be used to give a rough estimate of the costs of all the schemes (including the Oide one) up till then. Running costs work out at ¥3·30 and interest and capital repayments at ¥3·30 also,[y] giving total annual costs of ¥6·60.[57] Thus even the more expensive schemes achieved very substantial cost reductions for water-raising.

[x] More precise calculations of the financial profitability of the scheme reveal that it yielded a very high rate of return, even on fairly restrictive assumptions. It is possible to calculate the present value of the investment in the Oide scheme as follows:

$$\text{Present Value} = -\text{initial cost} + \sum_{i=1}^{n} \frac{\text{labour costs saved} - \text{pump operating costs}}{(1 + r)^i}$$

$$= -20\cdot63 + \sum_{i=1}^{10} \frac{8\cdot55 - 1\cdot62}{(1 + \cdot065)^i} \text{ ¥ per 10 ares}$$

$$= 29\cdot2 \text{ ¥ per 10 ares}$$

where: (i)n = 10. (The pump-sets probably lasted considerably longer than 10 years since they were guaranteed for that period and at least some original motors appear to have been still in operation at the time of the survey made in 1948, Saga-Ken Nōrin-bu, *Saga Heitan-bu ni okeru Denryoku ni yoru Yōsuikangai* (92).)

(ii) r = ·065. (There is only one reference to the rate of interest charged by the Hypothec Bank on its loans, giving it as 6½%. See Kyūshū Nōsei Kyoku, *Saga Heiya* (76), p.268. In fact the project only ceases to yield a positive present value at interest rates higher than 31%.)

(iii) The saving on labour costs uses the lowest estimate of the labour costs of pumping.

[y] At 6½% over 15 years.

The gains from late planting are by their nature almost impossible to value as an annual average figure, since it was the variability in the risk of crop loss which was the main problem. As a rough guide, though, the best estimate of annual average loss is put at 3·3% of the crop.[58] At current rice prices and yields, this gave a gain of ¥2·48 per 10 ares.[z] The chief gains from late planting, though, really lay in the improvements in the quality of rice grown and in the adoption of other yield-increasing techniques which it permitted, and these will also be dealt with in chapter 8.[aa]

Involvement in the mechanisation project thus appears to have been a profitable investment for all farmers to whom labour was a cost. However, since it involved factor substitution (capital for labour) and was clearly not neutral in its effects on farms owning different combinations of production factors, and since (looked at another way) the main motive for it was the solution of a particular, pressing technical problem which affected different farms to differing degrees, it is valid to ask which types of farm household would be expected to gain most from the project and to be most active in promoting and organising the innovation in the villages.

Given the nature of the available techniques for dealing with the problem of pumping and the existing structure of the irrigation network, the authorities could have made no choice of technique which would have been sufficiently labour-saving to reprieve the large-scale cultivator. After the mechanisation, the size of farm which could be managed with family labour alone, even supplemented by temporary hired labour at transplanting, was still below two hectares, and the innovation did nothing to halt the tendency for large-scale landowners to split up and rent out their holdings. At the other extreme, the small-scale cultivator gained the cost reductions for pumping on his own land, as well as the relief from the physical labour of working the wheels, and the benefits from late planting, but since he had not needed to hire labour before, he did not benefit as much as larger-scale farmers from the resolution of the problem of the availability of workers. Mechanisation may have deprived him of some opportunities for full-time agricultural employment, but it opened up scope for increased labour input

[z] The rice price was ¥30 per 150 kg and the yield 375 kg per 10 ares. Offsetting this gain was the fact that unified planting necessitated for many households the hiring of temporary labour for transplanting, as we shall see in the next chapter.
[aa] *Tenmatsu* (85), p.403, predicts an annual gain from improved rice quality (i.e. higher price obtainable) of ¥6 per 10 ares.

in other directions, just as it did for the family labour forces on larger-scale holdings.[bb]

What mechanisation did in fact was solve the problems of — and open up possibilities for — the middle-scale family farm. By reducing the labour requirements for pumping as sharply as it did, it raised the limit to the area which could be cultivated by family labour alone, and it opened up great scope for the profitable use of family labour time on farms of 1—2 hectares. Such households no longer needed to hire labour to be able to irrigate and, apart from the very busy peaks at transplanting and harvest time, family labour was freed to be applied to yield-increasing, labour-using techniques or to cultivating a larger area. It was therefore this sort of household — the one just about at the limit of the area which a family labour force could cultivate under the old technology — to whom the characteristics of the techniques selected were most suited, whom the authorities presumably had in mind when making the selection, and whom we would expect to be the strongest proponents of the innovation in the villages.

This prediction is borne out by what evidence we have concerning the administrative organisation of the mechanisation project in the villages, since it does indeed suggest that it was the middle-range farmers, predominantly part owner/part tenant, who stimulated and led the movement to achieve mechanisation in individual villages. This evidence consists in data on the characteristics of the leaders of the project in three Plain villages, in all of which mechanisation took place in 1922 or 1923 but within *kumiai* outside the Oide area.

The first example concerns North Kawazoe village (*mura*),[59] where the mechanisation project was set in motion in 1922 under the organisation of the village land re-organisation association (*kōchi seiri kumiai*). In May of that year a tenants' association was set up in the same village, with the express object of promoting the mechanisation project. 170 owner/tenant households and 98 pure tenant households made up the membership of this association. In the same month as the tenants' association was founded, its head became head of the land re-organisation association and in September of that year he became village head. This

[bb] It might be argued that some *nenko* who wished to remain as agricultural workers must have been thrown out of their jobs by the mechanisation. However, as we shall see in chapter 8, mechanisation and late planting gave such scope for profitable increases in labour input, on family holdings, in side-employment at home, and in more temporary employment for other households, that it is difficult to argue that such workers would be unable to find any alternative agricultural work (excluding the possibility of earning a higher income in industry). Agricultural wage rates in Saga did not fall after 1923 and remained high, despite the falling rice price, until the onset of the depression (see Table 6.7), indicating that the demand for labour remained high.

suggests that the political significance of the owner/tenant group was increasing and that it was behind the drive towards mechanisation in one of the villages that pioneered mechanisation in the Plain.

The second example is that of the same Sakaino village (*mura*) whose finances were described earlier in this chapter.[60] Yamada and Ōta have discovered the records of the land areas owned by the officers of the land re-organisation association which organised the mechanisation project in this village. They are set out in Table 7.6. The largest landowner in the area was an absentee landlord who owned 7·2 hectares, but he took no part in the association. Of the fourteen officers, the largest land-owner owned 2·1 hectares and another four owned more than one hectare. Five owned less than half a hectare and the remainder between a half and one. The association head and his deputy owned comparatively small areas. We do not know what areas these farmers actually cultivated, but it seems very likely that they must have been renting in considerable amounts of land in addition to what they owned and that they were thus middle-scale owner/tenants.

Table 7.6:   *Officers of the Land Reorganisation Association of Sakaino Village*

Position	Area owned (ha.)
Association Head	0·582
Deputy Association Head	0·212
Committee Member 1	2·120
” ” 2	0·691
” ” 3	1·350
” ” 4	1·610
” ” 5	1·840
” ” 6	0·782
” ” 7	0·702
” ” 8	1·293
” ” 9	0·491
” ” 10	0·060
” ” 11	0·003
” ” 12	0·122

Source: Yamada, T. and Ōta, R., *Saga-Ken Nōgyō Shi* (73), p.341.

The third example gives a good deal more detail about the proponents of the project, this time at the level of the natural village (*buraku*).[61] This village was within the area of one of the land re-organisation associations of Kanzaki County (that of village C in Table 7.4). Its mechanisation project was begun in March 1923 and completed in June of the

Table 7.7: *The Promotion of Mechanical Irrigation in a Village in Kanzaki County*
A. Officers of the Irrigation Association

		Area cultivated (ha.)	Area owned (ha.) 1919	1925	
Area Head Man		1·6−1·7	1·21	1·55	
Committee Member		Less than 1·0	0·40	0·40	
Assembly Member		1·2−1·3	1·49	1·80	
Construction					
Committee Member	1	1·7−1·8	1·71	1·32	
"	2	1·0	1·00	1·00	
"	3	1·0	1·00	1·19	
"	4	1·6−1·7	2·27	2·27	
"	5	1·7−1·8	0·12	2·02	
Consultative					
Committee Member	1	1·0	0·35	0·35	
"	2	1·0	−	0·43	
"	3	0·4−0·5	−	−	1934 owned 0·11
"	4	0·6−0·7	−	−	1934 owned 0·17
"	5	0·7−0·8	0·19	0·19	
"	6	1·2−1·3	0·14	0·14	
"	7	0·7	0·35	0·35	
"	8	1·3−1·4	−	1·47	
"	9	0·7	−	0·30	
"	10	0·8	−	0·14	
"	11	0·7	−	−	1934 owned 0·12
"	12	0·7−0·8	−	1·30	
"	13	1·2−1·3	−	1·43	

B. Other Residents

Cultivated Area (ha.)	Nature of Side-employment				
0	Stonemason	Straw weaver	Blacksmith	*Nenko*	*Nenko*
0−0·1	Factory worker	Disabled	None	*Nenko*	Unknown
0·1−0·3	*Nenko*	*Nenko*	Unknown	Carrier	
0·3−0·5	Prefectural employee	Straw weaver	Straw weaver	Straw weaver	Carpenter
0·6	Specialist farmer				
Unknown	Unclear	Unclear	Unclear		

Source: Yamada, T. and Ōta, R., *Saga-Ken Nōgyō Shi* (73), pp.352−3.

next year. The village made a memorial tablet to commemorate the mechanisation and, using the names on that, Yamada and Ōta were able to piece together, from village records and interviews, the information shown in Table 7.7 on the areas of land owned and cultivated by those who promoted the project. The village head and the two local government representatives, along with the members of the construction committee, were the main organisers of the implementation of the project. As can be seen, they were on the whole the larger cultivators in the village, all but one farming between one and two hectares. Most rented in some land over and above what they owned, but they tended to own considerably more land than most other farming households. According to Yamada and Ōta, they were the leading village households, who had been the main labour employers. Almost all the other full-time farm households belonged to the consultative committee. They tended to be farming slightly smaller areas and to be renting in much larger proportions of them than the organising households. Over half of them were pure tenant households. What is known of the other residents of the village is shown in the second half of the table. All but one of these 23 households farmed less than half a hectare and had some sort of side-occupation, a number being *nenko* households.

Various conclusions can be drawn from the picture of this village. All the full-time households cultivating more than 0·6 hectares, whether owners, owner/tenants or pure tenants, were involved in the organisation of the project, but the driving-force behind it was the group of middle-scale cultivators who were at the limits of what could be cultivated with family labour alone. They were cultivators too small to be able to carry out irrigation investment independently, but they were able to carry the other, smaller cultivators with them in the adoption of a new technique whose characteristics suited their needs and solved their problems, but which also provided benefits for all those whose primary interest was in agriculture. The village households not involved in the promotion of the project were almost all part-time farmers, many of whom worked at side-employments which were not directly agricultural. What the few remaining households with members who worked as *nenko* felt about the project is unfortunately lost to us.

This evidence suggests that the mechanisation project was carried through in the villages by the group of medium-scale owner/tenant households who appeared to have most to gain from the nature and characteristics of the new techniques and who, as a result of the developments of the previous twenty years or so, had risen to be the predominant group in the village structure. This chapter, having traced in detail the stages of the development and introduction of a particular technique in a particular environment, has sought to show how the choice-of-technique decision was conditioned by the prevailing technical and institutional situation, and by the structural change which this rise of the medium-scale owner/tenant household represented. We have seen how the decision was in fact compounded of a series of decisions, each concerned with one or another of the many characteristics of the technique. These decisions were taken by the members of a group of government officials and extension workers who had long experience of agricultural conditions in the area and close contact with working farmers, so that at each stage they were able to take into account the actual conditions of the local area. At each stage also, they consulted the opinions of the farmers concerned or their representatives, opinions increasingly coming to reflect the social and political rise of the middle-scale owner/tenant households within the village community, which the impact of industrialisation had brought about. Industrialisation in the surrounding region also helped to make available to them the services of a local firm with the knowledge necessary to translate industrial technology to agricultural uses.

The conclusions arising from this story could be summarised as follows: (a) that choice-of-technique decisions are complex compounds of decisions about the many technical and economic characteristics of new methods; (b) that in the case of Saga, the ability to make appropriate choices of all these characteristics was the result of a long investment in building up knowledge and contact between farmers and extension workers; and (c) that the way in which industrialisation affected the area had a strong influence over the forces which determined the choice of technique. These conclusions are clearly of some significance for the understanding of technical change and development in general, and this will be considered in more detail in chapter 9. Before that, however, we must go on to look at the further successes of the network of relationships between farmers, research and extension workers, and industrial suppliers, which the mechanisation and late planting projects had helped to build up, as it went into operation to deal with the dynamic problems generated by these fundamental changes in technology.

CHAPTER EIGHT

The 'Saga Stage' — the Culmination of the Process of Technical Change 1923–40

The innovations described in the last chapter overturned the basis of the technical system which, in its main outlines, had been in operation on the Saga Plain since the Tokugawa period. In this chapter I want to explore the ways in which other aspects of Saga Plain agricultural technology were adapted to the profound changes in irrigation infrastructure and crop rotation which had taken place in 1922 and 1923. In other words, I want to look at the ways in which one innovation led to other innovations, both technical and institutional — at what Hayami and Ruttan would call 'dynamic sequences', or what Rosenberg would call the 'internal compulsions and pressures' created by complex technologies. In what follows, I shall look first at the specific problems generated by the mechanisation of pumping and late planting, then at the development of technical solutions to those problems, and finally at the social and institutional changes induced in Saga Plain villages by the emergence of a new technical structure during the 1930s.

1. Immediate Problems

After the last chapter's glowing account of the successful introduction of mechanised pumping and late planting, we need to come down to earth somewhat, to the realisation that what was achieved was simply a reduction in the labour required for irrigation and the disappearance of the rice-borer. These did not in themselves lead to any immediate, dramatic increase in output (except the reduction in the loss from pest damage), only to the potential for such an increase, and indeed, when combined with the cultivation methods adapted to the old irrigation method and rotation, created new problems of their own.

The central issue governing these problems/potentials was that of the pattern of labour use. Mechanisation, as we have seen, resulted in an immediate drop in the number of labour days necessary to provide the required irrigation water. It also meant that, now that water could be supplied relatively easily and abundantly, there was less need for the elaborate processes of *tokojime* ploughing. Mechanisation therefore removed the causes of the long period of heavy labour through the spring and summer. Ploughing skills were no longer required to anything like the same extent, and the labour of family workers was freed from pumping to be applied to the other tasks of the main period of rice cultivation. The use of long-term hired labour therefore became unnecessary for all but very large-scale cultivators, and *nenko* workers began to disappear.

Despite this easing of long-term peak labour demands, however, the abandonment of the phased rotation, which had spread out over a relatively long period the operations, such as transplanting and harvesting, which in general caused the heaviest concentrations of labour demand in Japanese agriculture, meant that new short-term peaks were created. As Table 8.1 shows, these peaks occurred firstly in the early summer, at

Table 8.1: The Distribution of Labour Time Throughout the Year in a Saga Plain Village, 1931
(Units = average hours per household)

	Total labour time	Labour time in rice production	Labour time in rice production per 10 ares
January	475·3	203·8	11·1
February	392·7	98·7	5·4
March	430·9	89·7	4·9
April	617·0	217·1	11·9
May	580·0	146·4	8·0
June	750·6	373·8	20·4
July	687·9	522·9	28·6
August	461·1	195·6	10·7
September	433·5	91·2	5·0
October	457·6	130·2	7·1
November	514·9	296·0	16·2
December	546·4	145·1	7·9
Total	6,347·9	2,510·5	151·8

Source: Isobe, T., 'Iwayuru Saga Dankai' (70), p.37, from 'A Survey of Labour Conditions in Farm Households in Saga Prefecture', covering fifteen villages in the prefecture, and carried out in 1931 by the Saga Prefecture Industrial Society.

the time of transplanting, when the farmers in the villages surveyed put in five or six times as much labour per ten ares of rice cultivated as they did in the slack times of the year, and secondly in November and December, at the time of the rice harvest and the planting of the second crop.[a] These new peaks meant that middle-scale farmers cultivating over a hectare or so still could not, in most cases, manage entirely without hired labour, especially for transplanting. But they could now manage with labour hired just for the transplanting season. This enabled them to tap sources of labour outside the Plain itself and to hire temporary workers from other areas where transplanting had already been completed, who were much more easily recruited, and would work for much lower wages, than the skilled, permanent *nenko*.

The main source of supply of temporary transplanting labour open to Saga Plain farmers lay in the women-folk of the much poorer agricultural areas across the Chikugo in Fukuoka Prefecture. From 1923 onwards, large numbers of women and girls were recruited from the plain and mountain villages across the river where holdings were in general much smaller than on the Saga Plain.[1] Initially, even before 1923, some such workers had been recruited for larger-scale Saga farmers by agents, often horse-dealers who travelled about the region.[2] But after 1923 they began to come in large numbers, being met at the ferries or at Saga station by farmers or their agents, who negotiated with them over wages and length of employment and took them off to the villages. It became one of the familiar sights of the Saga Plain to see, in May or June, the groups of girls arriving for the transplanting, carrying their straw raincoats and changes of clothes wrapped in *furoshiki* bundles,[3] and there are many stories of romances between farmers' sons and the young transplanting girls.[4] During the depressed years of the 1930s especially, they worked for very low wages, often paid partly in straw which they carried home to work into bags to sell.[5]

Thus, although they no longer needed to hire *nenko*, Saga Plain farmers still relied heavily on hired labour. The girls from across the Chikugo were able to meet this requirement throughout the rest of the period with which we are directly concerned, but during and after the war it became much harder to find the labour necessary for transplanting, and this problem was not solved until the relatively recent development of the transplanting machine.

The severer problem for Saga Plain farmers in the years immediately after 1923 was the second peak at the time of rice harvesting and

[a] The spring peak under the old rotation had been spread over a period of two months (10 May – 10 July), but after 1923 the same operations had to be carried out between 27 May and 10 July. Kamagata, I., *Saga Nōgyō* (71), p.237.

second-crop planting. With the existing seed varieties, the time available for these operations under the new rotation was very short, and wheat and barley planted even a little late had not time to mature enough to be able to survive the winter. As a result, many farmers found themselves still without enough labour to be able to plant a second crop, especially of grain, and the rate of double-cropping did not immediately pick up after mechanisation from the low levels to which the outflow of labour had driven it (see Chart 6.3).

The new peaks in labour demand also had an obverse effect in creating periods of the year much freer from agricultural work than Saga farmers had known before. With the main agricultural operations over in comparatively short periods of time, Saga Plain farmers found themselves at other times of the year somewhat underemployed. To some extent they were able to take this increased leisure in the form of a relaxation of the pressure under which they had formerly worked. Before mechanisation and late planting, operations such as weeding had to be carried out at the right time as quickly as possible and everybody knew how long each task should take. After mechanisation, when there was no longer any pumping to be done at the same time, it ceased to matter nearly so much if a farmer got behind with his weeding, since there was plenty of time to catch up again.[6] But the freeing of labour time also offered scope for increased labour input, both in existing agricultural operations and in new ones, if profitable outlets were available. The techniques of the *Meiji Nōhō* which Saga farmers had previously found difficult to adopt offered some possibilities for this more intensive use of labour, for instance in transplanting methods, fertiliser use and so on. But beyond this, Saga farmers after mechanisation found themselves looking for ways in which to intensify the use of newly-available family labour time in the off-peak times of the year

In general, the problems which farmers and extension workers faced in adapting to the changed basis of the technology could be summarised as falling into two types. One was the type of problem faced by farmers in most areas of Japan, the type of problem to which the *Meiji Nōhō* was a solution, that of achieving the maximum yields possible and, to that end, making the most intensive use possible of available family labour time. In addition to catching up with the *Meiji Nōhō*, farmers were looking for adaptations to available techniques which would enable them to regain their former double-cropping rates and which would provide them with profitable occupations for their slacker times. The other type of problem was one faced by areas, like Saga, strongly influenced by modern industrialisation and its impact on the conditions of labour supply. This was the kind of problem which arose from the need to increase the area a family labour force could cultivate on its own, and this was a problem of the productivity of labour, especially in the peak operations of the farm year. Saga farmers also, therefore, sought the means whereby they could save labour and increase the area which a family labour force could manage. In the next section we shall see how the system of research and extension which had developed through the efforts to produce and diffuse earlier techniques to deal with Saga's particular problems was turned towards the solution of the new problems generated by previous successes.

2. Technical Change and the Role of Extension Institutions after 1923

(1) THE INTENSIFICATION OF LAND AND LABOUR USE

Mechanisation and late planting removed the barrier which had formerly prevented the full-scale adoption of the *Meiji Nōhō* package of intensive techniques on the Saga Plain. In the years after 1923, Saga farmers caught up with other areas in the use of such techniques, and, through the research and extension institutions, went on to develop them further to suit the requirements of Saga Plain agriculture.

Central to the package of intensive techniques were the high-yielding seed varieties. Before 1923, the improved varieties used on the Saga Plain had mostly been one or another of the members of the Shinriki family and it was to these, especially Shinriki No. 2, that farmers turned when, after the disappearance of the rice-borer, they found themselves able to switch uniformly to high-yielding, late-planted varieties without bothering about their resistance to the insect.[7] However, the experiment station had begun a series of tests to determine which were in fact the best varieties to use under the new rotation, and in 1928 it published results which showed that three varieties, Shinzan, Shintoku and Asahi No. 1, produced the highest yields under the conditions of the Saga Plain. Shinzan was best of all, producing very high yields of not particularly high-quality rice.[b] By 1932, according to a survey carried out by the experiment station, 90% of the paddy area of Saga County and Saga City was planted with improved varieties,[c] with 8,905 of the 10,310 hectares using high-yielding varieties planted to the three recommended

[b] Kamagata, I., *Saga Nōgyō* (71), p.225. Shinzan was a Shinriki cross, bred at the Kinai experiment station in the home ground of the *Meiji Nōhō*, and Shintoku and Asahi were similarly varieties largely produced by the official research establishment and transmitted through the network of experiment stations.
[c] 86·4% for the prefecture as a whole.

varieties above.[8] According to the prefectural interior department's survey, in 1936 nearly 75% of the area of improved varieties in Saga County was occupied by Shinzan, and in 1942 almost 85%.[9] Thus, from growing a wide range of assorted seed varieties, Saga farmers came to be uniform cultivators of the varieties recommended by the authorities.

Accompanying this was a steady increase in the input of fertiliser, particularly commercial organic and later chemical fertiliser. The prefectural yearbook shows both the total quantity and the real value of fertiliser input rising throughout the late 1920s and the 1930s.[d] Increased and efficient use of commercial fertiliser was strongly promoted by the authorities. In 1919 the experiment station had begun to work out and publish recommended fertiliser applications for each of the five areas into which it divided the prefecture.[10] After 1923 farmers began to demand more detailed and locally specific fertiliser recommendations, and the experiment station began to issue them for each administrative town and village (*chō* and *mura*) area, producing fifty-three different ones by 1935.[11] A surviving example of one of them shows that experiment station officials had surveyed the land types and particular problems of each *buraku* in the administrative village, and carried out soil analysis, and the document issued gives recommended seed varieties, cultivation methods, planting times and so on for each crop in each *buraku*, as well as the correct fertiliser combinations to use.[12] The combinations recommended for each area were made up and sold by the local *nōkai* or co-operative.[13]

One effect of increasing use of commercial fertiliser was a tendency for less effort to be put into mud-raising. A survey carried out in some Saga Plain villages in 1932–3 found that the amount of mud raised, per ten ares to be fertilised, was considerably less than the amount known to have been used around the late 1910s, and other surveys suggest that this decline continued quite fast as chemical fertilisers began to be used more and more.[14] Other factors also played a part in discouraging mud-raising. These included labour shortage, the revival of double-cropping, which meant that fewer fields were left in the fallow state required for mud application, and the fact that, after mechanisation, it became less vital to maintain the water storage capacity of the creeks through dredging. Thus, after mechanisation, commercial fertilisers were gradually substituted for communally-supplied natural fertiliser in Saga, just

---

[d] Although continuous series on consumption of fertiliser of different kinds do not exist, the prefectural yearbook (101) shows that the consumption of chemical fertiliser in Saga County increased from 1,543 tonnes in 1921 to 3,908 tonnes in 1929, and that of compound fertilisers from 1,149 tonnes in 1930 to 6,156 tonnes in 1936. See also similar figures from another survey shown in Kyūshū Nōsei Kyoku, *Saga Heiya* (76), p.319.

as they had been in more typical areas using grass and leaves instead of mud.

The use of high-yielding varieties and heavy fertiliser applications were complemented, in the *Meiji Nōhō* package, by various improved cultivation practices, such as straight-line transplanting and deep ploughing, and after 1923 Saga Plain farmers found that they had both the time and the incentive to use these much more consistently than they had done before. The most problematic of these practices had been deep ploughing, but after the mechanisation, with *tokojime* ploughing no longer necessary, the operations of land preparation were greatly simplified, and Saga Plain farmers began to buy improved, factory-made ploughs of designs suitable for deep ploughing.[15]

Another practice which increased the effectiveness of high-yielding seeds and heavy fertiliser application was careful control and variation of the water-level in the paddy fields, and the new irrigation technology on the Saga Plain allowed farmers there to move ahead of other areas in developing methods of doing this. Before mechanisation, farmers had had little choice but simply to pump as much water as possible into the fields and leave the growing plants standing in deep water. The new pumps, however, allowed much greater variation of the level of water in the field, according to the needs of the plant, and in addition more and more farmers began to improve their ability to control water levels by buying small-scale oil-driven motors and vertical pumps. As the technology for producing small-scale oil motors advanced and they became cheaper (both to buy and to run) and better suited to agricultural needs, they began to be bought both by those Saga Plain farmers unable to make use of the electric irrigation network and by others wishing to improve their ability to control their supply of water.[e] The number of oil motors in agricultural use in Saga Prefecture rose from 107 in 1923 to 13,483 in 1941, and that of individually-owned pumps from 721 in 1927 to 7,748 in 1941 (see Table 8.2 later). The authorities made considerable efforts to teach farmers to use the capacity which mechanised irrigation gave them for allowing water in and out of the fields as the plants required. The issues of the Saga Prefecture Nōkai Report between 1925 and 1927 are particularly concerned with explaining this.[16] As a result of it, Saga Plain farmers were not only able to avoid losses through drought, but also to become one of the first areas in the country to achieve the benefits of controlling the water-level in the fields.[17]

In all these ways, then, Saga Plain farmers were able to advance their techniques for the intensive use of land and labour in rice cultivation and, as a result, were able to achieve, as we shall see later, the highest

[e] N.B. the motors could be used to power threshers as well. See later.

levels of rice yields in the country during the 1930s. Much the biggest problem for them, though, in taking advantage of the scope for intensified use of family labour and land which mechanisation opened up lay in reviving the rate of double-cropping. As suggested earlier, the crux of the problem lay in the lack of time available for harvesting and threshing the rice crop and preparing the land for a second crop. The cultivation of second grain crops in general, and wheat in particular, remained difficult for many farmers, and the paddy area of Saga County planted to a second grain crop, which had stood at 5,378 hectares in 1904, was still below 3,500 hectares in 1927.[18] In essence this was a problem of labour shortage, intensified by the change in rotation, and much of the solution lay in the adoption of labour-saving machinery to be discussed in the next section. However, it could also be eased by any means which lengthened the time available for winter peak operations, and the experiment station attacked the problem by trying to develop varieties of wheat and naked barley which would mature in shorter lengths of time and thus could stand being planted a little later. In fact, the Saga experiment station was much more occupied with developing varieties of non-rice grain crops than it was with rice varieties, and the experiments it carried out under the central government's assigned experiment system were to do with wheat not rice.[19] In this it was not simply selecting the best available varieties as before, but was producing new varieties, reflecting its increasing scientific and technical capacity. In 1935 it produced a wheat variety, subsequently named Nōrin 20, which matured three or four days more quickly than previous varieties, and which was widely and successfully diffused. It also produced varieties of naked barley which matured about five days more quickly than prevailing ones, and which were named after Saga.

With these new varieties and with the spread of labour-saving machinery, the cultivation of second grain crops was able to pick up again, reaching a level of 6,080 hectares in Saga County by 1938.[20] The area under wheat rose from a low of 2,462 hectares in 1925 to 4,918 hectares in 1938, encouraged also by the government's campaign for self-sufficiency in wheat production in the 1930s. While grain crops were by far the most important second crops grown, beans continued to be grown on 4—5,000 hectares of the Plain until the mid-1930s, by which time the widespread use of commercial fertilisers had made the cultivation of nitrogen-fixing plants less important.[21] Overall double-cropping rates of around 65% were being achieved by the late 1930s.[22]

Finally we might note some of the ways in which Saga Plain farmers began to use the family labour time freed by mechanisation in activities outside traditional crop-cultivation. While remaining specialist grain-producers as far as their crops were concerned, increasing numbers of households began to move into activities, such as horse-breeding, silk production and dairying, which did not affect land utilisation but which provided an outlet for spare resources of capital and family labour time. For example, the revival of double-cropping meant an increased supply of fodder, and this enabled Saga farmers not only to stop sending their horses away into mountain areas in the summer, but also to begin to breed from them. The number of horses bred in Saga County rose from 78 in 1925 to 165 in 1936, overtaking the traditional horse-breeding areas in the mountains of the prefecture.

(2) MECHANISATION

The technical changes described above represent those whereby farmers sought to raise the yield of a given area and a given family labour force. But Saga farmers were also faced with the problems and the possibilities posed by a declining agricultural labour force and a relatively abundant supply, by Japanese standards, of paddy land. They therefore felt a considerable incentive to develop the means of maintaining or expanding the area which a limited family labour force could cultivate. In that the main obstacle to achieving this lay in the labour required at the time of the rice-harvest/second-crop planting peak, this aim coincided with that of raising the double-cropping rate. Most of the innovations described here therefore served both ends but, as we shall see in a later section, one of their results was certainly to increase the area which a family labour force could farm. There were, though, limitations to this process caused by the fact that the only operations for which machinery was available before the war were the ones which could be performed statically. The development of the power-tiller was only just beginning at this time, and the technical problems involved in producing rice-planting machines and tractors which could operate successfully under Japanese conditions were not solved until the end of the 1960s.

The main operation for which machines became available before the war was that of threshing. The traditional threshing tool was called a *senba* (1,000 teeth), and it looked like a large comb fixed to a trestle. With this it took between three and five people a day to thresh the grain from ten ares,[23] and this labour was required at the spring and autumn peaks to thresh the two grain crops, just when land preparation and harvesting were making their heaviest demands for labour. A pedal-driven threshing machine first came on to the market in the early 1920s, and there were eight different factories manufacturing it in Saga Prefecture.[24] The early models were not very successful, but towards the end of the 1920s their problems were ironed out and they began to spread. They reduced the labour required to thresh ten ares' worth of grain to two man-days.[25] The power-driven thresher first appeared around 1931. The types available in the early 1930s were powered by separate petrol-driven motors, which could be detached and used for other purposes, such as operating pumps. Much progress had been made in the design of these Japanese-made motors, and they were by now relatively cheap and easy to use. Later designs of thresher had their own built-in motors. Mechanical threshers became very widely used in Saga during the 1930s, their number in Saga Prefecture increasing from around 80 at the beginning of the decade to nearly 10,000 at the end, alongside the increase in the number of petrol motors (see Table 8.2). With the mechanical thresher, a group of five or six people could thresh the grain from fifty ares or more in a day.[26]

Pumps, threshers and the motors to power them were the most common pieces of machinery to be found on the Plain in the 1930s. In addition, mechanised hulling machines began to appear, but their capacity was large, relative to the average farm's harvest, and they were generally bought as a business proposition by those, not necessarily cultivators on any scale themselves, who received fees for hulling other people's grain.[27] The motorised pumps could be used to help raise water out of the creeks during the mud-raising operation, and in the mid-1930s a local firm began to produce a mud-raising machine which worked rather like an escalator.[28] The rotary weeder was widely diffused once straight-line planting became the rule, and a horse-drawn hoe was also developed to speed up land preparation.

All these kinds of machine, unlike the original irrigation machinery, were acquired by farmers themselves, individually or in small groups,

Table 8.2:   *Numbers of Agricultural Machines in Saga Prefecture*

	Petrol engines	Pumps	Mechanical threshers
1923	107		
1927	533	721	83
1931	867	792	86
1933	948	788	121
1935	1,516	1,279	151
1937	5,347		4,521
1939	7,860	5,112	7,289
1940	10,236		9,851
1941	13,483	7,748	

Source: Isobe, T., 'Iwayuru Saga Dankai' (70), p.39, from a study of the diffusion of agricultural machinery in Saga Prefecture, made by the Saga Prefecture Agricultural Labour Research Institute in 1943.

without the mediation of the authorities. By the 1930s there were agricultural machinery dealers in Saga, and new types of machine generally came to the area, according to Kamagata, as a result of Saga farmers' spotting them while travelling in other areas, and requesting local dealers to supply them.[29] However, the authorities did try to help farmers to make the best possible choice from among different designs and makes of machine. The experiment station conducted comparative trials of machines and published the results, and from 1922 it held open days at which farmers were able to inspect tools and machinery.[30] In 1923 regulations were passed to allow the experiment station to lend machinery to local *nōkai* to demonstrate.[31] Tanaka found, in the village he surveyed, that the threshers and motors which farmers had bought were almost all of a limited number of the best types or brands, despite a considerable range of choice, and he takes this as evidence of the knowledge and discrimination of farmers and of the technicians advising them.[32]

(3)   THE IMPACT ON YIELDS AND LABOUR PRODUCTIVITY

It was as a result of the process of technical change outlined here that, in the 1930s, Saga Prefecture moved to the top of the prefectural yield league table shown in Table 8.3. Apart from the early appearances of Ishikawa and Toyama, Saga is the only prefecture from outside the central Inland Sea area to appear in this table at all; but while its fertile soil, combined with such spread of the *Meiji Nōhō* as was achieved, put Saga among the top prefectures in the 1910s and 1920s, it was the much more rapid growth in the 1930s there than in other areas that singled out Saga as a pioneer of techniques of a new sort. The clearest indication of the breakthrough in yield levels, achieved as a result of the process of development of techniques adapted to the new irrigation technology, in specifically Plain areas, is the village-level data for Saga County shown in Table 8.4. During the 1930s, most Plain villages were achieving yields of over 450 kg/10 ares, and some more than 525, at a time when the official national average yield was less than 300 kg and the prefectural average less than 400.

More striking yet, and perhaps more significant in the light of Saga's relationship with the developing modern industrial sector, was the rise in labour productivity. According to the prefectural yearbook data, overall rice output per agricultural worker in Saga County rose from about 450 kg around 1900 to about 1,950 in the late 1930s. Much of this increase occurred before 1920, however,[f] as a result of the rapid labour outflow and was to some extent offset by declining second-crop output,

[f] Output per worker in 1920 was 1,500 kg.

Table 8.3: Prefectures with the Highest Average Rice Yields in the Country,
1883–1937
(Yields in kg/10 ares)

Position	1883–92	1893–1902	1903–12	1913–22	1923–32	1933–37
1.	Toyama 269	Nara 288	Nara 341	Nara 370	Ōsaka 362	Saga 390
2.	Shiga 267	Ōsaka 282	Ōsaka 328	Ōsaka 355	Nara 351	Nara 386
3.	Nara 266	Shiga 268	Kagawa 321	Kagawa 352	Kagawa 339	Ōsaka 369
4.	Ōsaka 263	Yamanashi 267	Saga 312	Saga 339	Saga 339	Kagawa 361
5.	Ishikawa 242 (Saga 9th 234)	Toyama 266 (Saga 12th 233)	Shiga 311	Shiga 331	Shiga 339	Yamanashi 359

Source: adapted from *Saga-Ken Shi* (80), p.612. Data originally official Ministry of
Agriculture statistics.

and by an increase in the work put in by those remaining. Table 8.5
summarises the data on output per labour day from the various surveys
used to make up Appendix Table 1, and shows that rice output per day
worked continued to rise steadily through the later 1920s and the 1930s
at the same time as second-crop output per labour day must also have
been increasing.

Examination of Appendix Table 1 shows the impact of the type of
mechanisation adopted in Saga on the pattern of labour use, and the
specific operations in which labour input was reduced. In particular,
man-days per ten ares spent on grain preparation had fallen from four
or more around the turn of the century to about one by the end of the
1930s. The time spent on weeding operations had also declined. Most
other operations, though, apart from pumping, and allowing for the
inconsistencies in the nature of the data, required much the same
amount of labour at the end of the 1930s as they had done in the 1910s,
and even in the 1850s. Thus the overall decline from around thirty man-
days per ten ares in the 1900s to twenty or less by 1940 can be seen to be the
result of a selective process of labour-saving innovation, attacking, where
technically feasible, the points in the cycle of operations which limited the
area a family labour force could manage. As a result of the labour outflow
to industry, the cultivated paddy area per farm household in Saga County

Table 8.4: *Village-Level Data on Rice Yields in the Saga Plain Area*
(Numbers of villages obtaining given yields, Plain areas of Saga County)

	kg/10 ares						
	225–300	300–375	375–450	450–525	525–600	600–675	Total
1912	4	14					18
1915		6	12				18
1916		4	13	1			18
1917		9	9				18
1918		10	8				18
1919		1	11	6			18
1920		1	13	4			18
1921		4	12	2			18
1922		5	12				17
1923			15	2			17
1924			11	6			17
1927		2	15				17
1928		8	8	1			17
1929		1	10	6			17
1930		1	13	3			17
1931		9	8				17
1932		2	11	4			17
1933			1	15	1		17
1934			2	14	1		17
1935		1	12	4			17
1936			8	8	1		17
1937			2	13	2		17
1938			1	12	4		17
1939			2	6	7	2	17

Source: Isobe, T., 'Iwayuru Saga Dankai' (70), p.6.

had risen from just over one hectare in 1900 to 1·3 hectares in 1920 and
1·4 in 1940,[33] and it was this selective mechanisation, beginning with
the mechanisation of pumping, which made it possible for family
labour forces to cope with the increased area to be farmed and even, at
the same time, to raise yields and cropping intensity. In the next section
I shall look at the way in which the agricultural structure was affected
by, and also in its turn influenced, the nature of the development of the
new technical system which made this possible.

Table 8.5:   *Increases in Labour Productivity in Rice Cultivation on the Saga Plain*

	Labour days per 10 ares	Yield (kg/10 ares)	Output per labour day (kg)
1857	38·65	333	8·6
1888	33·2	358	10·8
1909	29·25	370	12·6
1922	20·1	364	18·1
1936	18·18	403	22·2
1939	18·2	460	25·3

Source: various surveys covering different Plain areas as for Appendix Table 1.

3.   Structural Responses

In this section I shall begin by presenting the available data on the changes in the agricultural structure on the Saga Plain after 1923, and then go on to examine how these changes were related to the process of technical change described earlier. Finally I shall look at the way in which village groups and village social structure responded to these trends.

(1)   THE RISE OF THE MIDDLE-SCALE FARMER

We have already seen how the outflow of labour to industry led to a rise in the proportion of middle-scale, owner/tenant farm households within Saga Plain villages, and how it was these households who pressed for the mechanisation of irrigation pumping. The available data all go to suggest that this trend towards concentration in the centre of the size distribution of holdings continued during the 1920s and 1930s, resulting in the emergence of a structure in which most full-time farm households cultivated holdings of 1–3 hectares. This is clear from the data for the prefecture as a whole, shown earlier as Table 6.9, which reveal that, in the period between 1928 and 1938, the numbers of households at both extremes of the size distribution of cultivated holdings (under 1 hectare and over 5 hectares) were declining, while the numbers farming 1–5 hectares were increasing. The interesting feature of the data for this period is the new trend towards increase in the numbers farming 2–3 and 3–5 hectares, which had previously been declining. This suggests that the upper limit to the size of the family farm was indeed rising.

For the Plain itself, Chart 6.1 showed that the labour outflow tailed

Table 8.6:   *The Distribution of Households by Area Cultivated*
A.   1938, %:

Area cultivated (ha.)	Whole country	Saga Prefecture	Saga County	Honjō *Mura*
Under 0·5	33·6	25·5	21·7	19·3
0·5−1	32·8	32·2	25·0	9·6
1−2	24·3	32·9	34·6	41·5
2−3	5·7	7·8	14·2	24·8
3−5	2·2	1·4	4·4	4·8
Over 5	1·4	0·04	0·1	0·0

B.   A *Buraku* of Higashi Yoga *Mura*, no. of households:

Area cultivated (ha.)	1934	1939
Under 0·5	8	6
0·5−1	2	3
1−1·5	4	7
1·5−2	11	7
2−2·5	5	8
2·5−3	1	3
Over 3	5	2
Total	36	36

N.B. During this period four households left the village and four new ones were established.

Sources: A.: Kayō, N., *Nihon Nōgyō Kiso Tōkei* (68), p.135; *Saga-Ken Tōkei Sho* (101); Tanaka, S., *Saga Heitan Chitai* (95), p.230.
B.: Isobe, T., 'Saga Heitan Nōgyō' (89), p.133.

off after 1923, while continuing quite strongly in the prefecture as a whole, so that changes in the size distribution on the Plain must have been much more markedly the results of internal movements within the village. However the data shown in Table 8.6 suggest that these movements did in fact produce the same kind of concentration more strongly on the Plain than elsewhere. Almost half the farm households in Saga County in 1938, and two-thirds of those in the individual Plain village surveyed by Tanaka, farmed 1−3 hectares, compared with just 30% in the country as a whole. The proportions at the upper end of the middle-sized group were also substantially greater on the Plain than elsewhere. The data in the second part of the table, collected by Isobe from the records of one of the *buraku* of Higashi Yoga village just to the south of Saga City, show the same sort of pattern, and reveal the shift towards the 2−3 hectare level in the late 1930s.

These changes were accompanied by the same trend towards increase in the proportion of households both owning and renting in land as was observed in the 1910s. For the prefecture as a whole, the proportion of owner/tenants rose from about 47% in the late 1920s to 50·5% in 1940, and although we have no comparable data for households in Saga County, the available figures for farm workers by tenure status show the same movements.[34] The proportion of the paddy area which was tenanted, however, remained at or around 50% throughout the 1920s and 1930s. This leads to the conclusion that the mechanisms by which households moved into the 1−3 hectare class were the same as before. As before, larger landowners continued to split up their holdings, letting out parts of them to households moving into the middle-scale, owner/tenant group, selling pieces of land to their former tenants, and so on. This time, though, they were hit not only by labour shortage, but also by the effects of the depression, during which, for instance, two of the large-scale landowning households on the Plain suffered big losses from their banking and financial interests, one in fact going bankrupt.[35] In 1924 there were three landowners owning more than 50 hectares in Saga City and six in Saga County. By 1930, there remained only one in the City and three in the County.[36] Sales by big landowners meant that the number of medium-scale landowners, owning 1−5 hectares, increased, as owner/tenants reaching the limits of what they could farm began to use their savings to increase their landownership.[37]

The division of village society into two groups of households, the larger-scale employers and the small-scale cultivator/agricultural labourers, had thus completely disappeared by the 1930s. The new structure was dominated by the relatively homogeneous group of medium-scale cultivators, who made up 50% or more of village households. In Honjō village, households farming 1−3 hectares farmed 80% of the village's area.[38] The majority of the households farming less than this in fact farmed less than half a hectare, and probably had other part-time occupations.[39] In the village surveyed by Isobe to be described in detail later, most of the households farming small areas contained one or more members working off the farm. Households cultivating small areas therefore seem to have been generally in the process of moving out of agriculture altogether or becoming part-time farmers. Apart from the few remaining large-scale cultivators, almost all households which were committed to farming as a full-time occupation thus cultivated between one and three hectares. The implication of this is that by now the ability to adopt and operate the new technical package successfully depended less on the area of land which a household could command and more on the characteristics and structure of individual households, which determined the ability to gain access to capital and labour inputs as well as land. In what follows I shall look at the ways in which the set of new techniques which emerged to complement mechanised irrigation consolidated the position of the middle-scale farm households, and I shall examine the above implication by considering which sorts of middle-scale households were best able to take advantage of the characteristics of the new technology.

(2) THE NEW TECHNOLOGY AND THE CHARACTERISTICS OF
HOUSEHOLD ECONOMIES

Everything that has gone before leads up to the conclusion that farmers of middle-scale holdings of 1−3 hectares were best able to take advantage of the characteristics of the new technology, and that, as the technology developed, movement towards the upper end of this size-band became more and more feasible. Comparison of the results for the Saga Plain households sampled in the Rice Economy Survey of 1913−15 with those in the Middle-Scale Farmers Survey of 1940, all of which farmed areas between 1·5 and 2·5 hectares, shows that the profitability of such farms had risen substantially.[40] The surplus left to these households after meeting all expenses, including labour, measured as a percentage of their income from their rice crop, had risen on average from 14·5% in 1913−15 to 30·5% in 1940.[41] These surveys make clear that a major source of increase in income lay in earnings from activities outside crop cultivation, which were recorded as zero in the 1913−15 survey but brought in the equivalent of almost a quarter of the value of the rice crop in 1940. These were the earnings from diversified farm activities, such as horse-rearing, straw work and so on, and from the full- or part-time work of family members in industrial or service occupations, which the new technology made it possible to pursue. On the expenses side, the value of labour input was rising proportionately, while that of land in the form of rental payments was falling as rental rates declined (see later) and middle-scale households came to own more of the land they farmed. The relative cost of fertiliser input remained much the same as increasing input was offset by declining price. Altogether, these surveys confirm that middle-scale farmers were profiting substantially from the progress of technical change in the 1920s and 1930s.

   If we now turn to look at the factors conditioning access to the inputs required by the new technology and the changed structure of a profitable farm household economy, we can see why middle-scale households, and not smaller- or larger-scale households, were in the best position to take advantage of the changes going on. But we shall also see emerging during the 1930s differences between households within the middle-scale group in ability to exploit the new technology to the full. I shall look first at access to labour and capital inputs, and then at the changes in access to land which made it possible for households from other categories to move into the middle-scale group.

1.   Labour

The effect of the new technology was, as we have seen, to replace the heavy labour requirements over much of the year with two relatively short periods of peak labour demand, the latter of which (the autumn rice-harvest/second-crop planting peak) was substantially eased by subsequent mechanisation. Aside from these two peaks, a family labour force of, for instance, a househead couple and their successors had more than enough time, under the new technology, to farm a holding of a hectare or over, the upper limit rising to two hectares or even more with the mechanisation of the various grain preparation operations. On holdings which provided adequate employment for a family labour force over the year, though, additional hired labour remained essential for the transplanting peak.[g] This was not at this time a severe problem because it was now possible to tap the supply of temporary female labour from other areas in the well-organised manner described earlier. Therefore a holding of $1-2$ hectares and a compact family labour force of two couples represented an ideal land/labour combination.

What of those households who did not possess this ideal combination? Households with holdings larger than two hectares or so could continue to cultivate them as long as they had a suitable family labour force or could retain the services of permanently-hired workers. Clearly some households did continue cultivation in this way,[h] but, as we have already seen, their numbers were declining. The labour-saving machinery available was not designed for farms larger than two hectares or so, and did not represent a means of farming on a large scale. The increasingly meticulous and labour-using cultivation techniques which made up part of the new technology (e.g. careful water control, improved seed beds) intensified the existing problems of managing larger labour forces in Japanese agriculture. The pressure to provide younger sons with educations that did not fit them for agricultural work made it

[g] Households in West Kawazoe, surveyed in 1931, were employing on average 450 hours of temporary labour during the year. Isobe, T., 'Iwayuru Saga Dankai' (70), p.37. Those in Tanaka's survey hired an average 32 man/days per household in 1938. Tanaka, S., *Saga Heitan Chitai* (95), p.312.

[h] E.g. household 1 in Table 8.9, which employed two *nenko*.

harder to maintain a suitable family labour force structure. As a result of these forces, in the village surveyed by Isobe, for instance, all three households owning more than three hectares farmed less than that,[42] and other surveys similarly show that households which owned or came to own more than two hectares rented out their land above this level.[43]

At the other extreme, households with holdings less than a hectare could not provide full-time employment for a family labour force of two couples. Such households would therefore tend to seek either more land to farm (by the mechanisms to be examined in section 3), or employment away from the farm. Pure tenant households owning little or no land had both less incentive to remain in agriculture and more difficulty than other households in acquiring extra land, because of the drain of their rental payments, and would therefore be those most likely to seek outside employment. In Isobe's village in 1939, almost all the households farming less than one hectare were pure tenants and had members working away from agriculture.[44] In a number, the househead successor was working away, indicating that the household as a whole was probably moving out of agriculture. In a survey of another village, made in 1934, of the ten households farming less than a hectare, six were pure tenants and none owner/tenants, and only one household with more than one hectare was a pure tenant.[i] The conclusion follows that, in the 1930s, small-scale cultivators with the incentive of landownership to encourage them to stay in agriculture were able to acquire more land, usually by renting in,[j] and those owning little or no land were in the process of moving out, either full-time or part-time.

Finally, as households of all kinds moved in these ways towards the ideal land/labour combination of the new technology, there remained only those households who could reduce the holdings they cultivated to the ideal size but could not, for social and family reasons, trim their family structure down to the ideal pattern. These were the former central, labour-employer families in the village, with their extended households of relatives and dependents, with social obligations impossible to shed along with the land it was no longer profitable to farm.[k] As we shall see later, these households, while still central to the village lineage structure and able to farm the optimum area, were in fact less able than the

---

[i] Matoba, T., *Kyūshū ni okeru Keizai to Nōgyō* (90), p.251. The village contained 36 households in total.

[j] 20 out of the 26 households farming more than one hectare in the above survey were owner/tenants.

[k] See for instance the households 'with dependency rates over 60%' in Table 8.9. Similarly, in Tanaka's village the 1−2 hectare group had the lowest average number of dependents per household. Tanaka, S., *Saga Heitan Chitai* (95), pp.309−10.

younger, socially inferior households, who had more compact family labour forces, to take advantage of the new technology.

2.   Capital

What determined access to the capital equipment required as part of the new technology? The most important items to consider here are horses and motorised threshers. Hullers, as was pointed out earlier, were bought by a limited number of rural households with the purpose of hulling other people's rice as a business proposition. All households in most Plain areas had access to electric irrigation pumps. Petrol-driven pumps were in general acquired by households who had particular irrigation problems, so that access to them was largely associated with difficult water supply conditions. In some cases they were brought to use to avoid water shortage in times of drought or to facilitate better water control, and ownership of them and access to them were determined much as for mechanical threshers. Virtually speaking all households owned the necessary ploughs and weeders, and smaller tools such as hoes.[45]

The distribution of horse-ownership seems to have followed almost exactly the line dividing full-time farm households from part-time. That is to say, in each of the villages for which survey data exist, more or less every household farming more than a hectare owned a horse and almost all households farming less than that did not.[46] Thus, by the mid-to-late 1930s when these surveys were made, a horse had become a standard requirement for all households committed to full-time farming. This must have been made possible by the revival of double-cropping, which provided even relatively small-scale households with the fodder necessary for a horse. Thus one of the major factors differentiating the two groups of households making up the structure before mechanisation had ceased to operate, and the majority of households now had equal access to perhaps the most important capital input in Saga Plain agriculture.

Table 8.7 presents the results of a survey, carried out in Saga County in 1937, into the distribution of the ownership of mechanised threshers and pumps and the motors that powered them. From this it is clear that ownership of mechanised equipment was quite highly concentrated within the group of upper-middle-scale cultivators farming 2 hectares or more. This limitation of machine ownership is confirmed by the surveys of Isobe and Matoba, and is clear in Tanaka's village also, although, in this very highly mechanised village,[1] a significant

---

[1] There was one motor per 2·4 households, compared with the national average of one per 22·4 households. Tanaka, S., *Saga Heitan Chitai* (95), p.319.

Table 8.7: Distribution of the Ownership of Machinery by Area Cultivated
(10 villages in Saga County, 1937, machines as a percentage of the number of households)
A = petrol engine; B = mechanical thresher; C = privately-owned pump.

	owners			owner/tenants			tenants		
	A	B	C	A	B	C	A	B	C
Under ½ ha.	1·5	0·0	1·5	1·7	0·9	0·9	1·1	0·7	0·9
½ to 1 ha.	3·2	2·0	2·2	5·8	4·0	3·1	3·3	2·4	2·1
1 to 2 ha.	19·4	17·9	12·4	20·0	15·9	11·6	13·2	10·0	9·3
2 to 3 ha.	50·6	47·7	32·6	46·5	42·1	29·6	29·5	26·5	21·0
3 to 5 ha.	75·0	71·5	52·3	78·9	71·6	56·2	52·4	48·8	33·3
Over 5 ha.	116·6	100·0	115·0	100·0	100·0	100·0	100·0	100·0	100·0

Source: Yamada, T., and Ōta, R., *Saga-Ken Nōgyō Shi* (73), p.388.

proportion of the machines were owned by households in the 1−2 hectare class.[47]

If we look more closely at the village surveys, however, it becomes clear that access to powered machinery was not as limited as the pattern of ownership would suggest. In Tanaka's village, although owners of powered threshers farmed only 61% of the paddy area, rice from 96% of the area was threshed by machine, so that 35% of the village's rice was threshed with someone else's thresher.[48] Tanaka points out that this proportion would be much higher in villages in which ownership of powered machinery was less widespread. The nature of the relationship between the household owning a thresher and the other households which used it begins to emerge from Tanaka's finding that for over two-thirds of the time during which individual machines were threshing rice other than that of their owners they were being operated by the labour of the user household without fee to the owner household, i.e. the machines were being lent freely by owner-families to user-families.[49] In Isobe's village, ownership of threshers and pumps was concentrated within a relatively small group of households, who tended to own, but not necessarily to cultivate, larger areas than the other households in the village, but whose chief common characteristic was their position in the lineage structure of the village. That is to say, they were (with one exception) main households with branches within the village. This suggests that, while threshers were bought by the larger-landowning main households, they were used by the whole family grouping of main and branch households. In Tanaka's village, the first households to buy pumps were all owner/tenants, mostly farming middle-sized holdings, not the larger-landowning main households, suggesting that the real innovators in machine purchase were the middle-scale owner/tenants, even though later the actual purchases were made by the larger-landowning households.[50] These suggestions are borne out by Yoshida's study of post-war Saga Plain villages, in which he records that larger items of machinery, such as threshers and pumps and the post-war power-tiller, were still being operated by family groups of main and branch households, or by neighbourhood groups.[m]

The conclusion follows that, although the main households who had traditionally owned horses and the major items of capital equipment were called upon to buy the threshers and pumps required by the new technology, this probably did not restrict the use of them, and most households were able to gain access to powered machinery through their relationships with the purchasing families. While the increasingly independent branch households may, as Isobe suggests,[51] have disliked the dependent relationship into which this put them, and may have made every effort to acquire their own machinery when they could, it meant that the burden of purchasing the machinery which the middle-scale, owner/tenant, branch households were probably the most eager to use was transferred to the larger-landowning main households.

3. Land

The quite clear division, which had existed in Tokugawa and Meiji period Saga Plain villages, between those who owned and farmed relatively large holdings and those who owned very little land was broken down, as we have seen, by the impact of industrialisation on the village economy. Access to land, either to rent or to buy, had therefore, by the 1920s and 1930s, become much less of a problem for Saga Plain farmers. With rising yields generating savings for farm households, the possibility of being able to acquire more land in order to reach the ideal land/labour combination became much stronger, and, with larger landowners under pressure to re-organise their holdings and shed land no longer profitable to them, there was land available to be taken up. In general, as I shall go on to show, the position of the landlord, especially the non-cultivating one, was deteriorating, and, for those still unwilling or unable to buy more land, the position of having to rent in some of the land cultivated was no great barrier to reaping the benefits of the new technology.

[m] Yoshida, T., 'Integration and Change' (100), p.104. Joint-ownership of threshers by neighbourhood groups existed in Tanaka's pre-war village as well, although it was less common than ownership by main households. Tanaka, S., *Saga Heitan Chitai* (95), pp.332–3.

Larger landlords were, as we have already seen, often badly hit by the depression of the early 1930s, both through losses outside agriculture and through the drop in the value of the rice they received as rent. However this merely compounded the more general problems they faced as a result of the increasingly strong position of tenants. Widening job opportunities, increasing mobility, compulsory education, and the extension of the franchise to all males over twenty-five, together with the sheer decline in the numbers of those seeking agricultural employment, all meant that tenants were increasingly unwilling to accept former levels of rent and former tenancy conditions. Although the proportion of Saga Plain land tenanted probably did not decline, it was increasingly being let to those who already owned some land and who were in a much stronger position than the landless pure tenant.

The reflection of these forces in declining rental levels is shown in Table 8.8, from which it can be seen that rents in Saga County failed to keep pace with rising yields and were taking a declining proportion of the crop in the 1930s. Conditions of tenancy were probably also improving in other ways. For instance, it was increasingly becoming the custom for landlords to give tenants quite substantial gifts — generally around 10% of the value of rented land — for land improvement work which the tenant carried out, or as a kind of compensation when the tenant left.[52] Tenants' demands were expressed in Saga as elsewhere by tenancy disputes, but these were less common there than elsewhere, and it appears that in general tenants, on the Plain especially, managed to achieve substantial improvements in their position without strong opposition from landlords.[n]

The increasing unprofitability of land to own as an investment is also reflected in a change in the nature of the land reclamation projects carried out in the coastal plain areas.[53] In earlier periods, pressure on the land and high rents had provided the incentive for land reclamation projects, which had generally been carried out by landowners and businessmen with capital to invest in creating land to rent out. Projects in the 1920s and 1930s, however, were generally undertaken on the initiative of local farmers anxious to expand the area they could cultivate. In

[n] In 1918, when records of tenancy disputes began, two disputes were recorded in Saga County (out of nine in the prefecture as a whole). No more were recorded (although they continued in other parts of the prefecture) until 1927, and ten more took place between then and 1929. Others were recorded during the early 1930s, but they represented only a small proportion of the total occurring in the prefecture. By this time, as Waswo argues in *Japanese Landlords* (36), the nature of disputes had changed, and in Saga as elsewhere they had come to take place more commonly in the poorer parts of the prefecture. Data from *Saga-Ken Nōchi Kaikaku Shi* (79), p.404 and Kamagata, I., *Saga Nōgyō* (71), pp.244–8.

Table 8.8:   Rental Rates in Saga County
(Per 10 ares of middle-grade paddy)

	1909	1923	1937
Rents (kg)	180	193	193
Yields (kg)	370	375	549
Rental rate (% of crop)	48·6	51·6	35·2

Source: Isobe, T., 'Iwayuru Saga Dankai' (70), p.42, from Saga Prefecture Government Report (1909), a survey by the prefectural interior department (1923), and a survey by the Hypothec Bank (1937).

some cases, these cultivators lost financial control of the projects they had initiated, especially during the depression, and ended up renting instead of owning the new land, but even so, their position remained quite strong as a result of the trends described here.

*

This discussion of access to inputs produces the conclusion that few households with a full-time stake in agriculture would have experienced difficulties in acquiring the use of land, horses, or the capital inputs which embodied improved techniques. Rather, the key to economic success within the new technical framework was coming to lie more in the structure of the family labour force, with the newer, medium-scale, compact, branch households better able to operate the increasingly sophisticated technology than the still old-fashioned, rambling main households. The available studies of individual villages confirm this view and provide some evidence that the younger, up-and-coming branch households did indeed operate the new techniques more efficiently than those either above or below them in the social and economic hierarchy. This appears most clearly in the study by Isobe, the basic data from which are shown in Table 8.9.

The households labelled *honke* in this table are the central main families in the village, and most of the branch households in the village (labelled *bunke 1* and *bunke 2*) are branches of *honke 1* families. Only *honke 1* households (and household 14)° owned threshers and pumps. *Honke 2* households are like *honke 1* households in being larger-scale cultivators who are not branches of any other household, but only

° Household 14 was not a traditional *honke* household and had risen to equal the old main households in terms of asset ownership from being a tenant farmer. It was apparently considered to be a most remarkable household. Isobe, T., 'Saga Heitan Chitai' (88), p.224.

Table 8.9:   The Structure of a Saga Plain Village in 1939

Asset ownership group (1)	Household type (2)	Household number	No. of *honke* & year estd.	Owner or tenant (3)	Area owned (ha)	Area farmed (ha)	1934–9 increase (O) or decrease (X)		Labour structure (4)
							area owned	area farmed	
A	*Honke* 1	1		T/O	1·52	3·50	X		
		2		O/L	2·76	1·55	X	X	
		5		O/T	1·77	2·22	X	X	
		9		O/L	3·57	1·86	O	X	
		11		O/L	3·68	2·10	O	X	
	Other 1	14		O/T	1·11	2·10	O	O	
	Honke 2	3		O/L	3·62	2·95		O	O
		4		O/T	2·22	2·50	X	O	
		12		O/T	2·05	3·00	O	O	
B	*Bunke* 1	6	9, 1921	O/T	1·45	2·21	O	O	O
		7	12, Mei	O/L	2·59	2·10	O	X	
		8	1, Mei	T/O	0·32	1·40	X	X	
		10	5, Mei	O/T	2·06	2·71		X	
		15	9, Mei	O/T	1·40	2·04	O	O	O
		18	9, Mei	O	1·50	1·65		X	O
		19	1, Mei	T/O	0·91	2·03	O	O	O
		21	12, 1906	O/L	2·53	1·50	O		O
		22	5, 1938	O	1·20	1·20			
		25	14, 1923	T/O	0·41	2·00	X	O	O
	Other 2	13		O	1·29	1·12		X	
		16		T/O	0·26	1·40		X	O
		17		T	0·01	1·50		X	
		20		T/O	0·31	1·30		X	
		23		O/T	0·92	1·75	X	X	
		24		T/O	0·52	1·50		X	
		26	13, Mei	T/O	0·51	1·10	X	X	
C	*Bunke* 2	27	2, Mei	L/O	2·00	0·20			
		28	11, 1936	O	0·93	0·93			
		29	2, 1931	L/O	0·95	0·34	O	O	
		31	23, 1937	O/T	0·35	0·85			
	Other 3	30		T		0·40	X	X	
		32	another village 1907	O/T	0·81	1·34			
		33		T		0·46			
		36		T		0·62			
		37		T	0·02	0·20			
		39		T		0·45			
		40		T	0·01	0·12			

Source: Isobe, T., 'Saga Heitan Chitai' (88), pp.222–3.
Notes: see p.272

Dependency rate over 60% (5)	Over 40 labour days per 10 ares	Nenko	Temporary labour (days)	Part-time in agriculture (males) (6)	Office holding				Double cropping rate over 150% (7)
					Co-op director	Mayor	Deputy Mayor	Village council	
O		2	17			1929–32	1895–11	1895–11	
			125		1908–13	1908–11	1911–14	1914–22	
O						1911–14	1914–17	1922–26	O
	O				1908–15	1917–23			
O			10		1914–15	1894–98 / 1914–17	1904–08		
			29		1908–13	1923–26			O
O			21		1910–13	1902–08	1908–11		
O		1	18				1902–04		
	O								O
O			15						O
					1908–15	1926–29			
	O								O
	O			X		1935–38			O
	O			XX					O
	O				1914–15	1932–35			
	O								O
	O		16						
O									O
	O								O
	O			O					O
O	O		6						O
			2	⊙X					
	O		8	OXX					
O	O								O
O				⊙					
	O								O
O			5	⊙					
O			85						
O			29						
			20	OX					
	O			X					
			11	OXX					
				OXX					
				O					O

Notes to Table 8.9

(1) Asset ownership groups:
   A = household owns horse, mechanical thresher, mechanical pump, mat-maker.
   B = household owns horse, mat-maker.
   C = household owns mat-maker.
(2) *Honke* = main household.
   Bunke = branch household.
(3) O = owner, T = tenant, L = landlord.
(4) O = farm employing househead couple and their successor only.
(5) O = household where more than 60% of members are unable to work.
(6) Members of household employed off the farm:
   ⊙ househead
   O = successor
   X = someone else.
(7) Double-cropping rate = planted area as a proportion of cultivated area.

one has branches of its own and this represents the only larger-scale land-owning household with branches which does not own a thresher and a pump. *Bunke 2* households, with the exception of household 27 which is the household of the village priest, are branches established later than the *bunke 1* households and therefore of lower status and economic position. 'Other 2' and 'other 3' households have no particular family relationship to other households in the village (except for households 13 and 26).

The *honke 1* households were the former *nenko*-employing households in this village, farming 3–4 hectares in the Meiji period. Their traditionally superior status is borne out by the number of their branches and by their importance in providing political office holders. By the time of the survey, however, they had reduced the area they cultivated down to levels similar to those of their branch households, although they still tended to own more land than other households and to retain their position as landlords. Significantly, they tended to have more dependents and also to hire in more labour.

At the other end of the village social structure were the 'other 2', 'other 3' and *bunke 2* households. 'Other 2' households tended to own less land than other category B (horse-owning) households and, like category C (non-horse-owning) households, had more of the character of tenants. 'Other 2' households were all reducing the area they cultivated and a number of them had members working outside agriculture. In this also, they were coming to resemble category C (*bunke 2* and 'other 3') households, who were almost all on the way to becoming part-time farm households or moving out altogether.

This leaves the *bunke 1* households, who farmed middle-sized holdings with no particular tendency to increase or reduce them, and who were commonly owner/tenants. I have argued that this was the kind of household best suited to take advantage of the new technology, and in this village, as the table shows, these were indeed the households with the compact family labour forces committed to agriculture who seem to have been operating the new technology most efficiently. Unlike most households either above or below them, most of these households contained only the household couple and their successor. Few had members working away from agriculture, and almost all applied more labour to their land and achieved a higher double-cropping rate than other households. The fact that these were now the households providing the initiative and leadership in the village is reflected in their increasing importance as political office-holders, and, with one exception, no member of the traditional *honke* households held any of the political offices covered in the table after 1926.[P]

These findings are confirmed by Tanaka's study. He similarly found that the middle-scale owner/tenant group had the highest double-cropping rates, the highest labour productivity and the fewest dependents.[54] The connection between the spread of new, increasingly mechanised technology and the rising influence of branch households and younger men has been observed elsewhere in Japan,[55] and it became much more marked in Saga after the war.[56] But its origins can be seen to go back to the technical developments which sprang from the mechanisation of irrigation, and it leads to the conclusion that, although the new technical package suited all households with middle-scale, family-sized holdings, it brought to the fore a group with new characteristics better adapted to an agricultural sector now part of an industrial economy.

(3) THE ROLE OF VILLAGE INSTITUTIONS

Finally, what role did village institutions and local agricultural organisations play in the process of diffusion of the new technology and how did the changes described in this chapter affect the way in which they operated? I will look first at the official organisations—the *nōkai* and co-operatives—and then at community organisations within the village.

The prefectural and county *nōkai*, and the local village agricultural groups below them, had, as we have seen, played a very important role as intermediaries between farmers and the government in the course of the technical changes culminating in the mechanisation of pumping.

[P] Cf. Fukutake's description, in *Japanese Rural Society* (45), pp.146−7, of the shift of village political power away from the traditional leading families in the first twenty-five years of this century.

This role had both a technical side, with the government working through the *nōkai* to disseminate information and extension services, and an economic side, for instance through fertiliser marketing. However, as the 1920s and 1930s progressed, on the technical side, the *nōkai*, which had begun way back before 1900 as spontaneous organisations of innovative farmers, became more and more absorbed into the local government organisation as the main organs of the official extension system, epitomising the fact that technical progress in agriculture could no longer be of a kind which farmers could promote and develop themselves. On the economic side, the functions of providing farmers with assistance in marketing, finance and so on were passing more and more into the hands of local co-operatives, that is to say of organisations of more or less equal farm households grouping together to further their interests as farm businesses.

The government take-over, as it were, of the *nōkai* was facilitated by legislation, enacted in the early 1920s, which extended salary support to *nōkai* technicians at the town and village (*chō* and *mura*) level, in addition to that already given to county and prefectural *nōkai* technicians. The system of county-level government technicians was subsequently abolished and these technicians moved over into being *nōkai* technicians, although they continued to work in the county offices.[57] The supply of new local-level technicians was met from the graduates of expanded training courses run by the experiment station.[58] In 1928 the whole system of *nōkai* technicians was re-organised so as to provide specialised technical advice in areas such as animal husbandry. As the 1930s went on, government policy towards agriculture and rural life became increasingly interventionist, with measures to support the rice price, encourage wheat production, and so on, as well as to promote the government's political aims, and the *nōkai* were used as the means of administering these policies.

Meanwhile, as the *nōkai* became increasingly part of the bureaucracy, the co-operative movement, which had been slow to take off in Saga, began to develop. The number of co-operative members in Saga Prefecture rose from 12,572 in 1915 to 85,292 by 1936.[59] Fertiliser supply co-operatives began to compete with *nōkai* and local merchants and, with their favourable links with fertiliser producers through the national co-operative system, to obtain an expanding share of the market. Rice-buying, storing and marketing co-operatives also began to grow up and were so successful as to provoke the formation of an anti-co-operative movement among Saga traders.[60] Towards the end of the 1930s, informal co-operatives of cattle-producers, horse-breeders and so on also grew up.

In addition, co-operative finance played a role in facilitating the purchase of machinery. In Tanaka's village, over half the expenditure on petrol motors, for instance, was met by farmers' own cash, but most of the remaining borrowed finance came from co-operatives.[61] Tanaka's analysis of the recipients of co-operative lending for the purchase of threshers gives a clue as to the groups of farmers most aided by the growth of co-operatives. Three-quarters of this lending went to owner/tenant households, most of them in the 1−3 hectare class. A further 18% went to pure tenants, all farming 1−3 hectares, and very little went to pure owner farmers. This suggests that the growth of co-operatives was a further reflection of the initiative and requirements of the middle-scale owner/tenant group.

Finally, what effect did the spread of new technology and the changed village structure have on community relationships? In some respects, undoubtedly, the technical and structural changes which had been taking place in Saga since the 1910s destroyed the bases for intra-village economic co-operation. The departure of most of the *nenko* class, and the subsequent mechanisation of pumping, ended the old relationships between *nenko*-employer households and small-scale cultivator/agricultural labourer households. Most households now owned horses, so all the relationships based on the loan of horse-time also died out. The traditional village methods for ensuring that everyone got through with their transplanting were no longer adequate, after the change in rotation which concentrated peak labour demand in the spring.[62] Mud-raising remained a village responsibility, and where mud-raising machines were used they were bought by the village, but the incentive and pressure to carry out this operation were much reduced by the mechanisation of pumping and the spread of chemical fertilisers.[63]

In other respects, however, the new technical system created new bases for economic co-operation between households. We have already seen how the use of new items of machinery was organised through the traditional *honke/bunke* family groups. But the balance within these groups was shifting towards the more efficient, up-and-coming branch households, and the new technology was also bringing into existence other groups of farmers of more equal status. The pump-operating *kumiai* are an obvious example of this type of group, and similar neighbourhood groups were also founded for purposes such as machinery purchase. The spread of co-operatives reflects the same tendencies. Thus, in many ways, the new technology did not make the Saga Plain farmer less dependent on the help and co-operation of other households. It changed the functions which made co-operation necessary, and it made the relationships within the group less those between patron and client and more those of a cross between business partners and trade-union members, but in many ways it did not lessen the unity of the village group.[q]

As a result, when Yoshida made his survey of community relationships in post-war Saga Plain villages, he found intra-village organisations were much more active in the Plain village he studied than in the more remote but economically less advanced hill villages with which he compared it.[64] Because agriculture on the Plain prospered after 1923, there was much less incentive for the young to leave or to seek part-time work, and the differentiation of economic interests caused by some households' relegation of agriculture to the position of a side-occupation had not been strong enough to break up the village unity. As we have seen, the leading group of middle-scale owner/tenant households who predominated within the village were committed, with their successors, to full-time agriculture and for this they needed the maintenance of strong village ties.

*

In this chapter we have seen Saga Plain villages complete their transformation from societies composed of larger-scale, patron households and their client, employee/tenant households, to those made up of communities of farm households with similar economic interests, operating an increasingly mechanised and sophisticated technology and backed up by an increasingly scientifically-orientated government extension service. This transformation made Saga not only the most productive prefecture in the country, but also a pioneer in the development of the institutional organisation required by a small-scale mechanised agriculture. It was because of this that Japanese agricultural economists developed the idea of the 'Saga stage' to describe the kind of technical and institutional organisation which Saga pioneered, and towards which they saw Japanese agriculture moving in the years before the land reform.[65] The essence of this idea was that Saga represented the first evidence that Japanese agriculture was beginning to follow the path which the agricultural sectors of then-developed countries were believed to have followed, towards higher labour productivity, larger scale and the use of machinery. The 2−3 hectare, owner/tenant farmers of Saga were seen as pioneering the breakthrough away from the earlier stages of Japanese agricultural development, from the so-called 'Tōhoku stage' of large-scale, 'feudal' landowners ruling over low-productivity tenant

[q] On the continuing functions of village-based agricultural groups in post-war Japan, see Fukutake, T., *Japanese Rural Society* (45), pp.92−4, and many examples in Dore's *Shinohata* (43).

farmers, and the 'Kinki stage' of high-yielding, labour-intensive, commercialised farming on very small holdings. Saga farmers were beginning to show that, in Japan also, high yields were compatible with high
labour productivity, on the basis of the scientific management of relatively large-scale farms. The scholars who developed this view reckoned
without the land reform, the 'economic miracle' (which generated both
the great expansion of employment opportunities lying behind the
growth of part-time farming and the economic resources required to
preserve the interests of the ageing but influential farm sector), and perhaps also more fundamental features of rural attitudes and of the
Japanese agricultural environment. Nevertheless, they confirm the idea
that Saga farmers in the 1920s and 1930s did develop a set of techniques
and of individual and group farm management which was new in Japan
and which pointed towards a way in which a small-scale, rice-growing
agricultural sector might accommodate itself to the needs of a modern
industrial economy.

From the point of view of the issues raised in chapter 1, the evidence
presented here is also interesting in that it reveals how the progress taken
by technical change in Saga generated none of the kinds of distributional and structural problems emerging in some areas of the Green
Revolution today. The characteristics of both the initial and the subsequent, more mechanised, stages of technical change in Saga agriculture
were such that few farm households were technically unable to take
advantage of new methods, and the institutional organisation of extension work and of group activity within the village made sure that almost
all committed farmers were able to gain access to them. As I have frequently pointed out, the influence of industrialisation both structurally,
through the growth of employment opportunities for the poorer members of the village community, and technically, through the provision of
the knowledge and skills necessary to develop specific solutions to local
problems, remained an extremely important factor in explaining this,
and I will return to this issue in the final chapter, which brings together
the themes and conclusions of the whole study.

CHAPTER NINE
Some Concluding Thoughts

The purpose of this book has been to describe the economic workings of a rural community—the agricultural technology it used, the way it organised the production and distribution of output, and the forces conditioning changes in these things. Its purpose has not been to draw out 'lessons' for present-day developing countries from the experience of Saga Plain farmers, and indeed, as I shall go on to argue shortly, there are a number of factors which make that experience, in general terms, of little help to those faced with the problems of Asian agriculture today. Nevertheless, the story of the economic development of Saga Plain agriculture presents us with what was, by almost all criteria, a highly successful case of technical change, centring on the drawing up and implementation of a project whose results were all that present-day development administrators would ask of such a scheme. It has also shown us in action an early case of the much vaunted and envied Japanese success in adapting known technology, through consultation between workers, management and government, so as to be able to operate it highly efficiently within a particular economic and social environment. In this brief concluding chapter, therefore, while stressing that the economic circumstances of Japanese agriculture and of the Saga Plain in the prewar period differed in many ways from those of present-day developing countries, I will try to bring out the factors which seem to me to have been most significant in determining that success.

*

As chapter 2 suggested, it was once common to argue that the Japanese experience constituted a 'model' of the role which agriculture could play in economic development. We saw there how doubts were cast on the validity of a number of aspects of the model's conception of agricultural change in Japan, most notably on the apparently fast rate of agricultural output growth and the contribution of agricultural resources to industrial growth. Beyond this, however, a more funda-mental objection to the use of Japanese experience as a model for the present day lies in the more strictly historical argument that the econo-mic conditions surrounding Japanese agricultural development, both in the Japanese and in the world economies, differed so significantly from those surrounding today's developing agricultural sectors as to make comparisons irrelevant.[a] The substance of chapter 3 can be seen as, to some extent, corroborating this argument: the pattern and nature of technical change and economic development in Japanese agriculture depended heavily on the influence exerted by the growing industrial sector and this industrial growth differed significantly, both in its scope and in the type of technology on which it was based, from that exper-ienced in present-day developing countries. As we saw, in the early stages of development the bulk of industrial output was produced in small-scale, rural factories or workshops, and when modern industrial-isation began, the technology adopted was such that industry was able to absorb relatively large numbers of agricultural workers. Behind this lay the fact that Japan's industry developed at a time when there were growing world markets for simple manufactured goods (e.g. textiles) and when the best available techniques still offered scope for the use of relatively large amounts of labour. Thus, in the case of the Saga Plain, farm households were drawn into market relationships with the outside world not only by the increasing demand for food output, but also by the increasing demand for labour. The traditional system was disrupted not only by the increase in profitable opportunities for the sale of output, but also by the small farmer/agricultural labourer's finding his prospects sufficiently improved by the increase in employment opportunities to be able to opt out of the system which had assured him of a living, but little more than a subsistence one. In other developing countries (though possibly excepting the cases of some now-developed countries), this is not a typical way in which traditional rural economic systems are broken up and farmers drawn into commercial markets. More common causes of such changes would be such things as popula-tion growth, improvements in communications, impositions of taxes, changes in tenure and landownership systems, and the availability of new techniques.

[a] For the view that Japan's relative autonomy within the world economy was a crucial factor in explaining her successful industrialisation and differentiates her strongly from both nineteenth-century China and today's developing countries, see Moulder, F., *Japan, China and the Modern World Economy* (120).

But beyond this, what the case-study has shown, perhaps in an extreme form, are the mechanisms through which Japanese industrial growth influenced the direction of technical change in agriculture and thereby became crucial in determining many of the successful elements of agriculture's role in the development process. Two of these mechanisms stand out. Firstly, it was the absorption of agricultural labour into the industrial sector that produced the structural changes in agriculture whereby the middle-scale family farm became predominant. Even before 1868 in some areas, the expansion of non-agricultural employment opportunities had led to the decline of large-scale cultivation and the break-up of large holdings, but the case of Saga shows dramatically how the growth of modern industry provided poorer farmers and agricultural labourers with the means to escape the village economy and led to the emergence of an agricultural structure dominated by middle-scale owner/tenant farms using family labour. We have seen how Saga farmers of this latter sort were able to pioneer the development of mechanised technology suited to their needs and capabilities and to the scale of their farming, through their use of village organisations and through their influence on research and extension workers attuned to the structural changes taking place. The outflow of agricultural labour into industry, and the consequent shortage of hired workers, were thus crucial pre-conditions for the development of techniques which were labour-saving but which helped to preserve the small-scale family farm and make fuller use of its resources.[b]

The second mechanism is that whereby, in an area such as Saga not perfectly suited to the requirements of available new techniques, it was the development of industry which provided the technical knowledge and the material inputs necessary to overcome the environmental obstacles to higher output. We have seen in the case of Saga that the way in which Japan industrialised meant not simply that new techniques and inputs could be brought into rural areas from distant industrial centres or from abroad, but that there existed even in relatively insignificant country areas those with the training and experience necessary to find out about, adapt and even manufacture equipment and methods suitable for particular local conditions. This was perhaps partly the result of the lack of foreign influence over the Japanese economy, and also of the relatively long time-scale of

---

[b] For a description of a similar shift in the dominant group within the village, resulting from labour outflow and leading to the same kind of pressure for the development of new techniques meeting the needs of small- and medium-scale farmers, see Sansom, R., *The Economics of Insurgency* (170), pp.153–4.

industrialisation, compared with the industrialisation programmes of present-day developing countries, which allowed for the accumulation of technical experience and of sufficient numbers of trained personnel to make them available even to the experiment stations and small factories of remoter places.[c]

To a significant extent, therefore, the success of Saga in developing new techniques appropriate to the needs of the majority of smaller-scale farmers, and in preventing the emergence of differences between farmers in access to improved methods, was dependent on the way in which it was affected by Japanese industrialisation — on the fact that industry was able to absorb a substantial proportion of poorer farmers, on the applicability of the then-available industrial techniques to the solution of agricultural problems, on the emergence of a relatively wide range of people with basic technical or scientific training. Nevertheless, at a closer level, its success also depended on a number of factors applicable to the particular case and to the way in which the particular process of technical development and diffusion was carried out, and these reveal the importance of local skills and initiative and local responsiveness to the problems and potentials of a particular environment. These are factors which, within the generally favourable context described above, made Saga a particularly successful case.

The first point to stress here is the extent to which the environment of the Saga Plain forced officials and farmers to concentrate on the improvement of the irrigation system, with the result that an advanced and efficient irrigation technology was developed to overcome the barriers imposed by traditional methods. It is becoming increasingly unnecessary to emphasise the importance, in the process of economic development of a rice-growing area, of the state of irrigation technology and the organisation of the distribution of water. Since the advent of the Green Revolution, the spread of the tubewell, and so on, academic interest in the association between rising yields and not only the extent of irrigated area, but also the quality and reliability of water supplies and the factors affecting the distribution of water, has increased. In chapter 3 we saw how, in nineteenth- and early twentieth-century

[c] That sources of such technical skill may exist, and may be quite readily tapped, in present-day developing countries is suggested by Kaneda's study of the tube-well industry in Pakistan, which describes the quite rapid emergence of small firms capable of copying and adapting imported motors and branching out into the production of specialised agricultural machinery. See Kaneda, H., 'Mechanisation, Industrialisation and Technical Change' (160). Similarly the farmer and the small-engine merchant who both developed the mechanised irrigation pump in Vietnam are evidence of the existence of technical knowledge and skill in rural areas there. See Sansom, R., *The Economics of Insurgency* (170), pp.166–8.

Japan, just as in the rest of Asia today, the nature of irrigation organisation and the quality of the supply of water strongly influenced the social and economic relationships within villages and the ability to adopt improved methods and high-yielding seed varieties. In the case-study it was possible to see more closely how these forces operated in conditioning the possibilities for technical change.

Firstly, the case of Saga reveals strikingly the extent to which the nature of the irrigation system brought into being an agricultural technology and a set of economic and social relationships which complemented it and made production and survival possible within the constraints it imposed, but which equally presented formidable barriers to the adoption of methods designed to be used under different technical and economic conditions. The peculiarities of the irrigation method made necessary by the natural environment of the Plain resulted, as we have seen, in adaptations to the standard techniques of rice cultivation, which in turn necessitated economic and social relationships between village households designed to ensure the supply of inputs, maintain the irrigation infrastructure, and guarantee mutual survival and subsistence. While this system was able to absorb, in general unchanged, the effects of the gradual commercialisation of agricultural production, it represented a barrier to the adoption of parts of the package of improved techniques on which the development of agriculture in more advanced areas had been based. This placed Saga, despite its fertile soil and in some respects rather advanced economic and commercial arrangements, alongside the other outlying areas of Japan which environmental conditions and the quality of irrigation facilities (especially the inability to drain paddy fields when necessary) made unsuitable for the package of high-yielding techniques.

Secondly, however, as a consequence of this significance of irrigation technology and the barriers which it so clearly posed to technical change, the case of Saga shows how investment in irrigation improvement can act as a catalyst to a wide range of further technical and economic changes. Once the farmers of Saga were able to control the supply of water to their fields without the necessity for huge amounts of manual labour, they were able to abandon the technical practices which had stood in the way of higher yields, and go on to develop and adopt new improved methods of their own. Thus the return to the investment in irrigation improvements was very high and far-reaching, generating as it did the 'dynamic sequences' whereby a new technical system was developed. Because in Saga there was no choice but to confront the problem of the irrigation system if further progress was to be possible, the fundamental barrier to technical change was successfully removed.

The second factor to bear in mind in explaining Saga's success is the quality of, and balance between, the roles of governmental or research officials and farmers' organisations. The farmers of the Saga Plain, while probably from the early years of this century basically literate, had, by and large, no means of acquiring information about new techniques except through the instruction of officers of the local government, the semi-official extension organisations or the experiment station. What is perhaps remarkable about these officials, from early on in this century locally trained in basic agricultural science and technology, is the extent of their knowledge about local conditions and their close acquaintance with local farmers and their problems. This was the result of many years of government involvement in agricultural extension and of a substantial local investment in training and other facilities. It meant that, when the time came to carry out what was a relatively large-scale irrigation project, local government and extension workers were in a position to play a vital and successful role in the selection of techniques which met farmers' needs and in the organisation of their introduction. They were thus able to act as intermediaries between farmers and the sources of new knowledge, purchased inputs and machines, credit, and so on.[d]

On the other hand, though, this role was made possible by the existence at the village level of farmers' organisations through which extension officials were able to operate. These originated in the traditional solidarity of the village and in the requirements of the irrigation organisation, but became gradually part of the administrative structure of agricultural extension. These organisations provided the framework through which all cultivators were able to gain access to new techniques and to the credit to finance their introduction.

The balance between, on the one side, extension officials possessing both contact with the sources of new techniques outside the area and detailed local knowledge and connections, and, on the other, well-established farmers' organisations, representing the majority of small-to-medium cultivators, provided the means whereby appropriate new techniques could be developed and widely diffused to farmers of all kinds. On occasion, for instance over the implementation of the unified

[d] It is interesting here to contrast the case of the introduction of the tubewell in the Kosi district of Bihar in India, as described by Clay in *Planners' Preferences and Local Innovation* (141). Here, initially, decisions about the technical characteristics of the tubewells to be promoted by the extension services were taken high up at the state level. The model selected proved unnecessarily big and expensive for the local conditions of the Kosi area and few were bought despite credit provisions and extension work. However the promotion of the tube-well idea led to adaptations by local entrepreneurs, who produced the unofficial 'bamboo tube-well' which was well suited to local requirements and spread rapidly.

rotation, the balance tipped in an authoritarian direction, with officials resorting to the force of the law to obtain their objectives, but in general extension officials and farmers worked together with a degree of mutual respect. What must be remembered, though, is that this state of affairs did not arise overnight and only emerged out of the many years of uphill struggle on the part of local enthusiasts and officials to build up a body of knowledge about local agriculture and to overcome farmers' resistance to technical changes. In this it represents a prior investment which, like the investment in irrigation facilities in the country as a whole prior to 1868, was crucial in determining the ability to resond to new opportunities, but which few present-day developing countries are lucky enough to possess.

The third point in the explanation of Saga's success relates to the actual mechanisms of choice of technique and to some of the questions discussed in chapter 1, in relation to the development of the mechanised irrigation pump.[1] At the micro-economic level, the usual practice when trying to explain the emergence and spread (or lack of it) of a new technical system in agriculture (e.g. the Green Revolution) is to assume a certain package of new techniques, whose characteristics are defined, and then to ask why farmers do or do not adopt the package. This is generally done by comparing the characteristics of the technology with such things as the availability and distribution of production factors, risk-bearing ability, education, and so on. At the other extreme is the study of the determinants of the overall direction of technical change in an economy or a sector, in terms of concepts like relative factor supplies and prices at the macro-level. As Hayami and Ruttan have hypothesised, the responsiveness of the institutional links between these two aspects of the process, between the micro-economic conditions of actual farmers and the macro-economic determinants of the overall direction of technical change, are of crucial importance in determining the success of the adoption and diffusion of new technology. One of the objects of the present study has been to describe the operation of these links in a particularly successful case and it is perhaps worth summarising the main points and implications of that description once again here.

At the general level it is impossible to see the development of the mechanised irrigation pump in Saga as anything but the inducement of a labour-saving innovation in response to a rise in the relative price of hired labour, in the manner hypothesised by Hayami and Ruttan. However, chapter 7's detailed examination of the actual stages of the choice of technique showed that the particular form of the technical problem resulting from changed relative factor prices depended on particular local conditions, and that the decision as to the actual form in which the labour-saving bias was to be embodied involved consideration of a wide range of characteristics of possible techniques relative to the constraints imposed, on the one hand, by the macro-level state of technical development in Japan at the time, and, on the other, by the historically-determined conditions of Saga Plain agriculture. Examples of the first type of constraint included the stage of development of the use of motors and powered machinery in Japan at the time, hence the possibilities for acquiring either domestically-produced or imported equipment of suitable types; the possibilities of finding out about and acquiring such equipment in an area away from the main industrial centres; the state of power-supply facilities;[e] and so on. Into the second category fall constraints such as the availability in the local area of the skills required to install and maintain machinery; farmers' experience with and ability to operate machines; the existing irrigation infrastructure; the possibilities for group acquisition and operation of equipment; etc.

The existence of these varied constraints meant that the choice of a solution to a particular technical problem was not a straightforward choice from amongst a well-defined set of technical possibilities, but rather a series of decisions about a wide variety of technical characteristics. These decisions involved choices as to, for instance, the power source to be adopted; the scale or divisibility of the equipment relative to the size of holdings and the institutional ability to share the use of it; the mobility of equipment and the balance between efficient machine size and the loss of land for feeder channels; the technical complexity of the machinery relative to farmers' ability to operate it; etc. Thus a problem caused ultimately by a change in relative factor supplies at the macro level was solved by a series of detailed and locally specific decisions, and the ability to make the right decisions (i.e. to make an appropriate choice of technique) depended again on the depth of local knowledge and experience of the research and extension workers and local machinery producers who made the bridge between practising farmers and available technical knowledge. Because, in the case of Saga, this bridge had been carefully built up over many years through painstaking work and a substantial investment of time and resources, it was possible, after a relatively short period of trial-and-error experimentation, to select a technique which met what the officials concerned knew to be the requirements of local conditions, and which proved successful in its mechanical operation, in its distributional, social and economic effects

---

[e] Compare Kaneda, H., 'Mechanisation, Industrialisation and Technical Change' (160), pp.178–9, where he points out that, in his Pakistani case, electric motors would have powered the tube-wells more cheaply than the diesel motors actually used, but it was very difficult to obtain reliable access to electricity supplies.

on farmers, and in its stimulation of output growth and further technical change.

In summary, therefore, although the induced innovation hypothesis, based on changes in relative factor supplies, is a useful starting point in analysing the process of technical change in Saga, it is by no means the end of the story, and Saga's success in developing and diffusing appropriate new techniques depended crucially on the selection of a wide range of technical characteristics besides factor bias, suited to the particular conditions of the place and time.

*

Throughout I have been treating the process of technical change in Saga Plain agriculture as a successful one. It represented perhaps the most significant part of the transformation of Saga farmers from subsistence producers, locked within the village economy, with their livelihood still largely dependent on the vagaries of weather, water and pests, into rather sophisticated commercial farmers, familiar with the latest machinery and the application of scientific commercial inputs to their fields. In the course of this transformation, crop yields and labour productivity rose dramatically, freeing labour time for other activities. Yet all this was achieved without any fundamental change in the agricultural structure based on the small-scale family farm, with, if anything, an equalising rather than a polarising effect on income and land distribution, and with the maintenance of village cohesion and group activity.

In these respects, the pre-war development of Saga agriculture foreshadowed the shape of post-war Japanese agriculture as a whole. Although the trend towards larger scale came to nothing, within the structure of small-scale owner farms which emerged out of the land reform, yields began to rise dramatically again from their inter-war stagnation, as new seeds and new methods, notably the use of vinyl-covered seed-beds, permitted the spread of high-yielding techniques to the previously disadvantaged rice-growing areas of the north. As the power-tiller, and later other labour-saving machines adapted to small fields, spread through the country, labour productivity leapt up, releasing the time of the central members of the family labour force and giving rise to the phenomenon of part-time farming which characterises almost all of Japanese agriculture today. In the middle-scale owner/tenant farms of the Saga Plain in the 1930s, with their enthusiasm for machines and improved methods and their new activities outside rice cultivation, lie the seeds of the present-day Japanese farm, its hectare or so of owned land machine-tilled and planted by the head of the household in his free time from his office or factory job, and cared for the rest of the time by his wife or his elderly parents, sowing the seed-beds, weeding the paddies, tending the trees or plants of the currently favoured fruit or vegetable crop. Meanwhile, the marketing of crops, the supply of inputs, problems such as credit needs, even sometimes the preparation of the land itself, are all taken care of by the village co-operative through the national co-operative system.[2]

In this way Japanese farmers have discovered the means of surviving within a highly industrialised economy without any significant transformation affecting the scales of their farms or the internal structure of their households and their labour forces. In doing this, they have succeeded in causing their government most of the agricultural problems commonly faced by governments of industrialised countries, in particularly intractable forms. They continue to produce large surpluses of rice but manage only high-cost import substitutes for much of the meat, dairy produce, fruit and vegetables which Japanese consumers have come to demand in larger and larger quantities. Japanese consumers and taxpayers therefore support farm incomes much as their Western European counterparts do, and the progress towards the enlargement of farms and the modernisation of the ageing labour force has been painfully slow. These are problems which the governments of most of today's developing countries would no doubt gladly exchange for those which they currently face. Nevertheless, one day, happily, their countries may be rich enough to take into account the lessons to be drawn from the fact that the very success of areas like Saga in developing technology appropriate to prevailing conditions held within it the seeds of the problems of surplus faced by Japanese agriculture today.

APPENDIX TABLES

Appendix Table 1
Sources:
1857: Yamada, T., 'Saga Heiya ni okeru Bakumatsu-Ki' (98), p.53, from village records.
1888: Isobe, T., 'Iwayuru Saga Dankai' (70), p.10, Kyūshū Nōsei Kyoku, *Saga Heiya* (76), pp.288−9. Nōji Chōsa data for Saga County.
1908: Kamagata, I., *Nōgyō Sōgō Kenkyū*, vol. 1, 1947.
1909: Isobe, T., 'Iwayuru Saga Dankai' (70), p.10, from a prefectural government report for Saga County.
1922: Kyūshū Nōsei Kyoku, *Saga Heiya* (76), pp.288−9, original source not stated but clearly an area already mechanised.
1936: Kyūshū Nōsei Kyoku, *Saga Heiya* (76), pp.288−9. Teikoku Nōkai (Imperial Agricultural Association), Nōsakugyōbetsu Rōdō ni kan suru Chōsa (Survey of Labour Requirements by Agricultural Operation).
1938: Isobe, T., 'Iwayuru Saga Dankai' (70), p.10. Average of 17 Saga Plain villages from Nōsangyōson Jitsunō Chōsa (Survey of Conditions in Agricultural Villages).
1939: Kyūshū Nōsei Kyoku, *Saga Heiya* (76), pp.288−9. Average of 26 Saga Plain villages from Nōsangyōson Jitsunō Chōsa.
1941: Isobe, T., 'Iwayuru Saga Dankai' (70), p.10. Teikoku Nōkai, Nōsakugyō Kankō Chōsa (Survey of Agricultural Practices) for Saga County.

Appendix Table 1: *Assembled Data on Changes in Labour Requirements by Operation—Saga Plain Area*
(Units: Man/days per 10 ares)

	1857 Kawazoe Villages		1888	1908	1909	1922	1936 Saga Prefecture			1938	1939	1941
	West	East					South	North	West			
Land preparation	6·72	3·56	4·5	3·0	3·80	3·3	2·98	3·40	3·60	3·72	3·1	2·3
Seed beds	0·33	1·75	1·7	1·5	0·85	1·5	0·64	0·75	0·60	1·28	1·4	0·9
Transplanting	1·58	1·75	1·5	2·0	2·10	2·6	1·08	1·60	1·90	1·78	1·9	1·7
Pumping	10·00	15·00	(7·0)*	7·0	7·00	1·3	1·56	1·10	1·60	2·26	2·4	0·5
Weeding, fertilising & pest control	10·00	6·50	8·0	5·0	8·50	3·8	4·56	5·40	6·10	3·67	3·6	4·3
Harvesting	4·50	4·50	4·7	5·0	5·00	1·3	2·99	3·11	3·20	4·93	4·8	5·2
Grain preparation	6·87	6·00	4·8	4·0	2·00	6·3	2·63	2·64	3·10	1·05	1·1	0·6
Rice cultivation as a whole	40·00	37·31	(32·2)*	27·5	29·25	20·1	16·44	18·00	20·10	18·69	18·3	15·5
Output per man/day (kg)	8·47	8·76	10·8	—	12·66	18·07	24·00	21·52	21·45	26·08	25·5	28·06

*Pumping labour not recorded in the original data. Assumption of 7 man/days per 10 ares made on the basis of later data and Isobe, T., 'Iwayuru Saga Dankai' (70), p.10 and *Saga-Ken Shi* (80), p.611.

Appendix Table 2: *Areas Planted and Output of Rice and Other Grain Crops in Saga, 1890–1935*
(5-yearly averages for years shown; area in hectares; output in tonnes)

| | RICE | | | | OTHER GRAINS* | | | |
| | Area | | Output | | Area | | Output | |
	Saga-ken	Saga-gun	Saga-ken	Saga-gun	Saga-ken	Saga-gun	Saga-ken	Saga-gun
1890	49,895	10,615	118,821	31,232	33,583	—	35,163	—
1895	49,732	10,532	108,268	20,681	33,888	4,395	41,980	7,046
1900	50,535	10,547	125,675	25,945	37,629	4,871	48,928	7,846
1905	50,376	10,668	155,440	39,045	37,235	5,717	39,848	8,629
1910	50,956	10,825	161,022	36,406	37,864	5,014	48,587	8,260
1915	52,098	11,034	174,482	40,664	38,406	4,898	53,098	8,853
1920	52,922	10,941	174,773	41,559	34,745	4,473	46,847	7,597
1925	52,978	10,778	197,918	43,263	28,188	3,403	42,597	6,046
1930	54,245	11,045	180,757	42,367	29,506	4,281	47,808	7,899
1935	54,638	11,403	212,999	50,686	31,329	5,101	53,858	9,748

*Other Grains = wheat, barley and naked barley. (One *koku* of wheat = 136·9 kg, of barley 108·7 kg, of naked barley 138·7 kg.)
Source: *Saga-Ken Tōkei Sho* (101).

Appendix Table 3:   Rice Yields in Saga, 1890–1935
(5-yearly averages, kg/10 ares)

	Saga-gun	Saga-ken		Saga-gun	Saga-ken
1890	294·1	238·0	1913	351·4	329·2
1891	238·3	204·7	1914	360·2	333·4
1892	255·7	219·8	1915	368·6	339·2
1893	243·6	204·5	1916	352·0	328·8
1894	263·8	222·4	1917	368·9	327·9
1895	253·7	217·9	1918	377·6	335·6
1896	312·7	257·9	1919	376·3	328·9
1897	291·1	254·2	1920	379·7	330·2
1898	278·5	249·3	1921	390·3	362·4
1899	254·5	239·4	1922	387·5	366·9
1900	246·2	248·5	1923	386·3	362·5
1901	248·1	251·1	1924	393·3	370·3
1902	271·0	264·5	1925	401·4	373·6
1903	290·4	274·9	1926	395·1	339·8
1904	324·3	295·9	1927	396·7	340·6
1905	366·0	308·5	1928	395·2	341·6
1906	372·8	319·4	1929	383·9	332·8
1907	370·5	320·7	1930	383·5	333·0
1908	369·2	329·6	1931	402·9	353·7
1909	359·9	326·7	1932	411·7	360·1
1910	336·5	316·1	1933	415·4	362·0
1911	337·0	316·5	1934	431·2	378·1
1912	337·4	322·3	1935	444·3	389·8

Source: *Saga-Ken Tōkei Sho* (101).

Appendix Table 4: *Numbers of Agricultural Workers and Households in Saga,*
1890–1935
(5-yearly averages, thousands)

	Workers Ken	Gun	Households Ken	Gun		Workers Ken	Gun	Households Ken	Gun
1890	338·9	53·4	73·2	11·6	1913	272·2	38·0	69·6	10·7
1891	338·4	53·2	73·4	11·6	1914	269·5	35·8	70·4	10·4
1892	338·5	53·7	74·0	11·6	1915	262·9	32·1	70·5	10·1
1893	339·1	54·2	74·5	11·6	1916	258·2	32·3	70·7	9·9
1894	342·2	54·3	75·4	11·6	1917	250·1	32·3	70·8	9·8
1895	342·6	53·8	76·4	11·7	1918	247·3	31·0	70·8	9·6
1896	343·2	53·5	76·1	11·7	1919	239·3	30·4	69·5	9·6
1897	342·0	53·4	75·5	11·7	1920	234·6	29·5	69·1	9·5
1898	338·6	52·7	75·5	11·8	1921	230·2	28·4	68·9	9·4
1899	333·0	51·8	74·8	11·6	1922	225·1	27·3	68·6	9·3
1900	324·8	51·4	73·7	11·3	1923	220·8	26·7	68·5	9·2
1901	316·4	51·1	73·3	11·0	1924	219·1	26·4	68·4	9·2
1902	305·6	49·4	73·1	10·9	1925	217·0	26·5	68·4	9·3
1903	296·8	47·8	73·8	10·8	1926	215·7	26·9	68·3	9·3
1904	290·4	46·8	73·6	10·9	1927	215·0	27·4	68·3	9·3
1905	289·5	45·9	73·4	11·1	1928	214·4	27·7	68·4	9·4
1906	286·2	44·9	73·2	11·2	1929	213·0	27·9	68·5	9·4
1907	289·0	44·9	72·6	11·2	1930	211·8	27·7	68·4	9·3
1908	288·1	45·1	71·6	11·2	1931	209·9	27·5	67·0	9·3
1909	286·7	45·5	70·9	11·3	1932	208·4	27·4	66·7	9·3
1910	283·5	45·8	70·6	11·2	1933	206·8	27·5	66·4	9·4
1911	280·6	42·9	70·2	11·1	1934	205·3	27·5	66·1	9·4
1912	277·7	40·2	70·0	10·9	1935	203·9	27·5	65·8	9·4

Source: *Saga-Ken Tōkei Sho* (101).

Appendix Table 5: The Distribution of Households by Area Cultivated
(Saga Prefecture, %)

	Under ½ ha.	½ − 1 ha.	1 − 2 ha.	2 − 3 ha.	3 − 5 ha.	Over 5 ha.
1908	35·8	35·0	18·2	8·3	1·2	0·4
1909	31·4	33·6	23·3	9·7	1·7	0·2
1910	36·0	34·9	18·3	8·3	2·1	0·3
1911	35·0	35·7	20·5	6·9	1·7	0·1
1912	32·8	38·3	21·2	6·2	1·9	0·1
1913	33·2	38·3	21·0	6·0	1·3	0·1
1914	33·1	38·0	21·3	6·0	1·4	0·1
1915	32·3	37·8	22·4	5·7	1·6	0·2
1916	33·0	37·8	21·5	5·9	1·6	0·1
1917	31·0	36·2	24·5	6·6	1·6	0·1
1918	30·6	36·6	24·4	6·5	1·6	0·1
1919	31·2	37·7	24·3	5·4	1·4	0·1
1920	31·8	35·7	24·8	5·9	1·7	0·05
1921	29·7	35·5	27·1	6·5	1·2	0·04
1922	27·5	35·0	29·7	6·4	1·0	0·04
1923	29·1	37·1	26·5	5·9	1·3	0·04
1924	29·3	37·2	26·6	5·7	1·1	0·01
1925	28·7	37·3	27·2	5·6	1·0	0·02
1926	27·5	36·8	28·3	6·2	1·1	0·04
1927	27·4	36·7	28·2	6·4	1·2	0·05
1928	27·3	37·1	27·9	6·5	1·1	0·06
1929	26·7	35·0	29·6	7·1	1·4	0·05
1930	26·0	35·3	30·3	7·0	1·4	0·03
1931	26·3	35·4	30·6	6·5	1·1	0·02
1932	25·6	34·3	32·6	6·6	1·2	0·05
1933	25·0	33·8	32·9	7·0	1·3	0·04
1934	24·4	34·2	32·8	7·2	1·4	0·06
1935	24·3	33·5	33·1	7·7	1·3	0·07
1936	24·1	33·8	32·8	7·8	1·4	0·05
1937	25·5	34·0	32·0	7·0	1·4	0·04
1938	25·5	32·2	32·9	7·8	1·4	0·04
1939	25·5	31·0	33·8	8·0	1·6	0·03
1940	25·9	30·9	33·3	8·2	1·6	0·06

Source: *Saga-Ken Tōkei Sho* (101).

NOTES

Chapter 1

1. Brown, M., *On the Theory and Measurement of Technical Change* (138), p.9.
2. In *The Theory of Wages* (153) pp.124–5.
3. See e.g. Salter, who argued that entrepreneurs would be interested in *any* technique which reduced costs, regardless of its factor bias. Salter, W., *Productivity and Technical Change* (169), pp.43–4.
4. On the obsolescence of techniques, see Stewart, F., *Technology and Underdevelopment* (173), pp. 10–22.
5. Hayami, Y. and Ruttan, V., *Agricultural Development* (152).
6. Rosenberg, N., 'The Direction of Technical Change' (166).
7. Rosenberg, N., 'The Direction of Technical Change' (166), p.4.
8. Clay, E., *Planners' Preferences* (141) and Sansom, R., *The Economics of Insurgency* (170).
9. See Stewart, F., *Technology and Underdevelopment* (173), especially pp.3–10.
10. Stewart, F., *Technology and Underdevelopment* (173), p.3.

11. Stewart, F., *Technology and Underdevelopment* (173), p.185.
12. See Salter, W., *Productivity and Technical Change* (169), pp.48–65.
13. David, P., 'The Landscape and the Machine' (143).
14. Griffin, K., *The Green Revolution* (149).
15. For cases see Timmer, C., *The Choice of Technology* (175), also Clay, E., *Planners' Preferences* (141), and the reaction of the American engineers to the Vietnamese motor pump in Sansom, R., *The Economics of Insurgency* (170), pp.174–5.
16. As suggested by Thomas in 'The Choice of Technology for Irrigation Tubewells' (174), pp.51–7.
17. See Ishikawa, S., 'Technological Change in Agricultural Production' (158), Gotsch, C., 'Technical Change and the Distribution of Income' (147), and also Gotsch's attempt to apply his framework to the case of agricultural mechanisation in Pakistan in 'Tractor Mechanisation and Rural Development in Pakistan' (148).
18. See e.g. Mellor, J., *Economics of Agricultural Development* (163), especially pp.4–5.

19. For more on this see chapter 2, especially section 1 (1).
20. See Lewis, W., 'Economic Development with Unlimited Supplies of Labour' (161), and other dual economy approaches to development such as Ranis, G. and Fei, J., *Development of the Labour Surplus Economy* (164) and 'A Theory of Economic Development' (165).
21. For a full-scale discussion of the inequities and inefficiencies of policies which concentrate resources on the development of the industrial sector, see Lipton, M., *Why Poor People Stay Poor* (162).
22. Schultz, T., *Transforming Traditional Agriculture* (171).
23. Ishikawa, S., *Economic Development in Asian Perspective* (154).

Chapter 2

1. See, for example, Johnston, B., 'The "Japanese Model"' (9), and Ohkawa, K. and Rosovsky, H., 'A Century of Japanese Economic Growth' (15) and 'The Role of Agriculture in Japanese Economic Development' (16).
2. Yamaguchi, K., *Meiji Zenki Keizai* (64), p.38.
3. See, for example, Tussing, A., 'The Labour Force in Meiji Economic Growth' (19) and Smith, T., 'Farm Family By-Employments' (7).
4. Ohkawa, K. and Rosovsky, H., *Japanese Economic Growth* (124), p.11.
5. *Nōrinshō Ruinen Tōkeihyō* (65).
6. Hayami, Y. and Yamada, S., 'Agricultural Productivity at the Beginning of Industrialisation' (6), p.108.
7. Hayami, Y. and Yamada, S., 'Agricultural Productivity at the Beginning of Industrialisation' (6), p.110.

8. Nakamura, J., *Agricultural Production and the Economic Growth of Japan* (10).
9. Hayami, Y. and Yamada, S., 'Agricultural Productivity at the Beginning of Industrialisation' (6), p.110.
10. Ohkawa, K. et al, *Chōki Keizai Tōkei* (66), vol. 9.
11. For details see Ohkawa, K. and Rosovsky, H., *Japanese Economic Growth* (124), p.15.
12. This is discussed much more fully in chapter 3, especially section 1 (1).
13. Ohkawa, K. and Rosovsky, H., *Japanese Economic Growth* (124), p.35.
14. Data from *Chōki Keizai Tōkei* (66), vol. 1, and Ogura, T., *Agricultural Development in Modern Japan* (3), pp.40–1.
15. Oshima, H., 'Meiji Fiscal Policy' (17).
16. Sinha, R., 'Unresolved Issues in Japan's Early Economic Development' (130).
17. See Ishikawa, S., *Economic Development in Asian Perspective* (154), chapter 2, section 2 and pp.318–21.
18. Very briefly. For a fuller account see Hayami, Y., *A Century of Agricultural Growth in Japan* (1), chapter 2.
19. Hayami, Y., *A Century of Agricultural Growth in Japan* (1), p.26, calculated from data in *Chōki Keizai Tōkei* (66).
20. Hayami, Y., *A Century of Agricultural Growth in Japan* (1), p.25, calculated from data in *Chōki Keizai Tōkei* (66).
21. Tussing, A., 'The Labour Force in Meiji Economic Growth' (19).
22. Quoted in Hayami, Y., *A Century of Economic Growth in Japan* (1), p.24.
23. *Chōki Keizai Tōkei* (66), vol. 9.
24. Hayami, Y., *A Century of Agricultural Growth in Japan* (1), p.31.
25. Though Hayami, in *A Century of*

Agricultural Growth in Japan (1), pp.179—89, and Akino, in 'Land Infrastructure Improvement in Agricultural Development' (37), have attempted to estimate the returns to investment in land improvement in Japan.

26. Matsuo, T., *Rice and Rice Cultivation in Japan* (32), p.1.

27. Sawada, S., 'The Development of Rice Productivity in Japan' (28), pp.124—5.

28. See Hatate, I., *Irrigation Agriculture* (39) for a more detailed description of the stages of development of irrigation technology.

29. Nagata, K., *Nihon Nōgyō no Suiri Kōzō* (54), p.27.

30. For examples besides the case-study (chapter 5), see Eyre, J., 'Water Controls in a Japanese Irrigation System' (38); Nakane, C., *Kinship and Economic Organisation in Rural Japan* (46), pp.73—81; Shimpo, M., *Three Decades in Shiwa* (40); and Beardsley, R., Hall, J. and Ward, R., *Village Japan* (41), pp.113—44.

31. For a fuller discussion of the nature of the *ie*, see Fukutake, T., *Japanese Rural Society* (45), especially chapter 4.

32. Dore, R., *Land Reform in Japan* (34), p.17.

33. For the detailed and fascinating account, on which the following is based, of the traditional systems of land and labour use and of their transformation under the impact of the spread of the commercial economy, see Smith, T., *The Agrarian Origins of Modern Japan* (8).

34. For more on the *dōzoku* system see Fukutake, T., *Japanese Rural Society* (45), chapter 5.

35. Dore, R., *Land Reform in Japan* (34), p.29.

36. Fukutake, T., *Japanese Rural*

Society (45), p.82.

37. See also Fukutake, T., *Japanese Rural Society* (45), pp.83—4.

38. See Beardsley, R., Hall, J. and Ward, R., *Village Japan* (41), pp.274—5.

39. For ways in which Japanese landlords helped and protected their tenants, see Fukutake, T., *Japanese Rural Society* (45), pp.69—70 and Nakane, C., *Kinship and Economic Organisation* (46), pp.112—13.

40. Scott, J., *The Moral Economy of the Peasant* (172). For evidence that failure to fulfil obligations was a factor behind tenancy disputes in Japan, see Waswo, A., *Japanese Landlords* (36), pp.106—7.

41. See Dore, R., 'Agricultural Improvement in Japan' (26).

Chapter 3

1. Tussing, A., 'The Labour Force in Meiji Economic Growth' (19), p.220.

2. See Smith, T., *The Agrarian Origins of Modern Japan* (8) and 'Farm Family By-Employments in Pre-Industrial Japan' (7); Crawcour, E., 'The Tokugawa Heritage' (5); Hanley, S. and Yamamura, K., *Economic and Demographic Change in Pre-Industrial Japan* (110); Chambliss, W., *Chiarajima Village* (42); etc.

3. Hanley, S. and Yamamura, K., *Economic and Demographic Change in Pre-Industrial Japan* (110).

4. Smith, T., *The Agrarian Origins of Modern Japan* (8), p.67.

5. Smith, T., *The Agrarian Origins of Modern Japan* (8), p.68.

6. See e.g. Allen, G., *A Short Economic History of Modern Japan* (105), pp.17—19.

7. Hanley, S. and Yamamura, K., *Economic and Demographic Change in Pre-Industrial Japan* (110), chapter 6.

8. Rozman, G., *Urban Networks in Ch'Ing China and Tokugawa Japan* (128), p.273.

9. Yamaguchi, K., *Meiji Zenki Keizai* (64), pp.243—5.

10. See e.g. Shimpo, M., *Three Decades in Shiwa* (40), p.16, on the local *sake*-brewing industry as a source of employment for Shiwa villagers.

11. Smith, T., *The Agrarian Origins of Modern Japan* (8).

12. Allen, G., *A Short Economic History of Modern Japan* (105), pp.65—6 and 72—4.

13. For convenient descriptions of the *Meiji Nōhō* techniques, see Sawada, S., 'Innovation in Japanese Agriculture' (27), especially pp.331—9, and Crawcour, E., 'Japan 1868—1920' (25), especially pp.13—14.

14. Smith, T., *The Agrarian Origins of Modern Japan* (8), chapter 7.

15. Smith, T., *The Agrarian Origins of Modern Japan* (8), p.94.

16. Arashi, K., *Kinsei Inasaku Gijitsu Shi* (50), chapter 1.

17. Arashi, K., *Kinsei Inasaku Gijitsu Shi* (50), pp.36—50.

18. Arashi, K., *Kinsei Inasaku Gijitsu Shi* (50), map p.37.

19. Arashi, K., *Kinsei Inasaku Gijitsu Shi* (50), especially pp.322—52 and 366—84.

20. Arashi, K., *Kinsei Inasaku Gijitsu Shi* (50), p.371.

21. Arashi, K., *Kinsei Inasaku Gijitsu Shi* (50), p.405.

22. Arashi, K., *Kinsei Inasaku Gijitsu Shi* (50), p.95.

23. Sawada, S., 'The Development of Rice Productivity' (28).

24. Smith, T., *The Agrarian Origins of Modern Japan* (8), pp.128—31.

25. Ōuchi, T., *Nihon ni okeru Nōminzō* (58), chapter 2, pp.24—132.

26. Ōuchi, T., *Nōgyō Shi* (59), p.91.

27. Wataya, T., 'Shihonshugi no Hatten' (62), p.194.

28. See Dore, R., 'Agricultural Improvement' (26), pp.77—82.

29. Wataya, T., 'Shihonshugi no Hatten' (62), p.200.

30. Yamaguchi, K., *Meiji Zenki Keizai* (64), pp.127—8.

31. Allen, G., *A Short Economic History of Modern Japan* (105), p.72.

32. Allen, G., *A Short Economic History of Modern Japan* (105), pp.79—80.

33. Allen, G., *A Short Economic History of Modern Japan* (105), p.83.

34. Lockwood, W., *The Economic Development of Japan* (115), p.22.

35. Taira, K., *Economic Development and the Labour Market in Japan* (132), p.28.

36. Ohkawa, K. and Rosovsky, H., *Japanese Economic Growth* (124), Table 4.5 p.83, and Table 4.7 p.86.

37. Ohkawa, K. and Rosovsky, H., *Japanese Economic Growth* (124), Table 4.5 p.83.

38. Wilkinson, T., *The Urbanisation of Japanese Labour* (135), p.37.

39. Wilkinson, T., *The Urbanisation of Japanese Labour* (135), p.76.

40. Taeuber, I., *The Population of Japan* (131), p.155.

41. Taeuber, I., *The Population of Japan* (131), pp.133—4.

42. Ohkawa, K. and Rosovsky, H., 'Postwar Japanese Growth' (125), Table 1.4 p.14.

43. Ogura, T., *Agricultural Development in Modern Japan* (3), p.12.

44. Yamaguchi, K., *Meiji Zenki Keizai* (64), p.239.

45. Ogura, T., *Agricultural Development in Modern Japan* (3), p.24; Ohkawa, K. and Tōbata, S., *Nihon no Keizai to Nōgyō* (57), Vol. 1, pp.190—1.

46. Hayami, Y. and Ruttan, V., *Agricultural Development* (152), p.219.

47. Hayami, Y. and Ruttan, V., 'Korean

Rice, Taiwan Rice and Japanese
Agricultural Stagnation' (20).

48. Arashi, K., *Kinsei Inasaku Gijitsu
Shi* (50), p.117.

49. Hayami, Y. and Ruttan, V., *Agricultural Development* (152),
pp.352—3.

50. Ogura, T., *Agricultural Development in Modern Japan* (3), p.353.

51. Arashi, K., *Kinsei Inasaku Gijitsu
Shi* (50), p.371.

52. Ogura, T., *Agricultural Development in Modern Japan* (3), p.324.

53. E.g. Ohkawa, K., 'Phases of Agricultural Development' (13), p.19.

54. Arashi, K., *Kinsei Inasaku Gijitsu
Shi* (50), p.45.

55. Ogura, T., *Agricultural Development in Modern Japan* (3), pp.238—
43.

56. *Nihon Nōgyō Hattatsu Shi* (55), Vol.
4, p.225.

57. Hayami, Y., *A Century of Agricultural Growth* (1), p.172.

58. Calculated from *Nihon Nōgyō Hattatsu Shi* (55), Vol. 4, Table 9, p.228.

59. *Nihon Nōgyō Hattatsu Shi* (55), Vol.
4, p.217.

60. *Nihon Nōgyō Hattatsu Shi* (55), Vol.
6, p.201—2.

61. Ogura, T., *Agricultural Development in Modern Japan* (3), p.416,
Nihon Nōgyō Hattatsu Shi (55), Vol.
6, p.273.

62. Waswo, A., *Japanese Landlords*
(36), especially chapter 4.

63. Ōuchi, T., 'Agricultural Depression
in Japanese Villages' (21), pp.21—2.

64. Kayō, N., *Nihon Nōgyō Kiso Tōkei*
(68), p.94.

65. Wataya, T., 'Shihonshugi no Hatten'
(62), p.239.

66. See also Fukutake, T., *Japanese
Rural Society* (45), pp.138—43, on
the differences in village structure
between advanced areas influenced
by industrialisation ('south-western

type') and underdeveloped areas isolated from urban industrial influences ('north-eastern type').

Chapter 4

1. Kyūshū Nōsei Kyoku, *Saga Heiya*
(76), p.16.

2. Kyūshū Nōsei Kyoku, *Saga Heiya*
(76), map facing p.68.

3. Yamaguchi, K., *Meiji Zenki Keizai*
(64), p.231.

4. Ōta, R., 'Meiji Zenki' (91), p.213.

5. Kyūshū Nōsei Kyoku, *Saga Heiya*
(76), p.25.

6. Kyūshū Nōsei Kyoku, *Saga Heiya*
(76), p.118.

7. Eguchi, M., *Saga Nōgyō Oboegaki*
(82), vol. 1, p.131.

8. Kyūshū Nōsei Kyoku, *Saga Heiya*
(76), p.118.

9. *Saga-Shi Shi* (81), vol. 3, p.226.

10. Yamada, T., *Kyūshū Nōgyō Shi*
(74), p.231.

11. See, for instance, the illustration on
p.96 of Smith, T., *The Agrarian
Origins of Modern Japan* (8).

12. Yamada, T., *Kyūshū Nōgyō Shi*
(74), p.232.

13. Miyajima, S., *Kome Tsukuri* (72),
p.15.

14. Miyajima, S., *Kome Tsukuri* (72),
p.18.

15. Yamada, T., 'Saga Heiya ni okeru
Bakumatsu-ki' (98), p.50.

16. *Saga-Shi Shi* (81), vol. 3, p.663.

17. Arashi, K., *Kinsei Inasaku Gijitsu
Shi* (50), p.37, p.38, p.41.

18. *Saga-Shi Shi* (81), vol. 4, p.359.

19. Yamada, T., *Kyūshū Nōgyō Shi*
(74), pp.238—40.

20. Yamada, T., 'Saga Heiya ni okeru
Bakumatsu-ki' (98), p.48.

21. Kyūshū Nōsei Kyoku, *Saga Heiya*
(76), p.244.

22. *Saga-Ken Tōkei-Sho* (101).

23. *Nihon Nōgyō Hattatsu Shi* (55), vol. 6, p.434.
24. Kyūshū Nōsei Kyoku, *Saga Heiya* (76), p.239; *Saga-Ken Shi* (80), pp.378—9.
25. Eguchi, M., *Saga Nōgyō Oboegaki* (82), vol. 1, p.77.
26. Eguchi, M., *Saga Nōgyō Oboegaki* (82), vol. 1, p.184.
27. Especially chapter 2, section 2 (3) and chapter 3, section 1 (3).
28. *Saga-Ken Nōchi Kaikaku Shi* (79), chapter 8, section 3.
29. Kamagata, I., *Saga Nōgyō* (71), p.44.
30. Kamagata, I., *Saga Nōgyō* (71), p.182; *Saga-Shi Shi* (81), vol. 3, p.286.
31. From *Saga-Shi-Shi* (81), vol. 3, p.687.
32. *Saga-Shi Shi* (81), vol. 3, p.678.
33. *Saga-Ken Shi* (80), p.462.
34. *Saga-Shi Shi* (81), pp.233—4.
35. See Yamada, T., 'Saga-bei Ryūtsū' (99) and *Saga-Shi Shi* (81), pp.698—705.
36. Yamada, T., *Kyūshū Nōgyō Shi* (74), p.269.
37. *Saga-Ken Nōchi Kaikaku Shi* (79), p.390.
38. Ōta, R., 'Meiji Zenki' (91), p.223.
39. See *Saga-Ken Shi* (80), pp.467—72.
40. *Saga-Ken Nōchi Kaikaku Shi* (79), p.396.
41. Calculated from Yamada, T., 'Saga Heiya ni okeru Bakumatsu-ki' (98), Table 3, p.47.
42. Yamada, T., 'Saga Heiya ni okeru Bakumatsu-ki' (98), p.50; Isobe, T., 'Iwayuru Saga Dankai' (70), p.14.
43. Yamada, T., 'Saga Heiya ni okeru Bakumatsu-ki' (98), p.50; Isobe, T., 'Iwayuru Saga Dankai' (70), p.14.
44. Yamada, T., 'Saga Heiya ni okeru Bakumatsu-ki' (98), p.46.
45. *Saga-Shi Shi* (81), vol. 3, p.696.
46. Isobe, T., 'Saga Heitan Chitai' (88), Table 6, pp.222—3.
47. Yamada, T., 'Saga Heiya ni okeru Bakumatsu-ki' (98), p.47.
48. Kyūshū Nōsei Kyoku, *Saga Heiya* (76), p.265.
49. Kyūshū Nōsei Kyoku, *Saga Heiya* (76), p.265.
50. Yamada, T., 'Saga Heiya ni okeru Bakumatsu-ki' (98), p.51.
51. Yamada, T., 'Saga Heiya ni okeru Bakumatsu-ki' (98), p.47; *Saga-Shi Shi* (81), vol. 3, p.659.
52. Nagata, K., *Nihon Nōgyō no Suiri Kōzō* (54), pp.273—4.
53. Yamada, T., *Kyūshū Nōgyō Shi* (74), pp.239—40.
54. Isobe, T., 'Iwayuru Saga Dankai' (70), p.15.
55. Yamada, T., *Kyūshū Nōgyō Shi* (74), p.247.
56. *Saga-Shi Shi* (81), vol. 3, p.705.
57. *Saga-Shi Shi* (81), vol. 3, p.696.
58. Yamada, T., *Kyūshū Nōgyō Shi* (74), pp.246—7.
59. *Saga-Shi Shi* (81), vol. 3, p.706.
60. Yamada, T., *Kyūshū Nōgyō Shi* (74), p.274.
61. Yamada, T., *Kyūshū Nōgyō Shi* (74), pp.248—50.
62. *Saga-Shi Shi* (81), vol. 3, p.707.
63. See Chambers, R., 'Men and Water' (140), especially pp.340—2.
64. For other examples see Shimpo M., *Three Decades in Shiwa* (40); Eyre, J., 'Water Controls in a Japanese Irrigation System' (38); Beardsley, Hall and Ward, *Village Japan* (41).
65. Miyajima, S., *Kome Tsukuri* (72), pp.14—15.
66. *Saga-Shi Shi* (81), vol. 3, p.273.
67. Conversation with Professor Yamada, 20.12.80.
68. *Saga-Shi Shi* (81), vol. 3, p.272.
69. *Kasegawa Nōgyō Suiri Shi* (77), p.71. Cf. Shimpo, M., *Three Decades in Shiwa* (40), p.7, for the same procedure.

70. Kyūshū Nōsei Kyoku, *Saga Heiya* (76), p.352.
71. See chapter 2, section 2.
72. Yamada, T., *Kyūshū Nōgyō Shi* (74), p.250n.
73. 'Kangaekata.' *Saga-Ken Shi* (80), p.616.
74. *Saga-Ken Shi* (80), p.616. For other systems of exchanging labour still in use in Kyūshū villages in the 1930s, and for an enjoyable description of the social event that it was, see Embree, J., *Suye Mura* (44), pp.132–8.
75. *Saga-Shi Shi* (81), vol. 3, pp.262–3.
76. Yamada, T., 'Saga Heiya ni okeru Bakumatsu-ki' (98), p.49.
77. Yagi, H., 'Kinsei Makki Saga Heitan Nōgyō' (97), p.155; Tanaka, Y., 'Suiden Urasaku' (96), p.324.
78. Ōta, R., 'Meiji Zenki' (91), p.217.
79. Ōta, R., 'Meiji Zenki' (91), p.214.
80. Ōta, R., 'Meiji Zenki' (91), p.213 and p.220, and see footnote w.
81. The following relies mainly on Yamada, T., 'Saga-bei Ryūtsū' (99).
82. Yamada, T., 'Saga-bei Ryūtsū' (99), p.521.
83. Isobe, T., 'Iwayuru Saga Dankai' (70), p.23.
84. See Mathias, R., 'The Recruitment and the Organisation of Labour in the Coal-Mining Industry of Northern Kyūshū during the Meiji Period' (117), pp.25–6..
85. *Saga-Shi Shi* (81), vol. 3, p.619.
86. Ōta, R., 'Meiji Zenki' (91), p.223.
87. Described in Yamada, T. and Ōta, R., *Saga-Ken Nōgyō Shi* (73), pp.299–311.
88. Especially that in Yamada, T., 'Saga Heiya ni okeru Bakumatsu-ki' (98); Ōta, R., 'Meiji Zenki' (91); and Kyūshū Nōsei Kyoku, *Saga Heiya* (76), p.305.
89. Wheat yield: 1·7 *koku*/10 ares in 1882. *Saga-Shi Shi* (81), vol. 3, pp.262–3.
90. See e.g. Yagi, H., 'Kinsei Makki Saga Heitan Nōgyō' (97), p.161; Kyūshū Nōsei Kyoku, *Saga Heiya* (76), p.235 and p.313.
91. ¥4·25 per *koku*. Wages and prices from the Nōji Chōsa. See Ōta, R., 'Meiji Zenki' (91), p.223 and p.217.
92. Yagi, H., 'Kinsei Makki Saga Heitan Nōgyō' (97), p.161.
93. Yamada, T., *Kyūshū Nōgyō Shi* (74), p.256.
94. *Saga-Shi Shi* (81), vol. 3, p.619.
95. Yamada, T., 'Saga Heiya ni okeru Bakumatsu-ki' (98), p.45.
96. Isobe, T., 'Iwayuru Saga Dankai' (70), p.32.
97. *Saga-Shi Shi* (81), vol. 3, p.619.
98. *Saga-Shi Shi* (81), vol. 3, p.618.

Chapter 5

1. *Saga-Shi Shi* (81), vol. 3, pp.681–2.
2. For evidence see Isobe, T., 'Iwayuru Saga Dankai' (70), p.23 and the records of the Saga rice-trader to be described shortly.
3. Kayō, N., *Nihon Nōgyō Kiso Tōkei* (68), p.514.
4. *Saga-Shi Shi* (81), vol. 3, p.618.
5. Isobe, T., 'Iwayuru Saga Dankai' (70), p.23.
6. *Saga-Shi Shi* (81), vol. 3, pp.640–5.
7. *Saga-Shi Shi* (81), vol. 3, pp.699–701.
8. Quoted in *Saga-Shi Shi* (81), vol. 3, p.683.
9. Yamada, T., and Ōta, R., *Saga-Ken Nōgyō Shi* (73), p.161.
10. Yamada, T., and Ōta, R., *Saga-Ken Nōgyō Shi* (73), p.164.
11. *Saga-Ken Shi* (80), p.464.
12. *Saga-Ken Shi* (80), pp.464–5.
13. *Saga-Ken Shi* (80), p.462.
14. *Saga-Shi Shi* (81), vol. 3, pp.692–3.
15. See *Saga-Ken Shi* (80), pp.376–85.

16. *Saga-Ken Shi* (80), p.385; *Saga-Shi Shi* (81), vol. 3, p.630.
17. Kyūshū Nōsei Kyoku, *Saga Heiya* (76), p.296; *Saga-Shi Shi* (81), vol. 3, p.637.
18. Yamada, T., *Kyūshū Nōgyō Shi* (74), p.255.
19. *Saga-Ken Shi* (80), p.386.
20. *Saga-Shi Shi* (81), vol. 3, p.711.
21. *Saga-Shi Shi* (81), vol. 3, p.714.
22. *Saga-Shi Shi* (81), vol. 3, p.724.
23. Yamada, T., *Kyūshū Nōgyō Shi* (74), p.257.
24. *Saga-Shi Shi* (81), vol. 3, pp.719–20.
25. *Saga-Shi Shi* (81), vol. 3, p.648. Cf. Dore, R., 'Agricultural Improvement' (26), p.73.
26. *Saga-Shi Shi* (81), vol. 3, p.651.
27. *Saga-Shi Shi* (81), vol. 3, pp.651–2.
28. *Saga-Shi Shi* (81), vol. 3, p.203.
29. Kyūshū Nōsei Kyoku, *Saga Heiya* (76), pp.295–6.
30. *Saga-Shi Shi* (81), vol. 3, p.649.
31. *Saga-Shi Shi* (81), vol. 3, pp.650–1.
32. *Saga-Ken Nōgyō Shikenjo 50-nen Shi* (84), p.4.
33. *Saga-Ken Nōgyō Shikenjo 50-nen Shi* (84), p.8.
34. *Saga-Shi Shi* (81), vol. 3, p.652; *Saga-Ken Nōgyō Shikenjo 50-nen Shi* (84), p.8.
35. See *Saga-Shi Shi* (81), vol. 3, pp.649–51; *Saga-Ken Shi* (80), p.387.
36. The preceding description is based on *Saga-Gun Shi* (78), pp.270–2.
37. Kyūshū Nōsei Kyoku, *Saga Heiya* (76), p.339.
38. *Kasegawa Nōgyō Suiri Shi* (77), pp.63–6.
39. *Kasegawa Nōgyō Suiri Shi* (77), pp.66–7.
40. Kyūshū Nōsei Kyoku, *Saga Heiya* (76), p.341.
41. Kyūshū Nōsei Kyoku, *Saga Heiya* (76), p.72.
42. Kyūshū Nōsei Kyoku, *Saga Heiya* (76), p.73.
43. Yamada, T., and Ōta, R., *Saga-Ken Nōgyō Shi* (73), p.71.
44. *Saga-Shi Shi* (81), vol. 3, p.662.
45. *Saga-Shi Shi* (81), vol. 3, pp.656–7; Yamada, T., 'Saga Heiya ni okeru Bakumatsu-ki' (98), p.49.
46. Ōta, R., 'Meiji Zenki' (91), p.217; *Saga-Shi Shi* (81), vol. 3, p.656.
47. *Saga-Shi Shi* (81), vol. 4, p.341; Kyūshū Nōsei Kyoku, *Saga Heiya* (76), p.308.
48. *Saga-Shi Shi* (81), vol. 4, p.341; *Nihon Nōgyō Hattatsu Shi* (55), vol. 6, pp.615–29.
49. Yamada, T., and Ōta, R., *Saga-Ken Nōgyō Shi* (73), pp.308–9.
50. *Nihon Nōgyō Hattatsu Shi* (55), vol. 6, p.431 and p.434.
51. *Saga-Gun Shi* (78), p.120.
52. *Saga-Shi Shi* (81), vol. 4, pp.342–3.
53. Yamada, T., 'Saga Heiya ni okeru Bakumatsu-ki' (98), p.48; Yagi, H., 'Kinsei Makki Saga Heitan Nōgyō' (97), p.157.
54. See e.g. *Saga-Ken Tōkeisho* (101) or Hitotsubashi Keizai Kenkyūjo, *Nōgyō Keijōzai* (67) data on inputs of agricultural origin.
55. Yagi, H., 'Kinsei Makki Saga Heitan Nōgyō' (97), p.157.
56. Eguchi, M., *Saga Nōgyō Oboegaki* (82), p.144.
57. Kamagata, I., *Saga Nōgyō* (71), p.117.
58. Kamagata, I., *Saga Nōgyō* (71), p.119.
59. Kamagata, I., *Saga Nōgyō* (71), p.119.
60. *Saga-Gun Shi* (78), p.119.
61. *Saga-Gun Shi* (78), p.119.
62. Kyūshū Nōsei Kyoku, *Saga Heiya* (76), pp.301–2.
63. *Saga-Gun Shi* (78), pp.121–2.
64. Kyūshū Nōsei Kyoku, *Saga Heiya* (76), pp.301–2.
65. *Saga-Shi Shi* (81), vol. 4, p.336.

66. *Saga-Shi Shi* (81), vol. 4, p.336.
67. *Saga-Ken Shi* (80), p.38.
68. *Saga-Shi Shi* (81), vol. 4, pp.337−8.
69. *Saga-Gun Shi* (78), pp.122−3.
70. *Saga-Shi Shi* (81), vol. 4, p.338.
71. *Saga-Gun Shi* (78), p.123.
72. See Kyūshū Nōsei Kyoku, *Saga Heiya* (76), pp.246−8.
73. Kyūshū Nōsei Kyoku, *Saga Heiya* (76), p.239.
74. *Saga-Shi Shi* (81), vol. 3, p.722.
75. Kyūshū Nōsei Kyoku, *Saga Heiya* (76), p.239.
76. Kyūshū Nōsei Kyoku, *Saga Heiya* (76), pp.243−4.
77. *Saga-Ken Shi* (80), pp.379−80.
78. Kyūshū Nōsei Kyoku, *Saga Heiya* (76), p.245; Waswo, A., *Japanese Landlords* (36), p.37.
79. Kyūshū Nōsei Kyoku, *Saga Heiya* (76), pp.248−9.
80. Kyūshū Nōsei Kyoku, *Saga Heiya* (76), p.250.
81. Kyūshū Nōsei Kyoku, *Saga Heiya* (76), p.250.
82. *Saga-Shi Shi* (81), vol. 3, p.725.
83. *Saga-Shi Shi* (81), vol. 3, p.727.
84. *Saga-Shi Shi* (81), vol. 3, p.727.
85. Miyajima, S., *Kome Tsukuri* (72), pp.35−6.
86. *Saga-Gun Shi* (78), p.124.
87. See *Saga-Shi Shi* (81), vol. 4, p.347; Kamagata, I., *Saga Nōgyō* (71), p.181.
88. Kamagata, I., *Saga Nōgyō* (71), p.176.
89. Conversation 23 January 1981.
90. Conversation 26 December 1980.
91. See chapter 2, section 1 (1).
92. *Saga-Ken Tōkeisho* (101).
93. Isobe, T., 'Iwayuru Saga Dankai' (70), p.8.
94. *Saga-Ken Shi* (80), p.603.
95. *Saga-Shi Shi* (81), vol. 3, pp.663−4, and *Saga-Ken Tōkeisho* (101).
96. Yamada, T., and Ōta, R., *Saga-Ken Nōgyō Shi* (73), p.216, and *Saga-Ken Tōkeisho* (101).
97. Yamada, T., and Ōta, R., *Saga-Ken Nōgyō Shi* (73), p.218.
98. Kyūshū Nōsei Kyoku, *Saga Heiya* (76), pp.285−6.
99. See Ishikawa, S., *Labour Absorption in Asian Agriculture* (156), especially section 4, pp.40−79.

Chapter 6

1. Matoba, T., *Kyūshū ni okeru Keizai to Nōgyō* (90), p.67.
2. Isobe, T., 'Iwayuru Saga Dankai' (70), p.30.
3. Odaka, K., 'History of Money Wages' (121), Table A7, p.96.
4. Matoba, T., *Kyūshū ni okeru Keizai to Nōgyō* (90), p.68.
5. *Nagasaki-Ken Tōkei Sho* (103).
6. *Fukuoka-Ken Tōkei Sho* (102).
7. Isobe, T., 'Iwayuru Saga Dankai' (70), p.25.
8. Hayami, Y. and Ruttan, V., 'Korean Rice, Taiwan Rice and Japanese Agricultural Stagnation' (20).
9. See Odaka, K., 'History of Money Wages' (121), pp.82−3, also White, J., 'Internal Migration in Pre-War Japan' (134).
10. Matoba, T., *Kyūshū ni okeru Keizai to Nōgyō* (90), p.98n.
11. Isobe, T., 'Iwayuru Saga Dankai' (70), p.27.
12. Kyūshū Nōsei Kyoku, *Saga Heiya* (76), p.23.
13. Described in *Saga-Ken Shi* (80), pp.599−600.
14. Yamada, T., *Kyūshū Nōgyō Shi* (74), pp.302−3.
15. See Appendix Table 1.
16. Kamagata, I., *Saga Nōgyō* (71), p.186.
17. *Nihon Nōgyō Hattatsu Shi* (55), vol. 6, p.243.
18. Kamagata, I., *Saga Nōgyō* (71),

pp.184—5.

19. Kyūshū Nōsei Kyoku, *Saga Heiya* (76), p.236.

20. Kamagata, I., *Saga Nōgyō* (71), pp.239—40.

21. Kyūshū Nōsei Kyoku, *Saga Heiya* (76), p.236; Kamagata, I., *Saga Nōgyō* (71), p.184.

22. E.g. the household described in Yamada, T. and Ōta, R., *Saga-Ken Nōgyō Shi* (73), pp.258—9.

23. *Nihon Nōgyō Hattatsu Shi* (55), vol. 6, p.71.

24. *Saga-Ken Tōkei Sho* (101).

25. *Saga-Ken Tōkei Sho* (101).

26. See Isobe, T., 'Iwayuru Saga Dankai' (70), p.18.

27. Kamagata, I., *Saga Nōgyō* (71), p.184.

28. Yamada, T. and Ōta, R., *Saga-Ken Nōgyō Shi* (73), p.330.

29. Nōji Chōsa data from Ōta, R., 'Meiji Zenki' (91).

Chapter 7

1. *Nihon Nōgyō Hattatsu Shi* (55), vol. 6, p.225.

2. *Nihon Nōgyō Hattatsu Shi* (55), vol. 6, p.226.

3. For an interesting discussion of the causes and effects of this trend in the industrial context to compare with the agricultural trends discussed here, see Minami, R., 'The Introduction of Electric Power' (118).

4. *Nihon Nōgyō Hattatsu Shi* (55), vol. 6, p.226.

5. *Nihon Nōgyō Hattatsu Shi* (55), vol. 6, p.226.

6. *Nihon Nōgyō Hattatsu Shi* (55), vol. 6, pp.216—20.

7. *Nihon Nōgyō Hattatsu Shi* (55), vol. 6, pp.226—8.

8. *Saga-Ken Keizai Hyaku-nen Shi* (87), p.116.

9. *Saga-Shi Shi* (81), vol. 4, p.135.

10. Advertisement in the *Saga Shinbun* (Saga Newspaper), 1 October 1918.

11. See article in *Jigyō no Saga* (Business in Saga), 1 December 1919.

12. *Saga-Ken Shi* (80), p.606.

13. For example one in Yamagata described in *Nihon Nōgyō Hattatsu Shi* (55), vol. 6, pp.221—3.

14. *Saga-Shi Shi* (81), vol. 4, p.348; Kyūshū Nōsei Kyoku, *Saga Heiya* (76), p.252.

15. Kamagata, I., *Saga Nōgyō* (71), p.188.

16. *Saga-Shi Shi* (81), vol. 4, p.349; Kamagata, I., *Saga Nōgyō* (71), pp.188—9; Kyūshū Nōsei Kyoku, *Saga Heiya* (76), p.252; Miyajima, S., *Kome Tsukuri* (72), p.42.

17. Kamagata, I., *Saga Nōgyō* (71), p.188.

18. Kamagata, I., *Saga Nōgyō* (71), p.188.

19. *Saga-Shi Shi* (81), vol. 4, p.348; Kamagata, I., *Saga Nōgyō* (71), p.188.

20. Notably *Tenmatsu* (85), published in 1923.

21. *Tenmatsu* (85), p.381.

22. Kyūshū Nōsei Kyoku, *Saga Heiya* (76), p.253; *Saga-Shi Shi* (81), vol. 4, p.350—1; Kamagata, I., *Saga Nōgyō* (71), pp.189—90.

23. *Saga-Shi Shi* (81), vol. 4, p.353.

24. *Tenmatsu* (85), p.382.

25. Kyūshū Nōsei Kyoku, *Saga Heiya* (76), p.255.

26. *Tenmatsu* (85), p.381; Kamagata, I., *Saga Nōgyō* (71), p.195.

27. *Tenmatsu* (85), p.385.

28. *Tenmatsu* (85), pp.387—95.

29. *Tenmatsu* (85), pp.395—9.

30. Kamagata, I., *Saga Nōgyō* (71), p.196; Kyūshū Nōsei Kyoku, *Saga Heiya* (76), p.262.

31. Yamada, T. and Ōta, R., *Saga-Ken Nōgyō Shi* (73), p.337.

32. Nagata, K., *Nihon Nōgyō no Suiri Kōzō* (54), p.265.

33. Kamagata, I., *Saga Nōgyō* (71), p.195.

34. Data from Nagata, K., *Nihon Nōgyō no Suiri Kōzō* (54), pp.265—8.

35. Nagata, K., *Nihon Nōgyō no Suiri Kōzō* (54), p.269.

36. Kamagata, I., *Saga Nōgyō* (71), pp.213—18.

37. Kamagata, I., *Saga Nōgyō* (71), p.201.

38. *Saga-Shi Shi* (81), vol. 4, p.361.

39. Kamagata, I., *Saga Nōgyō* (71), pp.201—2.

40. *Saga-Shi Shi* (81), vol. 4, p.360.

41. Miyajima, S., *Kome Tsukuri* (72), p.48.

42. Kamagata, I., *Saga Nōgyō* (71), p.202.

43. *Saga-Ken Shi* (80), p.608.

44. *Saga-Ken Shi* (80), p.608.

45. *Saga-Shi Shi* (81), vol. 4, p.359.

46. *Saga-Shi Shi* (81), vol. 4, p.363.

47. Miyajima, S., *Kome Tsukuri* (72), p.49.

48. Kamagata, I., *Saga Nōgyō* (71), p.207.

49. *Saga-Shi Shi* (81), vol. 4, p.362.

50. Kamagata, I., *Saga Nōgyō* (71), p.220.

51. *Saga-Shi Shi* (81), vol. 4, p.365.

52. Miyajima, S., *Kome Tsukuri* (72), p.54.

53. Kamagata, I., *Saga Nōgyō* (71), p.223.

54. *Saga-Ken Shi* (80), p.610.

55. Kamagata, I., *Saga Nōgyō* (71), p.194; Kyūshū Nōsei Kyoku, *Saga Heiya* (76), p.259.

56. Kyūshū Nōsei Kyoku, *Saga Heiya* (76), p.265.

57. Kyūshū Nōsei Kyoku, *Saga Heiya* (76), p.268.

58. Kyūshū Nōsei Kyoku, *Saga Heiya* (76), p.269.

59. See Isobe, T., 'Iwayuru Saga Dankai' (70), pp.35—6.

60. See Yamada, T. and Ōta, R., *Saga-Ken Nōgyō Shi* (73), p.341.

61. See Yamada, T. and Ōta, R., *Saga-Ken Nōgyō Shi* (73), pp.351—3.

Chapter 8

1. See Kamagata, I., *Saga Nōgyō* (71), p.231; Tanaka, S., *Saga Heitan Chitai* (95), p.313.

2. Kamagata, I., *Saga Nōgyō* (71), p.231.

3. Kamagata, I., *Saga Nōgyō* (71), p.231.

4. *Saga-Shi Shi* (81), vol. 4, p.385.

5. Kamagata, I., *Saga Nōgyō* (71), p.231.

6. Kamagata, I., *Saga Nōgyō* (71), pp.235—6.

7. Kamagata, I., *Saga Nōgyō* (71), p.225.

8. Isobe, T., 'Iwayuru Saga Dankai' (70), p.37.

9. Kyūshū Nōsei Kyoku, *Saga Heiya* (76), p.318.

10. *Saga-Shi Shi* (81), vol. 4, p.369.

11. *Saga-Shi Shi* (81), vol. 4, p.370.

12. *Saga-Shi Shi* (81), vol. 4, pp.370—5.

13. *Saga-Ken Shi* (80), p.612.

14. Nagata, K., *Nihon Nōgyō no Suiri Kōzō* (54), p.280.

15. *Saga-Shi Shi* (81), vol. 4, p.383.

16. Nagata, K., *Nihon Nōgyō no Suiri Kōzō* (54), p.285.

17. Nagata, K., *Nihon Nōgyō no Suiri Kōzō* (54), p.286.

18. *Saga-Ken Tōkei Sho* (101), and see Chart 6.3.

19. Kamagata, I., *Saga Nōgyō* (71), p.239.

20. *Saga-Ken Tōkei Sho* (101), and see Chart 6.3.

21. Kamagata, I., *Saga Nōgyō* (71), p.240.

22. *Saga-Ken Tōkei Sho* (101).

23. Eguchi, M., *Saga Nōgyō Oboegaki* (82), vol. 1, p.182.
24. Kamagata, I., *Saga Nōgyō* (71), p.233.
25. Eguchi M., *Saga Nōgyō Oboegaki* (82), vol. 1, p.182.
26. Eguchi, M., *Saga Nōgyō Oboegaki* (82), vol. 1, p.182; Kamagata, I., *Saga Nōgyō* (71), p.238.
27. Tanaka, S., *Saga Heitan Chitai* (95), p.323.
28. Kamagata, I., *Saga Nōgyō* (71), p.233.
29. Kamagata, I., *Saga Nōgyō* (71), p.234.
30. *Saga-Shi Shi* (81), vol. 4, p.380.
31. Kamagata, I., *Saga Nōgyō* (71), p.234.
32. Tanaka, S., *Saga Heitan Chitai* (95), p.327.
33. *Saga-Ken Tōkei Sho* (101).
34. *Saga-Ken Tōkei Sho* (101); Isobe, T., 'Iwayuru Saga Dankai' (70), p.30.
35. *Saga-Shi Shi* (81), vol. 4, p.406.
36. Isobe, T., 'Iwayuru Saga Dankai' (70), p.43.
37. *Saga-Ken Shi* (80), p.472.
38. Tanaka, S., *Saga Heitan Chitai* (95), p.236.
39. Confirmed by Tanaka, S., *Saga Heitan Chitai* (95), p.319–20.
40. Isobe, T., 'Iwayuru Saga Dankai' (70), pp.20–1.
41. Isobe, T., 'Iwayuru Saga Dankai' (70), p.20.
42. See Table 8.9.
43. Matoba, T., *Kyūshū ni okeru Keizai to Nōgyō* (90), p.252.
44. See Table 8.9.
45. See e.g. Tanaka, S., *Saga Heitan Chitai* (95), p.315, p.317.
46. See Table 8.9; Tanaka, S., *Saga Heitan Chitai* (95), p.317; Matoba, T., *Kyūshū ni okeru Keizai to Nōgyō* (90), p.250.
47. Table 8.9; Tanaka, S., *Saga Heitan Chitai* (95), p.319; Matoba, T.,

Kyūshū ni okeru Keizai to Nōgyō (90), p.251.
48. Tanaka, S., *Saga Heitan Chitai* (95), pp.333–4.
49. Tanaka, S., *Saga Heitan Chitai* (95), p.325.
50. Tanaka, S., *Saga Heitan Chitai* (95), p.321.
51. Isobe, T., 'Saga Heitan Chitai' (88), pp.225–6.
52. *Saga-Ken Nōchi Kaikaku Shi* (79), pp.396–7.
53. What follows relies on Yamada, T., and Ōta, R., *Saga-Ken Nōgyō Shi* (73), chapter 9, section 12.
54. Tanaka, S., *Saga Heitan Chitai* (95), pp.305–6, p.308, pp.309–10.
55. Kawamoto, A., 'Socio-Cultural Adjustments of Farm Families' (30).
56. See Yoshida, T., 'Integration and Change' (100).
57. Kamagata, I., *Saga Nōgyō* (71), pp.261–2.
58. Kamagata, I., *Saga Nōgyō* (71), pp.261–2.
59. *Saga-Shi Shi* (81), vol. 4, p.414.
60. *Saga-Shi Shi* (81), vol. 4, p.415.
61. Tanaka, S., *Saga Heitan Chitai* (95), p.324.
62. *Saga-Ken Shi* (80), p.617.
63. Kyūshū Nōsei Kyoku, *Kasegawa Nōgyō Suiri Shi* (77), pp.81–2.
64. Yoshida, T., 'Integration and Change' (100), pp.110–15.
65. See Tanaka, S., 'Saga-Ken Nōgyō Ron' (94) and Yamada, K., 'Kome to Mayu no Keizai Kōzō' (63). The 'Saga stage' theory is summarised in *Saga-Shi Shi* (81), vol. 4, pp.386–93.

Chapter 9

1. See especially section 2 of Chapter 1.
2. For the feel as well as the facts of modern Japanese agriculture, see Dore, R., *Shinohata* (43), in this context especially pp.99–111.

BIBLIOGRAPHY

The following bibliography is by no means a comprehensive list of all the material available on the topics with which this book is concerned. Rather, it is an attempt to organise and present the bibliographic information which I have of necessity assembled in the course of the study in a form such that it might be useful as a guide to others approaching the subject. The works listed here are those which have been useful to me in the course of research for this book, and some items appear by virtue of having been cited in the text rather than because of their intrinsic significance for the subject. The notes are designed to try to help the user assess the relative importance of the entries for the various subjects covered. Works are cited in the notes by means of author, short title and the number against them in the bibliography list.

A.   Works in English on Pre-War Japanese Agriculture

The most up-to-date survey of many aspects of Japanese agricultural development is to be found in:

(1) Hayami, Y., *A Century of Agricultural Growth in Japan*, University of Tokyo Press, Tokyo, 1975.

In addition:

(2) Ohkawa, K., Johnston, B. and Kaneda, H., *Agriculture and Economic Growth—Japan's Experience*, University of Tokyo Press, Tokyo, 1969,

assembles many excellent and important articles on the subject, and:

(3) Ogura, T., *Agricultural Development in Modern Japan*, Fuji Publishing Company, Tokyo, rev. ed. 1967,

provides a very useful but inconvenient (index-less) basic reference source on the technology and institutions of Japanese agriculture.

(4) Nasu, S., *Aspects of Japanese Agriculture*, Institute of Pacific Relations, New York, 1941,

is difficult to obtain but a useful source, especially for technical and environmental information. Other literature is here assembled under specific topics.

(1)   AGRICULTURE AND THE ECONOMY

a)   The Tokugawa Heritage

(5) Crawcour, E., 'The Tokugawa Heritage' in (116), pp.17–44.

(6) Hayami, Y. and Yamada, S., 'Agricultural Productivity at the Beginning of Industrialisation' in (2), pp.105–35.

(7) Smith, T., 'Farm Family By-Employments in Pre-Industrial Japan', *Journal of Economic History*, Vol. 29, No. 4, Dec. 1969, pp.697–715.

(8) Smith, T., *The Agrarian Origins of Modern Japan*, Stanford University Press, Stanford, 1959. See also (110) and (42).

b)   The Role of Agriculture in Economic Growth

The literature in this area centres on the work of Professor Ohkawa and on studies arising from the growth-rate controversy.

(9) Johnston, B., 'The "Japanese Model" of Agricultural Development: Its Relevance to Developing Nations' in (2), pp.58–104.

(10) Nakamura, J., *Agricultural Production and the Economic Growth of Japan*, Princeton University Press, Princeton, 1966.

(11) Nakamura, J., 'Meiji Land Reform, Redistribution of Income and Saving in Agriculture', *Economic Development and Cultural Change*, Vol. XIV, No. 4, July 1966 pp.428–39.

(12) Ohkawa, K., *Differential Structure and Agriculture*, Kinokuniya Bookstore, Tokyo, 1972.

(13) Ohkawa, K., 'Phases of Agricultural Development and Economic Growth' in (2), pp.3–36.

(14) Ohkawa, K. and Mundle, S., 'Agricultural Surplus Flow in Japan 1868–1937', *The Developing Economies*, Vol. XVII, No. 3, Sept. 1979, pp.247–65.

(15) Ohkawa, K. and Rosovsky, H., 'A Century of Japanese Economic Growth' in (116), pp.47–92.

(16) Ohkawa, K. and Rosovsky, H., 'The Role of Agriculture in Japanese Economic Development', *Economic Development and Cultural Change*, Vol. 9, No. 1, part 2, Oct. 1960, pp.43–68.

(17) Oshima, H., 'Meiji Fiscal Policy and Agricultural Progress', in (116), pp.353–390.

(18) Rosovsky, H., 'Rumbles in the Rice Fields: Professor Nakamura vs. the Official Statistics', *Journal of Asian Studies*, Vol. XXVII, No. 2, Feb. 1968, pp.347–60.

(19) Tussing, A., 'The Labour Force in Meiji Economic Growth: A Quantitative Study of Yamanashi Prefecture', in (2), pp.198–221.

c)   The Inter-War Period

(20) Hayami, Y. and Ruttan, V., 'Korean Rice, Taiwan Rice and Japanese Agricultural Stagnation', *Quarterly Journal of Economics*, Vol. 84, Nov. 1970, pp.562–89, or (152) pp.218–28.

(21) Ōuchi, T., 'Agricultural Depression in Japanese Villages', *The Developing Economies*, Vol. 4, Dec. 1967, pp.597–627.

(22) Totten, G., 'Labour and Agrarian Disputes in Japan following World War I', *Economic Development and Cultural Change*, Vol. 9, No. 1, part 2, Oct 1960, pp.187–212.

d)   Miscellaneous

(23) Havens, T., *Farm and Nation in Modern Japan*, Princeton University Press, Princeton, 1974. (A study of agrarian thought.)

(24) Ogura, T., *Can Japanese Agriculture Survive?*, Agricultural Policy Research Centre, Tokyo, 1979. (An enormous and unwieldy book which can be made to yield useful information, especially on state involvement in agriculture.)

(2)   TECHNOLOGY

For overall description and analysis of technical change in pre-war Japanese agriculture, see (1), (3), (152) and:

(25) Crawcour, E., 'Japan 1868–1920', in Shand, R., ed., *Agricultural Development in Asia*, Australian National University Press, Canberra, 1969, pp.1–24.

(26) Dore, R., 'Agricultural Improvement in Japan', *Economic Development and Cultural Change*, Vol. 9, No. 1, part 2, Oct. 1960, pp.69–91.

(27) Sawada, S., 'Innovation in Japanese Agriculture 1880−1935' in (116), pp.325−51.

(28) Sawada, S., 'The Development of Rice Productivity in Japan − Pre-War Experience' in (159), pp.115−40.

On various particular aspects of technical change see:

(29) Ishikawa, S. and Ohkawa, K., 'Significance of Japan's Experience − Technological Changes in Agricultural Production and Changes in Agrarian Structure' in (159), pp.141−97, and reprinted in revised form in (155), pp.151−206.

(30) Kawamoto, A., 'Socio-Cultural Adjustments of Farm Families and Rural Communities in the Process of Mechanisation' in Southworth, H., ed., *Farm Mechanisation in East Asia*, The Agricultural Development Council, New York, 1972, pp.331−49.

(31) Kee Il Choi, 'Technological Diffusion in Agriculture under the Bakuhan System', *Journal of Asian Studies*, Vol. 30, No. 4, Aug. 1971, pp.749−60.

(32) Matsuo, T., *Rice and Rice Cultivation in Japan*, The Institute of Asian Economic Affairs, Tokyo, 1961. (For biological aspects.)

(33) Tsuchiya, K., *Productivity and Technical Progress in Japanese Agriculture*, University of Tokyo Press, Tokyo, 1976.

3. LANDOWNERSHIP AND TENURE

(34) Dore, R., *Land Reform in Japan*, Oxford University Press, 1967.

(The opening chapters still provide the best description of Japanese cultivation and landholding institutions.)

(35) Dore, R., 'The Meiji Landlord − Good or Bad?', *Journal of Asian Studies*, Vol. 18, No. 3, May 1959, pp.343−55.

(36) Waswo, A., *Japanese Landlords − the Decline of a Rural Elite*, University of California Press, Berkeley, 1977.

See also the review of (36) by Smethurst in *Journal of Japanese Studies*, Vol. 5, No. 2, Summer 1979.

4. IRRIGATION

(37) Akino, M., 'Land Infrastructure Improvement in Agricultural Development: the Japanese Case 1900−65', *Economic Development and Cultural Change*, Vol. 28, No. 1, Oct 1979, pp.97−117.

(38) Eyre, J., 'Water Controls in a Japanese Irrigation System', *Geographical Review*, Vol. 45, 1955, pp.197−216.

(39) Hatate, I., *Irrigation Agriculture and the Landlord in Early Modern Japan*, Institute of Developing Economies, Tokyo, Special Paper No. 9, 1978.

(40) Shimpo, M., *Three Decades in Shiwa*, University of British Columbia Press, Vancouver, 1976.

See also the relevant sections of (41), (45) and (46).

5. VILLAGE SOCIETY

(41) Beardsley, R., Hall, J. and Ward, R. *Village Japan*, University of Chicago Press, Chicago, 1959. Section on irrigation reprinted in Coward, E., ed., *Irrigation and Agricultural Development in Asia*, Cornell University Press, Ithaca, 1980.

(42) Chambliss, W., *Chiarajima Village − Land Tenure, Taxation and Local Trade 1818−1884*, University of Arizona Press, Tucson, 1965.

(43) Dore, R., *Shinohata*, Allen Lane, London, 1978.

(44) Embree, J., *Suye Mura − a Japanese Village*, University of Chicago Press, Chicago, 1939.

(45) Fukutake, T., *Japanese Rural Society*, Oxford University Press, London, 1967.

(46) Nakane, C., *Kinship and Economic Organisation in Rural Japan*, Athlone Press, London, 1967.

B. Works in Japanese on Japanese Agriculture

No attempt is made here to provide a guide to the enormous Japanese literature on agriculture. Bibliographies, none of them unfortunately covering very recent literature, are to be found in:

(47) Remer, C. and Kawai, S., *Japanese Economics: a Guide to Japanese Reference and Research Materials*, University of Michigan Press, Ann Arbor, 1956.

(48) Rosovsky, H., ed., *Quantitative Japanese Economic History*, Centre for Japanese Studies at the Institute of International Studies, University of California, Berkeley, 1961.

(49) Sumiya, M. and Taira, K., *An Outline of Japanese Economic History, 1630–1940*, University of Tokyo Press, Tokyo, 1979.

Other works cited or frequently used in the study are as follows:

(50) Arashi, K., *Kinsei Inasaku Gijitsu Shi* (History of Rice-Growing Technology in Recent Times), Nōsangyōson Bunka Kyōkai, Tokyo, 1975.

(51) Kanazawa, N., *Inasaku no Keizai Kōzō* (The Economic Structure of Rice Cultivation), Tōkyō Daigaku Shuppansha, Tokyo, 1954.

(52) Kitamura, T., *Nihon Kangai Suiri Kankō Shiteki Kenkyū* (Historical Studies of Japanese Irrigation and Water-Use Practices), Iwanami Shoten, Tokyo, 1950.

(53) Kondō, Y., ed., *Shōwa Zenki Nōsei Keizai Meisho Hen* (Famous Works of Agricultural Economics of the Early Shōwa Period), Vol. 6, Nōsangyōson Bunka Kyōkai, Tokyo, 1978.

(54) Nagata, K., *Nihon Nōgyō no Suiri Kōzō* (The Structure of Water-Use in Japanese Agriculture), Iwanami Shoten, Tokyo, 1971.

(55) Nōgyō Hattatsu Shi Chōsa Kai (Tōbata, S. and Morinaga, S. eds.), *Nihon Nōgyō Hattatsu Shi* (The History of Japanese Agricultural Development), 9 vols., Chūōkōronsha, Tokyo, 1953–6.

(56) Nōgyō Hattatsu Shi Chōsa Kai, *Shuyō Chitai Nōgyō Seisanryoku Keisei Shi* (History of Agricultural Productivity Formation in Various Regions), Nōrinshō Nōgyō Sōgō Kenkyūjo, 2 vols, Tokyo, 1958.

(57) Ohkawa, K., and Tōbata, S., *Nihon No Keizai to Nōgyō* (Agriculture and the Japanese Economy), 2 vols, Iwanami Shoten, Tokyo, 1956.

(58) Ōuchi, T., *Nihon ni okeru Nōminzō no Bunkai* (Analysis of Agricultural Stratification in Japan), Tōkyō Daigaku Shuppansha, Tokyo, 1969.

(59) Ōuchi, T., *Nōgyō Shi* (History of Agriculture), Tōyō Keizai Shimposha, Tokyo, 1960.

(60) Tōbata, S., 'Nihon Nōgyō no Ninaite' (Bearers of Japanese Agriculture), in (55), Vol. 9, pp.561–604.

(61) Tōbata, S., *Nōchi o meguru Jinushi to Nōmin* (Landlords and Farmers in relation to Agricultural Land), Kantōsha, Tokyo, 1947.

(62) Wataya, T., 'Shihonshugi no Hatten to Nōmin no Kaisō Bunka' (Agricultural Stratification and the Development of Capitalism), in Tōbata, S. and Uno, K., eds., *Nihon Shihonshugi to Nōgyō* (Agriculture and Japanese Capitalism), Iwanami Shoten, Tokyo, 1959, pp.191–257.

(63) Yamada, K., 'Kome to Mayu no Keizai Kōzō' (Economic Structure of Rice and Cocoons), in (53), pp.21–196, originally published by Iwanami Shoten, Tokyo, in 1942.

(64) Yamaguchi, K., *Meiji Zenki Keizai no Bunseki* (Analysis of the Economy of the Early Meiji Period), Tōkyō Daigaku Shuppansha, Tokyo, rev. ed., 1963.

Statistics:

The official agricultural statistics of Japan appear in the *Nōrinshō Tōkeihyō* (Statistical Yearbook of the Ministry of Agriculture and Forestry), and historical series from this are conveniently collected in:

(65) Japan: Nōrinshō Nōrin Keizai Kyoku Tōkei Chōsa Bu, *Nōrinshō Ruinen Tōkeihyō: Meiji-1-nen—Shōwa 28-nen* (Ministry of Agriculture Statistical Series: 1868–1942), Nōrinshō Nōrin Keizai Kyoku Tōkei Chōsa Bu, Tokyo, 1955.

The latest revised macro-level data appear in:

(66) Ohkawa, K., Shinohara, M. and Umemura, M., *Chōki Keizai Tōkei* (Long-Term Economic Statistics), Vol. 9, Agriculture and Forestry, Tōyō Keizai Shimpo Sha, Tokyo, 1966 (with English and Japanese text),

and the prefectural data collected as the basis for this are available at the Institute of Economic Research of Hitotsubashi University, Tokyo, as:

(67) Hitotsubashi Daigaku Keizai Kenkyūjo, *Nōgyō Keijōzai Tōnyūgaku no Fukenbetsu Suikei*, *1905—40*.

The ultimate collection of all kinds of agricultural statistics is:

(68) Kayō, N., *Nihon Nōgyō Kiso Tōkei* (Basic Statistics of Japanese Agriculture), Nōrinsuisangyō Seisansei Kōjō Kaigi, Tokyo, 1958. (This first edition is more useful for historical and prefectural statistics than the revised edition.)

A convenient source for the available farm survey data is provided by:

(69) Inaba, T., *(Fukkoku han) Nōka Keizai Chōsa Hōkoku—Chōsa Hōhō no Hensen to Ruinen Seiseki* (The Reports of the Farm Household Economy Surveys—Survey Methods and Series of Results), Nōgyō Sōgō Kenkyū Kankō Kai, Tokyo, 1953.

C. The Literature on Saga

As a result of the high yields and rapid technological progress achieved by Saga Plain agriculture in the 1930s, there has grown up a considerable body of agricultural economics literature in Japanese about it, in addition to the kinds of local history which are available for many areas. The overall story of agricultural change in Saga can be obtained from the following standard works, which have provided the basic foundation for the present study:

(70) Isobe, T., 'Iwayuru Saga Dankai no Keisei Katei' (The Process of Formation of the So-Called Saga Stage), in (56), Vol. 2, pp.4—48.

(71) Kamagata, I., *Saga Nōgyō no Hatten Katei* (The Process of Development of Saga Agriculture), Nōrinshō Nōgyō Sōgō Kenkyūjo, Tokyo, 1950.

(72) Miyajima, S., *Kome Tsukuri—sono Kunan no Ayumi* (Rice-Growing—a Story of Struggle), Aki Shobō, Tokyo, 1969.

(73) Yamada, T. and Ōta, R., *Saga-Ken Nōgyō Shi* (History of Agriculture in Saga Prefecture), Saga Prefectural Government, Saga, 1967.

(74) Yamada, T., *Kyūshū Nōgyō Shi Kenkyū* (Studies in the Agricultural History of Kyūshū), Nōsangyōson Bunka Kyōkai, Tokyo, 1977. (This contains essentially a shortened and revised version of the central part of (73).)

Since agriculture has always played such a large part in the life of the Saga area, local histories abound with material concerning it which can be used to add detail and colour to the more strictly academic studies above. In addition to the histories of geographical areas, there are also descriptive histories of the main irrigation networks of the area, and of the land development of the region:

(75) Kawazoe-Chō Shi Hensan Iinkai, ed., *Kawazoe-Chō Shi* (Memoirs of Kawazoe), Kawazoe-Chō Shi Hensan Jimukyoku, Kawazoe-Chō, Saga-Gun, 1979.

(76) Kyūshū Nōsei Kyoku, ed., *Saga Heiya ni okeru Suiri Jigyō no Enkaku* (The Development of Irrigation Facilities on the Saga Plain), Kyūshū Nōsei Kyoku, Fukuoka, 1967.

(77) Kyūshū Nōsei Kyoku Kasegawa Nōgyō Suiri Jigyō Jo Kasegawa Nōgyō Suiri Shi Hensan Iinkai, ed., *Kasegawa Nōgyō Suiri Shi* (History of Agricultural Irrigation Facilities on the Kase River), Kyūshū Nōsei Kyoku Kasegawa Nōgyō Suiri Jigyō Jo, Saga, 1973.

(78) (Shiritsu) Saga-Gun Kyōiku Kai, ed., *Saga-Gun Shi* (Memoirs of Saga County), Saga, 1915.

(79) Saga-Ken Nōchi Kaikaku Shi Hensan Iinkai, ed., *Saga-Ken Nōchi Kaikaku Shi* (History of Land Reform in Saga Prefecture), vol. 1, Nōchi Iinkai Saga-Ken Kyōgika, Saga, 1951.

(80) Saga-Ken Shi Hensan Iinkai, ed., *Saga-Ken Shi* (History of Saga Prefecture), vol. 3, Saga-Ken Shiryō Kankō Kai, Saga, 1967.

(80) Saga-Ken Shi Hensan Iinkai, ed., *Saga-Ken Shi* (History of Saga Prefecture), vol. 3, Saga-Ken Shiryō Kankō Kai, Saga, 1967.

(81) Saga-Shi Shi Hensan Iinkai, ed., *Saga-Shi Shi* (History of Saga City), vols. 3 and 4, Saga City Government, 1979.

In addition to these official works, there also exists a number of books of personal reminiscences or more popular local history which relate the stories of people or institutions involved either directly with agriculture or more generally with the economy of the area:

(82) Eguchi, M., *Saga Nōgyō Oboegaki* (Reminiscences of Saga Agriculture), 2 vols., Kinkadō, Saga, 1967.

(83) Nishimura, H. and Yoshitomi, N., eds., *Saga Keizai no Ayumi* (The Story of the Saga Economy), Saga Shōkō Kaigisho, Saga, 1966.

(84) Saga-Ken Nōgyō Shikenjo, *Saga-Ken Nōgyō Shikenjo Gojūnen-Shi* (The Fifty Year History of the Saga Prefecture Agricultural Experiment Station), Saga-Ken Nōgyō Shikenjo, Saga, 1954.

(85) Saga-Ken Saga-Gun Oide Futsū Suiri Kumiai Kanrisha (Hayada), *Saga-Ken Saga-Gun Oide Futsū Suiri Kumiai no Jigyō ni kakaru Kikai Kangai Jisshi no Tenmatsu* (An Account of the Actual Events of the Mechanisation of Irrigation Carried out by the Oide Irrigation *Kumiai* of Saga County, Saga Prefecture), Saga, 1923, reprinted in (76), pp.380–404.

(86) Saga Shinbunsha, ed., *Saga Shinbun Nanajūgonen Shi* (The Seventy-Five Year History of the Saga Newspaper), Saga Shinbusha, Saga, 1960.

(87) Saga Shinbunsha, ed., *Saga-Ken Keizai Hyakunen Shi* (The Hundred Year History of the Economy of Saga Prefecture), Saga Shinbunsha, Saga, 1974.

Finally, there is the academic work, mostly in the form of journal articles, of agricultural economists and economic historians concerned with Saga. In this the writings of Professor Yamada and Dr. Isobe stand out.

(88) Isobe, T., 'Saga Heitan Chitai' (The Saga Plain Region) in Isobe, H., ed., *Kazoku Nōgyō no Henbō Katei* (The Process of Change in Family Farming), Tōkyō Daigaku Shuppansha, Tokyo, 1962, pp.207–34.

(89) Isobe, T., 'Saga Heitan Nōgyō ni okeru Kantakuchi Keisei no Kadai' (Land Reclamation in Saga Plain Agriculture), *Nōgyō Sōgō Kenkyū*, vol. 15, March 1961, pp.127–64.

(90) Matoba, T., ed., *Kyūshū ni okeru Keizai to Nōgyō* (Agriculture and the Economy of Kyūshū), Nōrinshō Nōgyō Sōgō Kenkyūjo, Tokyo, 1959.

(91) Ōta, R., 'Meiji Zenki ni okeru Saga Nōgyō no Jōtai' (The State of Saga Agriculture in the Early Meiji Period), *Nōgyō Sōgō Kenkyū*, vol. 11, no. 1, 1957, pp.209–26.

(92) Saga-Ken Nōrin Bu, *Saga Heitan-bu ni okeru Denryoku ni yoru Yōsui Kangai no Jitsunō Chōsa Seiseki* (The Results of a Survey of the State of Electrically-Powered Irrigation Pumping on the Saga Plain), Saga Prefectural Government, Saga, 1948.

(93) Taki, T., 'Saga-Ken ni okeru Kikai Kangai Jigyō' (The Project for the Mechanisation of Irrigation in Saga Prefecture), *Teikoku Nōkaihō*, vol. 16, no. 8, 1926, pp.144–7.

(94) Tanaka, S., 'Saga-Ken Nōgyō Ron' (On the Agriculture of Saga Prefecture), originally published in *Keizaigaku Kenkyū*, vol. 9, nos. 3–4, 1939, and reprinted in (53), pp.221–79.

(95) Tanaka, S., *Saga Heitan Chitai Ichi Nōson no Bunseki* (Analysis of One Saga Plain Village), originally published by Saga-Ken Nōkai in 1939 and reprinted in (53), pp.281–345.

(96) Tanaka, Y., 'Suiden Urasaku no Seisan Kōzō' (The Structure of Production of Second Crops on Paddy Fields), in Tashiro, T. and Hanada, J., eds., *Gendai Nihon Shihonshugi ni okeru Nōgyō Mondai* (Agricultural Problems in Modern Japanese Capitalism), Ochanomizu Shobō, Tokyo, 1976, pp.311–53.

(97) Yagi, H., 'Kinsei Makki Saga Heitan Nōgyō ni okeru "Kandenka" Katei' (The Process of Creation of Drainable Fields in Saga Plain Agriculture in the late Tokugawa Period), *Nōgyō Keizai Kenkyū*, vol. 51, no. 4, March 1980, pp.155–62.

(98) Yamada, T., 'Saga Heiya ni okeru Bakumatsu-Ki no Nōgyō Gijutsu' (Agricultural Technology on the Saga Plain at the End of the Tokugawa Period), *Nōgyō Keizai Kenkyū*, vol. 28, no. 1, 1956, pp.44–55.

(99) Yamada, T., 'Saga Bei Ryūtsū Kikō no Seiritsu Katei' (The Establishment of the System for Trading in Saga Rice), in (56), vol. 2, pp.499–544.

(100) Yoshida, T., 'Integration and Change in Japanese Villages', *American Anthropologist*, vol. 65, no. 1, Feb. 1963, pp.102–16.

Basic statistical data have been assembled from:

(101) *Saga-Ken Tōkei Sho* (Saga Prefectural Yearbook)

for which copies for almost all years between 1888 and 1939 can be found. I have also made reference to:

(102) *Fukuoka-Ken Tōkei Sho* (Fukuoka Prefectural Yearbook), and

(103) *Nagasaki-Ken Tōkei Sho* (Nagasaki Prefectural Yearbook).

D. Other Works Used

1. On the Japanese Economy

(104) Abegglen, J., *The Japanese Factory*, The Free Press, Glencoe, Illinois, 1958.

(105) Allen, G., *A Short Economic History of Modern Japan*, Allen and Unwin, London, 2nd rev. ed., 1962.

(106) Beasley, W., 'Feudal Revenue in Japan at the Time of the Meiji Restoration', *Journal of Asian Studies*, vol. XIX, no. 3, May 1960.

(107) Beasley, W., *The Meiji Restoration*, Stanford University Press, Stanford, 1973.

(108) Chūbachi, M. and Taira, K., 'Poverty in Modern Japan', in (126), pp.391–437.

(109) Cole, R. and Tominaga, K., 'Japan's Changing Occupational Structure and its Significance', in (126), pp.53–95.

(110) Hanley, S. and Yamamura, K., *Economic and Demographic Change in Pre-Industrial Japan 1600–1868*, Princeton University Press, Princeton, 1977.

(111) Hazama, H., 'Historical Changes in the Life-Style of Industrial Workers', in (126), pp.21–51.

(112) Iwata, M., *Ōkubo Toshimichi—the Bismarck of Japan*, University of California Press, Berkeley, 1964.

(113) Kajinishi, M., *Nihon Shihonshugi no Botsuraku* (The Collapse of Japanese Capitalism), Tōkyō Daigaku Shuppansha, Tokyo, 1960.

(114) Levine, S., and Kawada, H., *Human Resources in Japanese Industrial Development*, Princeton University Press, Princeton, 1980.

(115) Lockwood, W., *The Economic Development of Japan*, Princeton University Press, Princeton, 1968.

(116) Lockwood, W., ed., *The State and Economic Enterprise in Japan*, Princeton University Press, Princeton, 1965.

(117) Mathias, R., 'The Recruitment and the Organisation of Labour in the Coal-Mining Industry of Northern Kyūshū during the Meiji Period', in Nish, I., and Dunn, C., eds., *European Studies on Japan*, Paul Norburg Publications, Tenterden, Kent, 1979, pp.24–9.

(118) Minami, R., 'The Introduction of Electric Power and its Impact on the Manufacturing Industries: with Special Reference to Smaller-Scale Plants', in (126), pp.299–325.

(119) Minami, R., *Water Wheels in the Pre-Industrial Economy of Japan*, Discussion Paper No. 7 of the Institute of Economic Research, Hitotsubashi University, Tokyo, December 1978.

(120) Moulder, F., *Japan, China and the Modern World Economy*, Cambridge University Press, Cambridge, 1977.

(121) Odaka, K., 'History of Money Wages in the North Kyūshū Industrial Area, 1898–1939', *Hitotsubashi Journal of Economics*, vol. 8, no. 2, Feb. 1968, pp.71–100.

(122) Ohkawa, K., et al., *The Growth Rate of the Japanese Economy Since 1878*, Kinokuniya Bookstore, Tokyo, 1957.

(123) Ohkawa, K., and Rosovsky, H., 'The Indigenous Components in the Modern Japanese Economy', *Economic Development and Cultural Change*, vol. IX, no. 3, April 1961, pp.476–97.

(124) Ohkawa, K., and Rosovsky, H., *Japanese Economic Growth*, Stanford University Press, Stanford, 1973.

(125) Ohkawa, K., and Rosovsky, H., 'Post-War Japanese Growth in Historical Perspective—a Second Look', in Klein, L., and Ohkawa, K., eds., *Economic Growth: the Japanese Experience Since the Meiji Era*, Richard D. Irwin, Inc., Homewood, Illinois, 1968.

(126), Patrick, H., ed., *Japanese Industrialisation and its Social Consequences*, University of California Press, Berkeley, 1976.

(127), Ranis G., 'The Financing of Japanese Economic Development', *Economic History Review*, vol. XI, no. 3, 1959, reprinted in (2), pp.37–57.

(128) Rozman, G., *Urban Networks in Ch'ing China and Tokugawa Japan*, Princeton University Press, Princeton, 1973.

(129) Silberman, B., and Harootunian, H., eds., *Japan in Crisis*, Princeton University Press, Princeton, 1974.

(130) Sinha, R., 'Unresolved Issues in Japan's Early Economic Development', *Scottish Journal of Political Economy*, vol. XVI, no. 2, June 1969, pp.109–151.

(131) Taeuber, I., *The Population of Japan*, Princeton University Press, Princeton, 1958.

(132) Taira, K., *Economic Development and the Labour Market in Japan*, Columbia University Press, New York, 1970.

(133) Tokutomi, K., *Footprints in the Snow* (Omoide no Ki), translated by Kenneth Strong, Allen and Unwin, London, 1970.

(134) White, J., 'Internal Migration in Pre-War Japan', *Journal of Japanese Studies*, vol. 4, Winter 1978, pp.81–123.

(135) Wilkinson, T., *The Urbanisation of Japanese Labour, 1868–1955*, University of Massachusetts Press, Amhurst, 1965.

2.   ON TECHNOLOGY AND AGRICULTURAL CHANGE

(136) Atkinson, A. and Stiglitz, J., 'A New View of Technological Change' *Economic Journal*, vol. LXXIX, Sept. 1969.

(137) Boserup, M., 'Agrarian Structure and Take-Off', in Rostow, W., ed., *The Economics of Take-Off into Sustained Growth*, Macmillan, London, 1963.

(138) Brown, M., *On the Theory and Measurement of Technical Change*, Cambridge University Press, Cambridge, 1968.

(139) Chambers, J. and Mingay, G., *The Agricultural Revolution*, Batsford, London, 1966.

(140) Chambers, R., 'Men and Water: The Organisation and Operation of Irrigation', in (145), pp.340–63.

(141) Clay, E., *Planners' Preferences and Local Innovation in Tubewell Technology in North-East India*, Discussion Paper no. 40 of the Institute of Development Studies, University of Sussex, 1974.

(142) David, P., *Technical Choice, Innovation and Economic Growth*, Cambridge University Press, Cambridge, 1975.

(143) David, P., 'The Landscape and the Machine' in (142), pp.233–90.

(144) David, P., 'The Mechanisation of Reaping in the Ante-Bellum Mid-West', in (142), pp.195–232.

(145) Farmer, B., *Green Revolution?*, Macmillan, London, 1977.

(146) Geertz, C., *Agricultural Involution*, University of California Press, Berkeley, 1963.

(147) Gotsch, C., 'Technical Change and the Distribution of Income in Rural Areas', *American Journal of Agricultural Economics*, vol. 54, no. 2, May 1972, pp.326–41.

(148) Gotsch, C., 'Tractor Mechanisation and Rural Development in Pakistan', in International Labour Organisation, ed., *Mechanisation and Employment in Agriculture*, I.L.O., Geneva, 1973, pp.129–62.

(149) Griffin, K., *The Green Revolution*, U.N. Institute for Social Development, Geneva, 1972.

(150) Grilliches, Z., 'Hybrid Corn and the Economics of Innovation', *Science*, 29 July 1960, reprinted in (167), pp.211–28.

(151) Harriss, B., 'Rural Electrification and the Diffusion of Electric Water-Lifting Technology in North Arcot District, India', in (145), pp.182–203.

(152) Hayami, Y. and Ruttan, V., *Agricultural Development: an International Perspective*, Johns Hopkins Press, Baltimore and London, 1971.

(153) Hicks, J., *The Theory of Wages*, Macmillan, London, 1932.

(154) Ishikawa, S., *Economic Development in Asian Perspective*, Kinokuniya Bookstore, Tokyo, 1967.

(155) Ishikawa, S., *Essays on Technology, Employment and Institutions in Economic Development*, Kinokyniya Bookstore, Tokyo, 1981.

(156) Ishikawa, S., *Labour Absorption in Asian Agriculture*, Asian Regional Programme for Employment Promotion, I.L.O. Bangkok, 1978, reprinted in (155), pp.1–49.

(157) Ishikawa, S., 'Peasant Families and the Agrarian Community in Economic Development', in Reynolds, L., ed., *Agriculture in Development Theory*, Yale University Press, New Haven and London, 1975, reprinted in (155), pp.253–348.

(158) Ishikawa, S., 'Technological Change in Agricultural Production and its Impact on Agrarian Structure', *Keizai Kenkyū*, vol. 22, no. 2, April 1971, pp.150−65.

(159) Japan Economic Research Center, ed., *Agriculture and Economic Development—Structural Re-Adjustment in Asian Perspective*, 2 vols, Japan Economic Research Center, Tokyo, 1972.

(160) Kaneda, H., 'Mechanisation, Industrialisation and Technical Change in Rural Pakistan', in Shand, R., ed., *Technical Change in Asian Agriculture*, Australian National University Press, Canberra, 1973, pp.161−82.

(161) Lewis, W., 'Economic Development with Unlimited Supplies of Labour', *Manchester School of Economics and Social Studies*, vol. 22, May 1954, pp.139−91.

(162) Lipton, M., *Why Poor People Stay Poor*, Temple Smith, London, 1977.

(163) Mellor, J., *The Economics of Agricultural Development*, Cornell University Press, Ithaca, 1966.

(164) Ranis, G., and Fei, J., *The Development of the Labour Surplus Economy*, Irwin, Homewood, Illinois, 1964.

(165) Ranis, G., and Fei, J., 'A Theory of Economic Development', *American Economic Review*, vol. 51, Sept. 1961, pp.533−65.

(166) Rosenberg, N., 'The Direction of Technical Change—Inducement Mechanisms and Focusing Devices', *Economic Development and Cultural Change*, vol. 18, no. 1, Oct. 1969, pp.1−24.

(167) Rosenberg, N., *The Economics of Technical Change*, Penguin Books, Harmondsworth, 1971.

(168) Rosenberg, N., *Perspectives on Technology*, Cambridge University Press, Cambridge, 1976.

(169) Salter, W., *Productivity and Technical Change*, Cambridge University Press, Cambridge, 1960.

(170) Sansom, R., *The Economics of Insurgency in the Mekong Delta of Vietnam*, M.I.T. Press, Cambridge, Mass. and London, 1970.

(171) Schultz, T., *Transforming Traditional Agriculture*, Yale University Press, New Haven, 1964.

(172) Scott, J., *The Moral Economy of the Peasant*, Yale University Press, New Haven and London, 1976.

(173) Stewart, F., *Technology and Underdevelopment*, Macmillan, London, 1977.

(174) Thomas, J., 'The Choice of Technology for Irrigation Tubewells in East Pakistan: Analysis of a Development Policy Decision', in (175), pp.31−68.

(175) Timmer, C., et al., *The Choice of Technology in Developing Countries—Some Cautionary Tales*, Center for International Affairs, Harvard University, 1975.

INDEX

This is a NORMAL LOAN item.

We will email you a reminder before this item is due.

Please see http://www.ssl.ox.ac.uk/lending.html
for details on:

- loan policies; these are also displayed on the notice boards and in our library guide.

- how to check when your books are due back.

- how to renew your books, including information on the maximum number of renewals. Items may be renewed if not reserved by another reader. Items must be renewed before the library closes on the due date.

- level of fines; fines are charged on overdue books.

Please note that this item may be recalled during Term.